anglistik & englischunterricht

Intercultural Studies: Fictions of Empire

Manfred Beyer · Hans-Jürgen Diller · Joachim Kornelius · Erwin Otto
Gerd Stratmann (Hrsg.)

anglistik & englischunterricht

Band 58

Intercultural Studies: Fictions of Empire

HEIDELBERG 1996
UNIVERSITÄTSVERLAG C. WINTER

Intercultural Studies: Fictions of Empire

Verantwortliche Herausgeber für den thematischen Teil dieses Bandes:
Vera und Ansgar Nünning

HEIDELBERG 1996
UNIVERSITÄTSVERLAG C. WINTER

Die Deutsche Bibliothek – CIP-Einheitsaufnahme

Anglistik & Englischunterricht: A & E. – Heidelberg: Winter.

Früher Schriftenreihe
ISSN 0014-2328

NE: A & E; Anglistik und Englischunterricht

Bd. 58. Intercultural studies: fictions of empire. – 1996

Intercultural studies: fictions of empire / verantw. Hrsg. für den themat. Teil dieses Bd.: Vera und Ansgar Nünning. – Heidelberg: Winter, 1996

(Anglistik & Englischunterricht; Bd. 58)
ISBN 3-8253-0390-X

NE: Nünning, Vera [Hrsg.]

ISBN 3-8253-0390-X
ISSN 0344-8266

Anschrift der Redaktion:
Dr. Ulrike Borgmann, Sandra Graßhoff, Ruhr-Universität Bochum, Englisches Seminar
Universitätsstraße 150 · 44801 Bochum
Verlag: Universitätsverlag C. Winter Heidelberg GmbH
Gesamtherstellung: Universitätsverlag C. Winter, Hans-Bunte-Str. 18, 69123 Heidelberg

Printed in Germany · Imprimé en Allemagne

anglistik & englischunterricht erscheint in drei Bänden pro Jahrgang. Der Gesamtumfang beträgt ca. 540 Seiten
Preis des Einzelbandes DM 35,–, des Doppelbandes DM 60,–
Jahresabonnement DM 80,–. Studentenabonnement DM 60,–, zuzüglich Versandspesen.
In diesen Preisen sind 7% Mehrwertsteuer enthalten
Für unverlangte Einsendungen von Manuskripten wird nicht gehaftet
Mitarbeiter erhalten von ihren Beiträgen 30 Sonderdrucke und 2 Freiexemplare. Honorar wird nicht bezahlt
Der Verlag trägt die Kosten für die von der Druckerei nicht verschuldeten Korrekturen nur in beschränktem Maße und behält sich vor, den Verfassern die Mehrkosten für Autorkorrekturen zu belasten

Inhalt

RUBRIK

Forum

Vera Nünning & Ansgar Nünning, Köln

Fictions of Empire and the Making of Imperialist Mentalities: Colonial Discourse and Post-Colonial Criticism as a Paradigm for Intercultural Studies

> More than any other, the Age of Empire cries out for demystification, just because we – and that includes the historians – are no longer in it, but do not know how much of it is still in us.
>
> (E. J. Hobsbawm)

> For fictions have their own logic and their own dialectic of growth or decline.
>
> (Edward Said)

1. Introduction: on the continuity of the imperial past in the present

The Age of Empire lies in the past, but its ambivalent heritage is still very much with us. The British Empire, like the colonial empires of the other European powers, came to an end when independence was granted to previously colonised countries. But colonialism and imperialism have left behind many social and political problems, and many of the values, preconceptions, and cultural stereotypes associated with the imperial world-view have been bequeathed to us. The reasons for this are not hard to determine. A plethora of books dealing with the British imperial experience as well as television, films, and the resources of other media heavily contributed to preserving the glories of the imperial past in Britain's cultural memory and to constructing highly standardized images by means of which the British Empire continues to be viewed. Moreover, a host of novels, plays, and poems[1], many of which reflect a persistent imperial world-view, testify both to the fascination that the British Empire still has for authors and to the great importance that the imperial heritage continues to have for the way Britain sees itself. It is largely due to culture that the perceptual and ideological fictions that form the conceptual matrix of imperialism live on as an integral part of what has been called 'collective memory and cultural identity'.[2] Referring to popular boys' adventure stories, Susan Bassnett recently pointed out that "the values of those stories, however we may wish to repudiate them on the grounds of racism, sexism and xenophobia generally, are encoded into our thought patterns".[3] This has, of course, nothing to do with a peoples' genes, but is the result of the discursive practices of cultural transmission.

One way of approaching the demystification of the Age of Empire is to take a revisionist look at the role that literary fictions have played in nurturing "the sentiment, rationale, and above all the imagination of empire" and in helping to create "imperialism's consolidating vision".[4] The essays in this issue try to explore the relationship between literature and the complex process that Mangan has felicitously called "making imperial mentalities".[5] The contributors look at the works of such authors as Tennyson, Rider Haggard, Kipling, Conrad, and Forster as examples of colonial discourse so as to shed light on the making of imperialist mentalities.

Since the articles are concerned with different works of fiction or poetry and with particular myths and metaphors of British imperialism, this introduction will attempt to outline the approach that informs and unites the different contributions, pursuing the goals of providing a general overview of the topic, exploring the connection between literature and imperialism, and giving a short overview of the essays. Section 2 will provide a brief discussion of post-colonial criticism and its impact on revisionist accounts of colonial discourse. Section 3 will be devoted to a preliminary explanation of the meanings of the term 'fictions of empire', i.e. of the ambiguous subtitle of this volume. Section 4 will then mainly deal with the relationship between culture and imperialism, and the creative role that works of fiction can play in the construction of the ideological fictions of imperialism. Section 5 discusses six of the main functions that both literary and conceptual fictions can fulfill with regard to the making of imperialist mentalities. A short overview of the essays in the volume will be given in section 6, and section 7 will conclude the introduction by offering some suggestions for dealing with the topic of fictions of empire in the upper grades of secondary schools.

2. *What is Intercultural Studies? A revisionist look at colonial discourse from the point of view of post-colonial criticism*

The above epigraphs, taken from E.J. Hobsbawm's all-encompassing study *The Age of Empire* and from Edward Said's seminal work *Orientalism*, reflect some of the issues that are of crucial importance for anyone trying to come to grips with the Age of Empire and the logic of the fictions which provided the ideological backbone of British imperialism. If one agrees with Hobsbawm and Said that "the Age of Empire cries out for demystification" and that "fictions have their own logic and their own dialectic of growth or decline"[6], one is faced with the question of how such a revisionist project of exploring and demystifying the fictions of British imperialism is to be undertaken.

The title of this introduction indicates the approach that the contributors to this volume have adopted in order to suggest possible answers to the question. The articles not only provide a reassessment, from the point of view of post-colonial criticism, of some of the most influential literary fictions that deal with the British Empire, but they also try to illuminate the role these works have played in the making of imperialist mentalities. They try to show how novels, poetry, and a wide range of other genres came to the service of creating Victorian England's imperialist view of the world. The essays thus attempt to demystify what Andrea White has poignantly called "the energizing myth of English imperialism", which, she argues, was "the culture's dominant fiction".[7] By focussing on the relationship between culture and imperialism, they also chart the dialectic of growth and decline that the fictions of empire have had since the heyday of British imperialism in the late nineteenth century.

Rather than attempting to contribute to the ongoing theoretical discussions about those recent developments in the humanities that have come to be subsumed under the label of 'cultural studies', the essays will try to illustrate how one can actually 'do' intercultural studies. Taking the British Empire and the fictions that are associated with it as their historical and literary paradigm, the contributors offer concrete and practical answers to the question raised on the title page of the *Times Literary Supplement* of May 27, 1994: "What is Cultural Studies?" This headline testifies to the popularity that the approaches subsumed under the label of cultural studies currently enjoy, but the fact that it is couched in the form of a question draws attention to the many theoretical and methodological problems of cultural studies which have yet to be resolved.

We will suggest an approach to doing intercultural studies within a multi- or cross-disciplinary framework.[8] In doing this, we will take up a suggestion made by Lynn Hunt in her introduction to a collection of articles on *The New Cultural History*. Hunt argues that "the more cultural historical studies become and the more historical cultural studies become, the better for both".[9] Similarly, it can be argued that what is needed for coming to grips with the complex relationship between literary fictions on the one hand and the making of imperial mentalities, the invention of traditions, and the constitution of a nation's cultural heritage on the other is a cross-disciplinary approach to cultural studies. Proceeding from the epistemological premises of radical constructivism, such an approach incorporates the anti-mimetic view of the relationship between literary texts and their extra-literary contexts, something which poststructuralism and the New Historicism have both argued for. Such a view rests on the assumption that, instead of conceiving of culture and imperialism as two distinct entities, it is more profitable to explore the ways in which literature as well as other media and the imperial project mutually influenced and reinforced one another. Moreover, the approach adopted is cross-disciplinary in orientation in that it draws on both the theoretical framework of the history of mentalities and the insights of post-colonial criticism.

One of the main goals of the volume is to explore those peculiarities of colonial discourse that are characteristic of British imperialism. Following Michael Titzmann, the term 'discourse' can be defined as a system of thought, feeling, and argument that is characterized by three features: a specific topic or subject-matter, regularities of speech, and interdiscursive relations to other discourses.[10] Colonial discourse can thus be defined as the set of codes, stereotypes, and vocabulary employed whenever the relationship between a colonial power and its colonies is written or spoken about.[11] An analysis of colonial discourse must therefore look at "the variety of textual forms in which the West produced and codified knowledge about non-metropolitan areas and cultures, especially those under colonial control".[12] Since any attempt at drawing up an encompassing and systematic inventory of the features of colonial discourse would be doomed to failure, this volume focusses on some of its most important features and on literary manifestations of the imperial idea.

As anyone familiar with current developments in literary theory will know, the approach outlined would be inconceivable without the insights provided by post-colonial criticism.[13] This takes in a number of theoretical and critical approaches used to explore both the complex relationship between culture and colonialism and imperialism's ambivalent heritage. They focus either on the cultural products of the former colonies of the European empires or on the problems inherent in imperialist views and representations of the colonies and their relationship to their mother countries. Both varieties of post-colonial criticism offer revisionist counter-narratives to the tradition of European imperial narratives. The roots of post-colonial criticism, or colonial discourse theory and analysis, as it is sometimes called, go back to the important work of Frantz Fanon and to Michel Foucault's work on the history of systems of thought, which has drawn attention to the fact that knowledge and power are articulated in discursive practices. Among the leading practitioners and theorists of post-colonial criticism at present are such well-known scholars as Gayatri Chakravorty Spivak and Homi K. Bhabha, but Edward Said is often regarded as its founding-father: "It is perhaps no exaggeration to say that Edward Said's *Orientalism*, published in 1978, single-handedly inaugurates a new area of academic inquiry: colonial discourse, also referred to as colonial discourse theory or colonial discourse analysis."[14] In this seminal study, which established a revisionist way of looking at the roots of imperialism in European culture and which has become one of the canonical texts of both post-colonial criticism and cultural studies, Said gives an overview of European representations of and attitudes towards the Middle East. He tries to reconstruct how a particular mind-set shaped not only Western conceptions of the Orient but also a tradition of academic study of the Orient. Adopting the approach inaugurated by Said and taken up by other practitioners of post-colonial criticsm, the essays in this issue take a revisionist look at colonial discourse in order to explore the role that fictions of empire have played in the making of imperialist mentalities.

3. *The fictions of empire and the empires of fiction*

The subtitle of this volume is *Fictions of Empire*, and one might begin by explaining what that phrase can mean. According to one of the standard works on the subject, "Empire is a relationship, formal or informal, in which one state controls the effective political sovereignty of another political society".[15] Although the meaning of the word 'empire' is as clear as its reference, in the present context, to Britain's overseas colonies or 'possessions', as they were often called, the British Empire's "diverse character" needs to be stressed. The empire was, as John M. MacKenzie has emphasized, "at least four separate entities. It was the territories of settlement [...]. It was India [...]. It was a string of islands and staging posts, a combination of seventeenth-century sugar colonies and the spoils of wars with European rivals, China and other non-European cultures. And finally, Empire was the 'dependent' territories acquired largely in the last decades of the nineteenth century".[16]

In contrast to the word 'empire', 'fiction' is an ambiguous term which can easily generate confusion. As the *Oxford English Dictionary* shows, the word 'fiction' has quite different meanings. On the one hand, the word can designate "[t]hat which, or something that, is imaginatively invented" or, more specifically, "[t]he species of literature which is concerned with the narration of imaginary events and the portraiture of imaginary characters", viz. "[a] work of fiction; a novel or tale".[17] On the other hand, 'fiction' refers to any "supposition known to be at variance with fact, but conventionally accepted for some reason of practical convenience, conformity with traditional usage, decorum, or the like".[18] In this latter sense, fictions are used in Law, for instance, with the fiction that a corporation is a person separate from its members being a case in point. Such legal fictions are theoretical constructs or rules that assume something as true that is clearly false or at variance with fact.

The subtitle of the volume is deliberately ambiguous in that it self-consciously alludes to the the double meaning of 'fiction': "the meaning of 'fiction' as literary, nonreferential narrative and its meaning (often [...] in its plural form) as theoretical construct".[19] This double meaning is essential for the questions that the articles try to answer in that they are concerned with the interplay between works of fiction that deal with the British Empire and those theoretical and ideological constructs which constituted the imperial idea.

First, then, the phrase 'fictions of empire' simply refers to those literary narratives that focus on the British Empire. Nineteenth-century travel writing, the adventure fiction of such authors as Frederick Marryat, Robert Ballantyne, G.A. Henty and H. Rider Haggard, Kipling's stories and poems, and Conrad's novels constructed not only the imperial subject, but also immensely popular and influential fictional models of imperialism and of the empire.[20] The articles in this volume are concerned with a number of such particularly literary fictions that deal with the experience of the empire. But such a limited definition does not adequately account for the complexity of the issues involved in the relationship between culture and imperialism. In a broader sense, the subtitle of this volume refers to the diversity of theoretical and ideological constructs which the colonial discourse projected. These constructs can be called fictions because they were clearly at variance with fact.

Such conceptual and ideological fictions can be defined as recurring images of the empire, of the imperialist, of what he regarded as his mission, and of the colonized, the 'Other'. Such fictions consist of predispositions, biases, values, and epistemological habits which provide both agreed-upon codes of understanding and cultural traditions of looking at the world. In their entirety these fictions constitute that culturally sanctioned system of ideas, beliefs, presuppositions, and convictions which constitutes imperialist mentalities. Such ideological fictions are closely connected with literary fictions because they find their most succinct expression in conventional plot-lines, myths, and metaphors that support and legitimize the imperial project.

It is this second meaning of fiction that Said has in mind when he calls Orientalism a "system of ideological fictions" and when he equates that phrase with such terms as "a body of ideas, beliefs, clichés, or learning", "systems of thought", "discourses of power", and with Blake's famous "mind-forg'd manacles".[21] Moreover, since the "scope of Orientalism exactly matched the scope of empire"[22], most of what Said says about those Western conceptions of the Orient he calls Orientalism is equally relevant for understanding the structure and functions of the ideological fictions of empire this volume is concerned with. Just as "the Orient is an idea that has a history and a tradition of thought, imagery, and vocabulary that have given it reality and presence in and for the West"[23], the empire can also be profitably understood as a set of ingrained and largely unconscious beliefs, ideas, feelings, and values.

What the present volume, then, mainly attempts to explore is not the colonial and foreign policy of England that created the actual British Empire, but manifestations of the imperial idea, "the rise and growth of an Imperialist spirit in England"[24], as reflected in or constructed by contemporary literature. As John MacKenzie has convincingly demonstrated in his seminal work *Propaganda and Empire*, in the late nineteenth century an ideological cluster of ideas known as the 'New Imperialism' took shape and forged new links between imperialism and patriotism. It was compounded of Social Darwinism, militarism, and Christianity, and it fostered and led to the propagation of the belief that Empire was an adventure and an ennobling responsibility. Moreover, MacKenzie argues that there was an extraordinary continuity in this system of ideas from late Victorian times until well into the twentieth century and that it was of central importance to British self-perception and pride.

What MacKenzie's work and that of other scholars on popular imperialism has also shown is that the ideological fictions that constituted the New Imperialism were not just reflected in or produced by the canonical works of 'high culture'. On the contrary, from the late nineteenth century to the second world war, nationalist and imperialist ideas were conveyed through various popular genres and media, e.g. boys' stories and other fiction for young people, the music hall, popular art, school books, postcards, packaging, cinema, exhibitions, parades, and a broad range of other genres and media.[25] In other words, the empires of fiction are not the only fictions of empire that one should take into consideration if one wants to come to grips with the questions of what made up the imperial idea and of how it manifested itself.[26]

What the essays in this issue are mainly concerned with is not the geographical or political extensions of the real British Empire but the relationship between literature and the mental realm that was discursively constructed and called 'the Empire' or the 'imperial idea', an empire 'of the mind' or of the imagination. They look at imperialism as a cultural or mental phenomenon, as a habit of mind or a structure of ideas and attitudes. Focussing on the images of the British Empire as they manifested themselves in textual representations, the articles try to throw light on both the ways in which the imperial idea was given literary form and on the question of how the British Empire was perceived, experienced, and understood by its contemporaries.

Instead of assuming that imperialism was merely reflected in literary works, the contributors argue that narrative fictions, patriotic poetry, boys' stories, history books, travellers' tales, and a host of overtly propagandistic genres played an active and constitutive role in creating the imperial idea and in making imperialist mentalities. Moreover, they maintain that literary as well as nonliterary fictions of empire have not only given the British Empire and the imperial idea reality and presence but that they have also secured the empire a lasting and significant place in England's cultural memory. The ideologial fictions of empire which such genres helped to create served as a filter through which the imperial experience came into the British public consciousness.

What are the most important ideological fictions that constituted the conceptual backbone of imperialism and that determined contemporary perceptions of the Empire? One of the dominating fictions of British imperialism was the ingrained belief in English superiority and the concomitant conviction that the native peoples in the various colonies were in need of elevation and civilization. Said even goes so far as to locate "the essence of Orientalism" in "the ineradicable distinction between Western superiority and Oriental inferiority", which was itself based on the "binary typology of advanced and backward (or subject) races".[27] Because of what Said has called "the structures of attitude and reference" that constituted the imperial world-view, this fiction went hand in hand with another assumption fostered by Social Darwinism, viz. the ingrained belief "that subject races should be ruled, that they *are* subject races, that one race deserves and has consistently earned the right to be considered the race whose main mission is to expand beyond its own domain".[28]

Moreover, Said has drawn attention to two other important conceptual fictions of empire or features that are characteristic of imperialism as a mode of thought and a set of attitudes: "stereotypes about 'the African' [or Indian or Irish or Jamaican or Chinese] mind" and "the notions about bringing civilization to primitive or barbaric peoples".[29] The colonized peoples were not only habitually regarded as inferior, but they were turned into undifferentiated types, the ingrained stereotypes about the Oriental or the African.

These processes of dividing up the world into 'them' and 'us', of fostering a sense of one's own superiority that was based on the principle of inequality, and of creating cultural stereotypes in turn brought forth and legitimized the notion of 'the White Man's Burden'. According to this fiction, it was the White Man's job, duty, or even mission to act as a bearer of moral and intellectual values, to bring humanity and civilization to primitive peoples, and to impose their benefits on a world of savagery. The deep-seated belief in European superiority over Oriental backwardness finds its most succinct expression in Kipling's idea of 'the White Man', whose (self-imposed) burden of fulfilling his civilizing mission was regarded as his unalterable destiny. What the ideological fiction of being a White Man entailed, is succinctly as well as critically summed up by Said:

> Behind the White Man's mask of amiable leadership there is always the express willingness to use force, to kill and be killed. What dignifies his mission is some sense of intellectual dedication; he is a White Man, but not for mere profit, since his 'chosen star' presumably sits far above earthly gain. [...]
> Being a White Man [...] meant specific judgments, evaluations, gestures. It was a form of authority before which nonwhites, and even whites themselves, were expected to bend.[30]

Another important ideological fiction of British imperialism was "the ideology of empire as family"[31], which was vividly expressed in the form of conceptual metaphors. The recurrent use of the family metaphor assigned the colonies the role of children dependent on the tutelage of the mother country. The widespread dissemination of this particular trope justifies calling the image of the British Empire as a world-wide family one of the metaphors that popular imperialism lived by.[32] Closely related to these ideological and metaphorical fictions was another recurrent feature of what Said has aptly called "the imperial lingua franca", namely the tendency to delineate the relationship between Britain and its colonies "in terms of possession, in terms of a large geographical space wholly owned by an efficient colonial master".[33]

As even a brief glance at a random selection of texts concerned with the British Empire will illustrate, talking about the relationship between Britain and its colonies in terms of possession often went hand in hand with another feature of colonial and imperialist discourse, viz. with denigrating or even erasing the native population of the countries that were colonized. What is implied in such a phrase as "many blank spaces on the earth"[34], which fascinate Conrad's Marlow, for instance, is that there are whole regions waiting desperately for the colonialist or imperialist to populate them: "Colonialism conceptually depopulated countries either by acknowledging the native but relegating him or her to the category of the subhuman, or simply by looking through the native and denying his/her existence."[35]

In addition to these fictions and rhetorical figures that one encounters in colonial discourse, there are a number of other more specific fictions of empire. In his thorough monograph *The Language of Empire*, R.H. MacDonald has provided an overview of some of the most influential myths and metaphors of popular imperialism. One of the main fictions imperialism lived by manifested itself in a "poetics of war" and in the "public school code of 'playing the game'". Both are based on the "metaphor of war as sport – and its corollary, sport as war", which encouraged people "to behave as though the battle-field was an extension of the playing field, requiring the same attitudes and spirit".[36] The vocabulary of war provided imperialism with a set of metaphors, of which "the trope of war-as-a-lesson" is another famous, or rather infamous, example. It also supplied the imperial project with stereotyped plots: "The framing narrative of imperialism, the ur-plot, was that of conquest: first came the traders and missionaries; the 'natives' resisted or 'rebelled'; then came the army to conquer and pacify."[37] Although the above brief overview of some of the main ideological fictions of popular imperialism is anything but complete, it may serve to convince the sceptic that there is more to the phrase 'fictions of empire' than meets the eye or than anyone thinking only in terms of narrative fiction may have anticipated.

4. Culture and imperialism: literature, the cultural construction of reality, and the making of imperialist mentalities

Making a distinction between the literary fictions that deal with the British Empire and the conceptual and ideological fictions of popular imperialism, of course, raises the question of how the relationship between literature and imperialism can be conceptualized. Despite the fact that in *Orientalism* Said suggested that an essay on culture and imperialism should be written, this suggestion was not taken up until he himself published a systematic study of that particular topic, namely his *Culture and Imperialism*, which appeared in 1993. In this important work, Said provides a methodological framework for applying the well-known epigraph of E.M. Forster's novel *Howard's End* – "Only Connect" – to the realms of culture and imperialism. The articles in the present volume follow the path laid out by Said in that they, too, consider literary fictions of empire within the context in which they were written and read, in order to "to show the involvements of culture with expanding empires, to make observations about art that preserve its unique endowments and at the same time map its affiliations".[38] Looking at the connections between fiction and the pursuit of imperial aims is, of course, something that has often been done before. Yet the question of how culture participates in imperialism has traditionally been posed only in a mimetic framework.

What has been less explored is the extent to which literature may have played a constitutive rather than a reflective role in colonial and imperialist discourse. The articles in this volume question the traditional assumption that the relationship between fiction and reality is based on mimesis. They argue that it is more rewarding to conceptualize fiction as an active force in its own right leading to the actual generation of ways of thinking and of attitudes and, thus, of something that stands behind historical developments.[39] Rather than being merely a passive vehicle that reproduced the imperial ideology of their time, narrative fictions need to be conceptualized as a productive medium that can play a creative role in the production of the ideological fictions that provide the conceptual framework of imperialism.

The articles argue that the imperial idea and the fictions it projected did not merely copy features of the 'objective' historical reality, but constructed an imperial ideology consisting of stereotypes, beliefs, feelings, and values. Although it would be wrong as well as patently absurd to argue that the British Empire was just an idea with no corresponding reality, it would be equally erroneous to assume that ideological fictions in any way represented real phenomena. Studies dealing with popular imperialism ought to take to heart what Peter Burke has called the "philosophical foundation of the new history", viz. "the idea that reality is socially or culturally constituted".[40] Such a view of the 'social construction of reality', to borrow Berger and Luckmann's well-known formula, has important and far-reaching consequences for the conceptualisation of the relationship between the language of popular imperialism and the reality of the British Empire: "Words did not just reflect social and political reality; they were instruments for transforming reality."[41] One needs to emphasize that the discursive practices of imperialism did not reflect objectively preexisting properties. On the contrary, the conceptual and ideological fictions of empire constituted the very reality they purported merely to reflect. Creating their own reality, they not only assigned roles to the colonizer and the colonized, but they also gave meaning to the imperialist project. What Said says about academic texts is therefore also true for most of the nonfictional and fictional works that deal with the British Empire: "Most important, such texts can *create* not only knowledge but also the very reality they appear to describe."[42]

On the basis of such a constructivist view of the relationship between colonial discourse and reality it can be argued that the forms of thought and sets of values that we have called conceptual 'fictions of empire' belong to those objects that "are made by the mind, and that these objects, while appearing to exist objectively, have only a fictional reality".[43] Moreover, colonial discourse is highly self-referential in that what it considers to be a fact does not reflect historical reality, but the preconceptions, values, and perceptions of the colonialist who produces the discourse in the first place. Just like Orientalism, the colonial discourse which projected such ideological fictions as those outlined above "responded more to the culture that produced it than to its putative object, which was also produced by the West": "it ascribes reality and reference to objects (other words) of its own making".[44] Such a constructivist conceptualisation of the relationship between culture and imperialism is indebted to the insights of a number of fairly recent approaches, especially to the New Historicism.[45] The New Historicism conceives of works of literature not as mirrors of reality, but as "historical and cognitive events in their own right"[46], "as texts which are involved in the actual production of history":[47]

> If texts exist in what – to be deliberately unfashionable – one could call a dialectical relationship with their social and historical context – produced by, but also productive of, particular forms of knowledge, ideologies, power relations, institutions and practices – then an analysis of the texts of imperialism has a particular urgency, given their implication in far-reaching, and continuing, systems of domination and economic exploitation.[48]

If one adopts such a view of the dialectical relationship between culture and imperialism, it becomes clear that fictional narratives or poetical works that deal with the British Empire need not necessarily just reflect imperialist issues and preconceptions. Instead of merely reproducing the imperial ideology of their time, literary fictions concerned with the empire can just as well contest, criticize, or deconstruct the ideological and racist premises on which imperialism rested. Joseph Conrad's and E.M. Forster's ambivalent fictions of empire are a case in point, whereas Rider Haggard's and G.A. Henty's works, for instance, show very little (if any) critical distance from the imperial project.

It is therefore not the question of correspondence, or the lack thereof, between the literary and ideological fictions of empire on the one hand and the 'real' British Empire on the other that is at issue, but the nature and internal consistency of that system of thought, feeling, and perception that constitutes the imperial idea and frame of mind. The disparity between texts or discourses and reality is the rule rather than the exception so far as colonial and imperialist discourse is concerned.[49] The significance of literary fictions of empire to an analysis of imperialist discourse is thus not in the historical accuracy of the accounts they give of colonialism, but in the light they throw on both the system of thought, attitudes, and values that informs imperialism and on the way fictions construct the past and shape cultural memory. Said has argued that such cultural forms as the novel "were immensely important in the formation of imperial attitudes, references, and experiences".[50] If the empire was viewed in a framework constructed largely out of literary and ideological fictions, then a revisionist analysis of the fictions, myths, and metaphors of British Imperialism is a good place to start in attempting to demystify the Age of Empire.

Anyone trying to connect literary fictions with the imperial process of which they were a part is, of course, faced with the difficult problem of how one can determine the imperialist, racist, or ideological bias of a given work. Since novels or poems do not generally do the critic the favour of making any direct statements for or against imperialism (or feminism, or anything else, for that matter), the critic has to expose them to detailed textual analysis. The things to look for, according to Said, "are style, figures of speech, setting, narrative devices, historical and social circumstances, *not* the correctness of the representation nor its fidelity to some great original".[51] If one substitutes the word 'empire' for 'Orient' in the following quote, one gets more than just an inkling of how to come to terms with the way in which the ideological fictions of imperialism implied or created in literary fictions that deal with the British Empire can be ascertained:

> Everyone who writes about the Orient must locate himself vis-à-vis the Orient; translated into his text, this location includes the kind of narrative voice he adopts, the type of structure he builds, the kinds of images, themes, motifs that circulate in his text – all of which add up to deliberate ways of addressing the reader, containing the Orient, and finally, representing it or speaking in its behalf.[52]

This means that an analysis of narrative structure, plot, point of view, narration, focalization and characterization is a prerequisite for determining the role that novels dealing with the empire may have played in the making of imperialist mentalities. Similarly, since poems restructure the empire through their use of metaphors, rhetorical tropes, and rhythms, it is these textual devices that provide insights into the complex relationship between culture and imperialism, between literary fictions of empire and the ideological fictions they project.

5. *Making imperialist mentalities, inventing cultural traditions, legitimizing imperialism, and other functions of fictions of empire*

The remarkable discrepancy between the often harsh and ignoble historical reality of the British Empire and the euphemistic myths and metaphors projected by colonial discourse raises the question of why the British were so prone to constructing complacent and self-congratulatory fictions of empire. At least part of the answer can be sought in the fact that the word 'empire' was generally regarded as an inappropriate term for designating the relationship between a mother country and her colonies. The same holds true of the word 'imperialism', which had a very bad press, as Laura Chrisman and Patrick Williams have recently pointed out: "In Britain, the term imperialism had never been a popular one – quite the reverse in fact, since it carried connotations of over-weening ambition and self-aggrandisement, the very antitheses of Britishness."[53] The connotations of the words empire and imperialism constituted a threat to the notion of Englishness, i.e. to those traditions that were regarded as specifically English.[54] Important though this insight into the unpopularity of the words empire and imperialism in Britain is, it hardly suffices to answer the question of what functions the conceptual and ideological fictions of empire outlined above may have fulfilled.

In the first place, by reducing both the complexity and the strangeness of the empire's diverse character such fictions imposed form upon an untidy reality and served as models for thought. They turned vast geographical areas into manageable entities, transformed complex series of diffuse events into simple imperialist myths, and made soldiers into heroes. Despite their inevitably reductive character, such conceptual fictions can fulfill heuristic or cognitive functions in that "they represent or stand for a very large entity, otherwise impossibly diffuse, which they enable one to grasp or see".[55] In their capacity as mental models, fictions of empire served as means for explaining complex historical processes and constellations. They helped to make sense of the imperial experience and "familiarised the public with the bearings of the question[s]"[56] that were raised by the debates and the agitation about the British Empire.

Secondly, the literary and conceptual fictions fulfilled normative functions because they authorized ideologically charged views of the relationship between the mother country and her colonies. Popularizing imperialist attitudes and norms, the myths and metaphors of popular imperialism established a configuration of values that was conducive to maintaining an imperial world view. Although colonial discourse purported merely to describe the empire and the relationship between the colonizer and the colonized, what it actually did was assign roles to them. Imposing not only structure but also transformations and corrections upon raw reality, the ideological fictions of popular imperialism shaped both the prevailing view of the relationship between the mother country and her colonies and the perception of the encounter between the colonizer and the colonized. By translating the foreignness of the imperial experience into a highly stylized language, literary as well as conceptual fictions of empire served to create habits of thought, feeling, and perception conducive to advancing the imperial project. More specifically, popular fictions helped to transform the public perception of the military which came to be viewed in a completely different light as a result of successful campaigns in the colonies.[57]

Thirdly, by establishing oppositions between 'us' and 'them', between self and other, fictions of empire served as an important means of maintaining an advantageous British self-image and of constructing Britain's national identity. The fiction of the White Man's burden, for instance, supported, or even created, a pronounced sense of self-regard as a nation of great power destined to wield its civilizing influence over 'an empire on which the sun never set' (as the famous formula had it). Colonial discourse and the fictions of empire it projected are closely bound up with the development of Britain's cultural identity, because a people's collective identity, just like personal identity, is neither natural nor stable, but discursively constructed: "In an important sense, we are dealing with the formation of cultural identities understood not as essentializations [...] but as contrapuntal ensembles, for it is the case that no identity can ever exist by itself and without an array of opposites, negatives, oppositions".[58] Emphasizing one's own superiority, enhancing Britain's self-pride in its achievements, or denigrating stereotyped Orientals or Africans was thus not an end in itself, but part of that complex political and cultural process that Linda Colley has aptly called 'Forging the Nation'.[59] In this respect, as in so many others, the so-called 'Indian Mutiny' was one of the most significant ideological and moral turning-points because this key event of imperial history transformed both the reputation of the army and the conception Britain had of itself, of its national characteristics, and of its role in the world.[60]

Fourth, many of the literary as well as of the conceptual fictions of empire constructed and propagated a patriotic view of imperial history and transmitted it from one generation to the next. Thus they played a significant part in the shaping of cultural memory that has been called the 'invention of tradition'.[61] Popular history, historical novels, and the official historiography of empire created what MacDonald – using Tennyson's phrase – has called "the Island Story", which had "very little to do with fact, but a great deal to do with metaphorical or imaginative reality [...]. Like all good stories, it had a plot, with a beginning and an ending, and in between, a series of crises".[62] It was in the framework of these patriotic myths of imperialism that officers acquired the aura of heroes and that these British heroes won each battle against native villains. The history of imperialism was thereby reduced to a series of memorable and heroic moments, each of which was endowed with patriotic meaning. MacDonald has called these mythologized events which made the 'Island Story' accessible and by which the imperial past has largely been remembered "Deeds of Glory", which "provided a pattern-book of heroism" and which were modelled on "an aristocratic sense of chivalry".[63] For obvious reasons, representations of such deeds of glory are of great interest to the cultural historian interested in the set of values underlying imperialism: "A hero is a product of his society, the culture gives the hero's life its particular meaning. The culture, ultimately, produces heroes who reflect its values".[64] The growth of legends about the exemplary lives and heroic deeds of such eminent Victorians as Lord Nelson and the Duke of Wellington, the two English champions of the Napoleonic wars, of General Charles Gordon, the epitome of the soldier as Christian martyr and gentleman, or of Sir Henry Havelock, who died a heroic death as a Christian soldier when he tried to relieve the besieged in Lucknow, provides typical examples of the role fictions of empire played in the construction of national identity and the shaping of cultural memory.

Fifth, fictions of empire fulfilled a legitimizing function because they provided rationalizations and justifications of imperialism. They legitimized colonial conquest and imperial rule by dignifying them with a high-minded mission which putatively aimed at conferring moral, religious, and material benefits onto the colonies. According to Said, the "important thing was to dignify simple conquest with an idea, to turn the appetite for more geographical space into a theory about the special relationship between geography on the one hand and civilized or uncivilized peoples on the other".[65] The ideological fictions that imperialism lived by served as means of retrospective and prospective justification, because they legitimized imperial rule in advance as well as after the fact.

Last but certainly not least, fictions of empire served as subtle means of propaganda and as ideological handmaidens of imperialism, because they glorified the imperial project, disseminated highly advantageous myths and metaphors of popular imperialism, and created a cult of exemplary heroes. The overtly propagandistic function that literary fictions played in the making of imperial mentalities is particularly obvious in Victorian popular literature. The popular fictions of prolific writers like G.A. Henty, Robert M. Ballantyne, Frederick Marryat, Cutcliffe Hyne and Edgar Wallace "became handbooks for the imperial programme".[66]

Literary fictions of empire, in particular, could fulfill such normative, legitimizing, and propagandistic functions because they shaped habits of thought, feeling, and perception. Their plots, myths, and metaphors played an important part in making imperialist mentalities because they organised "the metaphorical realities of empire" and "conditioned the way in which those who used them thought of the world".[67] The limited imagery, rhetoric, and vocabulary of popular imperialism provided conceptual and normative frameworks which functioned as more or less distorting lenses through which the empire was experienced.

6. *Essays in this Issue*

The articles that follow will explore the relationship between literature and the growth and decline of the imperial idea. The essays try to illuminate both the roles particular literary fictions of empire have played in the making of imperialist mentalities and the cognitive, ideological, and moral patterns by which the imperial world view was structured. Although the main focus lies on texts that appeared during the phase of late Victorian imperialism, the diachronic range of the contributions extends from the mid-Victorian period to the present. Most of the articles deal with novels and other narrative fictions, but other genres – e.g. travel literature, poetry, and history books – are also taken into consideration. In geographic terms, the articles range from English texts concerned with the colonial experience in India and Africa over South African literature to Indian-English novels and Chinese Canadian literature. Although the methods adopted by the contributors are diverse, they all focus on individual works and on the connections between literary fictions and the values, modes of thinking, and sentiments these texts reflect, criticize, or deconstruct, in order to throw light on the role literature played in the making of imperialist mentalities.

Adopting a historiographical approach, John MacKenzie surveys the development of scholarship in the area of popular imperialism and shows how fruitful the use of a wide range of non-official sources like school textbooks, juvenile and 'pulp' literature, music hall songs, advertising and other media of popular entertainment can be for promoting a more thorough understanding of British attitudes about the empire, particularly of ideas prevalent among the general population. In his broad overview of the complex relationship between imperialism and popular culture, MacKenzie shows that popular manifestations of the imperial idea often conveyed a similar set of ideas to those represented in the canonical literary works of authors like Rider Haggard or Kipling. In addition to discussing important recent approaches and their results MacKenzie indicates new directions for research that have opened up. The fairly extensive bibliography with which his article is supplemented is intended to give readers an ample guide to relevant books and articles on a quickly expanding and fascinating area.

The majority of the other articles focus on literary fictions dealing with the British Empire that appeared during the colonial or imperialist phase in the late nineteenth century, which was characterized by the acquisition of territories, mainly in Africa, by the European powers. British attitudes towards the empire and indigenous cultures were characterized by a number of conceptual fictions, three of which are analyzed in the articles by Vera Nünning, Bernhard Reitz, and Ansgar Nünning. In her article on the British reactions to the threat of losing the 'Jewel in the Crown', the Indian possessions, Vera Nünning shows how non-fictional texts – mainly diaries, letters, biographies, and history books – had their part in turning a real historical event into a powerful imperial myth. She argues that it was this process of mythologizing of imperial history, rather than the historical facts, which shaped cultural memory. Concentrating on a key event that took place during the Indian Rebellion in 1857, i.e. what has come to be known as 'the siege of Lucknow', the article investigates how the cruel, desparate, and inefficient acts of English soldiers and civilians were painted in heroic colours in a wide range of popular fictions and that such depictions were taken for historical 'fact' up to the 1950s, serving to justify British rule in India and elsewhere.

Exploring how a particular genre helped to shape imperialist mentalities, Bernhard Reitz concentrates on the role which popular adventure novels in general and the image of the Christian gentleman in particular played in the construction of imperial fictions. After delineating the Christian, moralistic, and nationalistic legitimation of the British Empire which was current in the second half of the nineteenth century, Reitz shows that Rider Haggard's *quest romances* moulded an imperial mentality by redefining and propagating imperial values while, at the same time, idealizing Englishness and constructing an idealized British past.

Focussing on metaphorical constructions of empire, Ansgar Nünning examines the structural properties and functions of the metaphor of the British Empire as a family in the poetry of Tennyson and Kipling. He argues that this rhetorical figure, which was used in a wide range of fictional and nonfictional genres, was no mere poetical embellishment, but a conceptual metaphor which affected the ways in which people perceived and thought about the Empire. The metaphorical uses of kinship terms provided a way of seeing one domain, namely the relationship between England (as the mother country) and her colonies, in terms of another conceptual domain, viz. our knowledge of kinship and family life.[68] Such kinship metaphors turned political conflicts into family squabbles, because they allowed people to endow the British Empire with the moral, emotional, and normative values of the family.

Whereas the texts dealt with in the essays already mentioned advanced a very favourable view of the British Empire, the two following articles delineate the gradual development of a more critical stance to British rule. Erhard Reckwitz provides an overview of three literary genres important for the thematization of colonial ideals in South African English literature. After explaining his theoretical framework by defining the terms discourse and colonial discourse with reference to current post-colonial theories, Reckwitz discusses the impact of the adventure novel, the "colonial pastoral", and the farm novel. Although the last genre was the most suitable mode for justifying the expropriation of land, Reckwitz shows that it also provided the germ of a strong counter-discourse which was critical of colonial exploitation and subjugation. Marion Gymnich discusses the construction and deconstruction of imperialist modes of thought in Rudyard Kipling's *Kim*, Joseph Conrad's *Heart of Darkness*, and E.M. Forster's *A Passage to India*. She shows that, in contrast to Victorian adventure fictions and to Kipling's *Kim*, the novels of Forster and, to an even greater degree, of Conrad imply an ambivalent view of the British domination of indigenous peoples. Since *A Passage to India* and *Heart of Darkness* do not merely reproduce the imperial ideology of their time, but question and criticize many of its assumptions, Conrad and Forster mark the transition from the imperial enthusiasm of the late nineteenth century, epitomized in Charles Dilke's vision of a 'Greater Britain', to the growing disillusion with the imperial project and the turning back to 'Little England', which came to be characteristic of the twentieth century.

The last two articles deal with different historical experiences of anti-colonial resistance to empire. They explore texts that belong to the post-colonial period and that reflect changed political and cultural realities. In these texts indigenous norms and values have come to dominate over British imperial ideals. Davids' investigation of the 'Amazing Mix', which characterizes the mixture of 'eastern' and 'western' concepts and values in Indian-English literature, discusses the various ways in which Indian conceptions of religion, politics, and everyday life are juxtaposed against English systems of thought. Looking at novels and short stories written in the twentieth century, Davids presents a spectrum of texts, ranging from the assertion of 'purely Indian' concepts to that 'amazing mix' in which cultural contradictions come together in complex mixtures. That the empire is indeed writing back, is demonstrated by Ronald Hatch, who looks at the literature Chinese writers have produced in Canada. Dealing with a former white settler colony with a history of both French and English colonialism, he examines the difficulties of overcoming the highly ambivalent heritage of empire and of finding an original voice. Whereas the other articles looked at the interaction between the native inhabitants of Africa or India and British rulers, Hatch discusses the impact of the racism of white settlers in Canada on Chinese immigrants, who came in great numbers from the middle of the nineteenth century onwards, but only found their own voice in the 1970s.

What Indian-English literature has in common with other post-colonial literatures is "that they emerged in their present form out of the experience of colonization and asserted themselves by foregrounding the tension with the imperial power, and by emphasizing their differences from the assumptions of the imperial centre".[69] What gives Davids' article a certain paradigmatic quality is that it explores the ways in which the ideological fictions of empire and the world-view they propagated have come to be deconstructed in post-colonial literatures everywhere. Moreover, many of the subversive strategies employed in the novels that Davids discusses can be related to those "two principles [...] which are central to all post-colonial writing: first, there is a repetition of the general idea of the interdependence of language and identity – you are the way you speak. [...] second, there is the more distinctive act of the post-colonial text, which is to inscribe difference and absence as a corollary of that identity".[70]

7. Some notes on teaching fictions of empire

Although the essays in this issue do not directly address the question of the possibilities of teaching fictions of empire, there can be little doubt that the subject of literary responses to the British Empire can be profitably dealt with in an intercultural framework in the upper grades of secondary schools. Despite the fact that intercultural approaches in foreign language teaching have recently been the subject of considerable debate, there is still a lack of practical suggestions for illustrating how such approaches could be applied in specific courses.[71] It is beyond the scope of this introduction to delineate a course calendar for an *Unterrichtsreihe* on the topic of 'fictions of empire' or to make detailed didactic suggestions, but a few concluding remarks about the selection of suitable texts may at least facilitate the preparation for those interested in teaching a course on this subject.

Teachers trying to select suitable texts will find two anthologies very helpful for providing literary glimpses of the British Empire and other textual material pertinent specifically to the relationship between Britain and India, viz. F. Jarmann's, G.H. Kämmer's, and D. Whybra's *Empire and After. Literary Glimpses of the British Empire* (Hannover, 1986) and R. Musman's *Britain and India – the love and the hate* (Paderborn, 1978). In addition to these useful collections and to the fictions analysed in the present issue, there are a number of other literary texts dealing with the British Empire that are eminently teachable. Two obvious cases in point are Ruth Prawer Jhabvala's novel *Heat and Dust* (1975) and Paul Scott's *Staying On* (1977), both of which were awarded the Booker Prize for fiction. Both of these novels are set in India and deal with the enormous changes in the relationship between England and India after the achievement of Indian independence in 1947. Moreover, there are many other relevant and teachable novels[72], and some are even readily available in inexpensive editions specifically designed for teaching purposes and supplemented with useful explanatory notes, coursework assignments and additional information on the author and the historical background.[73]

The list of books that may be taken into consideration as set texts in a course on the fictions of empire is, of course, anything but exhausted by these works or by the texts analysed by the essays in this issue. The growing awareness that "the Empire had not been built by choirboys"[74], already latently present in Conrad's fiction, has led to a wide range of post-colonial novels that provide revisionist accounts of the imperial experience. The works of authors from the former colonies, e.g. Chinua Achebe's, Peter Carey's, Nadine Gordimer's, Janet Frame's, Doris Lessing's, Timothy Mo's, V.S. Naipaul's, Ben Okri's, Caryl Phillips', Ngugi wa Thiong'o's, and, of course, Salman Rushdie's[75], to name but a few, come readily to mind as possible texts that might supplement (or even replace) the rather short list of somewhat outdated English classics that have been used in foreign language teaching in German schools for years. Moreover, well-known British writers like J.G. Ballard, William Boyd, J.G. Farrell, Paul Scott, Barry Unsworth, and many others have also provided revisionist fictional explorations of Britain's imperial past, most of which are anything but glorifications of the Empire. James Gordon Farrell, for instance, an author who won considerable acclaim in Britain during the seventies and who was awarded the prestigious Booker Prize for his novel *The Siege of Krishnapur* (1973), thematizes, satirizes, and debunks a wide range of clichés about imperialism in his historical novels by providing miniature versions of key episodes involved in the decline of the British Empire. In his novels such literary devices as the time-structure, the semantization of place and of material possessions, the use of illness and disease as recurring metaphors, and the inversion of roles, attitudes, and beliefs undermine the ideological justification of the British mission.[76] Like many of the works of the post-colonial literatures, Farrell's novels lay bare the values and unspoken assumptions that stand behind the British Empire.

In addition, anyone interested in teaching a course on the impact of literary fictions on the growth and decline of popular imperialism will find in the following essays suggestions for doing intercultural studies and food for thought about the question of why it is worthwhile to encourage students to explore the relationship between the imperial past and the present. By discussing and deconstructing the central ideological fictions of imperialism that are inscribed in many literary (as well as nonliterary!) works, the articles demonstrate that not only "the *guild* of Orientalists" but high and popular culture as well "has a specific history of complicity with imperial power, which it would be Panglossian to call irrelevant".[77] Moreover, only if we understand the logic and structure of what we have called conceptual and ideological fictions of empire will we be able to recognize "where and how our view of things is inflected (or infected) by colonialism and its constituent elements of racism, over-categorization, and deferral to the centre".[78] A great deal of the value and relevance of a course on such an unusual topic as 'fictions of empire' lies in this continuity between the past and the present: "Mentalities created by yesterday's certainties survive more frequently than some would like to believe. These mentalities still extensively influence those of today. The effort to collate and interpret such mentalities created in the past may well constitute in the present and the future, therefore, a moral prophylactic."[79] Anyone interested in these complex processes would therefore be well advised to heed the implied warning with which Said concludes his *Orientalism*: "systems of thought like Orientalism, discourses of power, ideological fictions – mind-forg'd manacles – are all too easily made, applied, and guarded".[80] If the discourse of popular imperialism cries out for demystification, then teaching a course on fictions of empire is surely as good a place to start as any.

Notes

* We should like to thank Jon Erickson for reading and commenting on an earlier draft of this article and for suggesting valuable improvements.

1 Cf. B. von Lutz: „Die Auseinandersetzung mit dem Britischen Empire in der zeitgenössischen englischen Lyrik". *Arbeiten aus Anglistik und Amerikanistik* 10,1-2, 1985, 109-121. – B. von Lutz: „Das Britische Empire in ausgewählten englischen Dramen der Gegenwart: Kritik und Nostalgie". *Literatur in Wissenschaft und Unterricht* 17,1, 1984, 21-35.

2 For these key concepts of cultural studies see J. Assmann: „Kollektives Gedächtnis und kulturelle Identität". – In J. Assmann, T. Hölscher (Eds.): *Kultur und Gedächtnis.* Frankfurt, 1988, pp. 9-19.

3 S. Bassnett: "Teaching British Cultural Studies: Reflections on the Why and the How". *Journal for the Study of British Cultures* 1,1, 1994, 63-74, here p. 71.

4 E. Said: *Culture and Imperialism.* London, 1993, pp. 12, 288.

5 Cf. J.A. Mangan: "Making Imperial Mentalities". – In J.A. Mangan (Ed.): *Making Imperial Mentalities. Socialisation and British Imperialism.* Manchester, New York, 1990, pp. 1-22.

6 Cf. E.J. Hobsbawm: *The Age of Empire 1875-1914.* London, 1989, p. 5. – E. Said: *Orientalism. Western Conceptions of the Orient.* Harmondsworth, 1995 [[1]1978], pp. 62, 328.

7 A. White: *Joseph Conrad and the Adventure Tradition. Constructing and Deconstructing the Imperial Subject.* Cambridge, 1993, p. 6.

8 For a theoretical and terminological outline of an interdisciplinary approach to cultural studies, see A. Nünning: „Literatur, Mentalitäten und kulturelles Gedächtnis: Grundriß, Leitbegriffe und Perspektiven einer anglistischen Kulturwissenschaft". – In A. Nünning (Ed.): *Literaturwissenschaftliche Theorien, Modelle, Methoden: Eine Einführung.* Trier, 1995, pp. 173-197.

9 L. Hunt: "Introduction: History, Culture, Text". – In L. Hunt (Ed.): *The New Cultural History.* Berkeley, 1989, pp. 1-22, here p. 22.

10 Cf. M. Titzmann: „Skizze einer integrativen Literaturgeschichte und ihres Ortes in einer Systematik der Literaturwissenschaft". – In M. Titzmann (Ed.): *Modelle des literarischen Strukturwandels.* Tübingen, 1991, pp. 395-438, here p. 406: „erstens durch einen *Redegegenstand*, zweitens durch *Regularitäten der Rede*, drittens durch *interdiskursive Relationen* zu anderen Diskursen".

11 Cf. the definition that E. Said: *Orientalism*, p. 71, gives of "Orientalist discourse".

12 L. Chrisman, P. Williams: "Colonial Discourse and Post-Colonial Theory: An Introduction". – In L. Chrisman, P. Williams (Eds.): *Colonial Discourse and Post-Colonial Theory.* New York, London, 1993, pp. 1-20, here p. 5.

13 For a concise and illuminating introduction to the theoretical assumptions of this approach, see E. Kreutzer: „Theoretische Grundlagen postkolonialer Literaturkritik". – In A. Nünning (Ed.): *Literaturwissenschaftliche Theorien, Modelle, Methoden*, pp. 199-213. – The following definition is indebted to J. Hart, T. Goldie: "Post-colonial theory". – In I. R. Makaryk (Ed.): *Encyclopedia of Contemporary Literary Theory. Approaches, Scholars, Terms.* Toronto, 1993, pp. 155-158.

14 L. Chrisman, P. Williams: "Colonial Discourse and Post-Colonial Theory", p. 5.

15 M.W. Doyle: *Empires.* Ithaca, 1986, p. 45.

16 J. MacKenzie: "Introduction". – In J. MacKenzie: *Propaganda and Empire. The Manipulation of British Public Opinion, 1880-1960.* Manchester, 1984, pp. 1-14, here p. 1.

17 *Oxford English Dictionary*, s.v. "fiction".

18 Ibid.

19 D. Cohn: "Optics and Power in the Novel". *New Literary History* 26, 1995, 3-20, here 18.

20 Cf. A. White: *Joseph Conrad and the Adventure Tradition.* – Z.T. Sullivan: *Narratives of Empire. The Fictions of Rudyard Kipling.* Cambridge, 1993.

21 E. Said: *Orientalism*, pp. 321, 205, 328. – Cf. also the use of the phrase "nationalist fiction" in E. Said: *Culture and Imperialism*, p. 20.

22 E. Said: *Orientalism*, p. 104.

23 Ibid., p. 5.

24 C.A. Bodelsen: *Studies in Mid-Victorian Imperialism.* London, 1960 [[1]1924], p. 7.

25 Cf. J.M. MacKenzie: *Propaganda and Empire.* – J.M. MacKenzie (Ed.): *Imperialism and Popular Culture.* Manchester, 1986.

26 The conceptual framework underlying this chiasm, which is more than a mere play on words, is indebted to M. Fludernik: *The Fictions of Language and the Languages of Fiction.* London, 1993, a wide-ranging narratological monograph, which also emphasizes pluralism, "the multiplicity of languages among different speakers" and the diversity of fictions "which language as a system projects in the course of narrative signification" (p. 2).

27 E. Said: *Orientalism*, pp. 42, 206.

28 E. Said: *Culture and Imperialism*, p. 62. – For the key phrase "structures of attitude and reference", cf. ibid., pp. 61ff., 73, 89, 114, 134, 157 and *passim.*
29 E. Said: *Culture and Imperialism*, p. xi.
30 E. Said: *Orientalism*, p. 226f.
31 Z.T. Sullivan: *Narratives of Empire*, p. 105.
32 This phrase is, of course, an allusion to an influential book on the theory of metaphor, viz. to G. Lakoff, M. Johnson: *Metaphors We Live By*. Chicago, 1980.
33 E. Said: *Orientalism*, p. 213.
34 J. Conrad: *Heart of Darkness* [1 1899]. – In *Youth and two Other Stories*. New York, 1924, p. 52.
35 C. Tiffin, A. Lawson: "Introduction: The textuality of Empire". – In C. Tiffin, A. Lawson (Eds.): *De-Scribing Empire. Post-Colonialism and Textuality*. London, New York, 1994, pp. 1-11, here p. 5.
36 R. H. MacDonald: *The Language of Empire: Myths and Metaphors of Popular Imperialism, 1880-1918*. Manchester, 1994, pp. 19, 20.
37 Ibid., pp. 27, 26.
38 E. Said: *Culture and Imperialism*, p. 5.
39 For a conceptual framework for literary history based on an alliance between narratology and the New Historicism, see A. Nünning: „Narrative Form und fiktionale Wirklichkeitskonstruktion aus der Sicht des *New Historicism* und der Narrativik. Grundzüge und Perspektiven einer kulturwissenschaftlichen Erforschung des englischen Romans im 18. Jahrhundert". *Zeitschrift für Anglistik und Amerikanistik* 40,3, 1992, 197-213.
40 P. Burke: "Overture: the New History, its Past and its Future". – In P. Burke (Ed.): *New Perspectives on Historical Writing*. Oxford, 1991, pp. 1-23, here p. 3.
41 L. Hunt: "Introduction: History, Culture, Text", p. 17.
42 E. Said: *Orientalism*, p. 94.
43 Ibid., p. 54.
44 Ibid., pp. 22, 321. – The authors of one of the canonical texts of post-colonial criticism, B. Ashcroft, G. Griffiths, H. Tiffin: *The Empire Writes Back: Theory and Practice in Post-Colonial Literatures*. London, New York, 1989, p. 59, make basically the same point when they warn against what they call the "danger in 'transcultural dialogues'", viz. "that a new set of presuppositions, resulting from the interchange of cultures, is taken as the cultural reality of the Other. The described culture is therefore very much a product of the particular ethnographic encounter – the text creates the reality of the Other in the guise of describing it".
45 For an informative and lucid overview of the basic tenets of this approach, see A. Simonis: "*New Historicism* und *Poetics of Culture*: *Renaissance Studies* und Shakespeare in neuem Licht". – In A. Nünning (Ed.): *Literaturwissenschaftliche Theorien, Modelle, Methoden*, pp. 153-172.
46 F.S. Schwarzbach: "London and Literature in the Eighteenth Century". *Eighteenth-Century Life* 7, 1982, 100-112, here 112.
47 T. Healy, J. Sawday (Eds.): *Literature and the English Civil War*. Cambridge, 1990, p. 2.
48 L. Chrisman, P. Williams: "Colonial Discourse and Post-Colonial Theory", p. 4.
49 E. Said: *Orientalism*, p. 71, has poignantly argued why it was futile to "look for correspondence between the language used to depict the Orient and the Orient itself": "not so much because the language is inaccurate but because it is not even trying to be accurate".

50 E. Said: *Culture and Imperialism*, p. xii.
51 E. Said: *Orientalism*, p. 21.
52 Ibid., p. 20.
53 L. Chrisman, P. Williams: "Colonial Discourse and Post-Colonial Theory", p. 1. – For a thorough investigation, see R. Koebner, H.D. Schmidt: *Imperialism: The Story and Significance of a Political Word, 1840-1960.* Cambridge, 1964.
54 Cf. the articles in *Anglistik und Englischunterricht* 46/47: *Englishness*, 1992.
55 E. Said: *Orientalism*, p. 66.
56 J. A. Froude: *Oceana, or England and her Colonies.* London, 1886, S. 390.
57 Cf. J. MacKenzie (Ed.): *Popular Imperialism and the Military, 1850-1950.* Manchester, 1992.
58 E. Said: *Culture and Imperialism*, p. 60.
59 L. Colley: *Britons. Forging the Nation 1707-1837.* New Haven, 1992.
60 Cf. V. Nünning: „'Daß Jeder seine Pflicht thue'. Die Bedeutung der *Indian Mutiny* für das nationale britische Selbstverständnis". *Archiv für Kulturgeschichte* 78, 1996 [forthcoming].
61 For the notion of Englishness as a set of 'invented traditions' see E. Hobsbawm, T. Ranger (Eds.): *The Invention of Tradition.* Cambridge, 1983, p. 1 and *passim.* – Cf. also J.A. Mangan: "'The Grit of our Forefathers: Invented Traditions, Propaganda and Imperialism". – In J.M. MacKenzie (Ed.): *Imperialism and Popular Culture*, pp. 113-129.
62 R.H. MacDonald: *The Language of Empire*, p. 51.
63 Ibid., pp. 81, 90.
64 Ibid., p. 82. – For the following, cf. ibid., pp. 83-111.
65 E. Said: *Orientalism*, p. 216.
66 R.H. MacDonald: *The Language of Empire*, p. 205, who focusses on "two of the most successful adventure writers of the high imperial age, Cutcliffe Hyne and Edgar Wallace" (ibid.). – On the significance of Henty's historical romances as imperialist propaganda, cf. V. Nünning: „Viktorianische Populärliteratur als imperialistische Propaganda: G.A. Hentys historischer Roman *In Times of Peril*". *Literatur in Wissenschaft und Unterricht* 28,3, 1995 5, 189–201.
67 R.H. MacDonald: *The Language of Empire*, p. 233.
68 For a general analysis of metaphorical uses of kinship terms, cf. M. Turner: *Death is the Mother of Beauty. Mind, Metaphor, Criticism.* Chicago, 1987, pp. 15-77.
69 B. Ashcroft, G. Griffiths, H. Tiffin: *The Empire Writes Back*, p. 2.
70 Ibid., p. 54.
71 For further information, see A. Nünning: „Das *British Empire* in der englischsprachigen Literatur. Theoretische Grundgedanken und praktische Hinweise zur Durchführung einer interkulturell orientierten Unterrichtsreihe". *Die Neueren Sprachen* 92,6, 1993, 567-586. – The article provides a theoretical outline of the possible goals of teaching literature in an intercultural framework as well as didactic suggestions for teaching a course on literary responses to the British Empire, for selecting suitable texts, and for applying new methodological approaches to literary works.
72 Cf. William Boyd's *A Good Man in Africa* (1981) and *An Ice-Cream War* (1982), J.G. Farrell's *Troubles* (1970) and *The Siege of Krishnapur* (1973), and Caryl Phillips' *Cambridge* (1991) and *Crossing the River* (1993),
73 Cf. N. Gordimer: *July's People.* J. Sidney (Ed.). Harlow, München, 1991 [London, [1]1981]. – R.P. Jhabvala: *Heat and Dust.* B. Bleiman (Ed.). Harlow, München,

1989 [London, [1]1975]. – P. Scott: *Staying On*. R. Samson (Ed.). Harlow, München, 1991 [London, [1]1977].

74 The phrase is a quote from P. Carey: *Oscar and Lucinda*. London, 1988, p. 475. – On Carey's revisionist fictional account of the colonial period in Australian history, see A. Nünning: „'The Empire had not been built by choirboys': Zur revisionistischen Darstellung australischer Kolonialgeschichte in Peter Careys *Oscar and Lucinda*". *Literatur in Wissenschaft und Unterricht* 27,3, 1994, 171-187.

75 For an excellent short survey, see E. Kreutzer: "Commonwealth-Literatur". – In H. U. Seeber (Ed.): *Englische Literaturgeschichte*. Stuttgart, 1991, pp. 394-438.

76 Cf. A. Nünning: „'Make miniatures of the once-monstrous theme...'. Formen und Funktionen der Auseinandersetzung mit dem Niedergang des Britischen Empire in J.G. Farrells Romanwerk". *Arbeiten aus Anglistik und Amerikanistik* 18,2, 1993, 159-179.

77 E. Said: *Orientalism*, p. 342.

78 C. Tiffin, A. Lawson: "Introduction", p. 9.

79 J. A. Mangan: "Making Imperial Mentalities", p. 20.

80 E. Said: *Orientalism*, p. 328.

John Mackenzie

Imperialism and popular culture: A historiographical Essay

'Reluctant Imperialists'?

It would surely be surprising if the possession of a vast empire had little or no effect upon the culture of the imperial metropolitan state. Yet it is a curious fact that for a long time British historians showed very little interest in studying such reflexive influences. There are a number of reasons for this. Those who wrote about empire from an imperial perspective in the late nineteenth and twentieth centuries (down to at least the 1950s) were anxious to emphasise its high-minded, quasi-religious and 'developmental' characteristics. From Sir John Seeley to Sir Reginald Coupland, they distrusted popular enthusiasms as dubious plebeian excitements to be decried rather than discussed. In any case the essence of empire was the radiating outwards of a series of moral and material benefits. Imperialism set up centrifugal rather than centripetal lines of force. If institutions, like the missionary societies, organised themselves for empire, or if scholarly disciplines, like geography or anthropology, prepared themselves to be the handmaidens of imperial rule, they did so in the pursuit of appropriate ideas and methodologies which would advance the imperial cause.

Second, there has been a long reaction in British imperial historiography to the writings of J. A. Hobson. Hobson's *Imperialism: a Study* and more particularly his *The War in South Africa* and *The Psychology of Jingoism*, all published at the turn of the century, became highly unrespectable works. Though Hobson himself was no Marxist – indeed he drew some of his inpsiration from such imperial figures as John Ruskin, and later wrote in what seemed like a pro-imperial manner – his theories of capital export and declining rates of return, rooted in classical economics, and his notion of working-class underconsumption inspired a succession of Marxist writers, culminating in Lenin's *Imperialism, the Highest Stage of Capitalism.* In *The Psychology of Jingoism* he seemed to be deeply dismissive of the malleability of popular culture, expressing views that were not likely to endear him to social historians or working-class sympathisers. Moreover, Hobson's barely concealed anti-semitism in identifying a group of Jewish financiers, particularly those located in South Africa, who alegedly sought to secure their ends by co-opting the British state and public through unwarranted influence in the press, helped to vitiate much else that he had to say. Historians writing outside Marxist traditions have generally been uncomfortable with conspiracy theories.

Yet as a third reason for this curious silence at the heart of British imperial historiography one can identify a strange and unspoken – and certainly unplanned and unforged – conspiracy between both right and left within the British political and intellectual tradition to play down any cultural effects of British imperialism. A group of historians, most notably A. J. P. Taylor and Henry Pelling, together with their students and disciples, imbibed many of their central ideas from the intellectual (though not popular) anti-imperial atmosphere of the inter-war years. They wrote within a 'soft left' tradition which emphasised 'England' over Britain and attributed more hard-headed domestic concerns to the British social classes, particularly the working class, as allegedly reflected in their voting characteristics. In the 1930s both George Orwell and the right-wing Esmé Wingfield-Stratford arrived at the same conclusion, that British patriotism had to slough off the imperial connection which compromised it before it could be fully effective in meeting the Nazi threat. Other right-wing commentators, of whom Max (Lord) Beloff is a notable and still active example, were anxious to suggest that the British never actually developed a true theory of empire or constitutional commitment to it. In this respect they were to be distinguished from the much more emotionally committed French or Portuguese. Moreover, the totalitarian states of Europe in the inter-war years had illustrated the vast dangers of public excitement directed to ideological ends. It was convenient to suggest that neither the propagandist techniques nor the popular enthusiasms should be ascribed to the cooler politics of Anglo-Saxondom, imperial power or not.

Thus the British Empire was not only distant, but also de-centralised and curiously de-coupled from metropolitan politics and society. Decolonisation, though painful at times, produced none of the dramatic political disruptions of Paris or Lisbon. There was no British equivalent to the French car-horn cry. 'Algérie française'. But as well as ideological, there were also technical reasons for ignoring popular imperialism. The serious and fully professional historian was inseparably wedded to the archive. Anyone who has ploughed through vast quantities of official colonial documents in the Public Record Office in London knows that popular interest and excitement features hardly at all. In my own case, I researched the records relating to the British South Africa Company between 1889 and 1923 and in that instance the natural tendency of mandarins to a cool scepticism was greatly enhanced by the fact that they were dealing with a commercial and administrative company which they were attempting to supervise while holding at arms' length. Insofar as public interest intruded at all, it was in the shape of the highly critical meetings of the 'Exeter Hall' faction of evangelical missionary societies, whose, prime movers tended to argue against company rule and in favour of direct (and hence theoretically disinterested and high-minded) imperial controls. It is perhaps not surprising that historians thus wedded to the archive and the document should have been so much more concerned with the 'official mind' than the popular psychology.

Even when the great log-jam of traditional historiography began to break up in the 1960s, more radical historians concentrated on peripheralist approches to the official dimensions of imperialism (for example, Robinson and Gallagher), on resistance and nationalism in individual colonial territories (like Ranger, Mazrui, Davidson), or on the origins of anti-imperial movements in Britain (as in Porter's *Critics of Empire*). Only those still writing within a Marxist tradition (notably Eric Hobshawm) were persistent in connecting imperialism not only to the domestic economy, but also to the interaction and co-optation of British social classes, particularly through the concept of the aristocracy of labour. Empire also came to be approached, by Corelli Barnett and by Bernard Porter in his *The Lion's Share*, for example – and more recently by Cain and Hopkins in their two-volume *Imperialism* – as the prime source of British eonomic weakness, from the 1870s a major symptom of decline rather than of continuing power. Politically, too, empire came to be seen as impacting upon the mother country. C.A. Bayly moved the high point of imperialism back to the turn of the eighteenth and nineteenth centuries and linked it to the development of more autocratic politics within the United Kingdom.

But even as these more radical approaches were gaining ground, history as a discipline had moved on into a succession of fresh fields: giving voice to the hitherto voiceless, particularly through the collection of oral material and the discovery of non-canonical texts, to studies of popular culture, sport, media, and the artifacts that reflected ideas as well as contemporary tastes. All that was needed was to put these interests, more generally studied in a domestic context, together with the record of empire and imperialism and some startling results were to ensue. At the same time new concerns with multi- and cross-disciplinary studies were developing and historians discovered that, at the very least, they could develop fresh insights as well as new sources through adopting relationships with other historicist disciplines.

Thus historians were weaned at last from their obsession with the official document. While they had long acknowledged the significance of such other sources as the press and contemporary texts, some at least now considered using oral evidence, materials associated with popular entertainment, artifacts, ephemera, images and advertising. All of this was perhaps stimulated by the knowledge that the contemporary electronic media would be vital sources for the historian of the future. Perhaps such reflectors of popular ideas and indicators of the inter-action between establishment and populace could also be found in the past. This has resulted in a positive explosion of studies of the popular cultural dimensions of imperialism, and the whole field has been further enriched by the examination of the role of empire in shaping a wide range of scholarly disciplines and institutional histories – not least that of museums – in the nineteenth and twentieth centuries. Partly through these developments, the history of science, formerly an esoteric and highly technical field, has entered into the mainstream of intellectual and cultural history. In all of these respects, the extensive multi-disciplinary and theoretical insights to be derived from imperial cultural history have much to offer other branches of historical study.

There can be little doubt that one of the seminal works in all of this activity was Edward Said's *Orientalism* of 1978. Said demonstrated what could be done if a blend of the theoretical positions of Michel Foucault and Antonio Gramsci was brought to bear upon the British and French orientalist texts which he was concerned to analyse. However, while Said's work was hugely suggestive and liberated a very extensive number of studies, it was also immensely limiting. It was purely textually based and operated only in the field of 'high culture'. It said little or nothing about social class or the articulation of the imperial ideology in relation to the political systems which practised and manipulated it.

Shortly after I read, and like everyone else was hugely impressed by, Said's book Britain embarked on what might be seen as its last great imperial adventure. I was already researching aspects of the popular cultural dimensions of empire when the Falklands War broke out in 1982. It was as though a nineteenth-century event had been re-created within a twentieth-century laboratory. A government immediately related patriotism to national pride in respect of the loss of a few small islands which the majority of its population had barely heard of and would certainly have been hard pressed to place on a map. All the media, with very few exceptions, swung their weight behind the patriotic project of re-conquest. The British Labour Party, led by an intellectual left-winger, Michael Foot, whose mindset was probably locked into his outrage at the appeasement of Hitler in the 1930s, lent its support, partly out of conviction, partly out of fear of electoral disaster (which happened anyway). Fervent public ceremonies took place in the dispatching of the troops and the ships, and above all on their return. The pride of the British merchant marine, particularly the great passenger vessels the *QE2* and the *Canberra*, returned to spectacular public receptions barely seen since the nineteenth century. Margaret Thatcher insisted on holding a ' triumph' which was positvely Roman in its scale and air of self-congratulation. She and the Archbishop of Canterbury clashed over whether prayers should be said for the countless young Argentinians who had lost their lives in the war.

Moral purpose, resistance to naked aggression, the need to protect the helpless islanders, a democratic system versus the dictatorship of General Galtieri, armed forces seeking to save themselves from extensive cuts through a successfull war – all these were closely bound up in the complex of emotions which that war engendered. While it helped to bring Galtieri's regime down, it undoubtedly contributed to Thatcher's major election victory of 1983 and to her ascendancy over British politics for the rest of the decade. My book, *Propaganda and Empire*, completed in 1983 and published in 1984, was unquestionably influenced by that sequence of events. I sought to use a wide range of sources, including archival evidence (on the Imperial Institute and imperial societies of the late nineteenth century), advertising, packaging, songs, ephemera, school textbooks, juvenile literature, material on the theatre and other media of popular entertainment, as well as on patriotic youth organisations.

It seemed to me that a number of conclusions could be drawn from such non-official and non-canonical sources. Appeals to empire and an imperial patriotism were everywhere in the visual and textual records of popular culture from at least the middle of the nineteenth century, with a considerable quickening of the impulse from the 1870s. The producers of such materials, the writers of school texts and the advertisers who linked products to the imperial project would not have done so had they not been drawing on what was in effect a dominant ideology which the majority at least of the populace found acceptable. What's more, there were a number of working-class sources that helped to confirm such fascinations. Thus, I have never accepted the objections of critics that, althouth you can demonstrate that there was a lot of it about, you cannot prove that it had any real influence.

Second, I considered that popular culture (particularly the theatre and 'pulp' literature) in the course of the nineteenth century had moved out of dramatic settings in which class conflict predominated into the imperial milieu where race could replace class as the source of hostility and tension. This had helped to change the public perception of the military, for example, as well as those classes which were involved in the imperial enterprise. The grandeur of the imperial project also fitted the Victorian tradition of spectacular entertainment, which had significant effects not only in the theatre, but in the remarkable tradition of exhibitions, both official and private, which became almost entirely imperial in their content from 1886 to 1938.

Third, the scale of its implied moral force seemed to act as the perfect vehicle for the socialisation of the young, both in the schools, where a number of disciplines could be linked to imperialism, and in the burgeoning youth organisations. The boys' brigade and other such youth brigades introduced military forms to the training of the young, which also found expression in the Empire Day movement. The Boy Scouts and the Girl Guides brought frontier images and techniques back to the metropolis, providing the perfect –

and immensely popular – vehicle for the Boer War and Mafeking experience of Baden-Powell to influence the First World War and the inter-war years.

Thus, while historians had been impressed by the lack of official propaganda and by the fact that so many elite societies had only limited success, they had failed to note that many of the prime instruments of propaganda in fact lay in private hands – the entertainment industry, the press, educationalists, the churches and youth organisations. In fact, imperialism had served to re-align the British press, link jingoism to the emergence of popular newspapers (an alliance re-forged in the Falklands War), and transform the fortunes of political parties (Disraeli's activities in the 1870s were crucial in this).

Such pervasive influences could not have failed to affect the political process and re-aligned politicians and parties in ways that were designed to ensure their political survival. Even the British Left found imperialism an unstoppable political force: they argued for ethical empire rather than anti-imperialism, but they were co-opted and deeply complicit until at least the Second World War and, in the case of Africa, the 1950s. Historians in the past had become bogged down in issues like the changing meaning of the word 'imperialism' (Koebner and Schmidt) and the various forms of empire and imperial issues which had deeply divided politicians. In fact, for the public the concerns were much simpler, a linking of imperial rule to patriotism, a sense of self-regard as a nation of overwhelming power and influence in the world, and a deep anxiety about anything that would detract from such authority.

Although some historians (notably Richard Price) had attempted to absolve the working class from patriotic enthusiasms. particularly during the Boer War, there seemed to be much evidence that pointed the other way. The attempt to accuse and acquit specific social classes was strikingly unconvincing. This argument suggested that jingoistic passions were the preserve of the lower middle class (a class whose ethos and tastes historians enjoy dismissing, even though so many of them come from its ranks), while the various elements of the working classes (so often distinguished as the 'rough' and the 'respectable') continued to pursue their own interests, the popular entertainments of sport and the pub or self-improving activities such as the educational and political objectives of the working men's clubs. In fact, the history of the working men's clubs provided convincing evidence the other way. As the nineteenth-century drew to a close, their self-improving elements tended to atrophy in the face of the transfer of music-hall entertainments, even stretching to the provision of larger rooms in which they could be enjoyed. In the clubs, as in the music halls themselves, patriotic songs and tableaux became the order of the day and while it is true that these were often also satirised such parodies were affectionate rather than undermining, only serving to confirm the popularity and familiarity of the originals. Those clubs which failed to make this transition went to the wall.

The complex of ideas which constituted this late nineteenth-century dominant ideology was made up. I suggested, of a linking of monarchism, militarism and social Darwinism to the imperial thrust. By the 1890s, Victoria was well clear of the unpopular phase of her 'widowhood at Windsor'; republicanism was in decline; and her image had begun to merge with that of Britannia herself. The 1897 Jubilee was received with scarcely any opposition throughout the country. Meanwhile her troops, whose image had been tarnished earlier in the century by billeting practrices and by their role in the suppression of civil disorder, and come to be viewed in a wholly different light as a result of their imperial activities, so much more conducive to providing them with a heroic halo. It is true that there remained many barriers to recruitment and the British army was among the smallest in Europe, but popular culture, including much visual imagery and advertising provided both army and navy with highly positive resonances. In colonial wars they were after all the instrument of social Darwinian laws in respect of other races, doing no more than to further and control the inexorable processes of natural selection and destruction. Such an ideology lay beneath much of the racial ideas which underpinned not only the 'New Imperialism', but also the sense of national self-regard which was its powerful concomitant. Anxieties that the British were ceasing to behave like the 'fittest' and were beginning to hand over the baton to their continental rivals, notably Germany, only served to re-emphasise this sense of being locked into a social Darwinian process.

The other conclusion I arrived at was a chronological one. It had been a long-held cliché of historical writing to suggest that the First World War represented a major watershed in imperial ideas as in so many other things. The carnage in the trenches of the Western Front destroyed the simple belief in an imperial patriotism which had encouraged so many to enlist in the first place. Simple faiths were replaced by a more sceptical and cynical approach to world (including imperial) affairs. The youth organisations, the churches and other bodies looked to a new spirit of internationalism as a source of idealistic values rather than to empire. The intelligentsia moved on into a notably radical and anti-imperial phase.

The testimony of popular culture, however, offered little confirmation of such a clear-cut break. Emphases changed, certainly (for example, the more naked examples of racist entertainment and advertising tended to be ameliorated), but school texts, juvenile literature, childrens' annuals, ephemera and major media like the radio and the cinema tended to continue to reflect an imperial world-view. Publications and societies emphasising empire as a source of idealism continued to be founded right up to the Second World War. Indeed, it seemed to me that one could go further: the first real check to this popular cultural expression of empire only came with the development of a more powerful decolonisation ethos at the end of the 1950s. It is certainly possible to find films perfectly representing the imperial ideology of the 1890s (Charlton Heston in *Khartoum* is an excellent example) being produced into the mid 1960s.

The book in which all these ideas were expressed, *Propaganda and Empire*, inevitably had a number of defects. It has been accused of being a survey and, while significant ideas are embedded in each of its chapters, it is certainly true that it had no overall theoretical framework. It hinted at Gramscian hegemonic theory while never fully working it through. However, it did argue that in the period studied there was an extraordinary convergence between intellectual and popular culture. Canonical literary output, as represented by Kipling for example, conveyed a similar set of ideas to those represented in popular and juvenile literature. A composer like Elgar could be regarded as a major classical genius while still having an extensive public following for his popular and patriotic works. It is true that a fin de siècle avantgarde and the onset of modernism cut across this, but it was not until the inter-war years that intellectual and popular culture began to diverge significantly.

Such a convergence cannot wholly be explained in terms of a hegemonic process. The agencies were private rather than public and while that does not necessarily inhibit the power of an Establishment to influence the content of their output, it is difficult to find evidence of an official hand working behind these expressions of imperial sentiment, this linking of patriotism to empire. It seems much more convincing that the extraordinary pervasiveness and persistence of this complex of ideas in the culture of the period represents an area of powerful negotiation among the social classes of Britain. The fact is tht the imperial ethos was a highly potent one, capable of originating, conjoining and also explaining and justifying so many of the ideas of the age. It constituted a circular chain of ideology which was only rent asunder through a sequence of disasters in the twentieth century. As a source of national pride and prejudice (as well as its concomitant anxiety), it had a striking capacity to create common ground among the classes.

Of course there were also sceptics, though they battled in vain at least until the inter-war years. There were also considerable class tensions with major outbreaks of industrial unrest and even violence throughout the period, but voting habits ran in essentially moderate channels and Establishment controls scarcely faltered. And while empire may have helped to ameliorate class tensions, there is also evidence to suggest that it helped to bind together the component parts of the United Kingdom. This has become a source of increasing interest to historians of late and I shall return to the subject below.

Imperialism and Cultural Studies

As so often happens in historical scholarship, it was soon apparent that *Propaganda and Empire* was merely part of a wave of new work being undertaken in the area of imperial culture. Thomas G. August examined parallel phenomena in his *The Selling of the Empire: British and French Imperial Propaganda, 1890–1940*, while William Schneider's study of the press in *An Empire for the Masses* offered many insights into the impulses behind French imperialism in the late nineteenth century. The Manchester University Press 'Studies in Imperialism' series was founded in 1985 to provide a forum for all this work and books swiftly appeared in it which explored various popular cultural media in relation to imperialism: juvenile literature, the theatre, exhibitions, images of the military, notions of patriotism, medicine, emigration, sexuality, education, travellers' accounts, the language of empire among several others. Meanwhile the work of Pieterse explored racial images in advertising, while Coombes embarked on highly suggestive explorations of ethnography and race in nineteenth-century museology.

Another highly significant new area was the exploration of gender issues in relation to empire. This is an expanding field in which a number of scholars have published on women and travel and women and the empire, notably Billie Belman, Sara Mills and Helen Callaway. An important work by Mrinalini Sinha is currently in the press and a collection of essays edited by Clare Midgley will be published in 1996. But empire was a notably male project, and a volume edited by Mangan and Walvin, *Manliness and Morality*, succeeded in drawing some interesting comparisons between Britain and the United States while contributing much to an understanding of imperial culture. Mangan also developed the field of sports history and empire, in his *The Sports Ethic and Imperialism* as well as in such edited volumes as *Sport in Africa* and *The Cultural Bond.* My own *The Empire of Nature* sought to connect the hunting ethic of metropolis and empire, the concepts of masculinity which it embodied, and the legal and cultural notions which were transferred to the colonial setting. It caught another great tide, that of imperial environmental history, which has major cultural connections that have not yet been fully explored.

The thrust of all this work was to unveil whole new areas of cultural and intellectual history relating to empire. It developed our understanding of the operations of an imperial ideology through a whole range of media and scholarly disciplines, and also extended its time-scale backwards. It was perhaps too restrictive to see all this cultural activity as an essential concomitant of the 'New Imperialism', as a cultural precipitation building up between the 1850s and the 1870s, as I argued in a German Historical Institute conference paper in 1987, subsequently published in a volume edited by Adolf Birke and Günther Heydemann in 1989. Some have pointed out that there were outbursts of popular excitement as early as 1765 when the East India Company acquired the diwani, or tax gathering rights, in Bengal. Even earlier, popular interest had been generated by the death of General Wolfe at Quebec in 1759, while the public also made a hero out of Captain Cook as his voyages of exploration seemed to reveal more and more of the South Pacific: after his death in Hawaii in 1779, he was apotheosised in images and poetry. These and other imperial events were encapsulated in paintings and associated lithographs and engravings which had some popular circulation. Thus the tradition of hero-worship, which I and others have identified as a characteristic of late nineteenth century empire, may well have significant precedents in the eighteenth century.

Wars against France in India fed into the elevation of the French into the major national and imperial 'Other' for the British in the late eigtheenth century. These concerns had much expression in the theatre during the Napoleonic wars and created a tradition of topical dramatic entertainment which was to continue throughout the nineteenth century, with high points during the Crimean War and the colonial wars of its last few decades. The British adversary during a number of late eighteenth century wars, Tipu Sultan of Mysore, became a significant figure in the popular imagination, featuring in several plays and much visual material, such that when the Indian reformer and philosopher Ram Mohan Roy visited Britain in the 1820s he was pursued by boys in the street shouting 'Tipu'. There was also a rich vein of melodrama set in India in the early decades of the nineteenth century, partly associated with Romanticism's fascination with the East, but seeking an essentially popular audience.

These interests certainly laid a powerful foundation for the infusion of popular culture by the imperial ideology in the late nineteenth century. Visual material particularly conributed to this, including for example the very popular panoramas, dioramas and cosmoramas which were displayed around the country in their striking and often dedicated buildings. Many of these illustrated military events, imperial journeys, colonial cities and the like. But all of this activity was greatly quickened by the development of the mass market and a whole range of new technologies that made printing, the reproduction of images, and the development of entertainment and advertising available in more widespread and potent forms.

There can be no doubt, too, that one of the most significant ideological turning-points in all of this came with the Indian 'Mutiny' of 1857. For the rest of the century this was seen as a great moral turning-point, a defining moment of empire when it faced its greatest test and survived. It was certainly that event which helped to transform the reputation of the army, already enhanced by the Crimean War: troops became heroic saviours of the besieged, avengers of the honour of the British, particularly in respect of the events involving women and children at Kanpur. While many paintings relating to empire can be identified from the earlier period, including the history paintings of Benjamin West, Robert Home, Ker Porter, Johann Zoffany, and David Wilkie, among many others, it was the Mutiny which helped to create a tradition of grand and sentimental imperial canvases by such artists as Frederick Goodall and Henry Nelson O'Neill. The Mutiny also helped to generate the atmosphere of hero-worship which was such a characteristic of late-nineteenth-century imperialism. The military leaders of its suppression, figures like Sir Colin Campbell, Sir James Outram (the 'Bayard of India'), Sir John Nicholson, Herbert Edwardes (whom Ruskin described as a 'military bishop... a captain whom all were proud to follow, a prelate whom all were eager to obey'), Sir Henry Lawrence (the most famous of the besieged in Lucknow), and above all Sir Henry Havelock became evangelical knights, defenders of the faith as well as of the empire.

In these ways religion, heroism and empire were conjoined in a potent mix. Nineteenth-century heroes, most notably Havelock, Livingstone and General Charles Gordon, were essentially religious figures, portrayed as moral titans facing dark forces which martyrised them in a Christ-like sacrifice. The church and missionary societies were not the least of the sources of the popular culture of empire. Moreover, to take another powerful evangelical figure of the age, it was perhaps the Mutiny (as Angus Calder has argued) which transformed Samuel Smiles from a radical, self-improving working-class propagandist to one who used empire as a prime source of moral uplift and self-help. He was certainly to make much of the Mutiny heroes (Campbell and Havelock both had relatively humble social origins) as well as the career of David Livingstone whose reputation was created contemporaneously with the Mutiny through his explorations in southern, Central and East Africa. The Indian revolt may also have helped to transform John Ruskin into a fervent imperialist, as later exemplified by his inaugural lecture as Slade Professor at Oxford in 1870.

Culture and Imperialism

While historians were thus inserting culture into imperialism, the literary critics set about injecting imperialism into culture. Said's *Orientalism* helped to stimulate a series of studies of the oriental interests of the Romantics, relocating such interests in the imperial thrust, the fame of the East India Company and the great debates among orientalists, as represented by Sir William Jones and his followers, and anglicists/utilitarians, as represented by philosophic radicals like Jeremy Bentham and James Mill and Whigs like Lord Macaulay. Patrick Brantlinger in his *Rule of Darkness* set about creating a sense of continuity in the imperial interests of British literature in the nineteenth century, seeking to escape from the notion that Kipling and his imperialist contemporaries represented some kind of new departure. Said's latest book *Culture and Imperialism* of 1993 has irrupted into these developments.

Said seemed to take these developments to their logical, or at least ultimate, conclusion. Using mainly British examples (with some attention to the United States in the later twentieth century), he argued that imperialism was the defining characteristic of almost all western culture in the nineteenth and twentieth centuries. It runs, he suggested, as a counterpoint through all the English literature of the period, often an unseen presence that nonetheless defines both plot and domestic space. He also suggested that the same impulses could be identified in other arts, and explored Verdi's Egyptian opera *Aida* with this end in view. *Culture and Imperialism* does not live up to Said's previous work. It is a sprawling and unfocused work, showing signs of the manner in which it has been delivered over the years as lectures for many different occasions. It aroused great controversy and some abusive reviews. Though Said intended it to be a highly historicist work, it actually shows many ahistorical tendencies – a failure to understand some of the necessary periodisations of nineteenth-century imperialism; an anxiety to create heroes and villains – for example Ruskin is a villain and Hobson a hero – which flies in the face of the complexities of Victorian thought; a refusal to recognise dissident voices (of which Verdi decidedly was one); and a failure to grasp much of the historical work laid out above. Moreover, as in *Orientalism*, Said is primarily concerned with high culture, and again avoids any analysis of the popular cultural elements which would have been significant grist to his mill.

Indeed. Said has always been too unidimensional in his consideration of what has come to be known as 'alterity'. He has concentrated on the Oriental Other to the exclusion of all alternatives. In fact, we have to recognise a highly complex process of 'othering' in all popular culture. We have to consider not only the British European Other – of whom the French were the most significant instance in the late eighteenth and early nineteenth centuries, later followed by the imperial Russians and, from the early twentieth, the Germans – but also domestic others like the Irish and the Scots. It is in the recognition of this process of self-definition, the identifying of community and national characteristics through comparison and contrast that historians have begun to make significant strides and in the process have once again connected metropolis to empire.

Culture, Ethnicity and the Metropolitan State

It was an imperial historian, Reginald Coupland, who as early as 1954 linked the processes of decolonisation to the stresses and strains of the metropolitan state. In his book, *Welsh and Scottish Nationalism*, Coupland wrote a paean of praise to the Union between Scotland and England of 1707, describing it as such a triumph that 'there is nothing in the history of international relations to compare with such an ending to so long and fierce a duel'. Unlike that with

Ireland, the relationship had been nothing but beneficial, and Scots – and by analogy the Welsh – would slough it off only at their economic and political peril. In writing this, Coupland was recognising that Irish independence (and her departure from the Commonwealth in the late 1940s) might not be the last act of metropolitan decolonisation, that, as in Ireland and the empire at large, popular culture had the capacity to switch from imperial to nationalist concerns.

It has certainly been one of the puzzles of Scottish history that the Scots seemed to be so willing to submerge their political (though not their legal, educational, religious or cultural) identity in the British state from the eighteenth century. What is now clear is that they did so partly to secure the considerable economic advantages of involvement in the British Empire. Scots were active – far beyond the numbers their population warranted – in the patronage systems of the East India Company from the 1720s. They contributed more than their fair share of soldiers and senior officers to colonial territories, and after the 1745 Jacobite Rebellion, many Highland families sought to restore their fortunes and reverse their attainders by founding regiments and pursuing military and political involvement in the empire. The clearances of Highland peasants to convert the land into sheep runs and later deer forests contributed emigrant population to territories of white settlement. This was soon followed by considerable emigration from the populous central belt and other parts of the country.

The wealth secured from Empire, by East India nabobs in the eighteenth century, for example, also contributed to the re-investment which fed the Scottish end of the industrial revolution. No wonder Sir Walter Scott described India as 'the cornchest for Scotland'. Throughout the succeeding century and beyond, Scottish industrialism (for example in shipbuilding, locomotive manufacture and other forms of engineering) was geared to imperial markets. The Scots featured prominently throughout the empire and had a high reputation within it (justified or not) as businessmen, doctors, botanists, engineers, clerics and other professionals.

It may be that this activity served to submerge Scottish separatist tendencies within the imperial state; it may be that it helped to convert Scottish culture into the obsession with tartanry which has been seen by some as fatal to the emergence of truly distinctive national forms; or it may be (as I have argued) that this helped to keep a sense of a separate Scottish identity alive. Although the empire was dominated by English administrative and legal systems, the Scots were often able to transfer aspects of their social ethic, notably in education, religion and radical approaches to land rights, the press and popular cultural activities, which helped to reinvigorate pride in their survival at home. Examples of such phenomena can be identified in India, New Zealand, Canada, South Africa, and some parts of Africa. In facing the problem of dominance by an adjacent and powerful nation, England, the Scots were able to carve out a wider global role, appealing to their contributions to a larger entity, the British (never the English) Empire. In the modern British state, with all the stresses induced by Northern Ireland, the equivalent larger form to which the Scots now cleave is the European Union. In the past, many patriotic Scots appealed to the concept of 'Scotland and the Empire'. Now the equivalent cry is 'Scotland and Europe'.

This relationship between empire, migration, and inter-active cultures (both within the metropolis and between ethnic components of the mother country and colonial territories) has become a major source of research interest in recent times. My book *Propaganda and Empire*, together with all the other equivalent and related studies largely failed to discriminate among the different parts of the United Kingdom. In *Culture and Imperialism*, Edward Said, writing from his rather slanted vantage point in the United States, has never made any attempt to understand the fact that the United Kingdom is itself a mini-empire with widely different imagined communities and a complex process of internal 'othering'. Yet this is the area which perhaps requires most attention and research in the future to understand the social and ethnic complexities of the popular culture of imperialism.

Fresh Fictional Fields

The other potentially highly productive field is again the one in which Said has least to offer, that of non-canonical literature and other aspects of popular reading and performance. While the song scenes, patriotic tableaux and other aspects of imperial music hall have received a good deal of atention, as have many of the juvenile journals and authors of the second half of the nineteenth century, adult 'pulp' fiction has been largely ignored. While canonical literature tells us a good deal about ideas debated among an intelligentsia and conceptualisations of rule, race, personal relations and the environment shared by a mainly upper and middle class audience, it is in popular literature that we are likely to find sets of ideas and attitudes prevalent among the wider population. From the point of view of the historian, rather than the literary critic, such 'pulp' material can be a much more productive study. As with popular visual materials, scholars often have to suspend the aesthetic judgments which have invariably been their stock-in-trade in the past. Different modes of analysis have to be brought to bear.

Excellent examples of such popular writing exist in the work of a group of women authors of the late nineteenth and early twentieth centuries who set much of their fiction in India. These included Mary Croker, Maud Diver, Sara Jeanette Duncan, Laurence Hope (Florence Cory), Katherine Mayo, Alice Perrin, Ethel Savi, Flora Annie Steel (perhaps the most famous of them), and Christine Weston, among others. Florence Riddell is a twentieth-century example who used Kenya as the setting for a great deal of her work. They generally enjoyed enormous readerships, were published in cheap editions, and were widely available in the private subscription and public municipal libraries. Although they may have had a shorter shelf-life than the classics, they certainly had a much deeper penetration of the social classes.

A number of questions immediately arise about these writers and their work. Did they merely illustrate the filtration downwards of canonical attitudes? Were they just pale reflections of the great imperial writers? Or do they embody wholly different approaches to empire, its politics, peoples, problems, and environments, its personal opportunities and tragedies? And what did the members of their extensive readerships derive from such work? To what extent was their view of empire shaped through such imaginative excursions into the exotic locales of India and Africa?

Benita Parry has briefly looked at some of these materials, but much more detailed research is now under way by Dominic Omissi and this promises to yield a whole range of exciting insights. The only preview that can perhaps be offered here is the strong indication that such popular writing actually contains powerful counter-canonical attitudes, some approaches at least that seem to run in a contrary direction to the standard obsessions of Kipling. This should help us to re-locate Kipling within precise intellectual and social contexts, recognising that women readers, the youth and people from a wider spectrum of the population may have been susceptible to different sorts of impressions. Moreover, such studies are likely to lead us to the re-thinking of standard periodisations of imperial literature that tend to run from confidence to doubt, apprehension and rejection. In 'pulp' literature, it seems that confidence and glorification of the imperial project may have continued for a much longer period, helping to confirm the idea that popular culture preserves ideas and disrupts them less readily than the 'high' culture of intellectuals and the upper classes.

Conclusion

Cultural studies, not least in relation to imperialism, have moved from being the Cinderella of historical scholarship to a princess at the court of Clio. The developments of the past fifteen years or so have been remarkable, yet they have represented little more than an era of exploration. New regions are being opened up almost daily and the scholarly literature is now vast. Said's *Orientalism* continues to stimulate a vast literature, which has moved out into several related disciplines, including geography and anthropology. His insights are also being debated in relation to a number of arts, including art, architecture, design, music and the theatre. We need more discussion of

Orientalism in popular culture, but Said's *Culture and Imperialism* seems more likely to stimulate hostile than favourable responses.

Work continues to be done on the full range of media through which imperial ideas were projected, not least in visual imagery, advertising and the like. We need more of these and in particular a greater awareness of parallel developments in France, Germany, Portugal, Italy and elsewhere. Divided ethnicities at home, the relationship of these to empire and to national identities involved in the processes of global dominance also require further study, as do the rich sources of non-canonical literature. Theorisation is also becoming much more complex (witness the now vast literature relating to Orientalism and British rule in India) and we can expect many debates about the applications of Foucault, Gramsci and the Frankfurt school to continue, with new applications and modifications to their frameworks. No doubt this issue of *Intercultural Studies: Fictions of Empire* will do much to advance these debates.

Bibliography

Anderson, Olive: "The growth of Christian militarism in mid-Victorian Britain". *English Historical Review* LXXXVI, 1971, 46–72.

August, Thomas G.: *The Selling of the Empire: British and French Imperialist Propaganda 1890–1940.* Westport/CT, 1985.

Baker, William J., and Mangan, James A.: *Sport in Africa: Essays in Social History.* New York, 1987.

Bayly, C. A.: *Imperial Meridian: the British Empire and the World, 1780–1830*, London, 1989.

Bell, Morag, Butlin, Robin and Heffernan, Mike (Eds.): *Geography and European Imperialism*, Manchester, 1995.

Beloff, Max: *Imperial Sunset.* London, 1969.

Brantlinger, Patrick: *Rule of Darkness: British Literature and Imperialism.* Ithaca, 1988.

Bratton, J. S., et al: *Acts of Supremacy: the British Empire and the Stage, 1790–1930.* Manchester, 1991.

Cain, P. J., and Hopkins, A. G.: *British Imperialism: I Innovation and Expansion, 1688–1914; II Crisis and Deconstruction. 1914–1990.* London, 1993.

Calder, Angus: "Samuel Smiles: the unexpurgated version". *The Raven Anarchist Quarterly* V, 1992, 79–89.

Callaway, Helen: *Gender. Culture and Empire: European Women in Colonial Nigeria*, London, 1987.

Colley, Linda: *Britons: Forging the Nation 1707–1837*, New Haven, 1992.

Coombes, Annie E.: *Reinventing Africa: Museums, Material Culture and Popular Imagination*, London, 1994.

Coupland, Reginald: *Welsh and Scottish Nationalism.* London, 1954.

Cunningham, Hugh: "The language of patriotism". *History Workshop* XII, 1981, 8–83.

Field, H. John: *Toward a Programme of Imperial Life: the British Empire at the Turn of the Century.* Oxford, 1983.

Godlewska, Anne, and Smith, Neil (Eds.): *Geography and Empire*, Oxford, 1994.
Greenhalgh, Paul: *Ephemeral Vistas: the Expositions Universelles, Great Exhibitions and World Fairs, 1851–1939*, Manchester, 1988.
Hichberger, J. M. W.: *Images of the Army: the Military in British Art, 1815–1914*, Manchester, 1988.
Hobsbawm, Eric: *Industry and Empire*, London, 1969.
Hobsbawm, Eric, and Ranger, T. O. (Eds.): *The Invention of Tradition*, Cambridge, 1983.
Hobson, J. A.: *The War in South Africa*, London, 1900.
–: *The Psychology of Jingoism*, London, 1901.
–: *Imperialism: a Study*, London, 1902.
Hyam, Ronald: *Empire and Sexuality, the British Experience*, Manchester, 1990.
Jeffery, Keith (Ed.): *An Irish Empire? Aspects of Ireland and the British Empire*. Manchester, forthcoming 1996.
Koebner, R. and Schmidt, H. D.: *Imperialism: the Story and Significance of a Political Word, 1840–1960*, Cambridge, 1964.
Leask, Nigel: *British Romantic Writers and the East*, Cambridge, 1992.
Lenin, V. I.: *Imperialism: the Highest Stage of Capitalism*, 1916.
Lorimer, D. A.: *Colour, Class and the Victorians*, Leicester, 1978.
MacDonald, Robert H.: *The Language of Empire: Myths and Metaphors of Popular Imperialism, 1880–1918*. Manchester, 1994.
McGilvary, George K.: "East India Patronage and the Political Management of Scotland, 1720–1774". PhD thesis, the Open University in Scotland, 1989.
MacKenzie, John M.: *Propaganda and Empire: the Manipulation of British Public Opinion, 1880–1960*. Manchester, 1984.
–: *The Empire of Nature*, Manchester, 1988.
–: *Orientalism: History, Theory and the Arts*. Manchester, 1995.
–: „Die Popularisierung des Empire". In Adolf M. Birke and Günther Heydemann (Eds.): *Die Herausforderung des europäischen Staatensystems: Nationale Ideologie und staatliches Interesse zwischen Restauration und Imperialismus*, Göttingen, 1989, pp. 216–40.
–: "Essay and Reflection: On Scotland and the Empire". *The International History Review* XV. 4, 1993, 714–739.
–: "Edward Said and the Historians". *Nineteenth-Century Contexts* 18, 1994, 9–25.
– (Ed.): *Imperialism and Popular Culture*. Manchester, 1986.
– (Ed.): *Imperialism and the Natural World*. Manchester, 1990.
– (Ed.): *Popular Imperialism and the Military*. Manchester, 1993.
Mangan, J. A.: *Athleticism in the Victorian and Edardian Public School: the Emergence and Consolidation of an Educational Ideology*. Cambridge, 1981.
–: *The Games Ethic and Imperialism*. Harmondsworth, 1987.
– (Ed.): *The Cultural Bond: Sport Empire and Society*. London, 1992.
– (Ed.): *Benefits Bestowed? Education and British Imperialism*. Manchester, 1988.
– (Ed.): *Making Imperial Mentalities: Socialisation and British Imperialism*. Manchester, 1990.
Mangan, J. A., and Walvin, James (Eds.): *Manliness and Morality: Middle-Class Masculinity in Britain and America, 1800–1940*. Manchester, 1987.
Marshall, P. J. (Ed.): *The Illustrated History of the British Empire*. Cambridge, forthcoming 1996.

Melman, Billie: *Women's Orients: English Women in the Middle East, 1718–1918.* London, 1992.
Mills, Sara: *Discourses of Difference: Women's Travel Writing and Colonialism.* London, 1991.
Nairn, Tom: *The Break-up of Britain.* London, 1977.
Omissi, Dominic: "The Mills and Boon Memsahibs: Women's Romantic Indian Fiction 1877–1947", PhD thesis, Lancaster University, 1995.
Orwell, George: *The Lion and the Unicorn.* London, 1941.
Parry, Benita: *Delusions and Discoveries: Studies of India in the British Imagination, 1880–1930*, London, 1972.
Pieterse, Jan Nederveen: *White on Black: Images of Africa and Blacks in Western Popular Culture*, London, 1992.
Porter, Bernard: *Critics of Empire: British Radical Attitudes to Colonialism in Africa, 1890–1914*, London, 1968.
–: *The Lion's Share.* London, 1975.
Price, Richard: *An Imperial War and the British Working Class.* London, 1972.
Reader, W. J.: *At Duty's Call: a Study in Obsolete Patriotism.* Manchester, 1988.
Richards, Jeffrey M.: *Visions of Yesterday.* London, 1973.
– (Ed.): *Imperialism and Juvenile Literature.* Manchester, 1989.
Richards, Thomas: *The Imperial Archive: Knowledge and the Fantasy of Empire.* London, 1993.
Roberts, Robert: *The Classic Slum.* Manchester, 1971.
Robinson, Ronald, and Gallagher, John: *Africa and the Victorians: the Official Mind of Imperialism.* London, 1963.
Said, Edward W.·: *Orientalism.* London, 1978.
–: *Culture and Imperialism.* London, 1993.
Schneider, William H.: *An Empire for the Masses: the French Popular Image of Africa, 1870–1900.* Westport/CT, 1982.
Senelick, Lawrence: "Politics as entertainment: Victorian music-hall songs". *Victorian Studies XIX, 1975, 149–80.*
Sinha, Mrinalini: *Colonial Masculinity: the 'Manly Englishman' and the 'Effeminate Bengali'.* Manchester, 1995.
Smiles, Samuel: *Self-Help.* London, 1859.
Stafford, Robert A.: *Scientist of Empire: Sir Roderick Murchison, Scientific Exploration and Victorian Imperialism.* Cambridge, 1989.
Thomas, Nicholas: *Colonialism's Culture.* Princeton, 1994.
Tidrick, Kathryn: *Empire and the English Character*, London, 1990.
Wingfield-Stratford, Esmé: *The Foundations of British Patriotism*, London, 1940.
Winks, Robin W., and Rush, James R. (Eds.): *Asia in Western Fiction*, Manchester, 1990.
Youngs, Tim: *Travellers in Africa: British Travelogues 1850–1900*, Manchester, 1994.

Vera Nünning, Köln

Vom historischen Ereignis zum imperialen Mythos: *The Siege of Lucknow* als Paradigma für den imperialistischen Diskurs*

> The little band in the Residency did more than make history. In a sense they made scripture, for their refuge became one of the holy places of British Imperialism and their struggle, reiterated and glamorised in verse and prose, re-enacted on the stage and refought in spirit, summarised the Imperial ethos and furnished the Imperial dogma with all the apparatus of miracles and martyrs.
>
> Pemble[1]

Die Belagerung der britischen Residenz in Lucknow, die viele Briten als eine der größten und glorreichsten Belagerungen in der Weltgeschichte ansahen, erweist sich aus militärgeschichtlicher Sicht als ein eher unwichtiges Ereignis. Daß sich ein paar hundert Europäer mit der Hilfe von indischen Soldaten einige Monate lang erfolgreich gegen einen Ansturm einer wesentlich größeren indischen Armee halten konnten, bis es britischen Truppen gelang, die Belagerten zu befreien, stellt bei nüchterner Betrachtung der militärischen Fakten nur ein nebensächliches Kapitel in der Geschichte der britischen Herrschaft in Indien dar. Nicht nur britische Historiker, auch zeitgenössische Beobachter in England und Europa hielten dieses Ereignis jedoch für überaus wichtig. Auch außerhalb von Großbritannien bestand großes Interesse an der Belagerung, und Leser in Europa und Amerika griffen „fast jeden Tag mit klopfendem Herzen nach den neuesten Blättern“[2], um zu erfahren, welchen Fortschritt die britischen Soldaten unter General Havelock bei ihrem Versuch machten, die Europäer in Lucknow zu befreien. Selbst in amerikanischen Häfen wie New York, Boston und Baltimore standen die Flaggen auf halbmast, um die Trauer über den Tod Havelocks kurz nach dem Ende der Belagerung zum Ausdruck zu bringen. Daß man in Großbritannien den Entsatz der eingeschlossenen Landsleute in Lucknow für genauso wichtig hielt wie die Siege von Trafalgar und Waterloo, zeigt sich nicht nur an den Feiern, mit denen die Soldaten in den verschiedenen Heimatstädten empfangen wurden, sondern auch daran, daß die Statue von Henry Havelock noch heute neben der von Admiral Nelson auf dem Trafalgar Square zu bewundern ist.[3]

Die große Aufmerksamkeit, mit der die *Siege of Lucknow* sowohl von Zeitgenossen als auch von Historikern bedacht wurde, beschränkte sich nicht auf die ersten Monate nach der Befreiung der Belagerten, in der Dutzende von

Tagebüchern und Briefen der Überlebenden und zahlreiche Biographien der beteiligten Generäle den englischen Markt überschwemmten. Vielmehr sorgte eine Flut von jugendlichen Abenteuergeschichten, Dramen, Balladen, Romanen, Bildern, Schulbüchern und Geschichtswerken dafür, daß diese "first and heroic siege", "one of the most famous in history"[4] in Großbritannien bis um die Mitte des 20. Jahrhunderts immer wieder als eines der glanzvollsten Ereignisse der Geschichte beschrieben wurde. Diese hohe Stellung der Belagerung im britischen kollektiven Gedächtnis steht nicht nur in krassem Mißverhältnis zu ihrer tatsächlichen militärgeschichtlichen Bedeutung; eine besonders große Diskrepanz besteht zwischen den historischen Ereignissen während der Belagerung und dem sich darum rankenden Mythos[5] der *Siege of Lucknow*, der das eigentliche historische Geschehen verklärte. Mißt man die britischen Darstellungen der Belagerung in Geschichtswerken, Literatur und Kunst daran, inwiefern sie faktische Beschreibungen eines historischen Ereignisses lieferten, so muß man sie als überaus verzerrt, glorifizierend und historisch falsch beurteilen. Aus mentalitätsgeschichtlicher Sicht sind die vielen unzutreffenden Schilderungen der Belagerung jedoch keineswegs bedeutungslos, denn "in dealing with the figures of national myth, one is confronted [...] by fictions which, by dint of their popularity, become realities in their own right."[6] Die Helden, die im Mythos von Lucknow weiterlebten, hatten zwar wenig Ähnlichkeit mit den Menschen, die 1857 in der Residenz von Lucknow eingeschlossen waren, im britischen kollektiven Gedächtnis waren sie jedoch insofern sehr wichtig, als sie gleichsam die in der zweiten Hälfte des 19. Jahrhunderts entstehenden *fictions of empire* personifizierten und mit konstituierten.

Die Diskrepanz zwischen dem realen historischen Ereignis und dem nationalen imperialen Mythos der *Siege of Lucknow* bildet den Ausgangspunkt des folgenden Artikels, der die Frage zu beantworten versucht, auf welche Weise und aus welchen Gründen die Belagerung von Lucknow im kollektiven Gedächtnis Großbritanniens eine so große Bedeutung gewinnen konnte und welche Funktionen diese propagandistische Fiktion erfüllte. Im ersten Teil wird untersucht, warum die Belagerung die Gemüter der Briten von Beginn an so sehr erregte, daß die Beteiligten sogleich in die Galerie der Nationalhelden aufgenommen werden konnten. Da die Bedeutung des Mythos sehr viel schärfer konturierbar ist, wenn der Kontrast zum historischen Geschehen verdeutlicht wird, sollen die Ereignisse während der Belagerung kurz beschrieben werden, um im Anschluß daran aufzuzeigen, welche Facetten britischen Verhaltens in den ideologisch aufgeladenen Erzählungen ausgelassen bzw. überhöht wurden. Die Bestimmung der Qualitäten, die besonders hervorgehoben und glorifiziert bzw. unterschlagen und negiert wurden, dient gleichzeitig als Grundlage für eine Untersuchung der verschiedenen Funktionen, die die *Siege of Lucknow* im britischen kollektiven Gedächtnis erfüllen konnte.

Die ersten Nachrichten über die *Indian Mutiny*, in der sich ein großer Teil der nordwestlichen Provinzen seit Mai 1857 gegen die britische Herrschaft auflehnte, trafen die englische Bevölkerung völlig unvorbereitet. Noch ein Jahr zuvor hatte man die Annexion der Provinz Oudh rückhaltlos befürwortet, die die indische Landbevölkerung vor den vermeintlichen Exzessen des dort regierenden Königs schützen sollte. Gerade Oudh war nun einer der Brennpunkte des Aufstandes, der die britische Fiktion, ein dankbares Indien allein zu dessen Wohl zu regieren, von Grund auf erschütterte. Der indische Aufstand stellte insofern einen schweren Schlag für die nationale Identität der Briten dar, als diese stolz auf ihren vermeintlich selbstlosen Einsatz für die Freiheit etwa im Zuge des Kampfes gegen die Sklaverei waren und sich als ein besonders humanes Volk verstanden.[7] Daß die Inder ihren Wohltätern nicht dankbar ergeben waren, sondern im Zuge der *Indian Mutiny* wahllos Briten töteten, rief in England ungeheure Empörung hervor.

Die Stimmung wurde weiter angeheizt durch Berichte von – zumeist frei erfundenen – Greueltaten, in denen mit unverkennbarer Sensationsgier geschildert wurde, wie wehrlose englische Frauen und Kinder geschändet und ermordet wurden. Diese Beschreibungen beruhten zwar großenteils auf in Indien kursierenden Gerüchten, zumindest ein Ereignis schien jedoch die schlimmsten Befürchtungen der Briten zu bestätigen.[8] Nicht nur war es im Juni immer noch nicht gelungen, Delhi und andere von Indern eingenommene Städte zurückzuerobern, auch die Lage der europäischen Bevölkerung in Cawnpore verschlechterte sich rapide. Dort versuchten die Briten, sich in einer nur provisorisch befestigten Stellung gegen den Ansturm indischer Soldaten zu halten. Nachdem der freie Abzug, der ihnen zugesichert worden war, aus ungeklärten Gründen in einem Massaker endete, wurden die überlebenden zweihundert Frauen und Kinder zunächst zwei Wochen in Gefangenschaft gehalten. Als die zur Rettung herbeigeeilten britischen Soldaten unter der Leitung von Henry Havelock vor Cawnpore ankamen, wurden auch diese Gefangenen ermordet und in einen Brunnen geworfen, so daß die Briten nur noch verstümmelte Leichen ihrer Landsleute vorfanden.

Die verzerrten und übertriebenen Nachrichten über diesen Massenmord riefen in der englischen Öffentlichkeit geradezu hysterische Rachegelüste hervor.[9] Da kaum Informationen über die berechtigten Beschwerden der Inder oder über die horrenden Grausamkeiten der britischen Armee bekannt waren, interpretierten Briten die vielen Berichte über die Brutalitäten der Inder insbesondere von Cawnpore als unmenschliche Exzesse eines undankbaren und blutrünstigen Volkes. Die englische Reaktion auf die Belagerung von Lucknow war von diesen aufgeheizten Gefühlen bestimmt. Zum einen waren Briten in Indien und im Mutterland fest davon überzeugt, daß ein indischer Sieg zu Schändungen der etwa 500 Frauen und Kinder führen werde, die neben knapp eintausend erwachsenen Europäern und 750 treuen indischen Soldaten in einigen notdürftig befestigten Gebäuden in Lucknow eingeschlossen waren. Zum anderen schien die Herrschaft über Indien, des *Jewel in the Crown* des britischen Empire, insgesamt auf dem Spiel zu stehen, denn die zahlenmäßig weit unterlegenen britischen Soldaten hatten trotz ihrer waffentechnischen Überlegenheit bis zum Sommer 1857 kaum Erfolge verzeichnen können. Dadurch wurde der Glaube an die prinzipielle Überlegenheit der Briten gegenüber den vermeintlich minderwertigen Indern zumindest implizit in Zweifel gezogen. Die Befreiung von Lucknow besaß daher auch deshalb so große Bedeutung, weil sie die militärischen und politischen Herrschaftsqualitäten der Briten bestätigen konnte, die durch die *Indian Mutiny* nachhaltig in Zweifel gezogen worden waren.

*

Die Belagerung der britischen Residenz in Lucknow begann am 30. Juni 1857, nachdem die Briten morgens die Kampfeshandlungen mit einem katastrophalen Angriff auf eine indische Stellung im nahegelegenen Chinhut begonnen hatten. Vermutlich war Martin Gubbins die treibende Kraft dieser Aktion, bei der 600 europäische Soldaten nach einem Gewaltmarsch auf einen zahlenmäßig weit überlegenen Gegner trafen. Da nur die Hälfte dieser Soldaten den Angriff überlebte, waren die Briten aufgrund ihres eigenen Verschuldens von Beginn an in einer relativ schwachen Position. Bereits am 2. Juli wurde der umsichtige Leiter der Briten, der rechtzeitig für die Herbeischaffung von Nahrungsmitteln, die Befestigung der Gebäude und die Einquartierung der europäischen Bevölkerung in die Residenz gesorgt hatte, tödlich verletzt. Nach dem qualvollen Tod von Sir Henry Lawrence ging die Verantwortung auf Major Banks und Colonel Inglis über.[10]

Das Leben in der Residenz war, wie aus den Briefen und Tagebüchern der Beteiligten deutlich hervorgeht, mühevoll und monoton. Der Gestank der verwesenden Tierkadaver und Abfälle, die übergroße Hitze, die Mücken bei Nacht und vor allem die Massen an Fliegen, die nicht von Nahrungsmitteln ferngehalten werden konnten, machten allen Anwesenden das Leben denkbar schwer. Selbst innerhalb der Gebäude wurden immer wieder Einzelne durch indische Schüsse verwundet oder getötet. Nahrungsmittel, Medikamente sowie insbesondere Tabak und Rum waren knapp und mußten rationiert werden. Die schlechten sanitären Verhältnisse sowie der Mangel an Obst und Gemüse bedingten viele Krankheiten, die im provisorischen Krankenhaus nur notdürftig behandelt werden konnten. Soldaten und männliche Zivilisten beteiligten sich an der Verteidigung der Außenposten und anderen notwendigen Aufgaben wie der Beerdigung von Menschen und der Beseitigung von Tierkadavern. Da relativ wenige indische Bedienstete zur Verfügung standen, mußten Frauen einige Hausarbeiten wie Waschen und

Kochen selbst verrichten. Dies fiel auch deshalb schwer, weil nötige Hilfsmittel, z.B. Seife, knapp waren und hauswirtschaftliche Grundkenntnisse fehlten.[11]

Da mit britischer Verstärkung auf unbestimmte Zeit nicht zu rechnen war und unklar blieb, wie lange die Nahrungsmittel ausreichen würden, war die Stimmung in der britischen Residenz in Lucknow sehr angespannt. Es kam zu einigen Selbstmorden, und ein Streit zwischen zwei Offizieren endete in einem Totschlag – "[b]ecause there are not murders enough done by the heathen"[12], wie eine Engländerin resigniert und sarkastisch in ihrem Tagebuch festhielt. Dennoch erstickten die Erinnerung an die Ereignisse in Cawnpore und der Glaube daran, daß indische Soldaten die europäischen Frauen und Kinder mißhandeln und ermorden würden, jeden Gedanken an eine Kapitulation im Keim. Vielmehr planten einige Briten in Übereinstimmung mit ihren Ehefrauen, diese kurz vor der endgültigen Niederlage selbst zu töten, um ihnen ein schlimmeres Schicksal zu ersparen.[13]

Obwohl die eingeschlossenen Europäer auf Gedeih und Verderb aufeinander angewiesen waren, machte niemand den Versuch, alle Betroffenen gleichermaßen zum Einsatz für das Gemeinwohl zu verpflichten. Vielmehr blieben soziale Unterschiede und die rigiden viktorianischen Umgangsformen auch bei der Belagerung von großer Bedeutung. Während viele einfache Soldaten und ihre Frauen bei ihrer Verpflegung ganz auf die täglichen Rationen angewiesen waren, besaßen andere große Vorräte an Nahrungsmitteln und Luxusgütern. Besonders gut ausgerüstet war Martin Gubbins, der sozial hochstehenden Gästen bis zum Ende der Belagerung täglich Delikatessen wie geräucherten Lachs, Champagner und Sherry anbieten konnte. Standesunterschiede wurden auch bei den Umgangsformen beibehalten; sobald etwa Katherine Harris sich mit den anderen Damen in ihrer neuen Umgebung eingewöhnt hatte, begannen sie damit, vor ihrem Haus "gentlemen visitors over from the 82nd"[14] zu empfangen.

Auch die tiefe Kluft zwischen Europäern und Indern blieb bestehen. Obwohl die verbleibenden loyalen Inder ihre Sozialkontakte opferten und ihr Leben für die Engländer aufs Spiel setzten, betrachteten die Briten sie bestenfalls mit Mißtrauen. Selbst Julia Inglis, die häufig beobachtet hatte, wie indische Soldaten mit englischen Kindern spielten und ihnen sogar von ihren mageren Rationen abgaben, konnte ihre Vorurteile gegen Inder nicht überwinden: "I said to John [Inglis] I wished we had no natives inside, but he checked me by answering, 'Do not say that; we could not hold the place without them'".[15]

Obgleich die Briten die Hilfe der Inder offensichtlich benötigten, finden sich in den Tagebüchern vor allem Klagen über die nachlässige Arbeitsweise und vermeintliche Aufmüpfigkeit der indischen Bediensteten, die darüber hinaus sehr schlecht behandelt wurden. Nicht nur wurden viele Inder weiterhin geschlagen, sondern man amüsierte sich etwa damit, Diener, die ihren Herren die Mahlzeiten zu den Außenposten brachten und dabei notgedrungen dem feindlichen Feuer ausgesetzt waren, mit Steinen und schwarzen Kugeln zu bewerfen, um sie zu erschrecken und zum Laufen zu bringen.[16] Während Verwundungen und Tode von Europäern in Tagebüchern festgehalten und offiziell verzeichnet wurden, versuchte offenbar niemand, die toten Inder zu zählen. Die dahinter stehende rassistische Denkweise, die auf dem tief verwurzelten Glauben an die natürliche Überlegenheit der Weißen beruhte, wurde von Rees prägnant formuliert: "[S]till our European deaths now average about ten a-day. The natives, of course, we don't count. We feel their loss is nothing very great; but it pains us all to hear of a poor European being knocked over."[17]

Auch die Bemühungen der britischen Truppen, nach Lucknow zu gelangen und die Belagerung zu beenden, zeichneten sich vor allem durch Ineffizienz aus. Seit Anfang Juli versuchte General Havelock mit 1.500 britischen und indischen Soldaten vergebens, durch feindliches Gebiet nach Lucknow vorzustoßen. Obwohl er seine Männer in keiner Weise schonte und hohe Verluste hinnahm, mußte selbst Havelock einsehen, daß er ohne Verstärkung nichts erreichen konnte. Nach vierwöchigem Warten verbanden sich seine Truppen mit denen von Sir James Outram, der als Major-General eingesetzt wurde, aber freiwillig auf diese Position verzichtete, um Havelock die Ehre zu lassen, die Residenz von Lucknow zurückzuerobern. Auch aufgrund von Mißverständnissen zwischen Outram und Havelock starben viele britische Soldaten bei dem schlecht geplanten Marsch durch die Straßen von Lucknow zur Residenz; als die Befreiungstruppen schließlich die Belagerten erreichten, mußten sie daher feststellen, daß inzwischen ca. 800 der 3000 Soldaten gefallen waren, und daß es ihnen nicht möglich sein würde, die Residenz wieder zu verlassen. Nicht nur moderne Militärhistoriker beurteilen diese Befreiungsversuche als inkompetent, auch ein britischer General "considered these attempts to have been mistakes – all bravado and no substance."[18] Daß die Belagerten dennoch über genügend Lebensmittel verfügten, um bis zu ihrer endgültigen Befreiung durch die Truppen von Sir Colin Campbell durchzuhalten, lag an einem glücklichen Zufall. Ende September fand man plötzlich große Getreide- und Alkoholvorräte, die noch von Henry Lawrence angeschafft worden waren. Obwohl Lebensmittel aufgrund der stark angewachsenen Zahl der Menschen, die versorgt werden mußten, weiter rationiert blieben, reichten die Transportmöglichkeiten von Campbells Truppen im November letztlich nicht aus, alles mitzunehmen.

Als der Kriegsberichterstatter der *Times*, William Russell, 1858 durch Indien reiste, erhielt er daher viele Informationen, die mit dem in England verbreiteten Geschichten so gar nicht in Einklang zu bringen waren. Nicht nur wurde der Ruhm von Havelock geringer, je näher er nach Lucknow kam, auch was er über die Verhaltensweisen der Belagerten erfuhr, verwunderte Russell sehr:

> From her [a lady who had been besieged in the Residency] I heard some strange tales respecting the internal condition of the garrison. Whilst some were starving, half fed on unwholesome food, and drinking the most unpleasant beverages, others were living on the good things of the land, and were drinking Champagne and Moselle, which were stored up in such profusion that there were cartloads remaining when the garrison marched out. There was a good deal of etiquette about visiting and speaking in the garrison! [...] It is a pity that our admiration for the heroism of that glorious defence should be marred by such stories as these; but I felt the lady was speaking the truth.[19]

*

Obgleich sich die Briten während der Belagerung und Befreiung von Lucknow in der Tat wenig ruhmreich verhalten hatten, bildete sich sehr schnell ein Mythos der *Siege of Lucknow*, in der sämtliche Aspekte britischen Verhaltens glorifiziert wurden. Russels Prophezeiung, daß kritische Berichte von Augenzeugen die 'Bewunderung für die Heldenhaftigkeit der glorreichen Verteidigung' beeinträchtigen würden, sollte sich nicht erfüllen. Vielmehr diente nur ein Teil der Informationen, die 1858 in Großbritannien über die Belagerung veröffentlicht wurden, als Grundlage für den Mythos der *Siege of Lucknow*. Wichtig für ein Verständnis der Bedeutung und der Funktionen dieses Mythos ist daher eine Beantwortung der Frage, durch welche Auslassungen und Überhöhungen es zu der Ausbildung des überaus positiven Bildes der Belagerung kommen konnte.

Voraussetzung für den Aufbau des Mythos war zunächst einmal das Tilgen fast aller Referenzen, die ein negatives Licht auf die Briten hätten werfen können. Militärische Fehler bei der Befreiungsaktion werden in den Schilderungen der Belagerung ebensowenig erwähnt wie die Probleme, die die gemeinsame Truppenführung durch Havelock und Outram mit sich brachte. Das Desaster des eigenen Angriffes auf Chinhut, mit dem die Briten selbst die militärischen Auseinandersetzungen begannen, wird nicht nur auf indische Spione und auf indische Heimtücke zurückgeführt, sondern es wird hervorgehoben, daß britische Soldaten dort "enormous acts of gallantry"[20] vollbrachten. Ein fast undurchdringlicher Mantel des Schweigens hüllte sich bis um die Mitte des 20. Jahrhunderts insbesondere um alle Schwächen und Fehlentscheidungen des wohl größten 'Helden' der Belagerung, Sir Henry Havelock.

Bei aller Verehrung von General Havelock ließ es sich jedoch kaum verschweigen, daß er sich als unfähig erwiesen hatte, die Belagerung zu beenden.

Es fanden sich aber Wege, sein Verharren in der Residenz als eine seiner Heldentaten darzustellen. Noch im 20. Jahrhundert begründeten einige Autoren Havelocks Entscheidung, seine Soldaten selbst zu Belagerten zu machen, mit dessen großem Verantwortungsbewußtsein und ritterlicher Fürsorge für Frauen und Kinder; "regard to the large number of women and children and wounded whom it would be necessary to guard through the terrible streets"[21] sei das wahre Motiv für Havelock gewesen, in Lucknow zu bleiben. Henty beurteilte Havelocks Ankunft sogar als gerade noch rechtzeitig. Anstatt darauf hinzuweisen, daß die Nahrungsmittel aufgrund der größeren Zahl an Menschen in der Residenz überaus knapp waren und nun auch Häuser bewohnt werden mußten, die nur sehr schlecht verteidigt werden konnten, behauptete Henty, daß die Briten in der Residenz durch Havelock vor dem sicheren Tod bewahrt worden seien: "[Havelock] fought his way through the streets of the town to the Residency, arriving there just in time, for the enemy had driven two mines right under its defenses. These would have been exploded the next day, and in that case the fate of the garrison of Cawnpore might have befallen the defenders of Lucknow."[22]

Menschliche Schwächen sucht man in den vielen Erzählungen des Mythos von Lucknow ebenfalls vergebens. Weder Selbstmorde noch Duelle werden erwähnt, die rigide soziale Hierarchie wird gleichfalls verschwiegen, weil sie nicht recht in das Bild der 'Helden' von Lucknow paßte; für soziale Etiquette und Besuche blieb den Belagerten zumindest im Mythos keine Zeit. Vertuscht wird in den meisten Werken, die bis um die Mitte des 20. Jahrhunderts veröffentlicht wurden, auch die ungleiche Verteilung der Lebensmittel. Obwohl immer wieder hervorgehoben wird, wie karg die Rationen und wie groß die Entbehrungen der britischen Soldaten waren, die nicht einmal mehr Tabak hatten und daher Teeblätter rauchen mußten, fehlt meist der Hinweis darauf, daß Einzelne weiterhin im Überfluß lebten. So versichert Ball seinen Lesern, daß mit der Knappheit der Nahrungsmittel und der Verbreitung von Krankheiten Unterschiede "of rank became almost obliterated, where all had to suffer alike".[23] Selbst 1938 bemäntelt eine Darstellung der Belagerung noch die ungleiche Verteilung der Nahrungsmittel. So betont Joyce unter Mißachtung vieler Aussagen aus den veröffentlichten Tagebüchern, daß Mrs Gubbins das Essen so großzügig verteilt habe, daß oft nichts für sie selbst übrig blieb, und daß die anderen Belagerten kaum neidisch auf den privilegierten Gubbins waren, weil sie sahen, wie freizügig er das Krankenhaus versorgt habe.[24] Von der arroganten und schlechten Behandlung der indischen Bediensteten fehlt in fast allen späteren Veröffentlichungen ebenfalls jede Spur. Fehler haben die Briten dem Mythos von Lucknow zufolge jedenfalls nicht.

Die Zeichnung der loyalen indischen Soldaten zeigt, wie sehr zeitgenössische politische Bedürfnisse den Mythos von Lucknow beeinflußten. Bis um die

Mitte des 20. Jahrhunderts werden die Leistungen der indischen Soldaten, sofern diese überhaupt erwähnt wurden, meist heruntergespielt. Diese Geschichtsverfälschung begann bereits mit den ersten Nachrichten aus Indien, die vor allem den verräterischen Charakter der undankbaren Sepoys hervorhoben. Der Geistliche Duff etwa zeichnete 1858 ein arg verzerrtes Bild der Situation: "[A]t Lucknow, a few hundred British men, [...] encumbered with women and children, held, for three months, a suddenly extemporised entrenchment, against an army of at least fifty thousand, backed by an armed and furiously hostile population of millions".[25] Duff unterschlug die Präsenz der anderen Europäer in der Residenz ebenso wie die der treuen Inder, während er die Zahl der indischen Soldaten, die Lucknow bedrohten, vervielfachte. Diese Verzerrungen dienten ebenso dazu, die große Überlegenheit der Fähigkeiten der Briten hervorzuheben, wie die dauernde Wiederholung der Tatsache, daß sich eine relativ kleine Zahl von Briten gegen eine viel größere Menge indischer Soldaten behaupten konnte.[26] Im 19. Jahrhundert erfüllte der Mythos von Lucknow daher sehr häufig die Funktion, die herausragenden Kampfesqualitäten der Briten zu beweisen. John Seeley, der den britischen Imperialismus insgesamt sehr positiv darstellte, machte sich schon 1883 über jene Historiker lustig, die aus Gründen nationaler Eitelkeit keinen Inder auf Seiten der Briten entdecken konnten: "No one who has remarked the childish eagerness with which historians indulge in their national vanity, will be surprised to find that our English writers in describing these battles seem unable to discern the sepoys."[27]

Obwohl Seeleys Werk sehr populär war, ignorierten die meisten Autoren im 19. Jahrhundert die Leistungen der Inder weiterhin. Oftmals wurden die indischen Soldaten in der Residenz nur zu Beginn der Erzählungen genannt, um die Zahlenverhältnisse zu verdeutlichen. Selbst bei der Aufzählung der verschiedenen Gruppen in der Residenz gelang es einigen Autoren, die Bedeutung der Inder herunterzuspielen. George A. Henty behauptete etwa in seinem *Sovereign Reader*, daß statt 750 indischen Soldaten nur 150 auf der Seite der Briten gekämpft hätten; da er parallel dazu die Zahl der Frauen und Kinder auf 1000 verdoppelte, handelt es sich wohl um einen gezielten Versuch, die übermenschlichen Leistungen der britischen Soldaten auf Kosten der an der Verteidigung beteiligten Inder hervorzuheben.[28] In seinem enorm populären Werk über die indische Rebellion von 1901 erreichte Fitchett eine ähnliche Wirkung, indem er in seinem Überblick über die Zahl der Belagerten die indischen Soldaten mit dem Nachsatz "of somewhat dubious loyalty"[29] versah. Im Gegensatz zu den Werken, die bis zur Zeit des Ersten Weltkriegs erschienen, werden die Leistungen der treuen indischen Soldaten in späteren Veröffentlichungen anerkannt und sogar hervorgehoben. Diese revisionistischen Darstellungstendenzen sind wohl vor allem darauf zurückzuführen, daß Großbritannien ab den 1930er Jahren auf die militärische Unterstützung der indischen Armee angewiesen war und verstärkt versuchte, einen möglicherweise erneut aufflammenden Rassenhaß zwischen beiden Seiten im Keim zu ersticken.[30]

Dem Mythos von Lucknow zufolge vollbrachten die Briten nicht nur übermenschliche militärische Leistungen, sondern sie wurden sogar allesamt als vorbildliche Menschen und wahre Helden dargestellt: "[E]very man who defended Lucknow was a hero, and the women were the equals of the men in unwearied fortitude and indomitable courage."[31] Diese Heroisierung der Frauen begann bereits mit einem offiziellen Bericht von Inglis, der in vielen Beschreibungen ausführlich zitiert und durch Anekdoten ausgeschmückt wird:

> The want of native servants has also been a source of much privation. [...] Several ladies have had to tend their children, and even to wash their own clothes, as well as to cook their scanty meals entirely unaided. [...] I cannot refrain from bringing to the prominent notice of his Lordship in Council the patient endurance and the Christian resignation which have been evinced by the women of this garrison. They have animated us by their example.[32]

Vor allem zwei Qualitäten britischer Frauen werden immer wieder genannt: ihre hausfraulichen und krankenpflegerischen Tugenden sowie ihr Mut und ihr geduldiges Ertragen der widrigen Umstände. Der Mythos von Lucknow bestätigte somit zugleich zentrale Züge des viktorianischen Frauenideals. In der Extremsituation der Belagerung zeigten die britischen Frauen vermeintlich die Qualitäten des *Angel in the House*, also jenes idealisierten Bildes der Frau, die für das Wohlergehen der Familie sorgt und dem – im wahrsten Sinne des Wortes abgekämpften – Ehemann ein sauberes und gemütliches Heim bereitet. In den Erzählungen wird meist betont, daß viele indische Bedienstete die Residenz verlassen hatten und selbst einige sozial höhergestellte Frauen nur noch wenige Diener hatten und daher selbst waschen, kochen und ihre Kinder versorgen mußten. Statt auf die Treue der vielen indischen Diener hinzuweisen, die trotz aller Entbehrungen weiterhin in der Residenz blieben wird stets hervorgehoben, in welch einer schrecklichen Situation jene Damen gewesen seien, die keinen einzigen Diener mehr hatten und die Hausarbeit selbst verrichten mußten. Selbst eine Schilderung aus dem Jahr 1938, als sich kaum noch eine britische Familie Bedienstete leisten konnte, beschreibt das vermeintlich so harte Los der englischen Ladies auf einfühlsame Weise:

> In a country where a junior chaplain, for instance, living very quietly with his wife and no children, had been used to employ twenty-three servants, it was hardship indeed for the wives of officers and civilians to clean their own rooms, draw their water, wash their clothes, attend to their children, and cook their food.[33]

Die Betonung der 'niederen' Arbeit von sozial Höhergestellten rief zum einen den Eindruck hervor, daß es keine sozialen Unterschiede mehr gab und alle Belagerten große Entbehrungen auf sich nehmen mußten. Zum anderen verstärkte sie das Bild einer gemeinsamen Anstrengung der Briten, die alle ihren Teil beitrugen, um das Leben in der Residenz erträglich zu gestalten. Außerdem verdeutlichte sie die Fähigkeit britischer Frauen, im Notfall ungewohnte und harte Arbeiten verrichten zu können.

Die aktive Mitarbeit der Frauen bei der Pflege der Verwundeten im notdürftig errichteten Krankenhaus war ebenfalls ein Bestandteil des Mythos, der kaum den historischen Ereignissen entsprach. In den Tagebüchern und Briefen finden sich zwar Hinweise auf einige wenige Frauen, die eine Zeit im Krankenhaus aushalfen; 'freiwillige' Pflege leisteten jedoch in erster Linie die dazu eingeteilten französischen Schüler der *Martinière*-Schule. In den ersten beiden Tagen kümmerten sich zwar auch britische Frauen um die Verwundeten im Krankenhaus, aber diese erste Welle der Hilfsbereitschaft ließ sehr schnell nach:

> It would have been well for the unfortunate sick and wounded if the same kindness had been shown to them by those whose professional duties did not oblige them to attend to the hospital; but unfortunately such scenes became so common that scarcely a thought was afterwards bestowed on the poor sufferers. People grew callous from a continued sight of pain.[34]

Dennoch behaupteten sehr viele Autoren, daß Frauen als Krankenpflegerinnen tätig gewesen seien: "Women [...] spent hours in the stifling hospital nursing the sick and wounded and speaking words of comfort to the dying".[35] Diese Glorifizierung der Leistungen von Frauen entsprach zum einen dem Ideal der 'Lady with the Lamp', das Florence Nightingale ein Jahr vor dem indischen Aufstand etabliert hatte und das durch den Mythos von Lucknow bestärkt und popularisiert wurde. Zum anderen diente diese Darstellung britischer Frauen als mitfühlende Krankenschwestern einmal mehr dazu, die Selbstaufopferung und Hilfsbereitschaft der englischen Frauen hervorzuheben, die im Notfall bereit waren, ohne Standesdünkel ihren Beitrag zum allgemeinen Wohl zu leisten.

Obwohl die Heroisierung der Frauen in Lucknow großenteils bestehende Züge des viktorianischen Idealbilds von Weiblichkeit bestätigte, trug sie gleichzeitig zur Erweiterung dieses Ideals bei. Frauen blieben in der Residenz zwar in der privaten Sphäre und halfen den Männern nicht bei der militärischen Verteidigung; in ihrem Bereich entwickelten sie aber Eigenschaften, die nicht zum viktorianischen Frauenbild gehört hatten: "The women too displayed an heroic patience and fortitude under the dangers and sufferings they underwent".[36]

Schon 1859 nutzte MacPherson das Potential dieser Erweiterung des britischen Frauenbilds, indem er dazu aufrief, das Verhalten der Frauen von

Lucknow von nun an als Leitbild bei der Erziehung von Mädchen zu verwenden. Wenn britische Frauen in der Lage sein sollten, ihre Ehemänner in kritischen Situationen bei der Bewahrung des Empire zu unterstützen, so müßten auch Mädchen systematisch dazu erzogen werden, zumindest passiven Mut zu zeigen. Obwohl MacPherson 'unweibliche' Härte als barbarisch ablehnte, pries er den "calm heroism of some of the most gentle of women"[37], die ihre Pflicht als britische Ehefrauen in herausragender Weise erfüllt hatten. Die mythisch verbrämten Erzählungen, die den heldenhaften Frauen in Lucknow Gleichmut und Aushaltevermögen zuschrieben, trugen daher dazu bei, das britische Frauenideal um Eigenschaften zu erweitern, die auf Englands Rolle als imperialistische Nation zugeschnitten waren.

Die männlichen 'heroes of Lucknow' verkörperten ebenfalls hohe nationale Werte. Neben ihren großen militärischen Fähigkeiten wird eine ganze Fülle von Eigenschaften hervorgehoben, die je nach Belieben des jeweiligen Verfassers einige herausragende Helden oder gleich alle britischen Soldaten auszeichneten: Sie besaßen eine scheinbar grenzenlose Fröhlichkeit, die verdeutlichte, daß sie ihre typischen Eigenschaften, ihren Humor, ihr Durchhaltevermögen und ihren Mut, auch in dieser angespannten Situation nicht verloren. Das Lachen der Briten verdeutlichte zudem, daß sie eine wahrhaft kämpferische Nation waren: "[O]n the whole the average Briton is apt to be grimly cheerful when a good fight is in progress, and even this dreadful siege was not without its humours."[38] An besonders guten Soldaten wird häufig hervorgehoben, daß sie "loved fighting for its own sake";[39] Offiziere hingegen zeichneten sich besonders durch eiserne Nerven, Selbstsicherheit und "cool courage"[40] aus. Ein idealer Offizier war dem Mythos zufolge "bold and daring in conception, prompt and sudden in execution, persistent and unshaken in his resolves".[41]

Viele Schilderungen der Belagerung wiederholten jedoch nicht nur sattsam bekannte Heldenqualitäten, sondern besonders in der Gestalt eines Generals – Sir Henry Havelock – wurde ein völlig neuer Heldentypus geschaffen, der in der zweiten Hälfte des 19. Jahrhunderts große Wirkung entfalten sollte. Havelock avancierte ungeachtet seiner Brutalität und seiner militärischen Fehlleistungen zum Symbol des vorbildlichen Soldaten. Im idealisierten Charakter dieses Helden zeigt sich besonders deutlich, daß nur das im kulturellen Gedächtnis einer Gruppe erhalten bleibt, was in die Kategorien der sich Erinnernden eingepaßt werden kann und deren gegenwärtigen Bedürfnissen entspricht.[42] Die Aura Havelocks und die ihm zugeschriebenen Eigenschaften, die nicht zum typischen Bild des Soldaten gehörten, aber im 19. Jahrhundert hoch angesehen waren, dienten vor allem dazu, den Ruf der britischen Armee stark aufzuwerten. Dies war nicht nur deshalb nötig, weil die traditionelle britische Abneigung gegen ein stehendes Heer überwunden werden mußte, wenn der schlechte Zustand der britischen Armee verbessert und die imperiale Macht Großbritanniens ausgeweitet werden sollten. Auch die große Bedeutung von Religion in der viktorianischen Zeit machte es erforderlich, den Beruf des Soldaten aufzuwerten und neu zu interpretieren.

Havelocks Verhalten während der indischen Rebellion war erst nach vielfältigen Auslassungen, Überhöhungen und Umdeutungen dazu geeignet, als strahlendes Vorbild zu fungieren. Seine makabren Scherze, mit denen er den blutbeschmutzten Maude empfing, der in seinem Auftrag eine brutale Hinrichtung durchgeführt hatte, paßten ebensowenig ins Bild eines viktorianischen Helden wie seine Härte den eigenen Soldaten gegenüber; beides wird in fast allen Erzählungen schlicht übergangen. In einer Biographie Havelocks, in der Forbes erstmals ein nicht idealisiertes Portrait vermitteln wollte, werden die Gewissensbisse und Skrupel Havelocks vor seiner Zustimmung zu einer einzigen Hinrichtung geschildert, ohne daß der Verfasser darauf hinwies, daß Havelock seinen Offizieren die Erlaubnis gab, alle Inder hinzurichten, die ihnen verdächtig erschienen.[43] Oftmals wird der christliche Held von Lucknow darüber hinaus mit der Eigenschaft der Milde ausgestattet, die ihn von den heidnischen und brutalen Indern abhebe.[44]

Da Havelock Zeit seines Lebens ein überzeugter Christ gewesen war, eignete er sich zur Veranschaulichung der These, daß ein guter Christ gleichzeitig ein guter Soldat sein könne. In allen Biographien, die noch 1858 auf den Markt kamen, wird betont, daß die christliche Religion immer sein Handeln bestimmt habe und daß es sein Ziel gewesen sei "to demonstrate that spiritual-mindedness was not incompatible with the energetic pursuit of a secular calling – that 'a saint could be a soldier.'"[45] In typisch viktorianischer Manier belehrten verschiedene Autoren ihre Leser darüber, daß Havelocks Leben ein Aufruf an seine Landsleute sei, die wahren Qualitäten von Soldaten anzuerkennen, deren Leben sich ebenso wie das von guten Christen durch Aufopferungsbereitschaft, Selbstverleugnung und Bereitschaft zum Gehorsam auszeichne. Mehr noch: "The heroism displayed in the life of this great soldier, furnishes a plea for religious men who follow the profession of arms; a plea addressed alike to their fellow-soldiers, and to civilians, many of whom look with horror on the profession to which they are indebted for their security."[46] Während Demut, Milde und Bescheidenheit vor der Belagerung von Lucknow nicht gerade zu den typischen Soldateneigenschaften gezählt wurden, trugen besonders die Schilderungen der Belagerung, die in den 1860er Jahren veröffentlicht wurden und die hervorkehrten, daß Havelock diese Eigenschaften im Übermaß besessen habe, maßgeblich zur Verbreitung der Vorstellung bei, daß diese Qualitäten einen heldenhaften Soldaten auszeichneten. Während frühe Schilderungen der *Siege of Lucknow* vor allem die Christlichkeit von Havelock und dem vorherigen Befehlshaber Sir Henry Lawrence betonten, galten zu Ende des 19. Jahrhunderts, als Religion nicht mehr eine so große Bedeutung hatte, andere Eigenschaften als die typischen Charakteristika der Helden von Lucknow. Die "heroic chivalry", die anfangs weniger wichtig gewesen war als die "benevolence of the Christian philanthropist"[47], trat zunehmend in den Vordergrund. Die Adjektive "gallant" und "chivalrous" fehlen in keiner der Erzählungen, die die Ritterlichkeit aller beteiligten Engländer hervorheben. Die britischen Helden werden als wahre Ritter gezeichnet, die selbst von den mythischen Taten der Ritter von Arthurs Tafelrunde nicht übertroffen wurden. Schon im Dezember 1857 stellte Froude in einem persönlichen Brief die rhetorische Frage: "We had been doubting, too, whether heroism was not a thing of the past: and what knight of the Round Table beat Havelock and Sir John Lawrence?"[48] Immer wieder wird betont, daß Havelock und seine Soldaten ihr Leben aufs Spiel setzten, um die in Lucknow eingeschlossenen Frauen und Kinder vor dem sicheren Tode zu bewahren. Bilder und Erzählungen feiern darüber hinaus die Art und Weise, in der die rauhen schottischen Soldaten, die allein in den letzten Stunden ihres Marschs nach Lucknow circa 2000 Inder getötet hatten, die Kinder in Lucknow auf den Arm nahmen und mit Tränen in den Augen streichelten. Die ängstliche Frage der Highlander "Are you one of them?"[49] geistert durch viele Erzählungen, die die Ritterlichkeit selbst der einfachen britischen Soldaten herausheben. Ungeachtet ihrer Konsequenzen wird auch Outrams Geste, Havelock freiwillig die Ehre zu überlassen, als der Befreier von Lucknow in die Nachwelt einzugehen, als großer Akt der Ritterlichkeit gewürdigt.[50]

Gleichgültig, ob christliche, ritterliche oder soziale Qualitäten im Mittelpunkt standen, besonders ein Schlüsselbegriff des viktorianischen Werte-und Normensystems wurde an den Helden von Lucknow gelobt: "[T]he strict performance of duty" war vermeintlich der "polar-star"[51], an dem sämtliche Helden ihr Handeln orientierten. Obwohl auch Havelock für seine "uniform submission to DUTY"[52] geehrt wird, erstrahlt der Ruhm von Sir Henry Lawrences Pflichtbewußtsein in noch höherem Glanz. In fast keiner Erzählung des Mythos von Lucknow fehlt der Hinweis darauf, daß der heroische und bescheidene Lawrence nur einen Wunsch bezüglich der Inschrift auf seinem Grabstein hatte: "Here lies Henry Lawrence, who tried to do his duty."[53]

*

Warum der Mythos von Lucknow eine so große Bedeutung erlangen konnte, wird erst verständlich, wenn man die vielfältigen Funktionen in Betracht zieht, die ein Vergegenwärtigen dieser Belagerung bis ins 20. Jahrhundert hinein erfüllen konnte.[54] Eine wichtigte Voraussetzung für die große Wirkung dieses Mythos war die Isolierung der Ereignisse in Lucknow von den zugrundeliegenden Ursachen der Rebellion, von den vielfältigen Ungerechtigkeiten der britischen Herrschaft und von den Grausamkeiten der britischen Soldaten in Indien, die für die indischen 'niggers' nur Verachtung übrig hatten. Dem nationalen Mythos zufolge erscheinen die Briten nicht als die Eroberer des indischen Kontinents, sondern als kleine heroische Minderheit, die verzweifelt versuchte, sich gegen die große Menge anstürmender indischer Soldaten zu verteidigen. Im Mythos von Lucknow sind damit nicht nur die Unterdrücker zu den Opfern geworden, sondern auch gut und böse sind klar verteilt: tapfere, christliche, ritterliche und milde Briten kämpfen gegen brutale indische Aggressoren.

Der Mythos von Lucknow eignete sich daher in hervorragender Weise dazu, etablierte britische Werte zu bestätigen und zugleich neue Ideale zu prägen. Während das idealisierte Verhalten der Männer Ritterlichkeit und kämpferische Qualitäten bekundete, die angesichts des wenig rühmlichen Auftritts im Krimkrieg und der anfänglichen großen Verluste in Indien schon verloren geglaubt waren, bestätigten die Aktivitäten der Frauen, daß Engländerinnen selbst unter widrigsten Umständen in der Lage seien, dem Ideal des *Angel in the House* gerecht zu werden. Außerdem lieferte der Mythos von Lucknow zwei neue Züge von guten Briten, die von großer Bedeutung für das britische Empire waren: Zum einen verbanden insbesondere die Truppen von Sir Henry Havelock Christlichkeit mit dem Beruf des Soldaten, wodurch die Vorstellung des *Christian Soldier* in einem Helden personifiziert und ein bedeutendes Hindernis für das Ansehen der britischen Armee beiseite geräumt wurde. Zum anderen bewiesen die Frauen in Lucknow, daß auch das weibliche Geschlecht passiven Mut zeigen und Männer aktiv bei der Ausübung ihrer imperialen Pflichten unterstützen konnte. Darüber hinaus veranschaulichte der Mythos von Lucknow eine bedeutende Uminterpretation des Pflichtbegriffs. In den Erzählungen trugen alle Belagerten unter großen Entbehrungen gemeinsam dazu bei, das britische Empire in Indien zu erhalten. Besonders Sir Henry Lawrence wurde zum Symbol eines Märtyrers, der selbstlos das Empire verteidigte. Die Bemühungen der Belagerten wurden nicht als nackter Kampf ums Überleben gezeichnet, sondern als Akte der Aufopferung zum Ruhme Großbritanniens.

Da alle beteiligten Briten – unabhängig vom Geschlecht – als Helden glorifiziert wurden, konnten die Erzählungen ihrer Taten mannigfaltige Funktionen übernehmen. Zum einen personifizierten sie Eigenschaften, die als typisch britisch angesehen wurden, und bildeten daher ein Sinnbild der nationalen Größe Englands. Zum anderen konnten sie zu Vorbildern für nachfolgende Generationen werden, denen der Mythos von Lucknow schon in Schulbüchern, Abenteuergeschichten und Romanen als leuchtendes Beispiel vor Augen gehalten wurde. Außerdem dienten ihre herausragenden Qualitäten dazu, die Größe des britischen Empire gleichzeitig zu erklären und zu bestätigen. Insbesondere durch die Betonung des Zusammenhalts der Belagerten, die vermeintlich alle gleichermaßen zum Sieg der Briten beigetragen hatten, wurden sie zu einer Verkörperung des kollektiven Willens Großbritanniens.[55]

Darüber hinaus bestätigte der Mythos von Lucknow den Glauben an die britische Überlegenheit. Gleichsam als Kompensation des großen Schocks, den die indische Rebellion der britischen Bevölkerung versetzt hatte, verdeutlichen die Erzählungen der Belagerung, daß es allen Grund dazu gab, stolz auf die Fähigkeiten der eigenen Landsleute zu sein. Der Erfolg der zahlenmäßig weit unterlegenen Briten in einer scheinbar aussichtslosen Situation wurde in diesem Sinne noch 1947 von einem angesehenen Historiker als ein bedeutendes Ereignis für Großbritannien interpretiert, denn "the relief and final capture of Lucknow, re-established the prestige of Britain not only in India, but in Europe also".[56] Daß der Mythos von Lucknow so lange eine bedeutende Stellung im nationalen Gedächtnis einnehmen konnte, verdeutlicht, daß er nicht nur das Prestige der Briten im Ausland hob, sondern vor allem der britischen Selbstbestätigung diente. Die Voraussage eines Zeitschriftenartikels von 1860, daß das Wort Lucknow "will be the symbol of heroism and devotion, the truest and the most noble, so long as there is one man to speak, and one other man to listen to the English language"[57], sollte sich fast ein Jahrhundert lang bestätigen.

Ein Teil der Attraktivität und Langlebigkeit des Mythos liegt darin, daß er leicht auf spätere Bedürfnisse zugeschnitten werden konnte. In allen Situationen, in denen Grund zum Zweifel an der britischen Überlegenheit bestand, konnte Lucknow als Symbol für die heroischen Fähigkeiten der Briten dienen, die selbst in aussichtslosen Situationen als Sieger hervorgehen würden. Der imperiale Mythos von der Belagerung von Lucknow bewies, daß die Briten ihre Pflicht, ein großes Empire zu regieren, in hervorragender Weise erfüllen konnten. Im britischen kulturellen Gedächtnis blieb Lucknow ein Symbol für

> a siege famous among the famous sieges of the Mutiny, wherein a handful of Europeans, filled with the fighting spirit of the master-race and the indomitable pride of Britain, made head against the overwhelming forces of murderous rebels [...] and would never confess defeat.[58]

Anmerkungen

* Für unerläßliche und unermüdliche Hilfe beim Aufspüren und Beschaffen von Quellen zum *Siege of Lucknow* danke ich Stefan Leonards und Karin Schültke.

1 J. Pemble: *The Raj, the Indian Mutiny and the Kingdom of Oudh, 1801-1859.* Sussex, 1977, S. 215.

2 J. F. Mürdter: *General-Major Sir Henry Havelock, Baronet von Landau, etc. als Kriegsheld und als Christ. Nach den Biographien von W. Brock, James Grant und John Marshman.* Stuttgart, 1859, S. 3.

3 Zum Ruhm Havelocks vgl. etwa J.C. Marshman: *Memoirs of Major-General Sir Henry Havelock K.C.B.* London, 1860, 1861, S. 452ff.

4 R. Hilton: *The Indian Mutiny: a Centenary History*. London, 1957, S. 129. Nicht nur aus stilistischen Gründen wird im folgenden 'englisch' teilweise als Synonym für 'britisch' verwendet, sondern auch um dem Umstand Rechnung zu tragen, daß schottische und irische Nationalcharakteristika nicht zum Bestandteil der gemeinsamen britischen Nationalidentität wurden.

5 Mythos wird hier im Sinne Peter Burkes verstanden als eine Geschichte mit symbolischer Bedeutung, die nicht eine exakte Abbildung von vergangenem Geschehen darstellt, sondern von stereotypen Begebenheiten und überlebensgroßen Figuren Gebrauch macht. Vgl. dazu P. Burke: „Geschichte als soziales Gedächtnis". – In A. Assmann/D. Harth (Eds.): *Mnemosyne. Formen und Funktionen der kulturellen Erinnerung*. Frankfurt a.M., 1991, S. 289-304, 295. R. Barthes: *Mythen des Alltags*. Franfurt a.M., 1964, bes. S. 97, 102, 109, geht davon aus, daß Mythen immer deformieren und meist mit Vereinfachungen und Überspitzungen arbeiten. Dies wird im folgenden ebenso bestätigt wie seine These, daß die Bedeutung des Mythos vom bloßen Sinn des Dargestellten zu unterscheiden ist.

6 R. Samuel: "Introduction: The Figures of National Myth". – In Ders. (Ed.): *Patriotism: The Making and Unmaking of British National Identity. National Fictions.* (vol. 3). London, 1989, S. xi-xxxvi, xxvii.

7 Zum Zusammenhang von Freiheitsideal und Einsatz für die Abschaffung der Sklaverei vgl. L. Colley: *Britons. Forging the Nation 1707-1837*. New Haven, London, 1992, S. 354, 359; zum Humanitätsideal vgl. V. Nünning: „Die Entdeckung der Humanität als kulturgeschichtliches Phänomen: Veränderungen in Menschenbild und Selbstverständnis von Engländern im 18. Jahrhundert". *Deutsche Vierteljahrsschrift für Literaturwissenschaft und Geistesgeschichte* 68,2, 1994, S. 214-37.

8 Zu der Reaktion auf die Nachrichten in Großbritannien und zu den Gerüchten über Vergewaltigungen und Schändungen vgl. etwa G.D. Bearce: *British Attitudes towards India, 1784-1858*. London, 1961, S. 233-38.

9 Zu einer knappen Darstellung der Ereignisse in Cawnpore vgl. M. Edwardes: *The Red Year. The Indian Rebellion of 1857*. London, 1973, S. 71ff.

10 Einen Überblick über die Ereignisse in Lucknow gibt etwa C. Hibbert: *The Great Mutiny, India 1857*. London, 1978, S. 223-52; 327-51.

11 Vgl. dazu etwa M. Germon: *Journal of the Siege of Lucknow*. Ed. M. Edwardes. London, 1958, die wie fast alle Belagerten die Tätigkeiten der Frauen immer wieder beschreibt, sowie M. Gubbins: *An Account of the Mutinies in Oudh and the Siege of the Lucknow Residency*. London, 1858, S. 239f., 364, der die schlechten sanitären Bedingungen und die mangelnden Kenntnisse über das Backen von Brot schildert.

12 K. Harris: *A Lady's Diary of the Siege of Lucknow, Written for the Perusal of Friends at Home*. London, 1858, S. 51.

13 Vgl. etwa J.K. Inglis: *The Siege of Lucknow: A Diary*. London, 1892, S. 129: "John [Inglis] said he had made up his mind that every man should die at his post, but what were the sick and wounded, the women and helpless children, to do? [...] At one time he talked of blowing us up at the last minute, but I have since heard this would have been impracticable."

14 K. Harris: *A Lady's Diary*, S. 44. Die 'snobbery' einiger Briten wird auch von R. Collier: *The Great Indian Mutiny. A Dramatic Account of the Sepoy Rebellion*. New York, 1964, S. 224, beschrieben.

15 J. Inglis: *The Siege of Lucknow*, S. 146. Vgl. zur Freundlichkeit der indischen Soldaten ebd. 22, 147f.

16 Vgl. entsprechende Zitate in E. Thompson: *The Other Side of the Medal.* London, 1925, S. 67-69, sowie C. Hibbert: *The Great Mutiny*, S. 56.

17 R. Rees: *A Personal Narrative of the Siege of Lucknow*. London, [2]1858, S. 137. So eklatant rassistisch wie Rees waren nur wenige der Verfasser von Briefen und Tagebüchern; meist wurden Inder einfach nicht erwähnt.

18 B. Watson: *The Great Indian Mutiny: Colin Campbell and the Campaign at Lucknow.* New York, London, 1991, S. 57. Die Zahlen variieren; nach J. Pemble: *The Raj*, S. 195, fielen 500 von 2000 Soldaten der britischen Truppen. Vgl. zu den Entsatzversuchen auch C. Hibbert: *The Great Mutiny*, S. 253-68, 327-51.

19 W.H. Russell: *My Diary in India in the Year 1858-9*. 2 vols. Ed. M. Edwardes. New York, 1970, vol. 1, S. 119. Vgl. auch ebd., S. 90ff., 195. Russells Werk, das viele Fehler der Briten offenlegte, wurde in England stark kritisiert und beeinträchtigte die Mythenbildung in keiner Weise.

20 W.H. Fitchett: *The Tale of the Great Mutiny*. London, [9]1911 (1901), S. 157. A. Duff: *The Indian Rebellion: Its Causes and Results, in a Series of Letters*. Edinburgh, London, 1858, S. 60, beschreibt dieses Debakel als Folge der "characteristic treachery" der indischen Soldaten. Vgl. auch R.P. Anderson: *A Personal Journal of the Siege of Lucknow*. Ed. T.C. Anderson. London, 1858, S. 26: "This disaster was caused by Sir Henry Lawrence having been deceived by his spies."

21 H. Gilbert: *The Story of the Indian Mutiny*. New York, London, 1916, S. 277; vgl. auch W. H. Fitchett: *The Great Mutiny*, S. 209: "Havelock fought his way through blood and fire into the Residency, but he shrank from leading a great procession of women and children and wounded men along that *via dolorosa*". Vgl. auch G.A. Henty: *The Sovereign Reader*. London, 1896, S. 123f. G.W. Forrest: *A History of the Indian Mutiny, Reviewed and Illustrated from Original Documents*. 2 vols., London, 1904-1912, vol. 2, S. vi, nennt die entsprechende Kapitelüberschrift "Outram concludes it is impossible to remove the sick, wounded, women and children".

22 G. A. Henty: *Sovereign Reader*, S. 123. Seit dem späten September trieben beide Seiten zwar Sprengstollen unter die gegnerischen Stellungen; aber kein anderer Autor setzte dies in Bezug zur Ankunft Havelocks.

23 C. Ball: *History of the Indian Mutiny*. 2 vols. London, n.d., S. 10.

24 M. Joyce: *Ordeal at Lucknow: The Defence of the Residency*. London, 1938, S. 65f. Obwohl M. Gubbins: *An Account of the Mutinies*, S. 366f. seine Gaben an das Krankenhaus und seine Großzügigkeit Gästen gegenüber hochspielt, behauptet er im Gegensatz zu Joyce nicht, auch Arme versorgt zu haben.

25 A. Duff: *Indian Rebellion*, S. 152. Duff war offensichtlich nicht klar, daß die Briten die grausame Niederschlagung des Aufstandes dadurch rechtfertigen würden, daß sie die Rebellion ausschließlich als den Aufstand einiger weniger fehlgeleiteter Soldaten kennzeichneten, während die Bevölkerung auf der Seite der Briten gestanden habe.

26 Vgl. etwa G. B. Malleson: *History of the Indian Mutiny, 1857-1858. Commencing from the Close of the Second Volume of Sir John Kaye's History of the Sepoy War*. 3 vols. London, 1878, vol. 1, S. 457: "The reader must never forget how the paucity of their numbers told against them".

27 J. R. Seeley: *The Expansion of England. Two Courses of Lectures*. London, 1900, (1. Aufl. 1883), S. 232.

28 G. A. Henty: *Sovereign Reader*, S. 116. Auch A. Duff: *Indian Rebellion*, S. 19 betont die "almost superhuman energy of the handful of British officers and soldiers" in Lucknow.

29 W. H. Fitchett: *The Great Mutiny*, S. 165. Außerdem reduziert er die Zahl der indischen Soldaten auf 700. Selbst bei den Zivilisten sah H. Gilbert: *The Story of the Indian Mutiny*, S. 33 große Unterschiede zwischen Briten und Indern: "There were tall, athletic Englishmen and fat Eurasians, all belly and no chest, some little more than boys and others bent with age."

30 Vgl. R. Hilton: *The Indian Mutiny*, S. 2f.: "Sinister influences are at work to spread hatred among white and coloured races. We must expect, therefore, to see some garbled versions of what, in reality, is an honourable tale. [...] it is a tale of heroism which both the contesting nations may share with justifiable pride." Ähnlich auch S. B. Chaudhuri: *Civil Rebellion in the Indian Mutinies (1857-1859)*. Calcutta, 1957. Ignoriert werden treue indische Soldaten hingegen von P. Landon: *1857. In Commemoration of the 50th Anniversary of the Indian Mutiny*. London, 1907.

31 *Art Journal*, News Series, 6 (1860), S. 159.

32 Zitiert in N.A. Chick (Ed.): *Annals of the Indian Rebellion, 1857/58*. London, 1859/60, S. 243.

33 M. Joyce: *Ordeal at Lucknow*, S. 53. Vgl. dazu auch C. Ball: *History of the Indian Mutiny*, vol. 2, S. 10, 53. A.G. MacPherson: "Englishwomen in the Rebellion". *Calcutta Review*, 33, S. 1859, 108-26, 115; G.B. Malleson: *History of the Indian Mutiny*, vol. 1, S. 487f.

34 R. Rees: *A Personal Narrative*, S. 92.

35 A. H. Miles, A.J. Pattle (Eds.): *Fifty-Two Stories of the Indian Mutiny and the Men Who Saved India*. London, 1895, S. 286. Vgl. auch A. G. MacPherson: "Englishwomen", S. 114: "There are few more touching pictures than that of the bereaved widows at Lucknow seeking consolation, not in the indulgence of grief, but in active service in the hospitals." C. Ball: *History of the Indian Mutiny*, vol. 2, S. 53, vergleicht die Frauen von Lucknow mit Florence Nightingale. Die unablässige Tätigkeit der Frauen werden auch in Hentys Roman über den indischen Aufstand betont; vgl. G.A. Henty: *In Times of Peril. A Story of India*. Illustrated in Colour by T.C. Dugdale. London, n.d., S. 212.

36 G. A. Henty: *Sovereign Reader*, S. 116f. Vgl. auch R. Hilton: *The Indian Mutiny*, S. 132: "All male survivors of the siege expressed amazement at the fortitude of the women. [...] In a remarkably short time they became inured to fear of death or wounds and played their valuable part in the daily routine of the place quite calmly and most courageously."

37 A. G. MacPherson: "Englishwomen", S. 108. Vgl. auch ebd., 109: "the woman so trained [in patient courage and endurance] will be very unlikely to incur the guilt and disgrace of failing in the wife's first duty of being a help-meet to her husband under all circumstances."

38 W. H. Fitchett: *The Great Mutiny*, S. 177. Das Lachen in gefährlichen Situationen beschreiben auch A. H. Miles, A. J. Pattle (Eds.): *Fifty-Two Stories*, S. 282 sowie M. Joyce: *Ordeal at Lucknow*, S. 132. S. Baldwin: *On England*. London, [4]1938, S. 18 bezeichnet "facing misfortunes with a cheerful face" als typisch britisch.

39 Vgl. H. Gilbert: *The Story of the Indian Mutiny*, S. 253 sowie W. H. Fitchett: *The Great Mutiny*, S. 173.

40 Vgl. etwa das Lob für Inglis in G.B. Malleson: *History of the Indian Mutiny*, vol 1, S. 481: "Daring obstinacy in resisting, his confident mien, his cool courage".

41 Ebd., vol 2, S. 220. Vgl. zu weiteren Beispielen etwa M. Gubbins: *An Account of the Mutinies*, S. 286f.

42 Vgl. J. Assmann: „Die Katastrophe des Vergessens. Das Deuteronomium als Paradigma kultureller Mnemotechnik". – In A. Assmann/D. Harth (Eds.): *Mnemosyne*, S. 337-55, 346f. Es gab immer einige Ausnahmen, die sich gegen den Strom stellten und kritisch berichteten; dazu zählten etwa Kaye und insbesondere Thompson. Während ein Band des Geschichtswerks von Kaye sofort von Malleson umgeschrieben wurde, nahm man Thompson kaum zur Kenntnis.

43 Vgl. etwa A. Forbes: *Havelock.* (English Man of Action). London, 1891, S. 109: "Havelock was as ever reluctant to sanction capital punishment." Vgl. dagegen J. Pemble: *The Raj*, S. 180: "But the pious Havelock was as ruthless, and sadistic besides. It was Havelock who told his artillery officer: 'My dear Maude, I give you leave to hang as many men as you like'; and it was Havelock who prescribed execution by the method of blowing from guns."

44 Vgl. etwa A.W. Brock: *Biographical Sketch of Sir Henry Havelock.* London, [7]1858 [1. Aufl. 1858], S. 192: Havelock "wished to restore liberty to the captive, children to their fathers, and wives to their husbands. He was a chivalrous soldier, whose sword had never been raised against the fallen. To him, therefore, these butcheries, which had given to this contest a character of blackest infamy, were cause of unspeakable grief." Vgl. auch J.C. Marshman: *Henry Havelock*, S. 460.

45 Ebd., S. 451. Vgl. auch W. Owen: *The Good Soldier. Memoir of Major-General Sir Henry Havelock.* London, 1858, S. 47, sowie A. W. Brock: *Henry Havelock*, S. 2f., 6, dessen ganzes erstes Kapitel um die Bedeutung der "Christian Soldiers" Havelock, Nicholson, und Lawrence kreist. A.G. MacPherson: "Englishwomen", S. 110, wies darauf hin, daß Havelock und die weiteren christlichen Soldaten wie Henry Lawrence dazu beigetragen hätten, Soldaten das ihnen gebührende Ansehen zu verschaffen, denn "[b]efore the Crimean campaign the army was looked down upon as more ornamental than useful."

46 W. Owen: *The Good Soldier*, S. 230. Vgl. auch A.G. MacPherson: "Englishwomen", S. 113. In ähnlicher Weise betonte noch 1957 J.C. Pollock: *Way to Glory. The Life of Havelock of Lucknow.* London, 1957, S. 2, 256, die symbolische Bedeutung Havelocks.

47 A. Duff: *Indian Rebellion*, S. 61. Die Bedeutung der Religion für den Charakter von Henry Lawrence wird in der späteren Biographie von C. Aitchison: *Lord Lawrence.* (Rulers of India), Oxford, 1892, S. 19 im Unterschied zu früheren Darstellungen nur sehr gering veranschlagt.

48 Zitiert nach M. Girouard: *The Return to Camelot. Chivalry and the English Gentleman.* New Haven, London, 1981, S. 220. Als Ritter wurden nach Girouard nur mittelalterliche Helden, Gordon von Khartum und die Helden der *Indian Mutiny* angesehen (vgl. ebd., 229). Vgl. auch A. W. Brock: *Henry Havelock*, S. 278: "True knights these three brave hearts! Each had periled his life to rescue the helpless".

49 M. Joyce: *Ordeal at Lucknow*, S. 333, vgl. auch J.C. Marshman: *Henry Havelock*, S. 418. Dieses Bild hielt sich bis in die 1960er Jahre; vgl. etwa R. Collier: *Great Indian Mutiny*, S. 277.

50 Vgl. M. Joyce: *Ordeal at Lucknow*, S. 326, sowie G. A. Henty: *In Times of Peril*, S. 280.

51 G.B. Malleson: *History of the Indian Mutiny*, vol. 2, S. 218.

52 A. W. Brock: *Henry Havelock*, S. 155. Vgl. auch die Verse auf dem Buchdeckel der Biographie von W. Owen: *The Good Soldier*: "And the prize he sought and won/Was the Crown for Duty done."

53 H. B. Edwardes, H. Merivale: *Life of Sir Henry Lawrence*. 2 vols. London, 1872, vol. 2, S. 375. Vgl. auch G. W. Forrest: *A History*. S. 260-2.

54 Seit Mitte des 20. Jahrhunderts herrscht ein anderes Bild vor. Zum einen zeigt sich in vielen Geschichtswerken ein Bemühen um Ausgeglichenheit; zum anderen liefert J. G. Farrell: *Siege of Krishnapur. A Novel*. London, [6]1990 [1. Aufl. 1973] eine dem Mythos von Lucknow in allen Details völlig entgegengesetzte fiktionale Veranschaulichung der Belagerung.

55 Vgl. zu einer ähnlichen Auflistung von Funktionen britischer imperialer Helden auch J.M. Mackenzie: "David Livingstone: The Construction of the Myth". – In G. Walker/T. Gallagher (Eds.): *Sermons and Battle Hymns. Protestant Popular Culture in Modern Scotland*. Edinburgh, 1990, S. 24-42, 26.

56 G.M. Trevelyan: *History of England*. London, New York, 1947, S. 674f.

57 *Art Journal*, News Series, 6, 1860, S. 224.

58 H. Gilbert: *The Story of the Indian Mutiny*, S. 242. Vgl. auch G.B. Malleson: *History of the Indian Mutiny*, vol. 1, S. 451 "It was the triumph of British coolness and pluck over Asiatic numbers and swagger; of the mind over matter. But in a moral point of view it was more important still."

Bernhard Reitz, Mainz

Der *Christian gentleman* als imperiales Konstrukt in den Afrika-Romanen Henry Rider Haggards

The Empire and all it means

Im Schlußwort der ausführlichen Studie *Rider Haggard and the Fiction of Empire* charakterisiert Wendy R. Katz Haggard als "imperial propagandist, a man who made use of every opportunity to advance matters relating to Empire".[1] Verwiesen wird in diesem Zusammenhang auf einen Leserbrief an die *Times* aus dem Jahr 1920, in dem Haggard eine Bilanz seiner schriftstellerischen Arbeit zieht:

> All my life, so far as opportunity was open to me, by means of fictional and other writings, and as a humble servant of the country, I have done my best to spread knowledge of the Empire and all it means or should mean to us.[2]

Für Katz sind diese Zeilen ein Beleg für Haggards "characteristically naive immodesty"[3]. Sicherlich war der 1912 in den Adelsstand erhobene Bestsellerautor, dessen erzählerische Begabung auch Kollegen wie W. E. Henley und Rudyard Kipling vorbehaltlos rühmten, von Selbstgefälligkeit nicht frei. Es ist jedoch zu fragen, ob hier tatsächlich nur naive Unbescheidenheit Haggard die Feder führte. Denn insbesondere der Schluß der Selbstcharakteristik erschließt sich nachzeitigen Lesern nicht auf den ersten Blick. Für einen überzeugten Propagandisten des Empire, als der Haggard nach Auffassung seiner Kritiker[4] gelten muß, erscheint die Formulierung "the Empire and all it means or should mean" zunächst eher ambivalent. Als Schriftsteller und als Publizist hat Haggard oftmals sehr kritische Worte für die koloniale Wirklichkeit gefunden. "Ignosi's Farewell", die Warnung des Kukuanaherrschers in *King Solomon's Mines*, er werde weder "traders with their guns and rum" noch Missionare in sein Land lassen[5], ist vielzitiert. Doch läßt sich aus Haggards Kritik an der kolonialen Praxis eine Abwendung von der imperialen Idee noch nicht folgern. Zudem erweist sich Haggards Selbstcharakteristik bei näherer Betrachtung keineswegs als ambivalent, sondern kann schlüssig als retrospektive Festschreibung einer sowohl literarischen wie ideologisch-teleologischen Programmatik interpretiert werden.

Mit dem Hinweis, er habe die Kenntnisse über das Empire erweitern wollen, postuliert Haggard zunächst auch für sein schriftstellerisches Werk den aufklärerischen und wissenschaftlichen Anspruch der viktorianischen Entdeckungsberichte und der Reiseliteratur. Daß deren hohe Akzeptanz beim Lesepublikum sowohl den Rezeptionshorizont der *adventure fiction* wie auch deren inhaltliche und narrative Strukturen entscheidend mitbestimmte, hat in einer neueren Untersuchung White dargelegt.[6] Wissensvermittlung allein genügt Haggard jedoch noch nicht als Legitimation der Unterhaltung des Lesers durch Exotik, durch *romance* und durch *fantasy*. Er weitet explizit die Grenzen eines auf die Schilderung unerforschter Kontinente und unbekannter Völker beschränkten Ansatzes. Wie seine Zufügung, "the Empire *and all it means or should mean to us*" ausweist, kann es aus seiner Sicht keine Kenntnis des Empire ohne eine gleichzeitige Auseinandersetzung mit dessen überpersönlicher Bedeutung, mit dessen Idee geben. Hieraus erklärt sich auch Haggards Annäherung an die theologisch-metaphysische Diktion. Sein und Wesen des Empire, Existenz und Essenz sind untrennbar verknüpft, und vor allem das Wesen des Empire bedarf der Vermittlung und wird zum darstellerischen Anliegen.

Der dem eher peripheren Thema "Air Exploration and Empire" gewidmete Leserbrief an die *Times* konkretisiert mit dem Bekenntnis zur Idee des Empire zugleich den politischen Standort Haggards. Seine Sympathien für die Konservativen, für die er 1895, wenngleich ohne Erfolg, bei den Parlamentswahlen kandidierte, hat Haggard nie verhehlt. Er unterstützte die expansive Kolonialpolitik, wie sie Disraeli formuliert hatte, und er befürwortete Annexion und militärische Intervention. Mit seinem Verweis auf das Wesen des Empire bekräftigt er für seine Zeitgenossen ganz unmißverständlich seine Zugehörigkeit zu den Reihen derer, die wie Lord Alfred Milner unermüdlich das Empire als teleologischen Entwurf propagierten. Im Vorwort zu *The Nation and the Empire*, der 1913 veröffentlichten Sammlung seiner Reden, schreibt Milner:

> Imperialism as a political doctrine has often been represented as something tawdry and superficial. In reality it has all the depth and comprehensiveness of a religious faith. Its significance is moral even more than material.[7]

Ebensowenig versäumte Milners Mitstreiter Lord Curzon eine Gelegenheit, dem Empire eine sakrale Aura zu verleihen:

> The British Empire has been signally blessed by Providence; and her eminence, her strength, her wealth, her prosperity, her intellectual, her moral and her religious advantages, are so many reasons for peculiar obedience to the laws of Him who guides the destiny of nations. These were given for some higher purpose than commercial prosperity and military renown.[8]

Diese idealistisch-teleologischen Überhöhungen des Empire waren gewiß auch stets zur Legitimation von dessen materialistischer Wirklichkeit instrumentalisierbar. Dennoch sind sie keineswegs nur Ausdruck viktorianischer Heuchelei, die von Gott und Moral spricht, aber Kattun und Geschäft meint. Nicht zufällig finden sich in den Reihen der engagiertesten Propagandisten des Empire zahlreiche Konservative, die mit Carlyle "cash payment" als "sole nexus of man with man"[9] verurteilten und für das Individuum "a higher purpose" als die Gewinnmaximierung einforderten. Sowohl bei Milner wie bei Curzon läßt sich dabei nicht übersehen, daß sie das Empire stets auch als einen sinnstiftenden Gegenentwurf zur gesellschaftlichen Wirklichkeit des späten 19. Jahrhunderts verstanden, die sie von moralischer Verwirrung und demokratischer Auflösung bedroht sahen.

Die Akzeptanz des Empire als teleologische Ordnung impliziert deshalb mehr als nur die Möglichkeit diesseitiger Erfüllung. Für Curzon handelt, wer sich im Dienst des Empire einem "higher purpose" verpflichtet, im Sinne der Vorsehung und des Allmächtigen. Aus seiner Sicht kann die Idee des Empire eine von den Naturwissenschaften und durch die Philosophie erschütterte christliche Glaubensgewißheit nochmals festigen. Auch bei Milner sind christliche Grundwerte noch insoweit impliziert, als er das Empire als eine moralische Ordnung begreift. Jedoch ist seine Position darin radikaler, daß er die explizit christliche Teleologisierung preisgibt und dafür die Ideologie in den Rang der Religion erhebt. Den frei gewordenen Platz Gottes besetzt bei Milner die Rasse. Imperialismus, so argumentiert er, sei nicht geographisch zu definieren, "not a question of a couple of hundred square miles more or less", sondern

> [...] a question of preserving the unity of a great race, of enabling it, by maintaining that unity, to develop freely on its own lines, and continue to fulfil its distinctive mission in the world.[10]

Aus nachzeitiger Sicht müssen das Gefahrenpotential und die Konsequenzen dieser Verschmelzung von religiösen und rassischen Vorstellungen, die dann zu rassistischen mutierten, in einer Teleologie des Empire nicht mehr ausführlich erläutert werden. Es ist aber auch nicht zu übersehen, daß vielen Viktorianern die scheinbar bruchlose Vereinbarkeit dieses zugleich christlich, rassisch und nationalistisch legitimierten Imperialismusverständnisses mit dem puritanisch fundierten Erwähltheitsbegriff den Blick für eine selbstkritischere Wertung verstellte. So wird einsichtig, weshalb sich Lord Rosebery vor den Studenten der Universität Glasgow in einem Atemzug auf "the energy and fortune of a race" und als überzeugter Christ auf "the supreme direction of the Almighty" berufen konnte.[11]

In bezug auf die hier skizzierten Vorstellungen ist Haggards eigener Beitrag allerdings nicht originär, sondern derivativ. Als sich Haggard mit seinen fiktionalen und journalistischen Texten in den achtziger Jahren in den imperialen und kolonialen Diskurs einschaltete, waren die ideologischen Positionen bereits besetzt. Dies mindert Haggards Beitrag zur Popularisierung und Plausibilisierung des Empire als ideologisch-teleologischem Entwurf jedoch ebensowenig wie die epistemologische Bedeutung, die seinem literarischen Werk zukommt. Es ist Teil des imperialen Diskurses und vermag dadurch dessen Strukturen zu verdeutlichen. Vor dem Hintergrund von Haggards Ausrichtung am teleologischen und ideologischen Vorverständnis des Empire soll deshalb nachfolgend jene ideologische Grundierung seiner Afrika-Romane untersucht werden, aufgrund derer erst sich diese Texte in einem mehr als nur geographischen Sinn als "fictions of the Empire" erweisen. Im Mittelpunkt stehen *King Solomon's Mines* (1885) und *Allan Quatermain* (1887). Es sind dies jene beiden Erfolgsromane Haggards, in denen er für seine Erzählerfigur Allan Quatermain und dessen Freunde Sir Curtis und Captain Good einen stimmigen Lebensentwurf zeichnet, der zugleich die Mechanismen der Konstitution des Selbst und des Anderen innerhalb eines teleologischen Überbaus offenlegt.

Men like Platonic ideas

Hinsichtlich der von Haggard insinuierten Annahme, er habe als "a humble servant of the country" von Beginn an seine Feder aus ideologischer Überzeugung in den Dienst des Vaterlands und der imperialen Idee gestellt, ergibt sich ein differenzierteres Bild, wenn man sowohl auf Haggards Karriere in Afrika wie auf seine Anfänge als Schriftsteller zurückblickt. Weder der eigene Antrieb noch familiäre Tradition führten Haggard in den Kolonialdienst. Vielmehr eröffnete die zufällige Konstellation, daß 1875 mit Sir Henry Bulwer ein Freund der Haggards zum Lieutenant-Govenor von Natal ernannt wurde, Haggards Vater die Möglichkeit, für den sechsten seiner sieben Söhne ein Auskommen zu finden. Nach dem wiederum unstrittigen Urteil seiner Biographen und Kritiker hat sich Haggard im Kolonialdienst bewährt. Zudem erwarb er mit einem für britische Kolonialbeamte keineswegs selbstverständlichen Wissensdurst fundierte Kenntnisse des südlichen Afrika. Sie begründen in seinen Afrika-Romanen den authentischen und plausiblen Kontext für *emplotments*, innerhalb derer Haggard seiner Phantasie kaum Zügel anlegte.

Mit der literarischen Verwertung seines Afrika-Aufenthalts begann Haggard jedoch erst, nachdem sein Versuch einer Existenzgründung auf dem schwarzen Kontinent endgültig gescheitert war. Der neu entflammte Widerstand der Buren, dem Gladstone aus innenpolitischer Rücksichtnahme nicht mit Gewalt begegnen wollte, hatte Haggards Beitrag zur Errichtung der britischen Herrschaft im Transvaal ebenso zunichtegemacht wie den Plan, sich auf einer Straußenfarm niederzulassen. Ein wesentlicher Anstoß für seine schriftstellerischen Versuche, die zunächst nur bescheidene Anerkennung fanden, war deshalb die Notwendigkeit, eine inzwischen vierköpfige Familie versorgen zu müssen. Erst *King Solomon's Mines* brachte den Durchbruch. Laut Haggards eigenen Angaben schrieb er den Roman in nur sechs Wochen, während er sich auf seine Zulassung als Anwalt vorbereitete. Der spektakuläre Erfolg bei den Kritikern und beim Publikum, das im ersten Jahr 31.000 Exemplare abnahm, beflügelte die Arbeit an der Fortsetzung. Auch *Allan Quatermain* entstand noch 1885, wurde aber erst zwei Jahre später und nach *She* veröffentlicht.

Zu Haggards Entschluß, sich ebenfalls auf dem Markt der *adventure fiction* zu versuchen, trug der noch wachsende Verkaufserfolg, den Stevenson seit 1883 mit *Treasure Island* erzielte, ganz unmittelbar bei. An das Lesepublikum, das Stevenson gewonnen hatte, richtete sich *King Solomon's Mines* unverblümt nicht allein in der äußeren Aufmachung des Bandes.[12] Stevenson hatte *Treasure Island* als "boy's book" bezeichnet, das aber auch Erwachsene noch fesseln könne. Eben diesem Leserkreis gilt auch die Widmung des Erzählers Quatermain. Er dediziert "this faithful but unpretending record of a remarkable adventure [...] to all the big and little boys who read it" (6). Wie Stevenson wählt Haggard einen Titel, der sagenhaften Reichtum suggeriert, und auch Haggard entfaltet innerhalb der für die *adventure fiction* geltenden Darstellungskonventionen der *romance* "a tale of adventure and heroic deeds"[13] ohne "love interest".

Stevensons jugendlicher Ich-Erzähler Jim teilt mit Allan Quatermain jene Disposition zum vorgeblich unprätentiösen Erzählen, die Quatermain in seiner Einleitung nochmals mit den Worten bekräftigt, er berichte "in a plain, straightforward manner" (9) und habe sich nach reiflicher Überlegung auch entschieden, seine Leser nicht allzusehr mit landes- und volkskundlichen Details zu behelligen. Nicht weniger explizit geht Haggard jedoch auch auf Distanz zu Stevenson. Angesichts des Zielpublikums ist der Kontrast zwischen Jim, der noch durch Erfahrung und Bewährung reifen muß, und dem lebenserfahrenen Quatermain augenfällig. Bereits im ersten Satz des ersten Kapitels gibt Quatermain sein Alter mit "fifty-five last birthday" (11) preis und etabliert sich trotz aller Bescheidenheitstopoi nachfolgend als rezeptionslenkende moralische Instanz. Zwar fehlt Quatermain jeglicher missionarische Eifer, aber durch seine persönliche Integrität, seine Reife und sein Verantwortungsbewußtsein hat er mehr gemein mit der Selbstdarstellung Livingstones in dessen Reiseberichten als mit den weißen Jägern und Abenteurern, die bis hin zu Indiana Jones nach seinem Vorbild geschaffen wurden.

Haggards Erzähler stellt sich vor als "Allan Quatermain, of Durban, Natal, Gentleman", relativiert aber jeden Verdacht auf Eitelkeit sofort mit der Einschränkung,

> And, besides, am I a gentleman? What is a gentleman? I don't quite know, and yet I have had to do with niggers – no, I'll scratch that word 'niggers'

> out, for I don't like it. I've known natives who *are*, and so you'll say, Harry, my boy, before you're done with this tale, and I have known mean whites with lots of money and fresh out from home too, who *ain't*. Well, at any rate, I was born a gentleman, though I've been nothing but a poor travelling trader and hunter all my life. (12-13)

Im Kontext des ersten Kapitels liest sich dieser Absatz wie die Abschweifung eines noch ungeübten Erzählers, der Mühe hat, bei seinem Thema zu bleiben. Tatsächlich jedoch präzisiert Haggard über die nur scheinbar rhetorische Frage, "What is a gentleman?", sowohl die soziologische wie die ideologische und in Konsequenz auch die literarische Strukturierung seines Romans.

Quatermain verweist auf die ursprüngliche Wortbedeutung, das lateinische *gentilis*, das die Zugehörigkeit zu einer *gens* und damit einer angesehenen Familie bezeichnet. Es konturiert diese Aufwertung der standesgemäßen Herkunft, daß Quatermain nur wenig später für den neuen Botanischen Garten Kapstadts lobende, für das ebenfalls dort neu errichtete Parlament als Symbol demokratischer Legitimation aber nur abschätzige Worte findet (vgl. 13). Indem Quatermain ungeachtet seiner materiellen Erfolglosigkeit darauf insistiert, als *gentleman* geboren zu sein, und im gleichen Zusammenhang "lots of money" als Qualifikationsnachweis verwirft, bekräftigt er eine Ausrichtung an einem vordemokratischen Standesdenken, das sich im Bekenntnis zu immateriellen Werten sittlich legitimiert und dabei die politisch reaktionäre Einstellung zugleich kaschiert. Teil dieser Legitimation ist die vorgebliche Überwindung von Rassenschranken, die mit der Anerkennung von "natives who *are* [gentlemen]" ausgesprochen wird. Jedoch funktioniert die soziologische Abgrenzung auch hier. Denn analog zu der Unterscheidung zwischen *gentlemen* und *mean whites* muß man jene Schwarzen, die keine *gentlemen* sind, wohl in der Gruppe der *niggers* vermuten.

Welches Gewicht der Selbstbestimmung als *gentleman* tatsächlich zukommt, verdeutlicht die später *Allan Quatermain* vorangestellte Widmung. Dort verzichtet Haggard auf die *persona* des Erzählers und wendet sich direkt an seinen Sohn:

> I inscribe this book of adventure to my son ARTHUR JOHN RIDER HAGGARD in the hope that in days to come he, and many other boys whom I shall never know, may in the acts and thoughts of Allan Quatermain and his companions, as herein recorded, find something to help him and them to reach to what, with Sir Henry Curtis, I hold to be the highest rank whereto we can attain – the state and dignity of English gentlemen.[14]

Das in *King Solomon's Mines* postulierte Kriterium der standesgemäßen Herkunft wird hier entscheidend erweitert. "Acts and thoughts", als beispielhaft verstandene Taten und Gesinnung weisen den *gentleman* aus und begründen seinen Anspruch auf "the highest rank whereto we can attain". Mit dieser Hervorhebung der meritokratischen Komponente wird das Kriterium der Herkunft jedoch keineswegs demokratisch nivelliert. Quatermain bekräftigt dies durch die Wahl seiner Gefährten, die ebenso nachdrücklich wie er selbst als *gentlemen* eingeführt werden. Das *Gentleman's Pocket Book of Etiquette* von 1840 definiert "good company" als "composed of persons of birth, rank, fashion and respectability".[15] Quatermains Begleiter werden dieser Definition in vollem Umfang gerecht. Sir Curtis ist adlig von Geburt, und wenn der Erzähler ihn mit unverhohlener Bewunderung für seine arische Ausstrahlung als "of Danish blood" vorstellt (14), so korrigiert ihn Haggard in der Rolle des fiktiven Herausgebers und hebt hervor, daß Sir Curtis zum sächsischen und damit ältesten Adel Englands gehört (ebd.). Captain John Good, mangels weiterer Beförderungsmöglichkeiten in der Royal Navy frühpensioniert, wird aufgrund seines Offiziersranges der Status des *gentleman* von Quatermain explizit zugesprochen (14). Unstrittig ist beider *respectability*, und der monokelbewehrte Good, der auch unter widrigsten Umständen Wert auf ein makelloses Erscheinungsbild legt, darf sogar als "man of fashion" gelten.

Quatermain nutzt die Einführung Goods zu einer weiteren erzählerischen Digression, um dessen Entlassung aus der Marine mit den Worten zu kommentieren,

> That is what people who serve the Queen have to expect: to be shot out into the cold world to find a living just when they are beginning to really understand their work, and to get to the prime of life. (15)

Über diese Kritik an einem gesellschaftlichen Mißstand in der Heimat wird zugleich die Bedeutung des Empire profiliert. Wenn sich in dessen Territorien Männer wie Quatermain, Sir Curtis und Captain Good zu einem gemeinsamen Handeln finden können, das ihnen als *gentlemen* ebenso wie ihrem Vaterland zur Ehre gereicht, dann kann und darf man dieses Empire nicht gleichzeitig abgeschobenen Sträflingen und profitgierigen *misfits* von der heimischen Insel überlassen. Durch sein Romanpersonal definiert Haggard Afrika und implizit das Empire als Ganzes als einen Ort der Bewährung für Eliten. Auf deren Ebene, aber auch nur dort, wird eine Überwindung von Rassenschranken möglich. Mit Ignosi, dem rechtmäßigen König der Kukuanas durch Geburt, aristokratisch in Erscheinung und Auftreten, und durch kriegerischen Mut wie durch Mäßigung zum Herrscher befähigt, ist ein Bündnis möglich. Dagegen gibt es keine Berührungspunkte mit dem Usurpator Twala, den Quatermain nur im Rückgriff auf die rassistischen Klischees vom auch physisch abstossenden *nigger* zu beschreiben vermag:

> [...] an enormous man with the most entirely repulsive countenance we had ever beheld. The lips were as thick as a Negro's, the nose was flat [...], and its whole expression was cruel and sensual to a degree. (115)

Im Sinne der Konstituierung des Empire als Ort der Bewährung für die Elite der wahren *gentlemen* ist Haggard ganz unübersehbar um den Nachweis bemüht, daß seine Protagonisten von immateriellen Motiven geleitet werden. Die sagenhaften Schätze Salomos, mit denen der Titel lockt, erwecken im Gegensatz zu Flints Piratenschatz in *Treasure Island* und zum anfänglichen Erstaunen des Lesers keinerlei materielle Begehrlichkeit. Als Ignosi seinen weißen Freunden anbietet, er werde sie für ihre Unterstützung bei seinem Kampf um den Thron mit Salomos Diamanten entlohnen, zögert Sir Curtis nicht mit seiner Antwort:

> 'Tell him,' answered Sir Henry, 'that he mistakes an Englishman. Wealth is good, and if it comes in our way we take it; but a gentleman does not sell himself for wealth.' (127)

Sir Curtis hat keinen anderen Wunsch, als seinen bei der Schatzsuche verschollenen Bruder George zu finden. Er bekräftigt diese ideelle Motivation mit der Erklärung, sofern man doch auf die Diamanten stoße, verzichte er vorab zugunsten Quatermains und Goods (31). Aber auch Captain Good träumt trotz seiner kargen Mittel nicht vom schnellen Reichtum. In vollem Einklang mit seinem suggestiven Namen begleitet er Sir Curtis allein aus Freundschaft und schwächt dieses honorige Motiv zudem noch bescheiden mit dem Hinweis ab, er habe ja sowieso derzeit nichts Besseres zu tun (20). Allein Quatermain bekennt sich zu materiellen Erwägungen. Doch haben auch für ihn die Diamanten, an deren Existenz er nicht glaubt, keine Verlockung. Seine Einwilligung, Sir Curtis und Good auf ihrer Suche zu führen, wird bestimmt von der Möglichkeit, die Zukunft seines Sohnes Harry absichern zu können. Mit den £500, die Sir Curtis noch vor dem Aufbruch zu zahlen bereit ist, will Quatermain seinen Sohn in den Stand setzen, sein Medizinstudium abzuschließen.

Indem Haggard Bruderliebe, Freundschaft und väterliche Fürsorge als handlungsleitende Motive der Protagonisten herausstellt, wird das Abenteuer, dem die *gentlemen* entgegengehen, zunächst zu einem ausschließlich altruistischen Unternehmen aufgewertet. Die von Quatermain angemahnte Gefahr eines tödlichen Ausgangs der Expedition dient dabei sowohl der Spannungssteigerung wie der Überhöhung der Motive, deren ethische Validität sich die Protagonisten sogar noch gegenseitig bestätigen (vgl. 36). Nicht aus Eigennutz, sondern für andere setzen Quatermain und seine Gefährten ihr Leben aufs Spiel.

Zu diesem hohen ethischen Ziel fügt sich schlüssig, daß sich die Protagonisten bei ihrem Unterfangen in Gottes Hand wissen, und es kennzeichnet Haggards narrative Strategie, daß er Sir Curtis in dessen Gebet vor dem entscheidenden Handlungsabschnitt nicht vom Aufbruch ins Abenteuer, sondern von einer "strange journey" sprechen läßt:

> [...] 'we are going on about as strange a journey as men can make in this world. It is very doubtful if we can succeed in it. But we are three men who will stand together for good or for evil to the last. And now before we start let us for a moment pray to the Power who shapes the destinies of men, and who ages since has marked out our paths, that it may please Him to direct our steps in accordance with His will.' (63)

Die altruistische Motivation der Protagonisten wird nicht allein durch Sir Curtis christlich validiert. Ausdrücklich betont Quatermain auch Goods Frömmigkeit und fügt hinzu, er selbst habe niemals "a better prayer in my life than [...] during that minute" (ebd.) gesprochen. Ebensowenig erscheint es zufällig, daß das Treuegelöbnis der drei an das christliche Eheversprechen erinnert und zudem explizit auf den göttlichen Heilsplan verwiesen wird.

Es läuft dieser altruistisch-christlichen Überhöhung der Handlungsträger keineswegs zuwider, daß sie die Diamanten dann doch finden und der pragmatische Quatermain sich mit einem kleinen Teil des Schatzes die Taschen füllt, bevor er mit seinen Gefährten den Ausweg aus der zur Falle gewordenen Schatzkammer sucht. Nur kurz dauert ihr "fit" angesichts des unermeßlichen Reichtums, zu dem die tückische Gagool geführt hat, denn der Augenblick der Faszination durch den Schatz erweist sich zugleich als Moment der größten Bedrohung. Danach läßt sowohl die Trauer über Foulata wie die vermeintliche Nähe des eigenen Todes Quatermain den Wert der Edelsteine relativieren:

> [...] the irony of the situation forced itself upon me. There around us lay treasures enough to pay off a moderate national debt, or to build a fleet of ironclads, and yet we would gladly have bartered them all for the faintest chance of escape. Soon, doubtless, we should be glad to exchange them for a bit of food or a cup of water, and, after that, even for the privilege of a speedy close to our sufferings. Truly wealth, which men spend all their lives in acquiring, is a valueless thing at the last. (230-31)

In Einklang mit ihrer Charakterisierung sehen Haggards Protagonisten den möglichen Nutzen der Diamanten nicht im privaten, sondern im öffentlichen Bereich. Reichtum wird definiert durch das Gute, das man damit tun kann, wenngleich nachzeitige Leser dieses im Bau von Panzerkreuzern vielleicht nur schwer erkennen können. Auch noch nach der Flucht aus Salomos Schatzkammer hält Haggard an der kritischen Konnotierung der Diamanten fest. Ignosi verdächtigt seine Freunde, sie verließen ihn nur deshalb, weil sie mit den Diamanten gefunden hätten, weswegen sie gekommen seien, und er verflucht die Steine, die wertvoller seien als Freundschaft (vgl. 244-245). Nur mit der Erklärung, ihre Sehnsucht nach ihrem Vaterland sei nicht geringer als jene, die Ignosi in seine Heimat zurückgeführt habe, kann Quatermain den König besänftigen.

Erst im letzten Kapitel, als die Gefährten auf ihrem Rückweg dann doch noch auf Sir Curtis' verschollenen Bruder stoßen, erfahren die Diamanten eine positive Umwertung. Bezeichnenderweise werden sie zu einer wiederum altruistischen Geste genutzt. Quatermain und Good teilen die Edelsteine mit George Curtis. Als *nabob* kehrt keiner dieser drei nach England zurück, wohl aber vermögend genug, um in der Heimat das einem *gentleman* standesgemäße Leben führen zu können.

Gemessen an der ausführlichen Darstellung der vorausgegangenen Abenteuer erscheint das nur kurze Schlußkapitel "Found" auf den ersten Blick als kaum mehr denn eine Coda, innerhalb der ein weitgehend aus dem Blickfeld geratener Handlungsstrang abgeschlossen wird. Zu dieser Folgerung kann allerdings nur gelangen, wer übersieht, wie Haggard mit dem *happy ending* der *adventure story* zugleich die exemplarische Präsentation seiner Protagonisten abrundet. Indem Quatermain und Good die Diamanten mit George teilen, verhelfen sie keineswegs einem gescheiterten Schatzsucher zu einem Teil dessen, wovon er noch immer träumt.

Beschenkt wird bei Haggard nicht der erfolglose Glücksritter, sondern ein Mann, dessen innere Wandlung einer Belohnung würdig ist. Für seine Hoffnung auf schnellen Reichtum hat George Curtis mit seinem Unfall gebüßt, von dem ihm ein lahmes Bein geblieben ist, und man kann diese Episode als eine Warnung Haggards an alle jene begreifen, die nur aus materiellen Motiven in Englands Kolonien gehen. Quatermain rafft George Curtis' Bericht bis hin zu dem Unfall, der George und seinen schwarzen Begleiter an die einsame Oase fesselte, läßt ihn den entscheidenden Satz aber dann selbst sprechen:

> 'And so', he ended, 'we have lived for nearly two years, like a second Robinson Crusoe and his man Friday, hoping against hope [...]. (253)

Die literarische Parallele ist hier zugleich eine moralische. Denn wie Defoes Robinson Crusoe hat die Vorsehung George Curtis an einen Ort geführt, der Gelegenheit zur Bewährung und zur Besinnung auf höhere Werte als Reichtum bietet. Zur Bestätigung, daß auch er eine Robinson vergleichbare Entwicklung durchlaufen hat, bezeichnet George seine Errettung ausdrücklich nicht nur als Glücksfall, sondern als "most merciful" (253) und damit als einen Akt der Vorsehung und der Gnade gegenüber seinem "worthless self" (254).

Mit dem Schlußkapitel wird deutlich, daß in *King Solomon's Mines* die Vorsehung gleich auf doppelte Weise waltet. Gerettet wird, wer die Rettung verdient, und die Vorsehung bedient sich hierfür derjenigen, die sich ihr aus uneigennützigen Motiven anempfohlen haben. Daß mit dieser Stilisierung der Protagonisten zu Agenten der Vorsehung zugleich eine moralische Hypostasierung einhergeht, die deren Glaubwürdigkeit beeinträchtigt, hat das viktorianische Lesepublikum ganz offensichtlich weniger gestört als nachzeitige

Leser. Deren gewandeltes Rezeptionsverhalten wird eher von Graham Greene angesprochen, wenn er erläutert, warum Quatermain und seine Gefährten ihn in seiner Jugend trotz aller ursprünglichen Begeisterung nicht dauerhaft fesseln konnten:

> They were men of such unyielding integrity (they would only admit to a fault in order to show how it might be overcome) that the wavering personality of a child could not rest for long against those monumental shoulders. These men were like Platonic ideas: they were not life as one had already begun to know it.[16]

Die von Greene zu Recht kritisierte exemplarische Abgehobenheit der *Christian gentlemen* Haggards trägt jedoch auch dazu bei, daß die literarische Organisation des Textes zunächst unscharf bleibt. Ungeachtet dessen, daß die in allen Situationen konstant untadeligen Helden, denen in Twala und Gagool ebenso eindeutig böse Widersacher entgegenstehen, für ein allein auf fesselnde *action* angelegtes Handlungsgeschehen wie prädestiniert erscheinen, läßt sich jedoch zeigen, daß Haggard um komplexere narrative Strukturen als die der *adventure story* bemüht war. Denn die christlich-moralische Grundierung der Protagonisten in *King Solomon's Mines* erweist sich bei Haggard zugleich als Voraussetzung und als Teil der Organisation des Textes als *quest romance*, die für die imperiale Propaganda instrumentalisiert wird.

Wie Nerlich dargelegt hat[17], entstammen seit den Ritterromanzen des 12. Jahrhunderts die Protagonisten der *quest fiction* der Oberschicht, und White weist im Zusammenhang ihres Strukturvergleichs von Reiseberichten und Abenteuerliteratur darauf hin, daß dort, wo sich beide Genres der Konventionen der *quest romance* bedienen, das Handeln der Protagonisten auch als "authorized, even divinely ordained" ausgewiesen wird.[18] Haggards Protagonisten entsprechen diesen Kriterien. Thematisch ist die *quest* als Suche nach einem hohen immateriellen Wert bestimmbar, der vom Helden jedoch erst durch Prüfung und Bewährung in heroischen Taten erlangt werden kann. Während für das *emplotment* einer *adventure story* Bruderliebe als handlungsleitendes Motiv genügt hätte, verlangt die *quest* eine höhere Zielsetzung. Sie ist allein in der ethischen Motivation von Haggards Protagonisten noch nicht gegeben, denn ihre guten Eigenschaften bringen Quatermain und seine Gefährten bereits als Voraussetzung mit ein.

In *King Solomon's Mines* etabliert Haggard jedoch dadurch ein der *quest* gemäßeres Ziel, daß er die Suche nach dem verlorenen Bruder zugleich als eine Wiederherstellung verletzten Rechts ausweist. Denn für Georges Versuch, als Schatzsucher zu Reichtum zu gelangen, trägt Sir Curtis insofern Mitverantwortung, als er seinem jüngeren Bruder wegen eines Zerwürfnisses die ihm aus dem väterlichen Erbe eigentlich zustehende Unterstützung verweigert hatte (vgl. 19). Für Sir Curtis ist die Expedition auch ein Akt tätiger Reue.

Indem Haggard die "strange journey" aus verletztem Recht und durch Wiedergutmachung begründet, wird es ihm zugleich möglich, die Handlung um George Curtis mit dem dominierenden Geschehen um Ignosi zu verzahnen. Der Aussöhnung der Brüder geht im Sinne der *quest* Bewährung voraus, die Haggard inhaltlich als die Wiederherstellung von Ignosis Erbrecht konkretisiert. Daß sowohl George Curtis als auch Ignosi in ihren legitimen Stand zurückversetzt werden, ist keine nur vordergründige Parallele. Denn mit der Wiederherstellung von Gerechtigkeit als dem beide Handlungsstränge übergreifenden gemeinsamen Ziel wird der für *King Solomon's Mines* konstitutive teleologische Anspruch Haggards explizit. Haggard erschafft einen imperialen Kontext, innerhalb dessen sittlich verantwortungsbewußte Protagonisten eine höhere, ausweislich des Bruderzwists auch in der Heimat schon bedrohte Ordnung verteidigen können. In diesem Tun offenbaren sie ihr wahres, ideales Selbst, das aber für die Anerkennung des Anderen dann auch keine anderen Maßstäbe als die eigenen mehr gelten läßt.

Im Land der Kukuanas beseitigen Quatermain und seine Freunde nicht nur einen Usurpator. Wie Bass[19] zutreffend dargelegt hat, resultiert der blutige, aber von Quatermain heroisierte Bürgerkrieg in einer gesellschaftlichen Transformation. Unter Twala verharrten die Kukuanas im Zustand abergläubischer Barbarei. Unter Ignosi sind sie ein stolzes Volk, dessen Würde in seiner Tapferkeit und Opferbereitschaft gründet. Bewirkt wird dieser Wandel jedoch von einer weißen Elite, die in der militärischen Konfrontation ihre Führungsqualitäten offenbart. Nicht Ignosi überwältigt den Usurpator, sondern Sir Curtis, "our great Englishman" (191), wie Haggard ihn beim Zweikampf mit Twala rühmt. Schöpfer der neuen Ordnung sind die *Christian gentlemen*, wodurch für Ignosi nur die Rolle des Hüters und Bewahrers bleibt. Dies aber schließt trotz aller Freundschaftsbekundungen eine wirkliche Anerkennung des Anderen als gleichwertig und eigenständig aus. Beim Abschied, als Quatermain den Kukuanaherrscher mit biblischer Emphase ermahnt, die Werte zu wahren, auf die er verpflichtet wurde, wird diese Differenz von Haggard nicht mehr verschleiert:

> Behold, Ignosi, with us thou camest as a servant, and now we leave thee a mighty king. If thou art grateful to us, remember to do even as thou didst promise: to rule justly, to respect the law, and to put none to death without a cause. So shalt thou prosper. (244)

Es entspricht dem gottähnlichen Schöpferstatus der Väter der neuen Ordnung, daß Quatermain zu Ignosi spricht wie Jahwe zu den Königen Israels, denen dieser den Sieg schenkte, damit sie seine Gebote befolgen. Man mag Bass nicht widersprechen, wenn er mit Blick auf eben diese Passage feststellt, "[Quatermain] is celebrating [...] cultural imperialism".[20] Verständnis für das Fremde ist in Quatermains Predigt, die allein das erhöhte Selbst als Maßstab zuläßt, nicht erkennbar. Jedoch verweist gerade die religiöse Emphase darauf, daß Haggards Imperialismusverständnis stärker teleologisch denn kulturell begründet ist.

Wenn Ignosi warnt, er könne die Integrität der ihm anvertrauten Ordnung nur dadurch schützen, daß er weder Händler noch Missionare ins Land lasse (vgl. 245), werden zugleich der Anspruch wie die Grenzen des von Quatermain und seinen Gefährten Erreichten sichtbar. Die Händler, die Alkohol und Waffen, und die Missionare, die Zwietracht bringen, verkörpern mehr als nur die Schattenseiten der kolonialen Wirklichkeit. Bei Haggard sind sie nicht Repräsentanten einer höheren, sondern einer gefährdeten Zivilisation und stehen für deren ungelöste Konflikte. Vor diesen gilt es die Reinheit des idealen Gesellschaftsentwurfs zu bewahren. Er ist anfällig, gerade weil ihn nur völlig integere Männer verwirklichen können, die wie Quatermain und seine Gefährten mit "the depth and the comprehensiveness of a religious faith" an die immaterielle Bedeutung des Empire glauben und als "men like Platonic ideas" dessen Idealität auch antizipatorisch verkörpern. Als Emanationen der imperialen Idee vermögen Haggards Protagonisten jedoch nur unter abstrahierten, von der Kontingenz und Komplexität der gesellschaftlichen Wirklichkeit abgelösten Bedingungen zu handeln, die eine eindeutige moralische Wertung zulassen.

Es ist Ignosi, der die Grenzen des teleologischen Anspruchs aufzeigt. Er verweist darauf, daß am Schluß von *King Solomon's Mines* die Distanz zwischen dem idealen Gesellschaftsentwurf für die Kukuanas und der englischen Wirklichkeit unüberbrückbar bleibt. Wenn allein gewaltsame Abgrenzung die Reinheit des Ideals bewahren kann, dann sind die Zweifel an der geschichtsmächtigen Kraft des von Quatermain und seinen Gefährten verkörperten Telos doch wohl größer, als die triumphale Heimkehr der Helden suggeriert. Bezeichnenderweise nutzen Haggards Protagonisten ihre in Afrika bewiesenen Führungsqualitäten in England denn auch nicht zum gesellschaftlichen Engagement, sondern verlegen sich, wie Sir Curtis' Brief an Quatermain offenbart, aufs Privatisieren (vgl. 255-56). Ihre Distanznahme ist Ausdruck einer tiefgehenden Skepsis gegenüber der Komplexität der gesellschaftlichen Wirklichkeit, die in der antidemokratischen Dimension des imperialen Telos ihren Ausdruck findet. An der ideologischen Perspektivierung von *Allan Quatermain* tritt dies noch eindeutiger zutage als in *King Solomon's Mines*.

Civilisation, what does it all come to?

Am Schluß von *Allan Quatermain* empfiehlt Haggards Erzähler seine Seele dem Allmächtigen und verabschiedet sich von seinen Gefährten mit den Worten, er gehe nun auf "a stranger journey than any we have taken together" (273). Im Bürgerkrieg der Zu-Vendis hat Quatermain Captain Good ebenso das Leben gerettet wie der Königin Nyleptha, an deren Seite Sir Curtis als Prinzgemahl herrschen wird. Danach erliegt er den Wunden, die er im Einsatz für andere und für eine gerechte Sache empfangen hat.

Auf Wunsch seines Lesepublikums hat Haggard den populären Helden in späteren Texten wiederbelebt. Demgegenüber läßt die unter dem Eindruck des Erfolgs von *King Solomon's Mines* zu Papier gebrachte Fortsetzung das Bestreben erkennen, die Protagonisten mit einem schlüssigen Lebensentwurf auszustatten. Allerdings weist *Allan Quatermain* auch die typischen Schwächen einer Fortsetzung auf, deren primäres Ziel die Fortschreibung eines Verkaufserfolgs war. Augenfällig wird dies in der Parallelität des *emplotment.* Auch bei ihrer zweiten Expedition in das noch unerforschte Afrika stoßen Quatermain und seine Gefährten nach einleitenden Abenteuern auf ein abgeschiedenes Volk, dessen Befangenheit in Aberglauben durch machtgierige Priester ausgenutzt wird. Gagools Entsprechung heißt Agon; er ist der tückische Oberpriester eines Menschenopfer fordernden Sonnenkults. Die Zu-Vendis von dieser Unterdrückung zu befreien, wird zur Aufgabe der Helden, wobei sie tatkräftige kriegerische Unterstützung durch Umslopogaas erfahren, einen "high-bred Zulu" (123), der Ignosis Platz einnimmt. Doch gibt es noch einen fünften Begleiter, den aus der französischen Armee desertierten Koch Alphonse. In *Allan Quatermain* dient dieser "constitutional coward" (95) an Stelle Goods, dessen heldische Natur nun akzentuiert wird, zum *comic relief.* Doch mißrät die Komik zur überwiegend peinlichen Demonstration chauvinistischer Überheblichkeit über den kleinen Froschfresser.

Während es für eine Kreatur wie Alphonse keinen Aufstieg geben kann, zeigt Haggard an Sir Curtis, daß einem prinzipienfesten Engländer jeder Rang offensteht. Schon in *King Solomon's Mines* ist nicht zu übersehen, daß Haggard die von ihm geschaffenen Königsmacher auch einer Krone für würdig erachtet. Aber dort verweist das Tabu der Rassenmischung darauf, daß Quatermain und seine Gefährten trotz ihrer Befähigung zum Herrschen in einem schwarzen Volk keine akzeptablen Untertanen hätten. So kann die "dusky beauty" (198) Foulata ihre unerfüllbare Liebe zu Good nur dadurch besiegeln, daß sie sich für ihn opfert. Die auch von Haggard als grundsätzlich unüberwindbar erachteten Rassenschranken schließen aus, daß die Repräsentanten der weißen Elite in einem schwarzen Stamm aufgehen.

Mit *Allan Quatermain* räumt Haggard dieses Hindernis aus, indem er die Zu-Vendis zu Weißen macht. Seine bemühte pseudo-ethnologische Argumentation, mit der die Zu-Vendis zu Nachfahren der Phönizier stilisiert werden, ist von unfreiwilliger Komik nicht frei, läßt aber eine schlüssige Programmatik erkennen. Ausweislich ihres Lebensstils und ihrer architektonischen Leistungen verkörpern die Zu-Vendis das kulturelle Potential der frühen Kulturen des Mittelmeerraumes. Gleichzeitig werden englische Vorbilder darin deutlich, daß es sich um eine im Kern noch bäuerliche, und das heißt bei Haggard unverdorbene Kultur handelt[21], deren politische Organisationsform die Monarchie ist. Diese wird dadurch gestärkt, daß mit Sir Curtis ein Mann an die Spitze gelangt, der nicht dem Eigeninteresse, sondern dem Allgemeinwohl verpflichtet ist und dem seine königliche Gattin im Einklang mit viktorianischen Rollenstereotypen bereitwillig die Staatsgeschäfte überläßt.

Im letzten Kapitel, in dem Sir Curtis die Erzählerrolle übernimmt, portraitiert er sich als Reformer, der zwei große Ziele verfolgt: "one strong central government" und "the sapping of the power of the priesthood" (276). Hinter der Begründung des ersten Ziels, nur eine starke Regierung könne die aus den Rivalitäten unter dem Adel resultierenden Bürgerkriege verhindern, tritt jedoch eine Rechtfertigung des Führerprinzips und der autokratischen Lösung gesellschaftlicher Konflikte zutage. Hierzu paßt, daß der mit "[the] increase [of] trade and commerce" beauftragte Good vorrangig mit dem Aufbau einer Kriegsmarine beschäftigt ist, die als "troublesome and warlike" eingestufte Grenzvölker in Schach halten soll (275). In Sir Curtis' kleinem Empire spiegeln sich die Probleme des großen.

Mit dem zweiten Reformprogramm handelt Sir Curtis im Geiste Quatermains, der ihn auf dem Sterbebett ermahnt hatte:

> I [i.e. Quatermain] went the length to exhort him not to be carried away in the future by the pride and pomp of absolute power, but always to strive to remember that he was first a Christian gentleman, and next a public servant, called by Providence to a great and almost unprecedented trust. (268-269)

Als *Christian gentleman*, der, wie Quatermain im gleichen Atemzug versichert, einer derartigen Mahnung eigentlich gar nicht bedarf, wird Sir Curtis auch der "true religion" den Weg bereiten und auf dem Sonnentempel das Kreuz errichten. Und natürlich wird er auch seinen neugeborenen Sohn, "a regular curly-haired, blue-eyed young Englishman in looks" (277), als "English gentleman" erziehen, denn dies ist "even a prouder and a finer thing than being born heir apparent to the great House of the Stairway" (ebd.).

Wie Moses hat Quatermain seine Gefährten in ein gelobtes Land geführt, in ein maßgeschneidertes Imperium, das ihnen ideale Entfaltungsmöglichkeiten für ihr idealisiertes Selbst bietet. Damit treten aber auch die utopischen Elemente der idealen Ordnung noch eindeutiger hervor als in *King Solomon's Mines*. Denn als Herrscher der Zu-Vendis wird Sir Curtis nicht anders verfahren können als Ignosi. Auch er wird sein Reich von äußeren Einflüssen abschotten:

> [...] I am convinced of the sacred duty that rests upon me of preserving to this, on the whole upright and generous-hearted people the blessings of comparative barbarism. [...] I cannot see that gunpowder, telegraphs, steam, daily newspapers, universal suffrage, &c., &c., have made mankind one whit the happier than they used to be, and I am certain that they have brought many evils in their train. I have no fancy for handling over this beautiful country to be torn and fought for by speculators, tourists, politicians and teachers, whose voice is as the voice of Babel, [...] nor will I endow it with greed, drunkenness, new diseases, gunpowder, and general demoralisation which chiefly mark the progress of civilisation amongst unsophisticated peoples. (276-277)

In seiner Schilderung der Gefährdungen durch die Zivilisation ist Sir Curtis präziser als Ignosi. Zugleich konkretisiert er auch die den Roman einleitenden Überlegungen Quatermains, der den in der Frage, "this civilisation, what does it all come to?" (4), gipfelnden Überdruß an der englischen Gegenwart als Motiv für den erneuten Aufbruch nach Afrika benannt hatte. Quatermains und Sir Curtis' Zivilisationskritik umrahmt das Handlungsgeschehen und verdeutlicht so den ideologischen und teleologischen Entwurf, auf den hin das Abenteuer zu lesen ist.

In Übereinstimmung mit *King Solomon's Mines* ist das Empire auch in *Allan Quatermain* ein Ort der Bewährung für Eliten:

> [...] all our magnificent muster-roll of colonies [...] testifies to the extraordinary value of the spirit of adventure which [...] implies a brave heart and a trust in Providence. (94)

Jedoch wird nun, wo es keine Heimkehr mehr, sondern nur noch Abgrenzung gibt, die Distanznahme zur komplexen und kontingenten Wirklichkeit finalisiert. Ob Agitation für ein allgemeines Wahlrecht oder auch nur Meinungsvielfalt der Presse, für Sir Curtis wie für Quatermain sind dies fragwürdige Manifestationen einer modernen Zivilisation, die laut Quatermain nur "savagery silver-gilt", "greed of money" und "vainglory" (4-5) hervorgebracht hat und die wie alle zu komplex gewordenen Kulturen zum Untergang verurteilt ist. Auch an der spätviktorianischen Umkehrung des technologisch fundierten Fortschrittsoptimismus in Fortschrittszweifel haben Haggards Protagonisten teil. Sir Curtis weiß um die verheerenden Folgen, die "field-guns" und "Martini-Henrys", d.h., Repetiergewehre für seine Zu-Vendis haben könnten. Wenn er trotzdem auf eine Politik der Stärke setzt und seine Marine aufrüstet, lenkt er den Blick auf Widersprüche, die zum Ersten Weltkrieg hinführten.

Einerseits läßt Haggard seine Protagonisten in ihrer Zivilisationskritik die für die spätviktorianische Gesellschaft konstitutiven Konflikte ansprechen.

Andererseits enthebt er sie aber konsequent der Notwendigkeit, diese auch austragen zu müssen. Von der Sinnkrise, die am Anfang der Moderne steht, bleiben die idealisierten *Christian gentlemen* Haggards im Gegensatz zu den zweifelnden Charakteren George Eliots, Hardys und Conrads unbelastet. Statt dessen verwirklichen sie ihr ideales Selbst in einem Empire, dessen *Englishness* Haggard zwar ununterbrochen beteuert, das er aber ebenso nachdrücklich als einen Gegenentwurf zur englischen Wirklichkeit organisiert. Diesem Ziel wird auch das kognitive Potential, das in der Begegnung mit dem Anderen liegen könnte, untergeordnet. Mit dem real existierenden Empire und seinen von Kipling wie von Conrad thematisierten Konflikten hat Haggards im Sinne Milners auf "moral significance" ausgerichteter Entwurf zumindest in *Allan Quartermain* nichts mehr gemein. Hier erweist sich Haggards Empire endgültig als ein ebenso wie seine Helden idealisiertes Konstrukt. Es ist ein utopischer Entwurf, der vorgibt, mit der Zukunft zu paktieren, um unter deren Deckmantel jedoch eine nunmehr eindeutig als restaurativ erkennbare Teleologie zu propagieren.

In Sir Curtis' Herrschaft über die Zu-Vendis konkretisiert sich als gesellschaftliches Ideal ein vordemokratisches, aristokratisch geführtes und christlich legitimiertes System, das von der "general demoralisation" des 19. Jahrhunderts noch unbefleckt ist. Die Zukunft liegt in der Rückkehr zu einer verklärten Vergangenheit, und diesen Gesellschaftsentwurf unterbreitet Haggard seinen Lesern zugleich als Mahnung, als Vorbild und als Hoffnung. Durch die Motive für ihre Abkehr von England lassen Haggards Helden keinen Zweifel daran, wie gefährdet die Heimat der *Christian gentlemen* bereits ist. Jedoch können die exemplarischen Helden den "big and little boys" als Vorbild dienen, und dies begründet Hoffnung gleich doppelt. Denn sollte sich die restaurative Reorganisation der englischen Gesellschaft als unmöglich erweisen, dann bleibt als Option das Empire, in dem sich auf der geistigen Grundlage der imperialen Teleologie das ideale England neu begründen läßt.

Graham Greene, der Haggard durchschaute, ging dann doch nicht in den Kolonialdienst.[22] Aber viele, die diesen Weg wählten, hatten Haggards Romane im Kopf und im Gepäck, und das mag mit erklären, weshalb Reformen, in denen England seinen Kolonien voranging, dort nicht durchsetzbar waren.

1 W. R. Katz: *Rider Haggard and the Fiction of Empire*. Cambridge, 1987, S. 153.
2 H. R. Haggard: "Air Exploration and Empire". *The Times*, 7.Februar 1920, 8.
3 W. R. Katz: *Rider Haggard and the Fiction of Empire*, S. 153.
4 Außer auf die Studie von Katz sei hier vor allem verwiesen auf die umfassenden Studien von M. Cohen: *Rider Haggard. His life and works*. London, 1960; N. Etherington: *Rider Haggard*. Boston, 1984; A. Sandison: *The Wheel of Empire*. New York, 1967, bes. Kap. 2.
5 H. R. Haggard: *King Solomon's Mines*. Harmondsworth, 1958, S. 245. Nachfolgende Seitenangaben beziehen sich auf diese Ausgabe. Etherington folgert mit Bezug auf diese Stelle, "The Book ends on a strongly anti-imperialist note [...]". *Rider Haggard*, S. 41.
6 Vgl. A. White: *Joseph Conrad and the Adventure Tradition. Constructing and Deconstructing the Imperial Subject*. Cambridge, 1993, Kap. 2.
7 Lord A. Milner: *The Nation and the Empire*. London, 1913, S. xxxii.
8 Zitiert nach A. Sandison: *The Wheel of Empire*, S. 7.
9 T. Carlyle: *Past and Present*. London, 1966, S. 32.
10 Lord A. Milner: *The Nation and the Empire*. S. xxxiii.
11 Zitiert nach A. Sandison: *The Wheel of Empire*, S. 7.
12 Vgl. M. Cohen: *Rider Haggard. His life and works*. London, 1960, S. 89.
13 Ebd., S.90.
14 H. R. Haggard: *Allan Quatermain*. London, 1909, S. ix. Nachfolgende Seitenangaben beziehen sich auf diese Ausgabe.
15 Zitiert bei M. Brander: *The Victorian Gentleman*. London, 1975, S. 95.
16 G. Greene: *The Lost Childhood and Other Essays*. New York, 1951, S. 14.
17 Vgl. M. Nerlich: *Ideology of Adventure*. Vol. 1. Minneapolis, 1987, S. 6.
18 Vgl. A. White: *Joseph Conrad*, S. 44.
19 Vgl. J. Bass: "The Romance as Rhetorical Dissociation: The Purification of Imperialism in *King Solomon's Mines*". *The Quarterly Journal of Speech* 67, 1981, 259-269.
20 Ebd., 267.
21 Vgl. H.R. Haggard: "The Land Question". *The Times*, 28. April 1886, 4, sowie "Liberalism and Land Reform". *The Times*, 1. Mai 1923, 15.
22 Vgl. *The Lost Childhood*, S. 14, wo Greene schreibt: "If it had not been for that romantic tale of Allan Quatermain, Sir Henry Curtis, Captain Good, [...] would I at nineteen have studied the appointments list of the Colonial office and very nearly picked on the Nigerian Navy for a career?".

Ansgar Nünning, Köln

Das Britische Weltreich als Familie: Empire-Metaphern in der spätviktorianischen Literatur als Denkmodelle und als Mittel der historisch-politischen Sinnstiftung

1. "What name shall be conferred/ On England's Ocean-state?" – Thema, Zielsetzung und Leitfragen

In seinem 1883 erschienenen einflußreichen Buch *The Expansion of England* betont der englische Historiker John Robert Seeley, das Wort 'Empire' sei eine unangemessene Bezeichnung für die Beziehungen zwischen England und seinen Kolonien: "The word Empire seems too military and despotic to suit the relation of a mother-country to colonies."[1] Seeley begründet diese Feststellung mit dem Hinweis, daß die Kolonialisierung Vorgängen in der Natur ähnele, und erläutert diese vermeintlichen Analogien durch Sprachbilder. Sowohl die konventionelle Metapher des Mutterlandes als auch weitere der von Seeley benutzten bildhaften Ausdrücke beziehen sich auf jene metaphorische Leitvorstellung[2], die für den Diskurs des britischen Imperialismus von zentraler Bedeutung ist: die Vorstellung vom Empire als einer Familie.[3]

Seeleys Ausführungen sind in zweifacher Hinsicht beispielhaft für die Art und Weise, wie sich die spätviktorianische Literatur mit den vom Empire aufgeworfenen Fragen auseinandersetzte. Typisch ist zum einen die verbreitete Neigung zur metaphorischen Umschreibung der Beziehungen zwischen England und seinen Kolonien. Zum anderen ist Seeleys Auswahl der Sprachbilder insofern repräsentativ, als vor allem organische Metaphern – allen voran Verwandtschafts- und Pflanzen-Metaphern – den Diskurs des britischen Imperialismus prägen. Welche Frage Metaphern implizit beantworteten, wird in John Davidsons Ekloge "The Twenty-Fourth of May" (1905) deutlich:

> Nobler than empire – word
> Ill-omened, out of date! –
> What name shall be conferred
> On England's Ocean-state?[4]

Ähnlich wie Seeley beklagt der Sprecher zunächst das vermeintlich unselige und veraltete Wort 'Empire'; sodann fragt er, welche Bezeichnung Englands

Weltreich verliehen werden solle. Aufschluß über die Antworten kann eine Analyse der Metaphern geben, die im ausgehenden 19. Jahrhundert zur Bezeichnung des Empire verwendet wurden. Obwohl gerade in der politischen Metaphorik jene kollektiven Denkmuster des britischen Imperialismus zum Ausdruck kommen, die in der spätviktorianischen Epoche als fraglos gültig galten und daher nicht auf die Ebene begrifflicher Reflexion gehoben wurden, hat sich die Forschung zum Verhältnis zwischen der englischen Literatur und dem britischen Imperialismus bisher noch nicht systematisch mit Empire-Metaphern als wesentlichem Bestandteil des imperialistischen Diskurses auseinandergesetzt. Zohreh T. Sullivan weist zwar auf die große Bedeutung und die Allgegenwart der Familien-Metapher hin ("The metaphor of the empire as 'family' was part of a colonial construct of imperialism in India"[5]), nennt aber keine konkreten Textbeispiele und untersucht weder die Struktur und Logik dieses Bildfeldes noch dessen Funktionen. Selbst eine unlängst erschienene Monographie über die Sprache des Empire geht trotz des vielversprechenden Untertitels nicht auf die Metaphern ein, die sich auf das Britische Weltreich beziehen.[6]

Aus diesem Defizit ergibt sich die Zielsetzung dieses Aufsatzes, der die Verwendung und die Funktionen jener Sprachbilder analysiert, mit denen das Empire in der spätviktorianischen Literatur bevorzugt umschrieben wurde. Es geht dabei zum einen um die Ermittlung und Analyse von Metaphern, die sich auf das Empire beziehen. Zum anderen soll das Leistungsvermögen der Empire-Metaphorik aus funktionsgeschichtlicher Sicht interpretiert werden. Dieser Versuch, durch die Analyse der metaphorischen Kennzeichnung des Britischen Weltreichs Aufschluß über epochenspezifische Vorstellungen, Denkweisen und Deutungsmuster zu gewinnen, orientiert sich in theoretischer und methodischer Hinsicht an neueren kulturwissenschaftlichen und mentalitätsgeschichtlichen Ansätzen.[7] Zugleich greift dieser Beitrag die Anregung des englischen Kulturhistorikers Peter Burke auf, die Mentalitätengeschichte solle sich stärker mit Metaphern beschäftigen, als sie es bislang getan hat.[8]

Zunächst wird anhand ausgewählter Gedichte von Alfred Lord Tennyson und Rudyard Kipling die Struktur des zentralen Bildfeldes des imperialistischen Diskurses – der Vorstellung vom Britischen Weltreich als einer Familie – aufgezeigt. Im zweiten Teil soll geklärt werden, wie das Verhältnis zwischen England und seinen Kolonien durch die metaphorische Vorstellung vom Empire als einer Familie strukturiert, gedeutet und bewertet wurde bzw. was die Empire-Metaphern im einzelnen zu leisten imstande sind. Die Hauptaufmerksamkeit gilt der Frage, inwiefern eine literaturwissenschaftliche Analyse des Metapherngebrauchs einen Beitrag leisten kann zur Bestimmung der Funktionen imperialistischer Lyrik und zur Geschichte der spätviktorianischen Vorstellungen vom Empire.

2. *"Sons be welded each and all,/ Into one imperial whole": Das Bildfeld des Empire als Familie am Beispiel von Tennysons patriotischer Lyrik*

Unter dem Begriff 'Empire-Metaphern' sollen sämtliche figurativen Ausdrücke verstanden werden[9], die zur bildlichen Kennzeichnung des Britischen Weltreichs dienen und die sich auf das Verhältnis zwischen England und seinen Kolonien beziehen. Es geht somit nicht um eine umfassende Ermittlung sämtlicher Sprachbilder des imperialistischen Diskurses, zu denen etwa die aus dem *public school*-Kodex stammende Metapher des Krieges als Sport oder die Jagdmetaphorik zählen. Zahlreiche Beispiele dafür finden sich in der Lyrik von Henry Newbolt, dessen Gedicht "Vita Lampada" mit der dreifachen Wiederholung des Verses "Play up! play up! and play the game!" das wohl bekannteste Paradigma für die Metaphorisierung des Krieges als Spiel und Sport in der spätviktorianischen Literatur ist.[10] Im Mittelpunkt der Analyse steht vielmehr ein bestimmter Bildempfänger, das Britische Weltreich, über das verschiedene metaphorische Äußerungen möglich sind und das im Untersuchungszeitraum vor allem durch organische Metaphern bildhaft bezeichnet wurde.

Es ist charakteristisch für Empire-Metaphern, daß sie von ganz bestimmten historischen Erfahrungen ausgehen.[11] Sie stellen zum einen Versuche dar, die geschichtliche Expansion Englands und dessen politisches Verhältnis zu seinen Kolonien bildlich zu erfassen. Zum anderen sind sie als Reaktionen auf die seit den 1870er Jahren verschärft geführten Debatten über die Zukunft des Britischen Weltreichs zu verstehen. Solche Metaphern für das Empire sind nicht als bloßer Redeschmuck aufzufassen, sondern als erkenntnisprägende 'Denkmodelle' bzw. als „Medien und Werkzeuge unserer Erkenntnis".[12] Dadurch wird hervorgehoben, daß diese Sprachbilder die Art und Weise, wie die historische Entwicklung des Empire und die vom Imperialismus aufgeworfenen politischen Probleme wahrgenommen und beurteilt werden, maßgeblich beeinflussen.

Empire-Metaphern finden sich in der spätviktorianischen Epoche in unterschiedlichsten Gattungen. Sowohl in Gedichten, Reiseberichten, politischen und historischen Werken als auch in politischen Reden, Vorträgen und Zeitungsartikeln wurde immer wieder eine Reihe von Sprachbildern verwendet, um die Beziehungen zwischen England und seinen Kolonien zu kennzeichnen. Von den literarischen Gattungen ist es vor allem die Lyrik, welche Empire-Metaphern in ebenso zahlreicher wie variantenreicher Weise verwendet.[13] Zu den Dichtern, die sich besonders intensiv mit dem Empire auseinandergesetzt haben, zählen vor allem der Hofdichter Alfred Lord Tennyson, Rudyard Kipling sowie weniger bekannte Lyriker des viktorianischen *Fin de siècle* wie William Ernest Henley, Henry Newbolt und John Davidson.

Überblickt man das breite Spektrum an Staats-, Herrschafts- und Geschichts-Metaphern[14], so ist zunächst bemerkenswert, daß in der spätviktorianischen

Literatur lediglich eine recht kleine Zahl von Sprachbildern rekurrent verwendet wurde, um das Empire zu charakterisieren. Viele der etablierten Herrschafts-Metaphern – etwa das Bild vom Hirten und seiner Herde, das Modell vom Bienenstaat, die Maschinenmetaphorik und die architektonische Metapher des Staatsgebäudes – spielen im Zusammenhang mit dem Britischen Weltreich so gut wie keine Rolle. Auch die Körpermetaphorik und die Metapher des Staatsschiffes sind für das Empire nur vereinzelt nachweisbar. Der in quantitativer und qualitativer Hinsicht vorherrschende Bereich, aus dem die bildspendenden Elemente für den Bildempfänger 'Empire' stammen, ist vielmehr das Feld der Verwandtschaftsbeziehungen. Metaphern aus diesem Bereich fügen sich zur Leitvorstellung vom Empire als Familie zusammen.

Besonders deutlich kommt die Metapher vom Empire als Familie in Tennysons patriotischen Gedichten zum Ausdruck. Daß Tennyson, der als *Poet Laureate* seit 1850 mit seinen Werken eine breite Leserschaft erreichte, im Jahre 1889 als "The True Poet of Imperialism" gepriesen wurde[15], ist Ausdruck der großen Bedeutung, die diesem Dichter für die Popularisierung imperialistischer Ideen beizumessen ist.[16] In einer für den imperialistischen Diskurs typischen Weise verdeutlicht etwa Tennysons Gedicht "Opening of the Indian and Colonial Exhibition by the Queen", das 1886 zur Kolonialausstellung erschien, wie Verwandtschafts-Metaphern in der spätviktorianischen Literatur verwendet wurden, um historisch-politische Zusammenhänge zu deuten. Die Sprechsituation dieses vierstrophigen Gedichts ist – dem Anlaß entsprechend – einer Begrüßungsrede nachempfunden, in der sich die namentlich nicht genannte englische Königin an ihre kolonialen Untertanen wendet. In der ersten Strophe heißt sie die Söhne und Brüder Englands willkommen, die aus allen Gegenden des Britischen Weltreichs Geschenke zusammengetragen haben.

In der zukunftsbezogenen zweiten Strophe von Tennysons Gedicht verleiht das lyrische Ich bzw. in diesem Fall besser das 'lyrische Wir', das durchgängig im Pluralis majestatis spricht, seiner Hoffnung Ausdruck, daß die Söhne auf die Mutter kommen und britischen Tugenden überall zum Durchbruch verhelfen werden. Wie Verwandtschafts-Metaphern zum Zwecke der Geschichtsdeutung funktionalisiert werden können, beweist die dritte Strophe, in der Vergangenheits-, Gegenwarts- und Zukunftsbezug eng verknüpft sind. Diese Strophe faßt die Lehre zusammen, die England aus dem Amerikanischen Unabhängigkeitskrieg gezogen habe:

> Britain fought her sons of yore –
> Britain failed; and never more,
> Careless of our growing kin,
> Shall we sin our fathers' sin,

Men that in a narrower day –
Unprophetic rulers they –
Drove from out the mother's nest
That young eagle of the West
To forage for herself alone;
  Britons, hold your own![17]

Zur Auslegung der Amerikanischen Revolution nutzt Tennyson hier die Bildlogik der Familienmetaphorik. Er greift damit ein konnotationsreiches Sprachbild auf, das im 18. Jahrhundert, wie die Historiker Gordon S. Wood und Jay Fliegelman gezeigt haben[18], das vorherrschende Deutungsschema für den Konflikt zwischen dem englischen Mutterland und seinen amerikanischen Kolonien war.[19] Die Familienmetaphorik liefert zum einen eine äußerst vereinfachte Beschreibung der vermeintlichen Sünde der Väter, den jungen Adler des Westens verfrüht aus dem Nest der Mutter vertrieben zu haben. Zum anderen bildet sie die Grundlage für die aus der Geschichte gezogene Lehre, sich fortan besser um die heranwachsenden Blutsverwandten zu kümmern. Diese Einsicht wird in der letzten Strophe auf die Gegenwart bezogen, indem das lyrische Ich in zwei rhetorischen Fragen den kolonialen Brüdern die glorreiche gemeinsame Vergangenheit in Erinnerung ruft und für den Zusammenhalt des Empire wirbt. Im letzten Teil dieses Gedichts erreicht die holistische Empiremetaphorik insofern ihren Höhepunkt, als die zentrale Frage nach der Einheit des Empire durch einen kollektiven Ruf beantwortet wird:

Britain's myriad voices call,
'Sons, be welded each and all,
Into one imperial whole,
One with Britain, heart and soul!
One life, one flag, one fleet, one Throne!'
  Britons, hold your own! (S. 1358)

Zum Zwecke der Emphase werden die Verwandtschafts-Metaphern hier mit dem aus der Technik stammenden Bild des Schweißens ("welded") verbunden sowie mit einer Aufzählung der Faktoren, die die Einheit und den Zusammenhalt des Empire garantieren. Daß Tennyson in diesem gemeinschaftlichen Ruf der britischen Kolonien dem Weltreich eine einzige Stimme verleiht[20], unterstreicht ebenso wie die Familienmetaphorik metonymisch die Einheit des Empire und die Zusammengehörigkeit seiner Teile. Sehr deutlich wird dieser Zusammenhang auch in Tennysons Gedicht "On the Jubilee of Queen Victoria", in dem die Kinder Albions dazu aufgefordert werden, in harmonischem Gleichklang ihre Stimmen zum Jubiläum der Königin zu erheben.

Die Art und Weise, wie Tennyson in diesen patriotischen Gedichten Verwandtschafts-Metaphern als Mittel der historischen Interpretation und der

Stärkung der Einheit des Empire verwendet, ist in mehrfacher Hinsicht typisch für viele andere patriotische Gedichte aus der spätviktorianischen Epoche.[21] Zum einen verdeutlicht Tennysons Metapherngebrauch, daß das Bild des Empire als einer Familie eine genaue Zuordnung der bildspendenden zu den bildempfangenden Elementen ermöglicht.[22] Der konventionellen Beschreibung von England als Mutter bzw. Mutterland entspricht die Charakterisierung der Kolonien als deren Kinder.

Zum anderen läßt Tennysons patriotische Lyrik deutlich erkennen, daß der Aussagewert nicht allein auf den einzelnen Metaphern beruht, sondern auf dem durch sie aufgebauten Bildfeld. Für die Analyse der Empiremetaphorik erweist sich daher der von Harald Weinrich eingeführte Begriff des Bildfeldes als geeignet. Dieser Terminus trägt der Tatsache Rechnung, daß Metaphern in übergeordneten Strukturen organisiert sind. In Bildfeldern, so Weinrich, sind „zwei Sinnbezirke durch einen geistigen, analogiestiftenden Akt zusammengekoppelt".[23] Bezogen auf den vorliegenden Fall folgt daraus, daß die Metapher des Mutterlandes nicht nur den weiblichen Elternteil mit der Kolonialmacht verbindet, sondern daß durch dieses Sprachbild auch die Sinnbezirke der Familie und des Kolonialismus miteinander verknüpft werden.

Durch das Bildfeld der imperialen Familie wird die Herrschaft Englands über seine Kolonien als ein soziales und persönliches Verhältnis gedeutet, das der Beziehung zwischen Eltern und ihren Kindern entspricht. Wie sich die Zeitgenossen die imperiale Familie vorzustellen hatten, geht beispielhaft aus der ersten Illustration hervor, die aus der Weihnachtsausgabe der populären Wochenzeitschrift *Punch* aus dem Jahre 1884 stammt. Sie trägt den bezeichnenden Titel "John Bull's Christmas Family Party" und zeigt, was für eine "Happy Family" John Bull, die etwas in die Jahre gekommene "Dame Britannia" und ihre zahlreichen Sprößlinge aus Übersee doch sind. Wem das Bild der ach so harmonischen Familienparty noch nicht reicht, der erhält durch ein die Illustration kommentierendes und erläuterndes Gedicht auch noch Einblick in die Gefühlswelt der Familienmitglieder, die – wie könnte es anders sein – natürlich überglücklich sind:

> All the brave young slips of her,
> Offshoots, every one, of her,
> Love the yet red lips of her,
> All the force and fun of her;
> Gather round her loyally.
> Proud she to possess them all,
> Greets them all right royally,
> Here's their health! God bless 'em all![24]

Dieses Beispiel der auf ihre tapferen Sprößlinge stolzen Britannia und ihrer treu ergebenen kolonialen Kinder verdeutlicht sehr gut, wie durch die Metapher des Empire als einer Familie emotionale Aspekte des Familienlebens auf den Sinnbezirk des Weltreichs projiziert werden. Ebenso wie andere Sprachbilder wirkt diese „Zentralmetapher"[25] insofern wie ein „Doppelfilter"[26], als sie nur noch für jene Merkmale des bildspendenden und des bildempfangenden Bereichs durchlässig ist, die für den vorliegenden Zusammenhang relevant sind. Der Gebrauch von Familienmetaphern zur Kennzeichnung der Beziehungen zwischen England und seinen Kolonien hat somit einerseits zur Folge, daß nur jene Aspekte des Weltreichs in den Blick rücken, die durch das Feld der Verwandtschaftsbeziehungen und des Familienlebens erfaßt werden. Andererseits sind aber auch nur jene Dimensionen des bildspendenden Feldes von Bedeutung, die sich auf die politischen Belange des Empire anwenden lassen.

3 "Because ye are sons of The Blood and call me Mother still": Verwandtschafts-Metaphern in der Lyrik Rudyard Kiplings, des "Laureate of Empire"

In besonders gehäufter und variantenreicher Form finden sich Empire-Metaphern aus dem Umkreis der Verwandtschaftsbeziehungen im lyrischen Werk des Nobelpreisträgers Rudyard Kipling. Daß zeitgenössische Rezensenten diesen Dichter als "Laureate of Empire", als "the poet of the empire" oder gar als "the approved and authoritative poet of the British empire"[27] bezeichneten, verweist auf den hohen Stellenwert, den die Auseinandersetzung mit dem Weltreich in Kiplings patriotischen Gedichten und Erzählungen hat. Kiplings Ruf, der Laureat des Britischen Weltreichs zu sein, beruht unter anderem auf einer Reihe von patriotischen Gedichten aus den 1890er Jahren. Vor allem in dem Gedichtzyklus "A Song of the English", der zuerst 1893 im *English Illustrated Magazine* erschien und zum Diamantenen Jubiläum von Königin Victoria als eigenständiger Gedichtband nachgedruckt wurde, übersetzt Kipling politische Beziehungen und historische Entwicklungen in Verwandtschaftsgrade.[28]

Obgleich Kipling das Empire meist im Rahmen des gleichen Bildfeldes evoziert wie Tennyson, unterscheidet sich seine Verwendung der Familienmetaphorik in dreifacher Hinsicht von der des viktorianischen Hofdichters. Erstens nutzt Kipling die Möglichkeit der Perspektivierung, die in Verwandtschafts-Metaphern angelegt ist, indem er – allerdings in stark vereinfachter Form – die Perspektive der Kolonien einbezieht.[29] Zweitens sind einige von Kiplings Empire-Gedichten – im Gegensatz zu Tennysons einstimmigen Lobgesängen auf England und sein Weltreich – mehrstimmig. Drittens entwerfen sie dadurch insofern ein vergleichsweise komplexeres Bild vom Empire, als die von der Metaphorik beschworene Einheit des Weltreichs durch die Andeutung der Unterschiede zwischen den Kolonien und durch die mehrstimmige Form zumindest teilweise relativiert wird.

Ein typisches Beispiel für die Einbeziehung der Perspektive der Kolonien ist das Gedicht "The Song of the Sons", dessen Titel auf die Sprechsituation und die Verwandtschaftsmetaphorik verweist. Dieser Text weicht insofern von dem von Tennyson popularisierten Schema ab, als nicht England, sondern die Kolonien als textuelle Sprecher fungieren. Dennoch unterstreicht auch dieses Gedicht die Zusammengehörigkeit der Teile des Weltreichs und die Verbundenheit der Kolonien mit dem Mutterland. Zum einen verdeutlicht bereits der Gebrauch der ersten Person Plural, daß die Kinder als Einheit auftreten, obgleich sie aus den entlegensten Teilen der Weltmeere stammen. Zum anderen unterstreicht das in diesem Gedicht entworfene Bild einer engen Mutter-Sohn-Beziehung, daß es sich um ein inniges persönliches Verhältnis handelt. Die geschickte Umkehrung der Sprechsituation und der Blickrichtung kann somit nicht darüber hinwegtäuschen, daß das Gedicht im Dienste der konventionellen Einheitsrhetorik des britischen Imperialismus steht. Daß Kipling die damals vorherrschende pro-imperialistische Haltung lediglich den kolonialen Söhnen in den Mund legt, wird sowohl in deren Aufforderung an die gemeinsame Mutter, doch bitte stolz auf ihre Nachkommenschaft zu sein, als auch in der rhetorischen Frage deutlich: "Judge, are we men of the Blood?" (S. 142)

Sehr viel komplexer sind der Gebrauch der Familienmetaphorik und die Struktur in dem mehrstimmigen Gedicht "The Song of the Cities", in dem ebenfalls die Kolonien als textuelle Sprecher fungieren. In diesem 15-strophigen Gedicht werden einige der großen Städte des Empire personifiziert und kommen nacheinander in jeweils einer der vierzeiligen Strophen einzeln zu Wort. Die Kolonien skizzieren die Beziehungen zum englischen Mutterland, das in einigen Strophen mit "Hail, Mother!" direkt angesprochen wird, somit scheinbar aus ihrer Perspektive. Dennoch zeigt allein schon die Auswahl der thematischen Details, mit denen die verschiedenen Städte sich zu erkennen geben, daß keine andere Sehweise übernommen wird, sondern daß der anglozentrische metaphorische Bezugsrahmen intakt bleibt. Besonders deutlich wird dies im Falle der Strophen, die den indischen Städten Kalkutta und Madras zugedacht sind. Wenn die imperialistische Eroberung metaphorisch als sexuelle Liebesbegegnung zwischen dem englischen Nationalhelden Clive und dem erotisch anziehenden Orient beschrieben wird, dann sagt dies wenig über die kulturellen Besonderheiten Indiens oder dessen Haltung gegenüber England, dafür aber umso mehr über den britischen Kolonialismus:

> Clive kissed me on the mouth and eyes and brow,
> Wonderful kisses, so that I became
> Crowned above Queens – a withered beldame, now,
> Brooding on ancient fame. (S. 142)

Daß somit trotz des punktuellen Perspektivenwechsels auch bei Kipling die Beschwörung der Einheit des aus englischer Sicht wahrgenommenen Empire im Vordergrund steht, wird in dem Gebrauch von Metaphern in dem Gedicht "England's Answer" nochmals sehr deutlich. Sowohl die Anordnung der Gedichte als auch intertextuelle Bezüge lassen erkennen, daß "England's Answer" als Entgegnung auf "The Song of the Sons" und "The Song of the Cities" zu verstehen ist. Das Prinzip der Mehrstimmigkeit weicht in Englands Antwort der mächtigen Stimme des Mutterlandes, das zugleich als lyrisches Ich in Erscheinung tritt. Durch die Sprechsituation, die Themenselektion und die Metaphorik verlagert sich die Aufmerksamkeit von Beginn an völlig von den zuvor zumindest angedeuteten regionalen Besonderheiten der verschiedenen Kolonien auf deren gemeinsame Abstammung: "Truly ye come of The Blood", so beantwortet England die ohnehin rhetorische Frage, die in "The Song of the Sons" den Kolonien unterschoben wurde, um sogleich emphatisch anzufügen: "Flesh of the flesh that I bred, bone of the bone that I bare." (S. 144)

Die Schlußfolgerungen, die das die Nation verkörpernde lyrische Ich in "England's Answer" aus dieser Tatsache zieht, verweisen außerdem auf die vielfältigen Möglichkeiten, wie die Familienmetaphorik als politisches Argument genutzt werden konnte. So richtet England etwa einen nostalgischen Appell an die kolonialen Söhne, sich im Mutterland über die politische Zukunft zu unterhalten, ohne freilich zu vergessen, diese zugleich an ihre Pflichten gegenüber ihrer inzwischen grauhaarigen Mutter zu erinnern. Sentimentale metaphorische Verse wie "Ay, talk to your grey mother that bore you on her knees!" (S. 144)[30] stehen somit im Dienst einer imperialistischen Ideologie, für die die emotionalen Konnotationen der Familien-Metaphern sehr nützlich sind. Das gleiche gilt für die inhaltsleeren Versprechungen, die das Mutterland seinen kolonialen Kindern macht. Die bildspendenden und bildempfangenden Bereiche durchdringen sich in diesem Fall so weit, daß sogar politische Zugeständnisse aus der Familienmetaphorik abgeleitet werden:

> The Law that ye make shall be law and I do not press my will,
> Because ye are sons of The Blood and call me Mother still. (S. 145)

Eine selbständige Legislative steht den Kolonien aus der Sicht des Mutterlandes somit allein deshalb zu, weil englisches Blut in den Adern der Kolonialbevölkerung fließt und weil die Söhne England noch immer 'Mutter' nennen. Die von einem Sprachbild geweckten Assoziationen, so kann man resümieren, haben hier die Logik und Sachebene so stark überlagert, daß eine Metapher bereits als politisches Argument erscheint. Insgesamt verdeutlicht Kiplings Verwendung von Familien-Metaphern, daß die emotionalen Aspekte dieses Bildfeldes jenen imperialistischen Ideenkomplex festigten[31], dem es um die Einheit des Britischen Weltreichs ging und den Heinz-Joachim Müllenbrock treffend als "Empire-Holismus"[32] bezeichnet hat.

4. Verwandtschafts-Metaphern als Denkmodelle und als Mittel der historisch-politischen Sinnstiftung: Die holistische Empire-Metaphorik aus funktionsgeschichtlicher Sicht

Da es einer kulturwissenschaftlich orientierten Metaphernanalyse nicht nur um die historisch-deskriptive Systematisierung der dominanten Bildfelder geht, sondern auch um die Funktionen der Metaphern, stellt sich die Frage, was die metaphorischen Umschreibungen des Empire leisten. Die offensichtlichste Funktion der Empire-Metaphern besteht darin, historisch-politische Zusammenhänge zu vereinfachen, veranschaulichen und verlebendigen[33], indem sie einem diffusen und heterogenen politischen Gebilde eine Struktur und inhaltliche Bestimmtheit verleihen.[34] In dieser Hinsicht ähnelt die Empire-Metaphorik insofern Modellen, als sie gleichfalls einen sehr vielschichtigen Objektbereich in vereinfachter Form darstellt.[35] Indem die Metaphern das nicht unmittelbar beobachtbare oder übersehbare Ganze des Weltreichs bildlich veranschaulichen, machen sie einen komplexen historisch-politischen Zusammenhang für die zeitgenössische englische Bevölkerung überhaupt erst vorstellbar.

Obgleich die Leistungen der Empire-Metaphern somit Parallelen zu den Funktionen von Modellen aufweisen, greift es aus zwei Gründen zu kurz, sie lediglich als Denkmodelle zu charakterisieren. Zum einen verkürzt der Modellbegriff insofern das Leistungsvermögen von Metaphern, als er nicht den für Sprachbilder charakteristischen Bedeutungsüberschuß zu erfassen vermag.[36] Zum anderen grenzt der Begriff des Denkmodells das Funktionspotential von Metaphern auf kognitive Aspekte ein. Vor allem Ricoeur hat jedoch überzeugend dargelegt, daß die Aktivierung von Gefühlen ein wichtiger Bestandteil des metaphorischen Prozesses sei.[37]

Empire-Metaphern fungieren daher nicht nur als Denkmodelle, sondern auch als kognitive bzw. schöpferische Mittel der historischen und politischen Sinnstiftung. Die erkenntnisprägende Leistung der Familien-Metaphern gründet darin, daß sie aufgrund der Denotationen und Konnotationen des bildspendenden Bereichs eine Fülle von neuen Informationen über das Empire liefern. Diese Empire-Metaphern bilden keine in der Wirklichkeit bereits vorhandenen Ähnlichkeiten ab. Ihre wirklichkeitskonstituierende Funktion gründet vielmehr darin, daß Metaphern, wie Harald Weinrich betont, „ihre Analogien erst stiften, ihre Korrespondenzen erst schaffen".[38] Empire-Metaphern legen bestimmte Sehweisen nahe, weil der Sinnbezirk der Familie das Britische Weltreich in einer neuartigen Weise strukturiert, deutet und bewertet.

Die schöpferischen Leistungen der Empire-Metaphern betreffen zum einen strukturelle Aspekte, weil die Familienmetaphorik aufgrund ihrer Bildlogik und Denotationen bestimmte Zusammenhänge zwischen den Bildelementen herstellt. Zum anderen liefern die bevorzugten Sprachbilder aufgrund ihrer Konnotationen inhaltlich bestimmte Konzepte für die Wahrnehmung und

Deutung historisch-politischer Zusammenhänge. Solche Deutungsschemata erfüllen nicht bloß kognitive Funktionen, sondern haben auch normative, emotionale und ideologische Implikationen. Ohne Anspruch auf Vollständigkeit sollen die wichtigsten der damit umrissenen Leistungen von Empire-Metaphern anhand der Leitvorstellung vom Weltreich als einer Familie exemplarisch verdeutlicht werden.

Erstens tragen die Verwandtschafts-Metaphern zur Entwicklung eines Familiengefühls innerhalb des Empire und zur Ausprägung nationaler Identität bei.[39] Diese gemeinschaftsstiftende und identitätsbildende Funktion gründet darin, daß Sprachbilder aus dem Umkreis der Familie natürliche Zusammengehörigkeit versinnbildlichen und damit den Zusammenhalt des Empire betonen.[40] Besonders deutlich wird dies etwa in Tennysons Gedicht "Hands All Round", das sich explizit an alle patriotischen Herzen richtet, die die Einheit des Empire bewahren wollen: "To all the loyal hearts who long/ To keep our English Empire whole!" (S. 1311) Diese holistische Rhetorik der Metaphern kann zugleich die Verbundenheit und den Gemeinsinn im Sinne einer selbsterfüllenden Prophezeiung stärken.

Zweitens fungiert die Verwandtschaftsmetaphorik als ein Medium der historischen Sinnbildung. Diese Funktion ist zwar eng verknüpft mit dem strukturellen Aspekt der Zusammengehörigkeit, aber durch das Bildfeld der Familie werden zwischen den einzelnen Bildelementen zusätzlich genealogische und genetische Beziehungen hergestellt. Zum einen postuliert die Metaphorik ein Abstammungsverhältnis zwischen den Kolonien und dem sogenannten Mutterland. Zum anderen wird durch Verwandtschafts-Metaphern und durch die Formel "English blood" das gemeinsame englische Erbgut der Kolonien hervorgehoben. Der durch die Familienmetaphorik hervorgehobene Aspekt der gemeinsamen Abstammung kann zwar im Bereich des Bildempfängers allenfalls für die weißen Siedlungskolonien eine gewisse Plausibilität beanspruchen, doch er wird immer wieder emphatisch als Grundlage und Garant der Einheit des Empire beschworen. Ebenso wie andere organische Metaphern unterstützt die Verwandtschaftsmetaphorik eine bestimmte Deutung historischer Zusammenhänge, die sich aus folgenden Denotationen und Konnotationen des Bildfeldes der Familie ableiten:

> The plant and parent metaphors stressed age, experience, roots, tradition, and, most importantly, the connection between antiquity and value. They implied the same distinctions as those existing between metropolis and frontier: parents are more experienced, more important, more substantial, less brash than their offspring. Above all they are the *origin* and therefore claim the final authority in questions of taste and value.[41]

Die patriotische Geschichtsklitterung der Familien-Metaphern besteht vor allem darin, daß sie historische Entwicklungen als das Ergebnis natürlichen

Wachstums umdeuten.[42] Das Bild des Empire als einer Familie impliziert ein entwicklungsgeschichtliches Erklärungsschema, das die Kolonialisierung als einen organischen Prozeß darstellt. Alexander Demandt zufolge verweisen Verwandtschafts-Metaphern generell auf ein Bedürfnis, „das Gemachte als *gewachsen* hinzustellen".[43] Erst im *Fin de siècle* wird in John Davidsons antiimperialistischer Lyrik durch Metaphern aus der Technik jenes 'Prinzip der Machbarkeit'[44] betont, das von den im imperialistischen Diskurs bevorzugten organischen Metaphern unterschlagen wird.

Drittens erfüllt das Bildfeld des Empire als Familie normative Funktionen, weil es bestimmte emotionale Bindungen und moralische Wertvorstellungen in bezug auf die Qualität der Beziehung zwischen den Beteiligten evoziert. Der Epilog zu Tennysons *Idylls of the King*, das Gedicht "To the Queen" aus dem Jahre 1873, verdeutlicht sehr gut, wie durch die Bildersprache emotionale Aspekte des Familienlebens auf die politischen Beziehungen zwischen Mutterland und Kolonien projiziert wurden: "The loyal to their crown/ Are loyal to their own far sons, who love/ Our ocean-empire with her boundless homes" (S. 1755). Die normative Funktion der Verwandtschafts-Metaphern besteht darin, daß diese England und den Kolonien bestimmte Rollen zuweisen und verbindliche Normen für deren jeweiliges Verhalten setzen. Im Gegensatz zu den strukturellen und genealogischen Konnotationen lassen sich diese Gebote und Verbote allerdings nicht unmittelbar aus der Bildlogik und den semantischen Merkmalen des Wortes 'Familie' ableiten. Die von der Empire-Metaphorik hervorgerufenen Erwartungen ergeben sich vielmehr aus dem besonderen Stellenwert von Ehe und Familie im viktorianischen England und werden durch das Werte- und Normensystem der Epoche bestimmt. Coventry Patmores berühmtes Gedicht *The Angel in the House* (1854) und John Ruskins damals überaus populärer Vortrag *Of Queens Gardens* aus dem Jahre 1864 verdeutlichen beispielhaft, wie sehr die Familie und das häusliche Leben in der zweiten Hälfte des 19. Jahrhunderts als ein Refugium und eine Quelle für jene Tugenden, Werte und altruistischen Gefühle verherrlicht wurden, die in der Gesellschaft und im Geschäftsleben vermeintlich nicht mehr zu finden waren. Die Familie, so schreibt John Stuart Mill in seiner Schrift *On the Subjection of Women* (1869), werde meist als "a school of sympathy, tenderness, and loving forgetfulness of self"[45] bezeichnet. Was in dieser Schule des Mitgefühls, der Zartheit und des liebevollen Altruismus nach Ansicht der Zeitgenossen gelehrt und gelernt wurde, geht aus einem Vortrag des positivistischen Philosophen Frederic Harrison über das Thema "Family Life" aus dem Jahre 1893 hervor. In der Familie, so Harrison, könne man folgendes lernen:

> sentiment (1) of *attachment*, comradeship, fellowship, (2) of *reverence* for those who can teach us, guide us, and elevate us, of *love* which urges us to protect, help, and cherish those to whom we owe our lives and better natures.[46]

Erst vor dem Hintergrund dieser viktorianischen 'Verherrlichung des Familienlebens'[47] erschließen sich viele der Assoziationen, die durch die Familienmetaphern mit dem Britischen Weltreich in Verbindung gebracht werden. Durch die Metaphorik werden die in der Privatsphäre des häuslichen Lebens geltenden Gefühle, Werte und Normen auf die Beziehungen zwischen England und seinen Kolonien projiziert. Die Vorstellung vom Empire als einer Familie läßt den britischen Imperialismus als eine Schule des Mitgefühls und des Altruismus erscheinen. In dieser Schule können die Kolonien Disziplin, Pflichtgefühl und Ehrfurcht vor dem geliebten Mutterland lernen, während dieses seinen Pflichten als Erzieherin und Beschützerin nachkommt. Durch die von der Familienmetaphorik evozierten Normen wurden somit jene Ideale bestärkt, denen die britische Mission zum Durchbruch verhelfen sollte und die Kipling in "McAndrew's Hymn" auf eine von Rezensenten oft zitierte Formel[48] brachte: "'Law, Orrder, Duty an' Restraint, Obedience, Discipline!'" (S. 102)

Die von den Familien-Metaphern erzeugte Analogie zwischen dem Privaten und dem Öffentlichen hat zum einen zur Folge, daß auch im politischen Bereich ein Gefühl der Zugehörigkeit und Gemeinschaft innerhalb des Empire etabliert wird. Zum anderen wird das Verhältnis zwischen Mutterland und Kolonien durch die Metaphorik implizit als auf Zuneigung und Liebe gründend hingestellt, während politische, ökonomische und militärische Aspekte der kolonialen Expansion durch die Bildlogik systematisch ausgeblendet werden.[49] Daß das Bildfeld der Familie die Beziehung zwischen England und seinen Kolonien als ein persönliches Vertrauensverhältnis darstellt, verdeutlicht etwa Kiplings Gedicht "The Young Queen". Es schildert, wie die im Titel genannte junge australische Königin von ihrer englischen Mutter, der "Old Queen", gekrönt wird. Die Leitvorstellung des Empire als Familie bildet zwar weiterhin den metaphorischen Bezugsrahmen, der jedoch durch die Worte der alten Königin und den darin implizierten Bildbruch gesprengt zu werden droht: "Daugther no more but Sister, and doubly Daugther so -/ Mother of many princes – and child of the child I bore" (S. 153). Daß die Familienmetaphorik den Akzent auf die beiderseitige Versicherung von Zuneigung, Unterstützung und Vertrauen legt, verdeutlicht etwa die in *Punch* im Jahre 1900 veröffentlichte zweite Illustration zum gleichen Thema, die Britannia im Gespräch mit ihrer australischen Tochter zeigt. Die koloniale Tochter hat sich inzwischen zu einer jungen Dame gemausert, die nun nach ein wenig mehr Freiheit strebt und sich einen eigenen Hausschlüssel hat anfertigen lassen, was Britannia natürlich gutheißt, da sie ihrer Tochter vertrauen kann.

Aus den normativen Implikationen der Verwandtschafts-Metaphern leitet sich noch eine vierte Funktion ab, die man als Legitimationsfunktion bezeichnen kann. Die Familienmetaphorik trägt maßgeblich dazu bei, die Autorität, die Rechte und die Pflichten der englischen Eltern gegenüber den kindlichen Kolonien hervorzuheben. Da das Bildfeld der Familie politisches Handeln zu einem hierarchisch strukturierten Erziehungsverhältnis umdeutet, stiftet es einen Bezugsrahmen für die Beschreibung der Rollen, die dem Mutterland als Erzieherin und den Kolonien als Zöglingen zugedacht werden. Auf der einen Seite vermittelt die Analogie zur Familie den Kolonien ein Gefühl der Ehrfurcht vor dem Mutterland, das sie lehrt und führt. Auf der anderen Seite gibt die Metaphorik den Briten implizit das Recht, diejenigen zu beschützen und zu lenken, die von ihnen abhängig sind. Jo-Ann Wallace geht sogar so weit, das historisch entstandene Konstrukt der Kindheit[50] als "a *necessary precondition* of imperialism"[51] zu bezeichnen, weil die Vorstellung von der Erziehbarkeit des Kindes den Kolonialismus überhaupt erst denkbar gemacht habe.

Da das Bild vom Empire als einer Familie den Kolonien die Rolle von unreifen Kindern zuweist und das Mutterland zu deren Erzieherin stilisiert, dient es als eine Rechtfertigungsformel für Englands Eingriffe in die Belange der Kolonien. Durch den von der Metaphorik vorgegebenen Erziehungsauftrag des Mutterlandes wird letztlich das Bestreben Englands legitimiert, die Kolonien zu bevormunden und zu gängeln.[52] Das Sendungsbewußtsein Großbritanniens, das sich aus der Familienmetaphorik ergibt, hat Kipling auf die einprägsame Formel "The White Man's Burden" gebracht, die die selbstauferlegte imperialistische Mission zu einem ebenso selbstlosen wie verdienstvollen Akt im Dienste der Zivilisation hochstilisiert:

> Take up the White Man's burden-
> Send forth the best ye breed-
> Go bind your sons to exile
> To serve your captives' need. (Kipling 1899/1990: 261)

Als letzte Funktion ist daher die propagandistische und didaktische Ausrichtung der imperialistischen Metaphorik hervorzuheben. Die Empire-Metaphern dienten insofern als ein Medium der politischen Meinungsbildung, als sie zur Verbreitung politischer Ideen beitrugen. Die skizzierten Funktionen, die die Metapher vom Empire als einer Familie erfüllte, zeigen sich auch in vielen bildhaften Darstellungen, denen oft ebenfalls metaphorische Beziehungen zugrunde liegen. Einige weitere Beispiele aus der populären Wochenzeitschrift *Punch* mögen verdeutlichen, wie die Werte und Normen des Familienlebens zu propagandistischen Zwecken auf die Beziehung zwischen England und seinen Kolonien projiziert wurden. Vor dem Hintergrund der Metapher des Empire als einer großen Familie erscheint es etwa nur folgerichtig, wenn sich der in die Jahre gekommene britische Löwe, der auf der dritten Illustration zu sehen ist, auf seine Jungs verlassen kann. Die kleinen Löwen, die dem stolzen Vater selbstredend aus dem Gesicht geschnitten sind, marschieren treu und brav in Reih und Glied auf, um ihm hilfreich zur Seite zu stehen.

Zehn Jahre später, so zeigt die vierte Illustration, sind auch die kleinsten Löwen erwachsen geworden, aber der Harmonie und der emotionalen Bindung der Familienmitglieder hat dies keinerlei Abbruch getan.

Die letzten beiden Illustrationen erweitern und variieren die von den Metaphern erzählten Familiengeschichten ein wenig, indem sie die der kolonialen Expansion vermeintlich zugrundeliegenden humanitären Motive ins rechte Licht rücken. Die eine zeigt Gladstone als Kinderfrau und Amme, die rührend um das Wohl des hilflosen ägyptischen Babys besorgt ist und es – wie ein dazugehöriges Gedicht erläutert – wie die leibliche Mutter liebt. Auch John Bull, so suggeriert die andere Illustration, kommt wie die Jungfrau zum Kind, als er – wie weiland Squire Allworthy in Fieldings *Tom Jones* – einen Findling vor seiner Haustür entdeckt. Daß ihm nichts anderes übrigbleibt, als die Bürde des weißen Mannes auf- und sich liebevoll des schwarzen Babys namens Uganda anzunehmen, verrät zwar ebenfalls wenig über die politischen Hintergründe, paßt aber bestens in das Bildfeld der Familienmetaphorik, die Englands Rolle als Kolonialmacht einmal mehr als einen humanitären und altruistischen Akt erscheinen läßt.

Obgleich sich die unmittelbare Wirkung der Empire-Metaphorik auf Zeitgenossen nicht eindeutig bestimmen läßt, kann an dem propagandistischen Potential der suggestiven Metaphern kein Zweifel bestehen. Daß es vor allem Tennyson und Kipling tatsächlich gelang, das politische Bewußtsein der Viktorianer zu beeinflussen und eine bestimmte Sehweise des Empire zu popularisieren, läßt sich durch viele zeitgenössische Quellen belegen. Stellvertretend für eine Vielzahl ähnlicher Äußerungen sei Edward Dowdens Einschätzung von Kiplings weitreichendem Einfluß zitiert, den Dowden im Jahre 1901 so beschrieb:

> It was long since a morsel of verse constituted an historical event of importance for two hemispheres; but this, without exaggeration, is what certain short poems of Kipling have been. They have served to evoke or guide the feelings of nations, and to determine action in great affairs.[53]

Ähnlich äußerten sich zahlreiche weitere Kritiker, die die enorme Breitenwirkung von Kiplings Lyrik würdigten und ihm eine entscheidende Rolle bei der Popularisierung imperialistischer Ideale zuschrieben. Kein Schriftsteller habe so viel für die Wiederbelebung des "Imperial sentiment" getan wie Kipling, denn er habe dem "average Englishman" überhaupt erst eine adäquate Vorstellung von der Bedeutung des Britischen Weltreichs vermittelt. Sir Walter Besant faßt diese damals verbreitete Einschätzung von Kiplings Wirkung anschaulich zusammen:

> He is a son of the empire; he has brought home to the understanding of the most parochial of Little Englanders the sense and knowledge of what

> the British empire means. What Seeley taught scholars, Kipling has taught the multitude. He is the poet of the empire.[54]

Die große Breitenwirkung, die Kipling zugeschrieben wird, ist nicht zuletzt darauf zurückzuführen, daß seine Werke maßgeblich dazu beitrugen, "the ideology of empire as family"[55] zu popularisieren. Die metaphorische Leitvorstellung des Empire als Familie ermöglichte es, politische Konstellationen in eine dem viktorianischen Bürgertum vertraute Sprache zu übersetzen. Daß die konnotationsreiche Familienmetaphorik ihre suggestive Wirkung nicht verfehlte, zeigt sich allein schon daran, daß sie auch von der zeitgenössischen Literaturkritik hervorgehoben und aufgegriffen wurde, wie etwa folgende Äußerung eines Rezensenten über Kiplings patriotische Lyrik verdeutlicht:

> The dominant tone of his verse is indeed the patriotic; and it is the tone of the new patriotism, that of imperial England, which holds as one all parts of her wide-stretched empire, and binds them close in the indissoluble bond of common motherhood, and with the ties of common convictions, principles, and aims, derived from the teachings and traditions of the motherland, and expressed in the best verses of her poets.[56]

5. *Ausblick: "Nicht nur Dichter [...] 'denken in Bildern', auch 'Kulturen' insgesamt"*

Ebenso wie diese Hinweise auf die enorme Breitenwirkung der imperialistischen Lyrik liefern die skizzierten Funktionen der Empire-Metaphorik in ihrer Gesamtheit auch eine Antwort auf die Frage, warum gerade Verwandtschafts-Metaphern im imperialistischen Diskurs des Spätviktorianismus eine so herausragende Rolle spielten. Vor allem die Leitvorstellung des Empire als Familie ermöglichte es, komplizierte historische Entwicklungen und politische Konstellationen in einer vertrauten Sprache darzustellen. Die weite Verbreitung dieses Deutungsschemas läßt sich darauf zurückführen, daß die Beziehungen zwischen England und seinen Kolonien durch den Rückgriff auf die moralischen Werte des Familienlebens in einer einfachen, klaren, stimmigen und der imperialistischen Ideologie eminent nützlichen Weise charakterisiert wurden.

Das besondere Leistungsvermögen der Verwandtschafts-Metaphern bestand darin, daß sie komplexe politische Prozesse in die Sprache, Denkweise und Normen der häuslichen Sphäre übersetzten und dadurch das Fremde mit dem Vertrauten in Beziehung setzten.[57] Aufgrund dieser Vermittlung zwischen dem Öffentlichen und dem Privaten war gerade die Familienmetaphorik dazu prädestiniert, jene Wirkung zu erzielen, die James Anthony Froude in seinem Buch *Oceana, or England and her Colonies* (1886) den hitzigen Debatten um das Empire zuschrieb: "the agitation has had its uses, for it has familiarised the public with the bearings of the question".[58] Die tote Metapher *familiarize* umschreibt nochmals sehr treffend jene Funktionen des Vertrautmachens, des Gewöhnens und des Veranschaulichens, die die Familienmetaphorik dadurch erfüllte, daß sie politische Beziehungen in Verwandtschaftsgrade übersetzte und die Werte des Familienlebens auf das Verhältnis zwischen England und seinen Kolonien projizierte.

Insgesamt bestätigt diese funktionsgeschichtliche Analyse des Gebrauchs von Metaphern zur Bezeichnung des Empire somit zum einen die These von Jürgen Link und Wulf Wülfing, daß die in einer Epoche verbreiteten Sprachbilder „in hohem Maße 'Mentalitäten' vor- und mitstrukturieren. Nicht nur Dichter [...] 'denken in Bildern', auch 'Kulturen' insgesamt."[59] Zum anderen gibt die Verwendung von Empire-Metaphern im imperialistischen Diskurs John Robert Seeleys Einschätzung recht, daß Metaphern einen unwiderstehlichen Denkzwang ausüben und sogar die Rolle eines politischen Arguments übernehmen können. Auf die in seinem eingangs zitierten Buch *The Expansion of England* aufgeworfene Frage, warum die obsolete Metapher von Kolonien als erwachsenen Söhnen nicht fallengelassen werde, gibt Seeley selbst die beste Antwort: "When a metaphor comes to be regarded as an argument, what an irresistible argument it always seems!"[60]

Anmerkungen

1 J. R. Seeley: *The Expansion of England. Two Courses of Lectures.* London, 1883, S. 44. Solche metasprachlichen Überlegungen über die Frage nach der Angemessenheit des Begriffs 'Empire' dienen vor allem der Betonung der vermeintlichen Besonderheiten des Britischen Empire sowie dessen Abgrenzung von allen früheren Weltreichen.

2 Der Begriff der Leitvorstellung geht zurück auf H. Blumenberg: „Paradigmen zu einer Metaphorologie". *Archiv für Begriffsgeschichte* 6, 1960, 7-142, hier 69. – Die Bezeichnung 'metaphorische Leitvorstellung' stammt meines Wissens von D. Peil: „Überlegungen zur Bildfeldtheorie". *Beiträge zur Geschichte der deutschen Sprache und Literatur* 112,2, 1990, 209-241, hier 219.

3 Aus Platzgründen muß leider auf Beispiele für den verbreiteten Gebrauch von Familienmetaphorik in nicht-fiktionalen Kontexten verzichtet werden; Belege und erste Hinweise zur Verwendung solcher Metaphern als politisches Argument finden sich in R. Hyam, G. Martin: *Reappraisals in British Imperial History.* London, Basingstoke, 1975, S. 102-107.

4 J. Davidson: *The Poems of John Davidson.* Ed. A. Turnbull. 2 vols, vol I. Edinburgh, 1973, S. 269.

5 Z. T. Sullivan: *Narratives of Empire. The Fictions of Rudyard Kipling.* Cambridge, 1993, S. 3.

6 Vgl. R.H. MacDonald: *The Language of Empire. Myths and Metaphors of Popular Imperialism, 1880-1918.* Manchester, 1994.

7 Vgl. J.A. Mangan (Ed.): *Making Imperialist Mentalities. Socialisation and British Imperialism.* Manchester, 1990. – A. Nünning: „Literatur, Mentalitäten und kulturelles Gedächtnis: Grundriß, Leitbegriffe und Perspektiven einer anglistischen Kulturwissenschaft". – In A. Nünning (Ed.): *Literaturwissenschaftliche Theorien, Modelle, Methoden: Eine Einführung.* Trier, 1995, S. 173-197.

8 Vgl. P. Burke: „Stärken und Schwächen der Mentalitätengeschichte". – In U. Raulff (Ed.): *Mentalitäten-Geschichte.* Berlin, 1987, S. 139f.: „Dennoch kann es für die Beschreibung der Unterschiede zwischen Mentalitäten sehr nützlich sein, sich an die wiederkehrenden Metaphern zu halten, insbesondere wenn sie das Denken insgesamt zu strukturieren scheinen". – Zur Mentalitätsgeschichte vgl. V. Sellin: „Mentalität und Mentalitätsgeschichte". *Historische Zeitschrift* 241, 1985, 555-598. – Zum Begriff 'Mentalitäten' vgl. auch U. Raulff: „Vorwort: Mentalitäten-Geschichte". – In U. Raulff (Ed.): *Mentalitäten-Geschichte.* Berlin, 1987, S. 7-17; Raulff betont, daß der Begriff der Mentalitäten nicht nur „Vorstellungen, Einstellungen und [...] Regeln" bezeichnet, sondern „auch gefühlsmäßig getönte Orientierungen"; er umschreibt somit „kognitive, ethische und affektive Dispositionen" (S. 10).

9 Vgl. analog dazu J. Schlobach: *Zyklentheorie und Epochenmetaphorik. Studien zur bildlichen Sprache der Geschichtsreflexion in Frankreich von der Renaissance bis zur Frühaufklärung.* München, 1980, S. 17, der unter dem Begriff 'Epochenmetaphorik' „ganz allgemein Bilder, die zur bildlichen Kennzeichnung von kulturellen und historischen Abläufen dienen", versteht. Vgl. auch die Definition des Begriffs 'Staatsmetaphern' von D. Peil: *Staats-und Herrschaftsmetaphorik in literarischen Zeugnissen von der Antike bis zur Gegenwart.* München, 1983, S. 12.

10 Vgl. H. Newbolt: *Collected Poems 1897-1907.* London, o.J., S. 130-132. In Newbolts Gedichten "The School at War" (S. 151-153) und "The Best School of All" (S. 166-169) deuten bereits die Titel an, daß die Normen der Schulwelt auf den Krieg projiziert bzw. nostalgisch verklärt werden. Typisch für Newbolts ideologisch geprägte Verwendung dieser Isotopieebene, deren Ausprägungen in der imperialistischen Lyrik Gegenstand einer eigenen Untersuchung sein müßte, sind euphemistische Metaphern wie "And he stooped, and finished the game" (S. 24), "But Captain Keats he knew the game, and swore to share the sport" (S. 42), "Now was the time for a charge to end the game" (S. 57), "To love the game beyond the prize" (S. 128) und "We held by the game and hailed the team" (S. 163). – Vgl. dazu auch MacDonald: *Myths and Metaphors of Popular Imperialism,* S. 18ff., der zwar nicht auf Newbolts Lyrik eingeht, aber "[t]he public school code of 'playing the game'" (S. 19) und "[t]he metaphor of war as sport" (S. 20) differenziert analysiert.

11 Vgl. Blumenberg: „Paradigmen zu einer Metaphorologie", 59; in dieser Hinsicht ähneln Empire-Metaphern der von Blumenberg analysierten *„terra incognita*-Metapher und der Metaphorik der '*unvollendenten Welt*'" (59).

12 F. Wessel: *Probleme der Metaphorik und die Minnemetaphorik in Gottfrieds von Strassburg 'Tristan und Isolde'.* München, 1984, S. 10; zum Begriff 'Denkmodell' vgl. ebd., S. 2, 7f., 10, 21, 45ff., 80, 98 sowie Peil: „Überlegungen zur Bildfeldtheorie", 230. – Auch Blumenberg: „Paradigmen zu einer Metaphorologie", 13, spricht von „ganz elementaren *Modellvorstellungen,* die in der Gestalt von Metaphern bis in die Ausdruckssphäre durchschlagen". – Zur kognitiven Funktion von Metaphern vgl. U. Eco: "The Scandal of Metaphor. Metaphorology and Semiotics". *Poetics Today* 4, 1983, 234f., der die Metapher als "a cognitive tool" (219)

bzw. "a tool of cognition" (232) bezeichnet. Der bisherige Stand der metapherntheoretischen Diskussion kann hier nicht im einzelnen referiert werden; vgl. aus der unübersehbaren Flut einschlägiger Publikationen neben den bereits erwähnten wegweisenden Studien von Hans Blumenberg, Joachim Schlobach, Umberto Eco, Dietmar Peil und Franziska Wessel vor allem die in den folgenden Anmerkungen genannten Arbeiten von Harald Weinrich, Wilhelm Köller, Alexander Demandt und Paul Ricoeur sowie die Themenhefte zur Metaphorik der Zeitschrift *Poetics Today* 13,4, 1992, und 14,1, 1993.

13 Vgl. H.-J. Müllenbrock: „Literatur als Politik: Zur Funktion imperialistischer Lyrik im viktorianischen England". *Anglia* 110, 1992, 119-142, hier 141: „Im viktorianischen Gattungsspektrum ist es jedenfalls die Lyrik, welche die interessantesten Einsichten in die genetischen Umstände, mentalitätsmäßigen Konstanten und stimmungsmäßigen Schwankungen des britischen Imperialismus gestattet." Müllenbrocks Artikel gibt einen guten Überblick über einige der Funktionen imperialistischer Lyrik im viktorianischen England, geht jedoch auf die Metaphorik des Imperialismus nicht ein. – Zu Kipling vgl. auch die Bemerkung von MacDonald: *Myths and Metaphors of Popular Imperialism*, S. 145: "in verse he could express the imperial idea in its simplest and most powerful form".

14 Von grundsätzlichem Interesse für ein Verständnis von Sprachbildern im historisch-politischen Denken sind die ebenso umfassenden wie vorzüglichen Studien von Alexander Demandt und Dietmar Peil, die systematische Bestandsaufnahmen der verbreiteten Metaphorik geben, allerdings nicht auf die Metaphorik des Imperialismus eingehen. Vgl. A. Demandt: *Metaphern für Geschichte. Sprachbilder und Gleichnisse im historisch-politischen Denken.* München, 1978. – Peil: *Staats- und Herrschaftsmetaphorik.*

15 Zitiert nach C.A. Bodelsen: *Studies in Mid-Victorian Imperialism.* London, 1960 [[1]1924], S. 126, der sich auf einen Artikel aus *Macmillan's Magazine* vom Juli 1889 bezieht. – Zu Tennysons zeitgenössischer Bedeutung und Repräsentativität vgl. auch den zuerst 1863/64 erschienen Beitrag von Hippolyte A. Taine: "Tennyson as the poet of Victorian England". – In J.D. Jump (Ed.): *Tennyson. The Critical Heritage.* London, 1967, S. 270-277.

16 Zu Tennysons eher ambivalenter Haltung zum Britischen Weltreich vgl. S. Shatto: "The Strange Charm of 'Far, Far Away': Tennyson, the Continent, and the Empire". – In M. Cotsell (Ed.): *Creditable Warriors 1830-1876.* London, 1990, S. 113-129.

17 A. Tennyson: *The Poems of Tennyson.* Ed. C. Ricks. London, 1969, S. 1358. Zitiert wird im folgenden aus dieser Ausgabe, auf die sich die in Klammern gesetzten Seitenzahlen im Text und in den Anmerkungen beziehen.

18 Vgl. G.S. Wood: *The Radicalism of the American Revolution.* New York, 1992, S. 165: "In the decades leading up to the Revolution scarcely a piece of American writing, whig or tory, did not invoke the parent-child image to describe the imperial relationship. The king was the 'father' and Great Britain the 'mother country' and the colonists were their 'children'. Because the image was so powerful, so suggestive of the personal traditional world in which most colonists still lived, almost the entire imperial debate was inevitably carried on within its confines. [...] The whole imperial struggle collapsed into a family squabble." Zu der Art und Weise, wie die Implikationen der Familienmetaphorik im Zeitalter der Amerikanischen Revolution als politisches Argument genutzt wurden, vgl. auch J. V. Jensen: "British Voices on the Eve of the American Revolution: Trapped by the Family Meta-

phor". *Quarterly Journal of Speech* 63, 1977, 43-50. – J. Fliegelman: "Familial Politics, Seduction and the Novel: The Anxious Agenda of an American Literary Culture". – In J.P. Greene (Ed.): *The American Revolution. Its Character and Limits.* New York, London, 1987, S. 331-354.

19 Auch in Tennysons "England and America in 1782" (S. 618-619) beruht die Geschichtsdeutung primär auf der Familienmetaphorik, wie die erste Strophe erkennen läßt: "O thou that sendest out the man/ To rule by land and sea,/Strong mother of a lion-line,/ Be proud of those strong sons of thine/ Who wrenched their rights from thee." (S. 618) In "Hands All Round!" (S. 1002-1004) beschreibt der Sprecher nicht nur die Vereinigten Staaten metaphorisch als "Gigantic daughter of the West", sondern erinnert auch durch eine rhetorische Frage an deren englische Abstammung ("For art thou not of English blood?") und leitet daraus eine unzweideutige Handlungsaufforderung ab: "Should war's mad blast again be blown,/ Permit not thou the tyrant powers/ To fight thy mother here alone,/ But let thy broadsides roar with ours." (S. 1003)

20 Vgl. auch Tennysons "Ode on the Death of the Duke of Wellington" (S. 1007-1117), die nicht nur mit den Versen "Bury the Great Duke/ With an empire's lamentation" (S. 1007) beginnt, sondern auch die Einheit des englischen Volkes beschwört: "A people's voice! We are a people yet" (S. 1012).

21 Stellvertretend für viele andere vgl. etwa Tennysons Gedichte "England and America in 1782" (S. 618-619), "'O mother Britain lift thou up'" (S. 622-623), "Hands All Round!" (S. 1002-1004) und "On the Jubilee of Queen Victoria" (S. 1369-1372). – Vgl. auch eine von Sir Lewis Morris zum Anlaß des Diamantenen Jubiläums von Königin Victoria im Jahre 1897 verfaßte Ode: "Mother of freemen! over all the earth/ Thy Empire-children come to birth/ Vast continents are thine, or spring from thee/ Brave island-fortress of the storm-vexed sea." – Zitiert nach M. Beloff: *Britain's Liberal Empire 1897-1921.* London, 1970, S. 21.

22 In begrifflicher und methodischer Hinsicht orientieren sich die folgenden Textanalysen an den wegweisenden Ausführungen von D. Peil: „Überlegungen zur Bildfeldtheorie", 220ff. sowie an H. Birus, A. Fuchs: „Ein terminologisches Grundinventar für die Analyse von Metaphern". – In C. Wagenknecht (Ed.): *Zur Terminologie der Literaturwissenschaft: Akten des IX. Symposions der Deutschen Forschungsgemeinschaft Würzburg 1986.* Stuttgart, 1988, S. 157-174.

23 H. Weinrich: *Sprache in Texten.* Stuttgart, 1976, S. 284. – Zum Begriff des Bildfeldes vgl. ebd., S. 283ff. Zu den Problemen und Vorzügen von Weinrichs Bildfeldtheorie vgl. die umsichtigen Überlegungen von Peil: „Überlegungen zur Bildfeldtheorie", dessen modifizierte Definition des Bildfeldbegriffes im folgenden zugrunde gelegt wird: „Das Bildfeld läßt sich als ein offenes, systemähnliches Gebilde auffassen, d.h. als eine unbestimmte Menge von verschiedenen (Bild-)Elementen in unterschiedlicher Ausprägung, zwischen denen verschiedene Relationen bestehen oder denen (im Sinne der Prädikatenlogik) verschiedene ein- oder mehrstellige Prädikationen zugesprochen werden können." (220) Zum Begriff des metaphorischen Bezugsrahmen vgl. B. Hrushovski: "Poetic Metaphor and Frames of Reference". *Poetics Today* 5, 1984, 5-43.

24 *Punch* 87, 1884, 306.

25 Vgl. zu diesem Begriff Peil: *Staats- und Herrschaftsmetaphorik*, S. 17, 24 sowie Peil: „Überlegungen zur Bildfeldtheorie", 219: „das Bildfeld ist die Summe aller möglichen metaphorischen Äußerungen im Umfeld der jeweiligen Zentralmetapher oder metaphorischen Leitvorstellung."

26 Peil: „Überlegungen zur Bildfeldtheorie“, 228, dessen Explikation der Metapher als „Doppelfilter“ in den folgenden Ausführungen auf die Empire-Metaphorik angewendet werden. Vgl. auch Hrushovski: “Poetic Metaphor and Frames of Reference”, 18, der von “mutual filtering” spricht. – Zur kognitiven Funktionsweise von Metaphern vgl. den sehr anschaulichen Hinweis von W. Köller: *Semiotik und Metapher. Untersuchungen zur grammatischen Struktur und kommunikativen Funktion von Metaphern.* Stuttgart, 1975, S. 201, „daß bei metaphorischen Prädikationen komplexe und nicht scharf konturierte Vorstellungsbilder aufeinander projiziert werden“.

27 W. T. Stead, *Review of Reviews*, XIV, Dezember 1896, 553; zitiert nach MacDonald: *Myths and Metaphors of Popular Imperialism*, S. 145, der Kiplings Beitrag zum Diskurs des Imperialismus differenziert herausarbeitet, auf dessen Gebrauch von Empire-Metaphern jedoch nicht eingeht. – Die Etiketten “the poet of the empire” bzw. “the approved and authoritative poet of the British empire” stammen von Sir Walter Besant und Robert Buchanan; zitiert nach R.L. Green (Ed.): *Kipling. The Critical Heritage.* London, 1971, S. 256 bzw. 238. William Dean Howells bezeichnete Kipling als “the laureate of that larger England whose wreath is not for any prime minister to bestow” (ebd., S. 195).

28 Vgl. R. Kipling: *The Complete Verse.* With a Foreword by M. M. Kaye. London: Kyle Cathie, 1990, S. 138ff. Kiplings Gedichte werden im folgenden nach dieser Ausgabe zitiert, auf die sich die in Klammern gesetzten Seitenzahlen beziehen. – Zur Publikationsgeschichte vgl. MacDonald: *Myths and Metaphors of Popular Imperialism*, S. 152. – Zu Kiplings politischer Lyrik vgl. die Studie von Ann Parry, *The Poetry of Rudyard Kipling. Rousing the Nation.* Buckingham, 1992, die vor allem im Hinblick auf Kiplings sehr ambivalente zeitgenössische Rezeption sehr aufschlußreich ist, aber dessen Verwendung von Familienmetaphorik nur an einer Stelle kurz kommentiert: “The verses stress, like Disraeli, Dilke and Froude had done before, that the essential character of the Empire was to be that of the family. It would be characterized by relationships, entered into willingly out of mutual respect, and with benefits for all concerned.” (S. 85)

29 Vgl. Kiplings Gedicht “The Native-Born” (S. 156-159), das im Kontext der imperialistischen Lyrik insofern eine Sonderstellung einnimmt, als es die Familienmetaphorik nicht bloß aufgreift, sondern auch auf die indische Bevölkerung ausweitet und deren äußerst ambivalentes Verhältnis zum englischen Mutterland nicht unterschlägt: “We’ve drunk to the Queen – God bless her!-/We’ve drunk to our mothers’ land;/ We’ve drunk to our English brother,/(But he does not understand);” (S. 156). Außerdem tragen metasprachliche Kommentare des lyrischen Ich dazu bei, die Künstlichkeit der Sprachregelungen bloßzulegen: “We learned from our wistful mothers/ To call old England ‘home’” (ebd.).

30 Vgl. zum folgenden etwa ebd., S. 144: “Also we will make promise. So long as the blood endures,/ I shall know that your good is mine: ye shall feel that my strength is yours:/ In the day of Armageddon, at the last great fight of all,/ That Our House stand together and the pillars do not fall.”

31 Zu dem oft als “Imperial ideal” bezeichneten imperialistischen Ideenkomplex vgl. Bodelsen: *Studies in Mid-Victorian Imperialism*, der sich zum Ziel setzt “to describe the rise and growth of an Imperialist spirit in England” (S. 7). – Vgl. auch A.P. Thornton: *The Imperial Idea and its Enemies.* London, New York, 1963. – Zahlreiche Belege für den Gebrauch von Familienmetaphorik im imperialistischen Diskurs finden sich auch in der Quellensammlung von G. Bennett (Ed.): *The*

Concept of Empire. Burke to Attlee 1774-1947. London, 1953, S. 48, 116f., 122, 134, 143f., 185, 200.

32 Müllenbrock: „Literatur als Politik", 120. – Besonders deutlich kommt dieser Empire-Holismus etwa in einem Band von Essays zum Ausdruck, der 1905 zur Einhundertjahrfeier der Schlacht von Trafalgar erschien; vgl. C.S. Goldman: "Introduction". – In *The Empire and the Century. A Series of Essays on Imperial Problems and Possibilities by Various Writers.* London, 1905, S. xiii-xxiii, bes. S. xviii: "It [Imperialism] desired to make the Empire a united and self-subsistent whole".

33 Zur Funktion der Veranschaulichung und Verlebendigung vgl. Wessel: *Probleme der Metaphorik*, S. 69. – Birus, Fuchs: „Ein terminologisches Grundinventar", 162. – Vgl. zum folgenden auch Blumenberg: „Paradigmen zu einer Metaphorologie", 20: „Sie [absolute Metaphern] geben einer Welt Struktur, repräsentieren das nie Erfahrbare, nie übersehbare Ganze der Realität."

34 Vgl. Wessel: *Probleme der Metaphorik*, S. 80: „Demgegenüber besteht die Leistung eines bildspendenden Feldes darin, den empfangenden Bereich allererst zu strukturieren, wobei freilich ihre Stärke nicht darin liegt, Präzision zu stiften, sondern Atmosphäre."

35 Zur Analogie von Metaphern und Modellen vgl. die einschlägige Studie von Max Black: *Models and Metaphors.* Ithaca/N.Y., 1962. – Demandt: *Metaphern für Geschichte*, S. 4f. – Peil: *Staats- und Herrschaftsmetaphorik*, S. 15ff. – Peil: „Überlegungen zur Bildfeldtheorie", 230, der von „ihrer Leistung als Denkmodell" spricht.

36 Zu dieser Kritik an der Beschreibung von Metaphern als Denkmodellen vgl. Wessel: *Probleme der Metaphorik*, S. 80, 98, die diesen Begriff jedoch im weiteren Verlauf ihrer Arbeit selbst verwendet (vgl. S. 118, 125, 132).

37 Vgl. P. Ricoeur: "The Metaphorical Process as Cognition, Imagination, and Feeling". *Critical Inquiry* 5, 1978, 143-159, bes. 143. – Vgl. auch Köller: *Semiotik und Metapher*, S. 202, der auf die Bedeutung der „konnotativen Komponenten und emotionalen Wertakzentuierungen" hingewiesen hat.

38 Weinrich: *Sprache in Texten*, S. 309. In enger Anlehnung an Weinrich bestimmen Köller: *Semiotik und Metapher*, S. 198ff. und Wessel: *Probleme der Metaphorik*, S. 62ff., 80 die schöpferische bzw. poietische Leistung von Metaphern ähnlich.

39 Vgl. B. Giesen: „Einleitung". – In B. Giesen (Ed.): *Nationale und kulturelle Identität. Studien zur Entwicklung des kollektiven Bewußtseins in der Neuzeit.* Frankfurt, 1991, S. 9-18, hier S. 16.

40 Vgl. Demandt: *Metaphern für Geschichte*, S. 28: „Die Innenbindung historischer Gegenstände, namentlich von Völkern und Herrschaften, wird auf diesem Wege verstärkt."

41 B. Ashcroft, G. Griffiths, H. Tiffin: *The Empire Writes Back. Theory and practice in post-colonial literatures.* London, New York, 1989, S. 16. – Ohne sich spezifisch auf Empire-Metaphern zu beziehen, betont auch Parry: *The Poetry of Rudyard Kipling*, S. 59, daß die imperialistische Lyrik einen Beitrag zur historischen Sinnstiftung und nationalen Identitätsbildung leistete: "the poetry of *The Seven Seas* attempted the same task by exploiting collectively shared symbols: symbols that called upon uncritical emotional responses in order to re-invent English identity and history".

42 Die Familien-Metaphern bestätigen damit implizit jene Form von Sinnbildung, die sich in verdichteter Form in Tennysons "Ode on the Death of the Duke Welling-

ton" findet und die dort als "our fair island story" umschrieben wird: "Not once or twice in our fair island story,/ The path of duty was the way to glory" (S. 1015). – MacDonald: *Myths and Metaphors of Popular Imperialism*, bezeichnet diese "island story" als "the paramount patriotic myth of the New Imperial age" (S. 51) und widmet ihr ein aufschlußreiches Kapitel.

43 Demandt: *Metaphern für Geschichte*, S. 28.

44 Vgl. ebd., S. 330: „Der wichtigste Gesichtspunkt, der Metaphern aus der Technik mit der Geschichte verbindet, auch im Sinne einer Primärbeziehung, ist das Prinzip der Machbarkeit."

45 J. S. Mill: *On the Subjection of Women*. London: Dent, 1974, S. 253.

46 F. Harrison, "Lecture II: Family Life". – In F. Harrison, *On Society*. London, 1918, S. 32-55, hier S. 33. Auch für Harrison ist die Familie eine Schule des Gefühls: "The Home is the primeval and eternal school where we learn to practise the balance of our instincts, to restrain appetite, to cultivate affection, to pass out of our lower selves – to *Live for Humanity*." (S. 42)

47 Vgl. die bis heute unübertroffene Studie über das viktorianische Weltbild von W. Houghton: *The Victorian Frame of Mind*. New Haven, London, 1957, der daher treffend von "the exaltation of family life" (S. 341) spricht.

48 Zu Rezensionen, in denen diese Zeile zitiert wird, vgl. Green (Ed.): *Kipling. The Critical Heritage*, S. 187, 212, 264.

49 Zur Bedeutung nationalistischer und wirtschaftlicher Faktoren vgl. den ausgezeichneten Aufsatz von W.J. Mommsen: "Nationale und ökonomische Faktoren im Britischen Imperialismus vor 1914". *Historische Zeitschrift* 206, 1968, 618-664.

50 Vgl. dazu im einzelnen die bahnbrechende Studie von P. Ariès: *L'enfant et la vie familiale sous l'ancien régime*. Paris, 1960 (dt. *Geschichte der Kindheit*. München, 1975), die auch die historische Entwicklung des Familiensinns aufzeigt.

51 J.-A. Wallace: "De-Scribing *The Water-Babies*. 'The child' in post-colonial theory". – In C. Tiffin, A. Lawson (Eds.): *De-scribing Empire. Post-colonialism and textuality*. London, New York, 1994, S. 171-184, hier S. 176; vgl. auch Wallaces These "that it is an idea of 'the child' which makes thinkable both nineteenth-century English colonialist imperialism and many twentieth-century forms of resistance to imperialism" (S. 171).

52 Dies wird bereits in Tennysons patriotischem Gedicht "'O mother Britain lift thou up'" (S. 622-623) aus den 1830er Jahren deutlich. Darin werden das Mutterland und dessen verdienstvolle Taten im Dienste der Zivilisation glorifiziert.

53 E. Dowden: "The Poetry of Mr Kipling". *New Liberal Review* XXVIII, Febr. 1901, 53-61; zitiert nach Green (Ed.): *Kipling. The Critical Heritage*, S. 259. – Zu Kiplings weitreichender Wirkung vgl. auch die Belege in C. Carrington: *Rudyard Kipling. His Life and Work*. London, 1978, S. 409.

54 Sir Walter Besant: "Is it the Voice of the Holligan". *Contemporary Review*, LXXVII, Jan. 1900, 27-39; zit. nach Green (Ed.): *Kipling. The Critical Heritage*, S. 256. Zu ähnlichen Äußerungen zeitgenössischer Rezensenten vgl. ebd., S. 200ff., 255, 258, 260.

55 Sullivan: *Narratives of Empire*, S. 105.

56 Charles Eliot Norton: "The Poetry of Rudyard Kipling". *Atlantic Monthly*, LXXIX, Jan. 1897, 11-115; zit. nach Green (Ed.): *Kipling. The Critical Heritage*, S. 187. Vgl. auch Dowdens Verwendung der Familien-Metapher (ebd., S. 261).

57 Zum Beitrag, den Metaphern zum Verstehen leisten, vgl. L. Bredella: „Ist das Verstehen fremder Kulturen wünschenswert?“ – In L. Bredella, H. Christ (Eds.): *Zugänge zum Fremden.* Gießen, 1993, S. 11-36, hier S. 32: „Die Metapher setzt das Vertraute mit dem Fremden in Beziehung, indem sie das Fremde unter einer neuen Perspektive erhellt“.

58 J. A. Froude: *Oceana, or England and her Colonies.* London, 1886, S. 390. – Ohne Bezug zur Empire-Metaphorik spricht auch Mangan von “familiarisation with empire and incipient jingoism”; vgl. J. A. Mangan: “‘The Grit of our Forefathers’. Invented Traditions, Propaganda and Imperialism”. – In J.M MacKenzie (Ed.): *Imperialism and Popular Culture.* Manchester, 1986, S. 113-120, hier S. 123.

59 J. Link, W. Wülfing: „Einleitung“. – In J. Link, W. Wülfing (Eds.): *Bewegung und Stillstand in Metaphern und Mythen.* Stuttgart, 1984, S. 7-14, hier S. 14.

60 Seeley: *The Expansion of England*, S. 344.

PUNCH, OR THE LONDON CHARIVARI.—DECEMBER 27, 1884.

JOHN BULL'S CHRISTMAS FAMILY PARTY.

PUNCH, OR THE LONDON CHARIVARI.—APRIL 25, 1900.

ADVANCED AUSTRALIA!

AUSTRALIA. "IF YOU PLEASE, MOTHER, I WANTED A LITTLE MORE FREEDOM, SO I'VE HAD THIS LATCH-KEY MADE. YOU DON'T MIND?"

BRITANNIA. "I'M SURE, MY DEAR, IF ANYBODY CAN BE TRUSTED WITH IT, YOU CAN."

[Clause 74, "Australasian Federation Bill," abolishes appeal to Privy Council.]

"MY BOYS!"

BRAVO, YOUNG 'UNS!

Young Cubs. "WELL DONE, DAD! WE'LL STICK TO YOU!"
British Lion. "THANK YOU, MY BOYS! I NEVER DOUBTED IT!"

PUNCH, OR THE LONDON CHARIVARI.—August 25, 1883.

NURSE GLADSTONE.

"OH, THE LITTLE DUCKY-WUCKY! NEVER WILL ITS NANA LEAVE IT TILL IT CAN RUN QUITE ALONE;—NEVER!!"

THE BLACK BABY.

Mr. Bull. "WHAT, ANOTHER!!—WELL, I SUPPOSE I MUST TAKE IT IN!!!"

Erhard Reckwitz, Essen

Colonial Discourse and Early South African Literature

I

The sweeping imperial gesture is there right from the beginning: In the very first literary text to be published on South African soil, a sonnet in High Dutch on the occasion of laying the foundation stone of Cape Town Castle as recorded in the *Dagregister* of 2 January 1666, mention is made of "spreading the empire" ("de rijcken uijtgespreijt"), of "scattering the blacks and yellows [i.e. the Khoi and San indigenes]" ("de swart en geluwen gespreijt"), and of "inspiring with terror Asians, Americans and savage Africans alike" ("schrich sowel [...] den Aes- Ameer- en wilden Africaen"). In the final quatrain the anonymous author praises the daring, the foresight and spirit of enterprise exhibited, through this venture, on the part of the governours of the Dutch East India Company, and in doing so he invokes, in classical fashion, the imperial European tradition associated with names like Augustus, Alexander and Caesar, none of whom, however, "had the glory of laying a cornerstone at earth's extremest end" ("zijn noijt daermee gswaerd/ Met't leggen van een steen op't eijnde van de Aerd").[1] The theme adumbrated in this rather clumsy praise poem is one that remains constant throughout South African writing, whether in Dutch or English, which from the very beginning is thus inscribed in the general discursive context of taking possession, of subjugating, taming and dominating both the foreign territory and the people living on it that is typical of any colonial encounter.

II

Before I turn to analyzing some early English literary manifestations of colonial discourse in South Africa a few observations about the theoretical concept of discourse in general – as evolved by Michel Foucault – and colonial discourse in particular seem to be in order. At its most fundamental level a discourse is a cognitive *a priori* regulating what – in a given historical and social context – can and must be said ("ce qui peut et doit être dit"[2]).

As such it is constitutive of what is to be regarded as 'truth' or 'reality', thereby depriving these concepts of their status as absolute ontological givens and making them contingent upon what Foucault has termed "truth-effects". Such an inversion of the hierarchical subject-object relation hitherto thought to exist between a 'primary' reality assumed to be 'out there' and its merely imitative and therefore 'secondary' mimesis causes any *representation* to be demoted to the status of a mere *presentation* to which is always attached the opprobrium of being nothing but a more or less willful imposition of meaning, hence, in the last resort, a *misrepresentation.* A discursive formation is thus a system of thought erected and pervaded by power, a power intent on carefully policing the borders of what it tries, through the use of language, to pass off as 'the self-evident', 'the commonsensical' or 'the natural'. This masking of its status as a mere signifier, with a signified that is devoid of any guaranteed reference, makes the notion of discourse complicit with that of ideology, or as Paul de Man puts it: "What we call ideology is precisely the confusion of linguistic with natural reality [...]."[3], and correspondingly Pêcheux subsumes the linguistic "formation discursive" under the more general and translinguistic "formation idéologique".[4]

One should beware, however, of not falling into the idealistic trap of assuming that discourse as well as the overarching notion of ideology are tantamount to being languages without a world. In the first place, this would be disregarding the "materiality of discourse" in that "[...] 'discourse' makes possible disciplines and institutions which, in turn, sustain and distribute those discourses."[5], so that discursive or linguistic practices and non-discursive or material practices are closely and dialectically intertwined. Secondly, although it may be dealing with reality only at one remove, it is the normalizing or naturalizing function of discourse, as the language of ideology, that ensures the interrelatedness of material situations and ideological discourse: In spite of the fact that ideological language may cause a certain kind of reality to come into being, as has been stated earlier on, this does not amount to a *creatio ex nihilo* that is totally arbitrary. On the contrary, we must presuppose that there is a preexisting material situation upon which ideological discourse goes to work in a transformative way, thereby "explaining, rationalizing, concealing, legitimating and so on"[6] that situation.

It is this legitimating function of discourse and its attending involvement with a certain power constellation that is responsible for its divisiveness: "[...] l'histoire de l'ordre des choses serait l'histoire du Même", says Foucault, thus setting 'the order' of things, the identifiable 'sameness' of the world (and by implication that which is deemed to be 'normal'), over against "l'histoire de l'Autre"[7], that which is the 'abnormal' and hence excluded Other of the normalizing discourse of the self – those who are either unruly, or mad, or of a different colour, or all taken together. This is precisely the juncture where the concept of discourse merges with that of colonialism to become united as 'colonial discourse', i.e. the discourse through which the colonized become 'othered' by the colonizers, as has first been developed by Edward Said who conceives of this type of discourse as "[...] a collective notion identifying 'us' Europeans as against all 'those' non-Europeans"[8], whether it be intellectually, morally, technologically, or economically.

It is one of the important insights provided by Lacanian psychoanalysis that colonial discourse, like any other ideological discourse based on an explicit or implicit "theory of otherness"[9], is mainly grounded in the specular fascination of the 'imaginary phase' where a sense of identity on the part of the self is only achieved by identifying with, as well as setting itself off against, the mirror image of an Other which, in the process, becomes a strangely ambivalent Self/ Other. The ideological quality of the simple binarism inherent in imaginary thought patterns becomes evident in all ethical or value judgements, i.e. in those "[...] valorizations or repudiations in which 'good' and 'bad' are simply positional descriptions of the geographical relationship of the phenomenon in question to my own Imaginary conception of centrality."[10]

What, therefore, the entire "psychopathology of the colonized and the colonial other"[11] with its strange intermingling of fascination and aggression amounts to, is the assumed centrality of the colonizer's 'here and now' and the ensuing denigration and marginalization of the colonized's 'there'. More specifically, the Other gets constructed, via colonial discourse, within the economy of what JanMohammed, taking up Frantz Fanon's formula of the "manichean delirium" of the colonizer's obsession with binarism, has termed "the manichean allegory" of the opposition between the entirely positive values of the European and the correspondingly negative ones of 'the Native'. This opens up "[...] a field of diverse yet interchangeable oppositions between white and black, good and evil, superiority and inferiority, civilization and savagery, intelligence and emotion, rationality and sensuality, self and Other, subject and object."[12]

The ideological function of any discourse invoking this economy with its almost obsessive insistence upon the savagery and evilness of the natives is evident: "[...] to justify imperial occupation and exploitation."[13] The reduction of the native to the status of a stereotyped object commodifies him in semiotic terms, in the process depriving him of any semantic individuality or subjectivity of his own because he is automatically typified as worthless in terms of what Frantz Fanon has referred to as "the epidermal schema" – an extremely reductive signifying system with 'skin' as its key signifier. This is the point where discursive and material practices coalesce, as has been posited above, to form the "dispositif" (Foucault) of colonialism: "[...] the discursive practices do to the symbolic, linguistic presence of the native what the material practices do to his physical presence".[14] Another famous theoretician of colonialism, Homi K. Bhabha, has offered a similar definition of colonial discourse: "The objective of colonial discourse is to construe the colonized as a population of degenerate types on the basis of racial origin, in order to justify conquest and to establish systems of administration and instruction."[15]

III

In spite of the obvious similarities between both definitions, including their theoretical underpinnings – Althusserian post-Marxism, Lacanian psychoanalysis, Foucaultian archeology of power – there is one central difference in that JanMohammed is quite clearly more traditionally structuralist in his approach, whereas Bhabha is equally as clearly motivated by a poststructuralist, deconstructivist impulse. JanMohammed is definitely intent on upholding the unbridgeable difference between colonizer and colonized – given his materialist leanings colonial discourse for him is nothing but an ideological camouflage of colonial exploitation. Bhabha, however, with his deconstructivist approach, argues in favour of upsetting the Derridean "violent hierarchy" of a colonizer unilaterally dominating the colonized in order to replace it with a more ambivalent relationship in which both sides are mutually dependent on each other, thereby positing a dialectical relationship in which the colonized's values and culture also impinge upon those of the colonizer: Before the colonial encounter takes place, the colonizer's identity is an unquestioned, symbolic 'presence'; the moment, however, it solely defines itself by setting itself off against that of the colonized, it becomes an 'absence' or a sign whose meaning, in truly Derridean fashion, becomes split off from itself.

Where, as in all binary oppositions, each opposing term becomes the clandestine accomplice of the other because each one of them is only defined by what it is not, the inevitable result is what Bhabha has termed the "hybridity"[16] of the colonial subject. It is important to note that colonizer and colonized alike are affected by the ensuing "displacement" of their respective identities, i.e. the specular fascination with the Other typical of the imaginary phase results in an ambivalent "identité aliénante"[17] for both sides concerned.

Another reason responsible for the alienation of the colonizer resides in the fact that the colonized 'savage' is, psychoanalytically speaking, more or less implicitly equated with the 'id', as Octave Mannoni has convincingly argued.[18] This means that "mastery" of the dominant over the dominated has as its exact counterpart the "selfmastery"[19] of the dominant, which involves the careful repression and control of his own unconscious or underground self. Consequently, the colonizer is torn between the duty to correct the native's faults (which, by implication, are also his own), in the process denigrating him as utterly worthless, or the desire to see him as the adamic incarnation of some lost paradise. "L'autre, c'est mon propre inconscient"[20], thus Julia Kristeva succinctly sums up this sentiment, and hence the native becomes the screen onto which the colonizer's conflicting desires are projected, causing him to vacillate between "fear and temptation"[21]: The alternative between the *temptation* to go native, to shed his clothes "and join the skip and dance", as Conrad's Marlowe confesses in *The Heart of Darkness*, and, more specifically, to succumb to the allure of dark skin and swaying hips, or the *fear* to give in to what his entire socialization has taught him most to abhor – the savagery of his own uncontrolled urges, especially those of a sexual nature. Even though idealizing the indigene as the noble savage may be nothing but racism in reverse and the 'positive' commodification of the native, it is nevertheless concomitant with the dominant civilization's questioning of its own worth; it is the sign of a civilization afflicted with a deep "melancholia".[22] Because of their complementarity, the myths of the good and the bad native are indicative of the essential ambivalence of colonial discourse.

IV

Literature as a special kind of discourse is quite obviously capable of contributing its share to the overall discursive formation of colonialism, such as it has just been analyzed in the light of recent theoretical insights, and accordingly Edward Said includes literary texts in his list of discursive practices devoted to promulgating a colonial view of the world: "[...] philosophy, lexicography, history, biology, political and economic theory, novel-writing, and lyric poetry".[23]

What Said fails to recognize by indiscriminately putting literary texts side by side with other more pragmatic discourses is their „Eigensinn" (Jürgen Habermas), i.e. "the relative autonomy of aesthetic production".[24] This means that one would have to pay attention to the mediating qualities of literature in terms of genre, mode and internal structuration, all of which combine to give a specific shape to whatever ideological content they may or may not try to convey. What is at stake here is to make visible their "ideology of form" (Fredric Jameson). This means that no matter what ideology certain literary texts are called upon to reproduce, they submit it to a process of 'transcoding', thus conforming to the old structuralist insight that, in the last resort, form and content are indistinguishable: "Content receives its reality from its structure, and what is called form is a way of organizing the local structures that make up the content."[25]

Quite apart from the possibility of texts involuntarily getting caught up in structural contradictions, there exist numerous literary works that are clearly "interrogative"[26] in purpose in that they are bent on exposing the inviability of certain ideologies. The intimate as well as dialectical relationship existing between literature and ideology, and the important part played by literature in reproducing the ideology prevalent in a given society, becomes evident in Tzvetan Todorov's insight that "[...] une société choisit et codifie les actes qui correspondent au plus près à son idéologie; c'est pourquoi l'existence de certains genres dans une société, leur absence dans une autre sont révélatrices de cette idéologie et nous permettent de l'établir avec une plus ou moins grande certitude."[27] Bearing this in mind I now wish to examine three specimens of genres typically employed to encode the colonial mentality from the earlier stages of South African literature in English.

V

In his magisterial study *Culture and Imperialism* Edward Said maintains that stories of adventure and discovery "[...] stand guard over the imagination of the New World"[28], i.e. the quest or voyage motif has proved to be of particular importance for non-literary as well as literary manifestations of colonial control and authority. The literary code most consistently employed for this purpose has been, right from the beginning, the one established by the genre of quest-romance. It is not for nothing that one of the most virulent metaphors used to express the need for the cognitive as well as physical appropriation of the colonial *terra incognita*, the "blank space" of Conradian fame, should have been the one of *mapmaking*.[29] Explorations of the interior with a view to charting the terrain therefore form a very important discursive strand within the general context of colonial discourse[30], and the tale of adventure, cast in the mould of the quest-romance, is the literary extension or continuation of this type of discourse. Gareth Cornwell has gone so far as to suggest that the novel of adventure was "the literary adjutant of Empire"[31], transmitting to a largely metropolitan readership the 'truth' or 'reality' of imperial conquest. There are a few salient features that make the genre singularly suited for imperial purposes, as we shall see. It is no surprise, therefore, that the adventure story should have flourished in South Africa throughout the latter part of the second half of the last century, mostly connected with the names of Victorian writers like William Charles Scully, John Buchan, G.A. Henty, Ernest Glanville or Rider Haggard, and the genre has persisted right until the present time with novelists like Laurens van der Post, Stuart Cloete or Wilbur Smith acting as more contemporary exponents.

A novel like Henry Rider Haggard's (1856-1925) *Allan Quatermain* (1887)[32] will serve as a prototypical example of the romantic 'frontier tale' because it exhibits all the specific traits of the genre. First of all, there is the 'forward-carrying' momentum (Roland Barthes' "code proairétique") of the quest plot that only gets arrested by the attainment of the final goal. Hence departure and arrival, beginning and end, fulfill an important function in demarcating the syntagmatic boundaries of the story. Within those rigid boundaries, however, the romance is rather loosely structured. Whereas in more realistic plots the narrative difference between the initial and the final situation, for instance with regard to the hero's fortunes, has to be made interactionally and psychologically plausible in the sense of explaining why and how such a change has come about, this kind of causal logic or "motivation", as the Russian formalists have called it, is totally absent in the in the present case.[33] One episode just follows another: The decision to leave England for Africa, the first conflicts with the native tribes; the bloody battle at the Mission and its various stages; the perilous journey into the interior; the encounter with the Zu-Vendi nation, a mysterious white tribe somewhere in the middle of Africa; the events associated therewith, such as Quatermain's fellow explorers, Good and Curtis, falling in love with "the Sister Queens" Nyleptha and Sorais, plus the various intrigues and battles ensuing from this.

This sequence of events, so haphazardly strung together and following no other logic than that of a purely temporal "and then"[34], is the Barthesian "structure diagrammatique" of the ultimate lack of causality of the adventure tale. This is neatly summed up in the way Quatermain outlines his proposed route to his fellow travellers at the very beginning:

> Now listen. What I propose is this. That we go to Lamu and thence make our way about 250 miles inland to Mt Kenia; from Mt Kenia on inland to Mt Lekakisera, another 200 miles, or thereabouts, beyond which no white man has to the best of my belief ever been; and then, if we get so far, right on into the unknown interior. What do you say to that, my hearties? (p. 12)

The motivation for the entire venture is sheer *wanderlust*, or as Quatermain puts it: "We want a change of scene, and we are likely to get one – a thorough change." (p. 12). Accordingly, 'change' as well as 'coincidence' are the narrative principles propelling the action and the characters. As soon as one episode is over, the story moves on to the next one, especially when some coincidence brings about a new turn of events, as in the political as well as amourous intrigues between the Sister Queens or the changing fortunes of war in the battle scenes.

This potentially endless metonymic deferral of adventurous desire – theoretically any romance could go on and on with ever new permutations of basically the same adventures – only gets arrested by the rather willful imposition of an end which marks the final destination of the quest. In *Allan Quatermain* the search for a "lost white race" deep in the heart of Africa finds its consummation when one of Quatermain's companions, Sir Henry Curtis, in true romantic fashion, gets married to Queen Nyleptha of the Zu-Vendi: The plot thus conforms to the cyclical movement of perilous descent (in the present case quite literally into an underworld network of subterranean caves) and jubilant ascent typical of the genre.[35]

This is the happy ending that so effectively frames the story and towards which, like a river, all the events and actions, in spite of their apparent randomness, have to take their course. It is at this point that the semantics of colonial discourse get grafted onto the seeming superficiality and absence of meaning of the adventure plot in which confrontation with all kinds of enemies is the most recurring narrative syntagm: Whatever new situation the adventurers may find themselves in, they have to fight their way through. Northrop Frye has suggested that the aggressive actionism of romance with its insistence on fighting and killing is deeply symbolic of an ascendant class or society, and if one takes into account that all of the fighting is done in a good cause, then what initially looks like wanton aggressiveness automatically becomes converted into idealized, as well as justifiable, acts of protection and responsibility which, in the present case, amount to a justification of British imperial rule over the lesser breeds.[36] One only has to replace the slaying of dragons and the saving of damsels in distress of classical romance with the appropriate acts of colonial conquest – subduing the savages, saving white women from their clutches, and so on – for this to become strikingly evident. Accordingly, an adventure story like the present one is capable of "incorporat[ing] the dreams of British imperialism"[37], in that Curtis' marriage with the, in spite of her white skin, rather barbarous Queen Nyleptha is expected to temper her native cruelty through exposure to the beneficial influence of the Christian English Gentleman. Especially the rather 'uncivilized' propensity of the Zu-Vendi for internecine warfare is to be remedied, as Curtis in his new role as Queen Consort suggests, through a governmental reform designed to strengthen the role of the central government and weaken that of the 'heathen' priesthood. The very culmination of the civilizing mission of the *Pax Britannica* would be to introduce the Christian religion, or as Curtis puts it: "I yet hope to see the shadow of the cross of Christ lying on the golden dome of the Flower Temple" (p. 275).

Here adventure becomes invested with the dignity of the civilizing mission in order to justify the bloody business of imperial conquest, or as Quatermain puts it: "But then that is what Englishmen are, adventurers to the backbone; and all our magnificent muster-role of colonies [...] testifies to the extraordinary spirit of adventure which at first sight looks like a mild form of lunacy." (p. 94) Therefore the chance element inherent in the semantics of 'adventurer' – "[...] he who goes out to meet whatever may come" (p. 94) – gets subsumed under the teleological concept of "Providence" (p. 94) – Britain's imperial role. Even though the story may thus – in accordance with the generic rules of romance – appear to strike, in the end, a comfortable balance between prospective contingency and retrospective necessity, the structural contradiction is there all the same – the self-serving and random forward drive of the adventure plot (which could easily be supplanted by the equally as self-serving economic motive of colonialism) stands in stark contrast with the meaningfulness of the fulfilled civilizing mission. All this points to an internal conflict or "complexité réelle" (Pierre Macherey) within the structure of the adventure tale that the ideological project of colonial discourse is so intent on glossing over.

Because of the confrontational nature of its action, however, adventure romance literally lends itself to a neatly ideological division of the world into good and bad, as has been observed by Fredric Jameson.[38] Put otherwise, in the measure that the colonized Other gets denigrated the colonizing self gets valorized. This is transformed into narrative structure mainly by means of a magical conception of the usual "parcours syntagmatique" (A.J. Greimas) of *vouloir*, *savoir* and *pouvoir*: Where in realistic narratives the attempt to move from desiring something to the actual fulfillment of that desire often gets thwarted because the actant's *savoir faire* and abilities prove to be insufficient, this is definitely not the case in a "magical narrative" (Jameson) like adventure romance. Accordingly, Quatermain and his companions, although they may encounter plenty of difficulties, always miraculously manage to overcome all obstacles because of their superior resourcefulness, courage and willpower, whereas their foes are invariably represented as spectacularly lacking in those qualities – the natives are just no match for the English.

On the other hand, as Homi Bhabha has argued, the colonizer can never be entirely certain of his superior identity because of the Hegelian dialectic inherent in the master-slave relationship. It is in this context that the half-redeemed status of the Zu-Vendi and their white skin-colour has to be seen: Within the specular identifying game of the imaginary phase, the colonizer's recognition by the colonized is only worth getting if the other is not entirely worthless, in the sense that he must be deserving of the colonizer's civilizing efforts, or else these would be rendered meaningless. By the same token the Africa represented in the novel is strangely double-edged by vacillating between utopian delights and dystopian horrors. There are several passages where Quatermain, in his capacity as first person narrator, voices some of the more typical Victorian anxieties culminating in an explicit civilizatory *ennui* which is particularly prominent in the "Introduction" (pp. 3-6). In going to Africa the adventurer, therefore, speaks of throwing himself "in the arms of nature" (p. 6). Sometimes he even strikes an almost Carlylean note when he castigates an England dominated by the cash-nexus: "How can a world be good in which Money [sic!] is the moving power, and self-interest the guiding star?" (p. 269) A heroically romanticized Africa, therefore, stands for the liberation from the reality principle, and it is the genre of quest-romance that is the apt expression of "[...] the search of the libido or desiring self for [...] fulfillment".[39]

This implicitly erotic motive becomes most evident in the metaphoric substitution of Africa with the female principle: „Ein sonderbares Buch," says Sigmund Freud about Haggard's novel *She*, „aber voll von verstecktem Sinn

[...], das ewig Weibliche, die Unsterblichkeit unserer Affekte [...]."[40] Africa as woman, woman as Africa – this is a topos that keeps recurring throughout the history of South African literature, and colonial conquest is thereby put on a par with "[...] man's desire of mastery over woman."[41] In keeping with this all three English adventurers in *Allan Quatermain* cannot take their eyes off the female Zu-Vendians, especially the Sister Queens. There are frequent archly coy references to their "ivory skin", their "deeply blue eyes" or their custom of wearing a Cretan-style toga that leaves their right breast uncovered. This erotic fascination is intermingled with civilized disgust, as for instance when Nyleptha summarily wants to have a servant put to death for a minor offence (pp. 177-178). When the Englishmen interfere on the servant's behalf, the Queen throws a tantrum and is subsequently laid up with a headache for three days, after which time she reappears as sweet and kind as ever before. The message to be derived from this is obvious: Women are rather sweet, but at times they tend to be somewhat wayward and irrational, particularly if it is their time of the month. Curtis, after his marriage to Nyleptha, admits to her "not being perfect" (p. 274) and to her also being "a little *exigeante* at times" (ibid.). However, he is certain of instilling some English good sense into her. This is precisely what, in terms of colonial discourse, Africa stands in need of: having – in spite of possessing a few minor virtues – her numerous faults corrected. The erotic element contained in the ambivalent attitude of the colonizer towards Africa becomes evident in almost all tales of exploration where – suspended between fear and temptation – he feels the irresistible male urge to penetrate ever deeper into the dark interior.

VI

The conflict between the necessity of exercising cognitive, as well as physical, control and the problems of cultural and psychological identity the colonizer finds himself confronted with in his encounter with 'wild nature' and 'the savages', and the difficulties arising from this – that is the subject-matter of a genre which, at least superficially, is far less confrontational than the quest-romance: It is a class of texts that, for want of a better word, goes by the name of "colonial pastoral".[42] An early exponent of this genre is the poet Thomas Pringle (1789-1834) who came to South Africa as leader of the Scottish party of 1820 settlers that were given land grants in the Eastern Cape by the British colonial government. There is one longer piece from Pringle's collection bearing the title *Poems Illustrative of South Africa* (1834)[43] that I wish to analyze in the following.

As opposed to the literature of adventure romance for which Africa is nothing but "[...] an exotic alternative to a 'real' existence elsewhere, and never to be taken entirely seriously in its own right"[44], Pringle's poems tend to be more realistic – if not in result, but by intention. Quite significantly, the adventure romance is the product of writers who, like Haggard, Buchan and others, only stayed in South Africa temporarily and who could therefore well afford to indulge in projections of Africa as an exotic, erotic, heroic etc. alternative to Europe because they ultimately had their roots 'at home' in Britain. The settler, however, is not a fligh-by-night sojourner, but one to whom Africa is an everyday reality in his pursuits as farmer or tradesman, therefore "[...] enforcing negotiations [with the country] on which depend both physical and spiritual survival."[45] This sentiment, transcoded in literary terms, gives rise to an *écriture* which eventually comes to fruition in the shape of one of the most prolific and influential literary genres in South Africa – of what in Afrikaans goes by the name of *plaasroman* (farm novel). All this is, to some extent, foreshadowed in Pringle's literary attempts to come to terms with a situation for whose representation he – a minor Scottish romantic poet who was a contemporary of Scott, Campbell and Wordsworth – was somewhat ill equipped given the symbolic systems at his disposal for such an enterprise of colonial mimesis.[46] "How oft 'tis said, 'this is a songless land.'" – thus runs a famous and much quoted line by the South African poet Francis Carey Slater (1876-1958). What is adumbrated here is the challenge with which English poetry in the Cape was faced right from the beginning – the vast emptiness of the landscape and the intractibility of its inhabitants, both of whom appear, as Pringle himself puts it in his poem "Cape of Storms", as "naked", "cheerless", "fierce" and "faithless". This is, quite evidently, not the stuff that new Arcadias are made of, and it is consequently no surprise that, unlike in America with its myth of 'the Virgin Land', the edenic or adamic myth of mankind reborn or paradise regained should never have gained currency in Africa: "[...] Africa was not a new world."[47]

Even so, it is new to the settler, and hence there are some good reasons why in South African poetry "The dominant concerns were topographic and ethnographic"[48]: First of all there was the problem, in an essentially alien environment, "[...] of finding a language to fit Africa, a language that will be authentically African."[49], thereby allowing the colonial to identify with Africa, or, in the words of another South African poet, Jeremy Cronin, "To learn how to speak/With the voices of the land". Secondly, there was the colonial inferiority complex born of the fear that the colonial material might be "[...] too exiguous for the European [literary] form".[50] This fear derived from the fact that European literature developed its codes from its interaction with a dense and complicated network of historically grown social relations that was more or less entirely missing in a colonial context – hence the emphasis on what was genuinely new and original, namely a strange landscape peopled by even stranger humans. This emphasis, in its turn, caused early colonial versification to link up with travel writing with which it shared its desire cognitively to appropriate what appeared as strange.

This is the more general context in which Pringle's poem, "The Emigrant's Cabin. An Epistle in Rhyme" (1822), takes its place. The epistle takes the form of an imaginary dialogue between P. (i.e. Pringle) and F. (his old Scottish friend John Fairbairn). The literary code the poem invokes is that of the pastoral which gets adapted to a colonial situation: Fairbairn, who represents a 'metropolitan' British viewpoint, takes the part of what in Classical or Renaissance pastoral would have been that of the city dweller, whereas Pringle, as the colonial, casts himself in the role of the person who fled from the bustle of the city to lead an existence of rustic simplicity and honest (but not back-breaking) labour. The latter sentiment, incidentally, is an attempt to pass off as civilizatory *ennui* what was primarily motivated by economic considerations since Pringle, like so many other settlers, left Britain because he was in dire straits financially. However this may be, the poem starts with the following idyllic scene:

Where the young river, from its wild ravine,
Winds pleasantly through Eildon's pastures green, –
With fair acacias waving on its banks,
And willows bending o'er in graceful ranks,
And the steep mountain rising close behind,
To shield us from the Snowberg's wintry wind, –
Appears my rustic cabin, thatched with reeds,
Upon a knoll amid the grassy meads;
And close behind it, looking o'er the lea,
Our summer-seat beneath an umbra tree.

The diction is as clearly romantic ("knoll", "meads", "lea") as the descriptive mode is picturesque, which in painting can be defined as follows: "Landscape is picturesque when it composes itself, or is composed by the viewer, in receding planes".[51] The opening stanza, allowing for the peculiarities of linguistic representation, more or less completely conforms to this definition; because linguistic description is faced with the problem of expressing in terms of its linear temporality that which is spatial and non-temporal, the poet employs an old trick in order to submit the contemporaneous visual world to a temporal schema by causing the reader, in his imagination, to follow the course of the river [the Pringle family settled in the Baviaans River Valley]: From the background of the dark ravine, with the Sneeuberg in the far distance, to the middle plane showing the cottage and the summer seat in the foreground.

In his famous essay "The Picturesque and the South African Landscape"[52] John M. Coetzee has argued that all landscape painting, as well as writing, in South Africa were doomed to failure because of the utter incommensurability of the African landscape with an aesthetics that was developed upon a totally different material which lent itself to the framing effect of the picturesque. By contrast, the South African landscape is, in the Kantian sense of the term, "sublime", i.e. in its emptiness it defies all representation, "[...] it refuses to emerge into meaningfulness as a landscape of signs."[53] This means that Pringle, in idyllizing the landscape, submits it to a semiotic system that is clearly metropolitan: Like any colonizer from Columbus onwards he only sees what he wants to see, and therefore he expresses, in truly colonial fashion, everything in terms of what he already knows, thereby reducing the alterity of the unknown. It is not for nothing that the 'reality effect' thus produced should have been criticized by all postcolonial theorists as the most insidious form of exercizing colonial control – it is an act of "kidnapping language".[54]

I have analyzed the opening stanza in such detail because its effect of civilizing the wilderness sets the tone of the ensuing dialogue which is determined by Fairbairn's implicit charge that, in having removed himself to Africa, Pringle has succumbed to the allure of barbarism, which would be something deeply 'anti-pastoral' because the pastoral approach to nature is, paradoxically, a highly civilized one. Pringle, of course, is at pains to refute the charge of barbarism by demonstrating that the exact contrary is the case. He therefore emphasizes that the nature he is forced to live in close contact with is a highly benificent one, and that, even though having renounced the bustle of metropolitan Britain (in his case Edinburgh), he does not lead a life of unrefined laziness. Accordingly, he ticks off his list of cultural achievements: His cabin, although simple, has 'all mod. cons.', it is "clean-swept, and cool", and the imaginary visitor is invited to take a seat on "a jointed stool" or recline on a "couch of leopard skin". Fairbairn, though grudgingly admitting that the cabin is "snug enough", points out a few of its shortcomings, especially that Pringle's home-made furniture that he is so proud of is nothing but "rough-hewn sticks and spars". Next comes the question of the culinary delights Africa has to offer when Fairbairn asks "how manage ye for food?". To this Pringle retorts by presenting the "best bill of fare" the land has to offer – an abundance of food, mutton, fowl, venison, fruit, that would put any British farmer's table to shame ("A pauw, which beats your Norfolk turkey hollow"). Even local wine, "the old *Kaap smaak*", is there to lighten the spirit.

Even though Fairbairn seems half-convinced of the fact that his friend has not degenerated to the depths of barbarism, he feels himself constrained, after the ladies have left the dinner-table, to enquire after the state of intellectual affairs in the Colony:

> But can the comforts of your wattled den,
> Your sylvan fare and the rustic tasks, suffice
> For one who seemed finer joys to prize?

This is a serious charge, indeed. Obviously a man cannot just leave British culture behind and rest content, like a brute, to have a roof over his head and a full stomach. Correspondingly, Fairbairn invokes the very best metropolitan culture has to offer in order to point out a serious deficiency of colonial life: "like Vergil's swains", i.e. in true pastoral fashion, the friends used to sit on the banks of the rivers Esk or Tweed (one should note here the way in which Scottish culture is equated with that of Imperial Rome) and converse on finer matters, but how does he fare now in terms of intellectual intercourse? The seriousness of the charge of having relapsed into intellectual torpor draws from Pringle a veritable barrage of arguments: He takes Fairbairn on an intellectual *tour d'horizon* of the whole northern part of the Eastern Cape – from Craddock to Graaff-Reinet and back again via Somerset (i.e. Somerset-East), naming every dignitary – judges, colonial officials, gentlemen farmers, missionaries – pointing out the excellence of each and every one, and specifying which particular intellectual need of his each person satisfies.

Then, without the least provocation on Fairbairn's part, Pringle raises the matter of work, thereby anticipating possibly the worst charge, namely that the pastoral existence he is leading as a colonial may be nothing but a life of leisure, of sheer uncivilized *otium*. At once he adduces numerous reasons why his farming occupation is a Ciceronian *otium cum dignitate*, if not a downright *negotium*:

> Nor wild Romance nor Pride allured me here:
> Duty and destiny with equal voice
> Constrained my steps: I had no other choice.

Having cleared up that matter, he then goes on to relate what he conceives of as his duty, which is principally that of the civilizing mission, although of a more benign nature than in the 'High Imperialism' of adventure romance:

> For in this wilderness there's work to do;
> Some purpose to accomplish for the band
> Who left with me their much loved Father-Land;
> Something for the sad Natives of the soil,
> By stern oppression doomed to scorn and toil;
> Something for Africa to do or say –
> If but one mite of Europe's debt to pay –
> If but one bitter tear to wipe away.

What he does here is to distance himself from the oppressive regime the indigenes previously had to suffer at the hands of the Dutch colonial government and the thoughtless cruelty of the Boer-farmers of the region. What he cannot fail to raise in this context, however mildly disposed towards the blacks he may feel, is the vexed question of who is actually going to *do* the work to be done both on behalf of the Scottish settlers and the poor natives. On the one hand he professes a great deal of sympathy for the blacks – he counts the

Xhosa "Among earth's noblest sons" and muses about the fact that they appear to him as "*our* sires appeared in Caesar's eyes". On the other hand, a nasty suspicion raises its head: "The 'work' Pringle has in mind will increasingly depend [...] on the 'toil' of the subjected races."[55]

This means that any colonial encounter is perforce a violent one, however charitably the settlers may be disposed towards the natives. In spite of his commitment to the Anti-Slavery Campaign and his stylization of the Xhosa as Noble Savages – what Pringle cannot get around participating in is the old South African drama, "[...] the great drama of appropriation and dispossession that South African writing in English has been enacting for so long."[56] In Pringle's poem that drama is remarkably low-key: When a few Xhosa of the AmaTembu tribe with their chief Powana visit the Scottish settlement, he talks of this being "a friendly visit" and he invites the Xhosa to "smoke the Pipe of Peace with Scottish men", and he asks him to stay overnight; accordingly he instructs one servant: "Prepare the Stranger's bed/in the spare hut, – fresh strewn with fragrant hay." Peaceful and on equal terms though the encounter may seem to be, there occurs one important slip in Pringle's discourse that unwittingly reveals a subtext that he is at pains to repress: He calls the AmaTembu chief, to whom the land he settles on originally belonged, a "stranger", which is tantamount to calling someone a stranger in his own house. The subtext repressed here is one of armed conflict over the same land, a continued strife that was to last for over seventy years, and that required seven (!) 'Kaffir wars' to be fought in order to quell the Xhosa's resistance.[57] That relations are not all that friendly as he claims them to be one can see from the fact that Pringle is initially alarmed about the AmaTembu being "armed" and "in earnest talk" with his servant, so he rather anxiously "mark[s] their mien". Only after their (initially doubtful) good intentions have been verified does the much vaunted friendly spirit reign. There is, however, no getting away from the fact that the "destiny" the 1820 settler claims for himself, automatically implies the "doom" of the Xhosa and the other dispossessed peoples of the Cape such as the Khoi and San who are almost extinct by that time or have already been fed into the labour process as 'Hottentots' such as the servant girl or the shepherd mentioned in the poem, a fate that also lies in store for the Xhosa.

What is the conclusion to be drawn from all this? On the one hand Pringle's poem is in many ways a typical representative of colonial discourse in that he brings everything and everyone within the purview of his controlling, dominating colonial gaze, at the same time marginalizing, however innocently, the Other. On the other hand his discourse is fraught with uncertainties: It is one of the justificatory commonplaces of every colonial conquest that the colonizer's rightful claim to the land he takes away from the feckless savages lies in his turning the land to good use, i.e. cultivating and tilling the soil that has hitherto lain fallow. The moment, however, the Marxian definition of *praxis*, of converting nature into culture, does not apply because it is not the colonizer himself but the subjected objects of empire who do the work, then his right to the land becomes ethically untenable.[58] Especially the ideal of the pastoral invoked in the poem requires at least a small input of work, and the undeniable history of sloth in South Africa marks the failure on the part of the settler to live up to this ideal.

Another reason for a good deal of colonial unease lies in the secondary nature of the poet's culture vis-à-vis the metropolitan one he is so intent upon imitating, thus causing his position to be marked by a Derridean 'doubleness'. This becomes evident in the way he continually emulates British culture with the crude means at his disposal without ever quite making it: the rickety furniture, the lack of culinary refinement counterbalanced by sheer quantity, the close friends it takes eight days' journey to see, all this points to the fact that any colonial culture is but a poor substitute for the metropolitan original, it is "the same but not quite" (Homi Bhabha). This is what lies at the heart of the colonial's lack of 'centredness', of identity: the contradiction between his on the one hand "[...] moving out to civilize what must be seen as inarticulate"[59], on the other hand his "[...] feeling impelled by the inherent deficiencies of colonial life to return 'home'."[60] – if not bodily, so at least intellectually.

It has to be borne in mind that Pringle's discourse with Fairbairn is an imaginary one – they meet, as the speaker says, "in Fancy's bower" – and the poem, far from being a real dialogue between real people, is a typical specimen of „Rollenlyrik“[61], i.e. a fictitious dialogue enacted between two conflicting selves – colonial vs. metropolitan – striving for dominance within the lyrical I that, at one or two removes, can be equated with the poet Pringle. That the internal contradiction should remain unresolved is not surprising in view of the literary mode employed: Even in a European context the pastoral was conceived of as utopian, an ideal never to be realized. The application of this ideal to the infinitely harsher conditions of South Africa is even less viable, thereby exposing the representation of the settlers in terms of arcadian inhabitants of an idyllic landscape, leading simple but refined lives, watching their herds, tilling the soil and living in harmony with nature as a figment of the imagination, a purely intellectual schema as alien to Africa as the English language with its romanticized "leas" and "meads".

In the last resort, the settlers in South Africa are, therefore, extremely "unsettled settlers"[62], people to whom applies what Laura Trevelyan, the central character in one of the greatest novels of colonial conquest and its strange reverses, Patrick White's *Voss*, has to say about her native Australia: "It is not my country, although I have lived in it." This is the most succinct expression of the colonial subject's predicament: It is doubly "displaced" (Homi Bhabha) in being far from home and, in spite of its urge to control and dominate, in being a self that is 'split off' from itself, a self upon which the alienating forces of the Other (another climate, another landscape, other human inhabitants) impinge in unforeseen ways.[63]

VII

One of the most persistent literary genres in South Africa both in Dutch/Afrikaans and English has been, as already indicated, the *plaasroman* or farm novel. The prevalence of that genre has something to do with the fact that, after the initial colonial phases of conquering and exploring – as represented in *Allan Quatermain* – and a rather tenuous hold on the land – as in "The Emigrant's Cabin" – it is the most suitable literary code in which to negotiate what in a stable and historically more advanced colonial society is of prime importance, namely to justify and perpetuate the appropriation of the land. "Land is ownership, and in colonial times land was allocated according to the laws of the colonists, and disregarding the customs of the original inhabitants. The law and its justification for ownership was synonymous with power."[64] This alliance of the law with power became most brutally clear in the 1913 Native Land Act which, at one stroke, debarred blacks from owning land, thus creating a vast, uprooted proletariat that could easily be fed into the labour market. Even though the title deeds of the land the colonizer has thus been able to acquire may be legally valid, there does lurk at the back of his mind the lingering suspicion that before he or his ancestors appeared on the scene, the land to which he holds the legal title was someone else's grazing ground, and that, in the last resort, he is something of an interloper. Bearing this in mind, the farm novel is the apt literary codification of a fairly advanced stage of the South African drama of dispossession and appropriation mentioned above, and the farm with its fenced-in territory stands metonymically for South Africa at large. It is thus symbolic of the colonizer's urge to control and subdue the wilderness so as to make it manageable, or as Jacobus Coetzee, the central character of the second part of John M. Coetzee's novel *Dusklands* puts it:

> We cannot count the wild. The wild is one because it is boundless. We can count fig-trees, we can count sheep because the orchard and the farm are bounded. The essence of orchard and farm sheep is number. Our commerce with the wild is a tireless enterprise of turning it into orchard and farm. When we cannot fence it and count it we reduce it to number by other means.[65]

Inclusion within the fence therefore means ownership for the colonizer, who thereby *excludes* and marginalizes those to whom the land used to belong, without their knowing such a concept of ownership, by means of drawing boundaries.[66] The circumstance that the dispossessed are only granted admittance to the land within the pale in their capacity as workers, again raises the delicate matter of the proprietary role played by work, as discussed earlier on in the context of Pringle's idealized vision where, however, work was more an object of philosophical speculation than something that really had to be done.

In the more realistic mode of the farm novel, by contrast, it would have to be made more specific in the sense of showing how work in the day-to-day running of the farm is divided up, and what kind of work is done by whom. This also, at least implicitly, poses the problem whether "[...] those inherit the earth who make the best use of it."[67] So in the farm novel the questions of ownership and work are closely interconnected.

Because of the problems it is, through its specific code, capable of addressing, the farm novel has proved to be an extremely effective gearbox for transmitting and giving meaning to those problematic areas that are of central importance to the South African body politic. Therefore, it is also the one genre that genuinely grew out of the South African experience. This means that in addressing that experience, there was no falling back on aesthetic models brought in from outside, from the metropolis, but that it meant discovering the colonial context as one which, because of its inherent qualities, was worthy of literary representation. The farm novel thus plays an important part in reclaiming for South Africa what in America goes by the name of 'Native Muse', a voice distinctly South African. In some respects the farm novel is the South African variety of a genre that in British literature is designated as 'domestic novel' because of its supposedly realistic depiction of everyday middle-class life. This is definitely a departure from the chauvinistic heroism of the adventure tale as well as from the facile idealizations of the pastoral.

Olive Schreiner's (1855-1920) *The Story of an African Farm* (1883)[68] is commonly assumed to be the first novel in English written in South Africa by a South African. The descriptive opening of the novel is strangely double-edged by showing the eponymic sheep farm in two different kinds of light: The first view of the farm, in a kind of cinematographic sweep, is in the light of "the full African moon" (p. 26) which, because it "lovingly hid defects" (p. 30), almost makes the homestead conform to the picturesque through a scenic composition with a careful arrangement of foreground and background. The overall effect is one of "a kind of dreamy beauty" (p. 29), and the reader is obviously meant to conceive of the quiet moonlit farm with its peacefully sleeping population, whether human or animal, as 'home' in the sense of a place not only providing food and shelter but also a sense of belonging, of permanence and human companionship.

This impression, however, is dispersed in what can be regarded as the novel's second opening when the farm is shown in the glare of the relentless Karoo sun beating down: "The farm by daylight was not the farm by moonlight."(p. 32) This is the negation of everything the homestead by night might be made to stand for: What could initially pass as "a kind of beauty" is now converted to an empty landscape ("the plain") devoid of vegetation ("No tree or shrub was to be seen far or near." [p. 32]), and the homeliness previously evoked has given way to a sense of primitive shabbiness ("the red walls", "the zinc roofs" [p. 32]). This double beginning informs the "code herméneutique" (Roland Barthes) underlying the entire novel by begging the question why and by what means the inhabitants are capable of turning the farm into a home where people have their roots - physically, emotionally and culturally. Put otherwise, the double beginning renders the farm strangely ambivalent, thus investing its status as a kind of spatial actant within the story to be told with a sense of "le double" (Julia Kristeva) so that none of its inhabitants are capable of forming a lasting impression of its qualities as 'home'.

There are five people initially living on the farm: the fat Boer woman Tant' Sannie, her stepdaughter Emily, Emily's orphan-cousin Lyndall, the old German overseer and his son Waldo. In addition, there are a few temporary sojourners, especially Bonaparte Blenkins, the Irish impostor who, with his blustering cowardice, is a parodic intertextual reference to the imperial adventurer of Haggard fame, and Gregory Rose, Em's fiancé and later husband. The presumably large contingent of black workers only get mentioned in passing as the inhabitants of the "kaffir huts" (p. 29) within the precinct of the farm. What is surprising in the first exponent of a genre whose main concern is with staying put in one place or with the right of residence, is the fact that the main narrative verbs propelling the action are 'arriving' and 'leave taking', or in A.J. Greimas' terminology, the semantic opposition of 'the farm as home' and 'the farm as non-home' gets projected onto the syntagmatic plane as a succession of "syntagmes contractuels" and "syntagmes disjonctionels".

This theme of entering into a lasting kind of relationship versus the impossibility of doing so is sounded in the first dialogue between Em and Lyndall when the latter is asking her cousin:

> 'And you think that I am going to stay *here* always?'
> The lip trembled scornfully.
> 'Ah, no,' said her companion. 'I suppose some day we shall go somewhere; but now we are only twelve, and we cannot marry till we are seventeen. Four years, five - that is a long time to wait.[...]'
> 'And you think that I am going to stay here till then?'
> 'Well, where *are* you going?' asked her companion. (p. 38)

There is a strange conflict in the daydreaming of the two girls about their future between somehow wishing to get away from so desolate a place, and of wanting to stay on the other hand, of somehow having to make a go, however resignedly, of living on the farm for good which is far removed from the cozy, oldworldly concept of 'home is where the heart is'.

The first new arrival on the farm is Blenkins who, through courting Tant' Sannie, ousts the old German from his job as overseer. Next he also manages to drive Waldo from the farm, only to be driven off himself a short while later after having fallen from Tant' Sannie's grace. Next Tant' Sannie moves to a neighbouring farm after getting married. Then Lyndall leaves for Cape Town, only to come back on a short visit (when she also meets Waldo) and never to return thereafter. Another new arrival is Greg Rose who, however, leaves in pursuit of Lyndall with whom he has fallen in love and whom he, later on, nurses until her death. Greg eventually returns to the farm where Em has been the only – and lonely – permanent sojourner, as does Waldo after a long itinerant period spent as a transport rider, and who, after having heard of Lyndall's fate, dies himself. Accordingly the novel ends on an extremely pessimistic note as to the fulfillment of human aspirations:

> Well, to die then; for, if you live, so surely as the years come, so surely as the spring succeeds winter, so surely will passions arise. They will creep back, one by one, into the bosom that has cast them forth, and fasten there again, and peace will go. Desire, ambition, and the fierce agonizing flood of love for the living – they will spring again. Then Nature will draw down her veil: with all your longing you shall not be able to raise one corner; you cannot bring back those peaceful days. Well to die then! (p. 279)

The authorial comment only systematizes what the story, in its unfolding, is all about: Man is nothing but a wanderer upon the face of the earth, engaged in a constant quest for meaning and permanence without ever getting there. The suitable emblem for this ever renewed cyclical quest, for arriving and going away again, is the sea with its surf constantly breaking and receding, to which Waldo feels himself strangely drawn when he first gets to see the Indian Ocean. (p. 238)

That the inhabitants of the farm are settlers unsettled in the extreme also becomes evident in the way they work upon the land. That theirs is not the kind of farm work capable of reclaiming the land from its inert state of nature by cultivating it is underlined by the kind of farming they are engaged in, namely sheep farming. The way that activity is represented in the novel comes very close to being total inactivity. Obviously the sheep, "a small and dusty herd" (p. 32), require very little work:

> His flock gave him [Waldo] little trouble. It was too hot for them to move far; they gathered round every little milk-bush as though they hoped to find shade, and stood there motionless in clumps. He himself crept under a shelving rock that lay at the foot of the 'kopje' [Afrikaans for 'hillock'], stretched himself on his stomach, and waved his dilapidated little shoes in the air. (p. 33)

So, most of the day is spent dozing and daydreaming, and the settlers are little or no better than the Hottentots whom they always charged with being idle, indolent, slothful and lazy – in other words barely human.[69] The same applies to the other inhabitants, for instance Tant' Sannie who is too fat to move anyway, or Blenkins who delegates what little work there is either to Waldo or the native servants. What is represented with this state of affairs is something that throughout the whole history of colonial discourse had been feared most, i.e. that the colonizers might not prove worthy or capable of the civilizing mission conferred upon them, that they might relapse into barbarism – just like Crusoe who, instead of cultivating his plantation, would simply prefer to doze in the sun, living upon gathered fruit and mussels. This also means that there is very little justification for having taken the land away from the indigenes. This is, then, what in the present case the civilizing mission has come to: a few bedraggled sheep, a few ramshackle buildings in a primal landscape that has not changed in thousands of years, and one can easily follow J.M. Coetzee's assessment that "[...] the farm mimes the idleness, ignorance, and greed of colonial society. To Schreiner the Cape Colony, and perhaps all colonies, are in truth anti-Gardens, dystopias."[70] The first farm novel to have been written in South Africa in the English language is thus a rather prescient analysis of a terrific failure of the whole enterprise of colonialism, thus proving to be postcolonial *avant la lettre*.

The much vaunted claim to realism of Schreiner's farm novel that Stephen Gray attributes to the fact that, in the present case, Africa, the "once mystically exotic inland of the adventure story" had become "the datum of existence"[71] for characters like Waldo, Em or Lyndall is somewhat dubious. Certainly *African Farm* is realistic, as has been shown, by engaging, in conformity with the tradition of the genre, with a "[...] bewilderingly empirical, 'meaningless', and contingent *Umwelt* – of which [it] [...] will then claim to be the 'realistic' reflection."[72] Quite apart, however, from the truth claim of realism having been deconstructed as being nothing but an artificially produced "effet de réel" (Roland Barthes), there is missing in Schreiner's text the narrative stance so typical of the realist novel: The authorial "meta-discourse" (Colin MacCabe) that, from the vantage point of superior wisdom integrates and orders the diversity of all the other social, psychological, professional, institutional etc. discourses to form one coherent representation of the world. As opposed to this, Schreiner's story is a highly complex text consisting of – but never unifying – a host of conflicting representational modes – "[...] allegory, lyricism, mysticism, farce, satire and parable, as well as realism."[73] The "monological" (Mikhail Bakhtin) realistic novel obviously presupposes a stable, homogeneous society which, in a South Africa with its numerous interfering ethnicities who all have a different story of their own to tell, simply does not exist. Therefore her novel is a "discontinuous text" (Wolfgang Iser) made up of various conflicting modes of representation.

VIII

The foregoing analyses of three exemplary texts from the three most important South African literary discourses have been intent on showing that these are all inscribed, one way or another, within the overarching discursive ideology of colonialism. It was also intended to show that literature, through its materiality as doubly encoded language, is capable, even though openly complicit with colonial discourse, of sometimes becoming structurally involved in unwanted contradictions, quite apart from the possibility of being explicitly and downright critical of colonialism as non-viable. It should be noted in this context that the farm novel in its subsequent development as the most virulent South African genre has branched out in two directions – one affirmative, the other critical. The affirmative 'pastoral' branch basically becomes a nostalgic, idealizing celebration of a lost world, a "herinneringskuns"[74] devoted to invoking an idyllic life in cozy Cape Dutch farm houses, an existence of social harmony and of turning, through honest labour, the recalcitrant soil of Africa into a garden. It is typical that in such novels the blacks should be conspicuous absentees. Where in *The Story of an African Farm* at least the outsiders Waldo and Lyndall are aware, through looking at the Bushmen's rock paintings, of the previous existence of indigenes who have been annihilated ("Now the boers have shot them all [...]." [p. 42]) and dispossessed of their land, the 'idyllic' farm novel is intent on carefully repressing the existence of the black labour that went into creating the idyl: "[...] the black man becomes a shadowy presence flitting across the stage now and then to hold a horse or serve a meal."[75] The subtext that gets repressed here is the one that is foreshadowed in Pringle's early version of colonial pastoral, as has been shown.

The most prominent example of later South African pastoral in English is Pauline Smith's (1882-1959) novel *The Beadle* (1926) with its evocation of a benign Dutch farming autocracy in the Aangenaam Valley of the Little Karoo. There is, however, a serpent in *la bonne vallée* of Aangenaam in the person of the Englishman Henry Nind who seduces the Dutch girl Andrina, thereby disrupting the community's old-fashioned way of life. Possession of the land is here again equated with possession of a woman, and the novel has accordingly been read as a story of a continuing chain of dispossession: After the Anglo-Boer war and during the Great Depression, the Dutch/Afrikaners with their subsistence farming economy were increasingly displaced by British investors interested in capitalist modes of agricultural production. In the novel, this contemporary conflict gets both personalized and projected into the past. However, the fate the Dutch are suffering is no different from the one they inflicted, only a few generations ago, on the blacks so that one act of dispossession and appropriation proceeds from the other.[76]

A famous exponent of the critical branch is Percival Gibbon's (1879-1926) novel *Margaret Harding* (1911), a text that contains a clear intertextual reference to Schreiner's *African Farm* and is every bit as caustic in its criticism of colonialism as its pretext: The setting is also that of a farm in the Karoo, in actual fact two adjacent farms, one of which has been converted into a sanatorium for tuberculosis patients from England, and in addition there is Boy Bailey, in his blustering ways an exact copy of Schreiner's caricature of the colonial adventurer. The difference in Gibbon's novel lies in the explicit mention of the natives in that Kamis, a chief's son who as a child was taken to England and later studied medicine at London University, comes back to his old 'home' as an utter stranger; although he does not actually reclaim as his the land now settled upon by the whites, his arrival on the scene throws the entire community into considerable confusion. It is Margaret Harding, the eponymic female protagonist of the novel, who recognizes Kamis' worth both as a human being, as well as a professional man, and befriends him, which in turn causes her to be ostracized by almost everyone. Again the whole situation is emblematic of the non-viability of a colonial situation – the dispossession of the rightful owners of the land, and the sterility, even moribundity of the intruders who, symbolically represented as TB-patients, are doomed to failure right from the start. Quite typically it is a woman, the member of another marginalized majority, who rebels against the prevailing state of affairs and is eventually forced to return to her native England – like the author Gibbon himself who, quite significantly, only had the nerve to write and publish his novel outside South Africa.

IX

The most invidious literary encoding of colonial discourse is certainly manifested in what goes by the designation of 'novel of race', which is mainly connected with the name of Sarah Gertrude Millin (1889-1968) and her novel *God's Step-Children* (1924). Where previously it was skin-colour – in keeping with Frantz Fanon's "epidermal schema" – that served as the basis of racial discrimination, it is now 'blood' or, more specifically, the genes a person inherits that determine his or her worth.[77] In *God's Step-Children*, it is the fate of the offspring of the Rev. Andrew Flood, a missionary who succumbed to temptation and had intercourse with a Hottentot woman, that is followed through several generations, right down to the last one where it is no longer skin-colour, but some inherited deficiency, that causes the person concerned to be branded for life: This shows up colonialism and the identity of the colonizer at its most vulnerable – where racial difference is no longer visible in terms of stereotyped images, the Other is semiotically constructed by having recourse to the semes of 'foreignness', 'mixedness', 'impurity' which are perceived as "transgressive and corrupting"[78] of the colonizer's carefully maintained sense of superiority. This new discursive move with its attending literary codification of 'scientific racism', which eventually led to the systematic racism of apartheid-legislation, was again, like all varieties of colonialism, closely linked to economic considerations:

> The question of how to secure South Africa for the future as a 'white man's country' loomed particularly large in the first decade of this century, as economic expansion and the after-effects of the war brought masses of landless blacks and numbers of poor whites to the towns.[79]

The counter-discourse, although it emerged, as has been shown, fairly early on, became more prominent, widespread and vociferous in later years: Sol T. Plaatje wrote with *Native Life in South Africa* (1916) what amounts to a black South African pastoral, a lament upon a lifestyle destroyed by white expropriation, and in his novel *Mhudi* (1930) he presents the black man's view of the history of white conquest. From today's perspective one can safely say that South African literature, whether by white or black writers, has been locked in the vicious circle of specular fascination, of being fixated – mostly negatively, sometimes positively – on the Other, whether in Nadine Gordimer's liberal attempts at breaking out of this circle or J.M. Coetzee's attempts at deconstructing the South African myths of conquest and of the right of possession: Gordimer's *The Conservationist* (1974) is an apocalyptic contemporary rewriting of the farm novel as is Coetzee's *In the Heart of the Country* (1982), while his novel *Dusklands* (1983) is a postmodern questioning of the whole business of colonial conquest. Most of all, and not surprisingly, all the literary manifestations associated with the Black Consciousness Movement amount to a wholesale refutation of the white settlers' right of abode, eventually culminating in political slogans like "One settler, one bullet", or the political demand reiterated by the PanAfricanist Congress (PAC) time and again: "The land first, all else will follow." – So much by way of indicating to what an extent South African history and literature have throughout been imbricated with the discourse of appropriation and dispossession.

Notes

1 For the full text of the sonnet cf. the anthology edited by J. VanWyk, P. Conradie and N. Constandaras: *Suidafrika in Posie/South Africa in Poetry*, p. 9.
2 M. Pêcheux: *Les vérités*, p. 144.
3 P. de Man: *Resistance*, p. 11.
4 M. Pêcheux: *Les vérités*, p. 144.
5 A. Bové: "Discourse", p. 57.
6 T. Eagleton: *Ideology*, p. 209.
7 M. Foucault: *Les mots*, p. 15.
8 E. Said: *Orientalism*, p. 7.
9 F. Jameson: "Imaginary", 379.
10 Ibid., 369.

11 Ibid., 379.
12 A. R. JanMohammed: "Economy", 63.
13 Ibid., 62.
14 Ibid., 64.
15 H. K. Bhabha: "The other question", p. 154.
16 H. K. Bhabha: "Signs Taken for Wonders", 155.
17 J. Lacan: "Le stade du miroir", p. 91.
18 Cf. O. Mannoni: *Psychologie*, pp. 20ff.
19 P. Brantlinger: *Crusoe's Footprint*, p. 3.
20 J. Kristeva: *Etrangers*, p. 271.
21 Cf. T. Goldie: *Fear and Temptation.*
22 Cf. H. Fink-Eitel: *Die Philosophie und die Wilden*, pp. 56ff.
23 E. Said: *Orientalism*, p. 15.
24 D. Porter: "*Orientalism* and its Problems", p. 153.
25 C. Lévi-Strauss, quoted from R. Con Davis, R. Schleiffer: *Criticism and Culture*, p. 7.
26 C. Belsey: *Critical Practice*, p. 90.
27 T. Todorov: *La notion*, p. 35.
28 E. Said: *Culture*, p. 254.
29 Cf. G. Huggan: "Decolonizing".
30 Cf. M. L. Pratt: *Imperial Eyes.*
31 G. Cornwell: "Novel of Race", p. 76.
32 All quotations will refer to the Puffin Classics edition, London, 1990.
33 Cf. N. Frye: *The Secular Scripture*, pp. 44ff.
34 Ibid., p. 47.
35 Cf. ibid., p. 54.
36 Cf. ibid., pp. 56-57.
37 Ibid., p. 57.
38 F. Jameson: *Political Unconscious*, pp. 103ff.
39 N. Frye: *Anatomy of Criticism*, p. 193.
40 S. Freud: *Traumdeutung*, p. 437.
41 D. Bunn: "Embodying Africa", 14.
42 Cf. D. Klopper: "Politics of the Pastoral".
43 All quotations will refer to the edition by J.R. Wahl, Cape Town, 1970.
44 M. VanWyk Smith: *Grounds of Contest*, p. 9.
45 Ibid.
46 Cf. E. Pereira: "Thomas Pringle".
47 J. M. Coetzee: *White Writing*, p. 2.
48 M. VanWyk Smith: *Grounds of Contest*, p. 19.
49 J. M. Coetzee: *White Writing*, p. 7.
50 Ibid., p. 24.
51 Ibid., p. 39.
52 Ibid., pp. 36-62.
53 Ibid., p. 9.
54 Cf. S. Greenblatt: *Marvellous Posessions*, pp. 86-118.
55 D. Klopper: "Politics of the Pastoral", 37.
56 M. VanWyk Smith: *Grounds of Contest*, p. 130.
57 Cf. Mostert: *Frontier.*
58 Cf. J. M. Coetzee: *White Writing*, pp. 12-35.
59 S. G. M. Ridge: "The Meaning of the Map", 89.

60 Ibid.
61 D. Lamping: *Gedicht*, p. 119.
62 J. M. Coetzee: *White Writing*, p. 4.
63 Cf. H. K. Bhabha: "Signs Taken for Wonders".
64 A. Coetzee: "The South African Farm Novel", p. 13.
65 J. M. Coetzee: *Dusklands*, p. 80.
66 A. Coetzee: "The South African Farm Novel", p. 13.
67 J. M. Coetzee: *White Writing*, p. 3.
68 All quotations will be from A.D. Donker Paper Books edition, Johannesburg, 1986.
69 Cf. J. M. Coetzee: *White Writing*, pp. 12-35.
70 Ibid., p. 4.
71 S. Gray: *Southern African Literature*, p. 156.
72 F. Jameson: *Political Unconscious*, p. 152.
73 S. A. Murray: "Olive Schreiner", p. 22.
74 J. C. Kannemeyer: *Geskiedenis*, II, p. 302.
75 J. M. Coetzee: *White Writing*, p. 5.
76 Cf. M. VanWyk Smith: *Grounds of Contest*, pp. 51ff.
77 Cf. K. A. Appiah: "Race".
78 H. K. Bhabha: "The other question", p. 152.
79 G. Cornwell: "Novel of race", p. 84.

Bibliography

Appiah, K. A.: "Race". – In F. Lentricchia, T. McLaughlin (Eds.): *Critical Terms for Literary Study*. Chicago, 1990, pp. 274-287.

Belsey, C.: *Critical Practice*. London, 1980.

Bhabha, H. K.: "Signs Taken for Wonders: Questions of Ambivalence and Authority". *Critical Inquiry* 12, 1985, 144-165.

–: "The other question: difference, dissemination and the discourse of colonialism". – In F. Barker (Ed.): *Literature, Politics and Theory. Papers from the Essex Conference 1976-1986*. London, 1986, pp. 148-172.

Bové, A.: "Discourse". In F. Lentricchia, T. McLaughlin (Eds.): *Critical Terms for Literary Studies*. Chicago, 1990, pp. 50-56.

Brantlinger, P.: *Crusoe's Footprint. Cultural Studies in Britain and America*. New York, 1990.

Bunn, D.: "Embodying Africa: Women and Romance in Colonial Fiction". *English in Africa* 15, 1988, 1-28.

Coetzee, A.: "The Geneology of the South African Farm Novel, from Land Colonization to Apocalypse". – unpublished manuscript of a lecture held at Essen University in November 1994, 18pp.

Coetzee, J. M.: *White Writing. On the Culture of Letters in South Africa*. Johannesburg, 1988.

Con Davis, R., Schleifer, R.: *Criticism and Culture. The Role of Critique in Modern Literary Theory*. London, 1991.

Cornwell, G.: "The Early South African Novel of Race". – In M. Chapman, C. Gardner, E. Mphahlele (Eds.): *South African English Literature*. Johannesburg, 1992, pp. 75-93.

Eagleton, T.: *Ideology. An Introduction.* London, 1991.

Fink-Eitel, H.: *Die Philosophie und die Wilden.* München, 1994.

Foucault, M.: *Les mots et les choses. Une archéologie des sciences humaines.* Paris, 1966.

Freud, S.: *Die Traumdeutung.* Studienausgabe, vol. II, Frankfurt, 1972.

Frye, N.: *The Anatomy of Criticism.* Princeton, 1957.

–: *The Secular Scripture. A Study in the Structure of Romance.* Cambridge/Mass., 1976.

Goldie, T.: *Fear and Temptation. The Image of the Indigene in Canadian, Australian, and New Zealand Literatures.* Montreal, 1989.

Gray, S.: *Southern African Literature. An Introduction.* Cape Town, 1979.

Greenblatt, S.: *Marvellous Possessions. The Wonders of the New World.* Oxford, [2]1992.

Huggan, G.: "Decolonizing the Map: Post-Colonialism, Post-Structuralism and the Cartographic Connection". – In I. Adam, H. Tiffin (Eds.): *Past the Last Post. Theorizing Post-Colonialism and Post-Modernism.* London, 1991, pp. 125-138.

Jameson, F.: "Imaginary and Symbolic in Lacan". *Yale French Studies* 55-56, 1977, 338-395.

Jameson, F.: *The Political Unconscious. Narrative as a Socially Symbolic Act.* London, [3]1989.

JanMohammed, A. R.: "The Economy of Manichean Allegory: The Function of Racial Difference in Colonialist Literature". *Critical Inquiry* 12, 1985, 59-87.

Kannemeyer, J.C.: *Geskiedenis van die Afrikaanse Literatuur.* 2 vols., Pretoria, 1983.

Klopper, D.: "Politics of the Pastoral: The Poetry of Thomas Pringle". *English in Africa* 17, 1990, 21-59.

Kristeva, J.: *Etrangers à nous-mêmes.* Paris, 1988.

Lacan, J.: "Le stade du miroir comme formateur du Je". – In J. Lacan: *Ecrits I.* Paris, 1966, pp. 89-97.

Lamping, D.: *Das lyrische Gedicht.* Göttingen, 1989.

de Man, P.: *The Resistance to Theory.* Minneapolis, 1986.

Mannoni, O.: *Psychologie de la colonisation.* Paris, 1950.

Mostert, N.: *Frontiers. The Epic of South Africa's Creation and the Tragedy of the Xhosa People.* New York, 1992.

Murray, S.A.: "Olive Schreiner: A Soul Struggling with its Material Surroundings". – In M. Chapman, C. Gardner, E. Mphahlele (Eds.): *South African English Literature.* Johannesburg, 1992, pp. 19-36.

Pêcheux, M.: *Les vérités de La Palice.* Paris, 1975.

Pereira, E.: "Thomas Pringle. An Introductory Guide". – In M. Chapman, C. Gardner, E. Mphahlele (Eds.): *South African English Literature.* Johannesburg, 1992, pp. 1-36.

Porter, D.: "*Orientalism* and its Problems". – In P. Williams, L. Chrisman (Eds.): *Colonial Discourse and Post-Colonial Theory.* London, 1994, pp. 150-171.

Pratt, M. L.: *Imperial Eyes. Travel Writing and Transculturation.* London, 1992.

Ridge, S.G.M.: "The Meaning of the Map. Considerations for a History of South African Literature". *English in Africa* 18, 1991, 87-97.

Said, E.: *Orientalism. Western Concepts of the Orient.* Harmondsworth, [2]1991.

–: *Culture and Imperialism.* London, [2]1994.

Todorov, T.: *La notion de littérature.* Paris, 1987.

VanWyk, J., Conradie, P., Constandaras, N. (Eds.): *Südafrika in Posie/South Africa in Poetry.* Pinetown/South Africa, 1988.

VanWyk Smith, M.: *Grounds of Contest. A Survey of South African English Literature.* Cape Town, 1990.

Marion Gymnich, Köln

Von *Greater Britain* zu *Little England*: Konstruktion und Dekonstruktion imperialistischer Denkweisen in Rudyard Kiplings *Kim*, E. M. Forsters *A Passage to India* und Joseph Conrads *Heart of Darkness*

Ausgehend von der Annahme einer komplexen Wechselwirkung der in fiktionalen Texten erzeugten Wirklichkeitsmodelle und der außerliterarischen Wirklichkeit sind seit dem Aufkommen der postkolonialen Literaturtheorie Ende der 70er Jahre verstärkt die Werke englischer Autoren, die den britischen Imperialismus zum Thema haben, zum Gegenstand revisionistischer Interpretationen geworden. Im Zentrum steht dabei das Verhältnis fiktionaler Texte zum imperialistischen Diskurs. Solche Interpretationen verfolgen das Ziel, die in literarischen Werken implizierten „imperialistische[n] Denk- und Ausdrucksmuster offenzulegen und sie [...] zu hinterfragen."[1] Da der imperialistische Diskurs grundsätzlich ein Diskurs der Ungleichheit ist, der Hierarchisierung von Kolonialherren und einheimischer Bevölkerung, setzt sich postkoloniale Literaturkritik mit der Frage auseinander, wie das historische Faktum der der Kolonialgesellschaft inhärenten Hierarchie im fiktionalen Text gestaltet wird, und ob diese Hierarchie etwa durch Legitimierungsstrategien unterstützt oder ob sie in Frage gestellt wird. Die Hierarchisierung von Kolonialherren und einheimischer Bevölkerung setzt eine klare Dichotomisierung des Eigenen und des Fremden voraus und geht daher mit einer Affinität zur Bildung und Tradierung von Kollektivvorstellungen einher. Die drei im folgenden unter diesen Fragestellungen zu untersuchenden Romane, Rudyard Kiplings *Kim* (1901), E.M. Forsters *A Passage to India* (1924) und Joseph Conrads *Heart of Darkness* (1902) - Werke, die zweifellos zum etablierten Literaturkanon zählen - sind in der Forschung hinsichtlich ihrer Relation zum imperialistischen Diskurs durchaus kontrovers diskutiert worden. Da alle drei Werke im ersten Viertel des 20. Jahrhunderts erschienen sind, können sie im Kontext einer Bilanzierung der imperialen Vergangenheit gesehen werden. In literarischer Form dokumentieren und kommentieren diese Klassiker des britischen Romans jenen komplexen historischen Entwicklungsprozeß, in dessen Zuge die von Charles Dilke geprägte und popularisierte Vision eines *Greater Britain* fragwürdig wurde und der Vorstellung eines *Little England* wich, wie sie bereits in der 2. Hälfte des 19. Jahrhunderts von Gegnern des Imperialismus vertreten wurde.

Rudyard Kiplings *Kim* – sicherlich einer der bekanntesten der englischen Romane, die sich mit der britischen Herrschaft in Indien beschäftigen – ist in der Forschung immer wieder als paradigmatisch für die Konstruktion eines positiven Indienbildes, ja sogar als frei von Stereotypen gesehen worden.[2] Diese Lesart hält jedoch einer kritischen Betrachtung im Sinne postkolonialer Literaturkritik kaum stand, wie vor allem Williams und Said überzeugend gezeigt haben.[3] Der große Anteil indischer Figuren am Romanpersonal und die offensichtliche Konzeption vieler dieser Figuren als Sympathieträger – hier ist vor allem, aber nicht nur, an den Lama sowie Mahbub Ali zu denken – erscheinen zwar auf den ersten Blick als Indikatoren für eine indienfreundliche Darstellung.

Bei einer genaueren Analyse werden jedoch Themen und Strukturen des Romans deutlich, die sich eindeutig auf imperialistische Denkweisen zurückführen lassen. Die Darstellung indischer Figuren als Sympathieträger ändert etwa nichts daran, daß die Einstellungen und Verhaltensweisen indischer und britischer Figuren in einer Weise miteinander kontrastieren, die mit gängigen Stereotypen vom „typisch Orientalischen“ und „charakteristisch Britischen“ korreliert. Diese Kontrastrelation hinsichtlich der Mentalitäten, die im Text durch das verbale und non-verbale Handeln der Figuren sowie durch generalisierende Kommentare der Erzählinstanz etabliert wird, rekurriert beispielsweise auf die Stereotypen, daß Inder -als Orientalen – zu Übertreibungen und Lügen tendierten und irrational, unpünktlich und langsam seien.[4]

Diese Kollektivvorstellungen werden gerade im Zusammenhang mit dem Protagonisten immer wieder angesprochen, dem aufgrund seiner britischen Herkunft und seiner Sozialisation in einer nahezu ausschließlich indischen Umgebung Kennzeichen beider Mentalitäten zugeschrieben werden. Der Erzähler streicht immer wieder heraus, daß Kims Verhaltensweisen typisch britisch bzw. orientalisch seien; dadurch wird betont, daß diese Figur eine ideale Demonstrationsfläche für die Dichotomie von orientalischer und britischer Mentalität bildet. So kann Kim beispielsweise die für den Europäer „natürliche“ Angst vor Schlangen nicht überwinden (S. 91) oder zeigt aufgrund von “the white man's impatience” (S. 126) ein aktiveres Verhalten als die Inder um ihn herum (S. 94, 126, 261). Dagegen manifestiert sich der orientalische Aspekt seiner Persönlichkeit beispielsweise in seiner Fähigkeit, „wie ein Orientale“ zu lügen (S. 71).

Die Tatsache, daß Kim bereits vor der Konfrontation mit europäischen Werten durch den Schulbesuch Verhaltensweisen zeigt, die vom Erzähler als „typisch britisch“ eingestuft werden, verweist auf einen fundamentalen Grundsatz imperialistischen Denkens, auf die Annahme nämlich, daß eine natürliche und unabänderliche Ungleichheit der Rassen bestehe und menschliches Verhalten zumindest in demselben Maße durch die Zugehörigkeit zu einer Rasse wie durch die Sozialisation bestimmt werde.[5] Obgleich ihm vom Erzähler auch orientalische Züge zugeschrieben werden, setzt sich Kim von Handlungsbeginn an durch die Effizienz seines Handelns von seiner Umgebung ab, wenn er sich beispielsweise um den weltfremden Lama kümmert, zunächst noch unwissentlich als Kurier für den britischen Geheimdienst tätig ist oder sogar Mahbub Ali das Leben rettet. Diese Tätigkeiten deuten bereits die Stellung an, die Kim gegenüber den anderen (indischen) Figuren einnimmt: er ist ihnen überlegen. Seine Stellung entspricht daher wohl kaum der eines armen indischen Waisenjungen, sondern viel eher der eines "Sahibs". Dies zeigt sich bereits in der Eingangsszene, in der er einen indischen Jungen von der *Zam-Zammah*, der Kanone, die die Herrschaft über das Punjab symbolisiert, vertreibt; Kim erscheint hier als "emblem of British authority"[6].

Die Überlegenheit des Protagonisten ist zwar ein Merkmal des Abenteuerromans, aber Kims besondere Qualitäten entsprechen den Eigenschaften der anderen britischen Figuren, so daß der Eindruck von der rassischen Überlegenheit der Angelsachsen vermittelt wird. So lenkt Colonel Creighton souverän das *great game*, d.h. die Aktivitäten des britischen Geheimdienstes in Indien, und der Kurator des Lahore Museums demonstriert sein überlegenes Wissen, indem er den Lama, einen buddhistischen Gelehrten, über den Buddhismus, also dessen eigene Religion, belehrt, was von dem Belehrten mit Bewunderung aufgenommen wird.[7] Im Gespräch mit dem Lama beweist der Kurator außerdem die Überlegenheit europäischer Technik, denn er schenkt ihm eine neue Brille, die wesentlich leichter ist und deren Gläser nicht zerkratzen. Diese Geste kann metonymisch für die Aufgabe der Kolonialherren, den kolonialisierten Völkern die „Segnungen der Technik" zu bringen, gesehen werden – eine Aufgabe, die zu den Legitimierungsstrategien imperialistischer Expansion zählt.[8] Eine weitere technische Errungenschaft Europas, auf die im Text wiederholt Bezug genommen wird, ist die Eisenbahn, über die die indischen Figuren sich stets bewundernd äußern und so der britischen Überlegenheit im Bereich der Technik Tribut zollen.

Die britische Kolonialherrschaft wird aber in *Kim* nicht nur durch überlegenes Wissen der Briten, sondern auch durch das väterliche und wohlwollende Verhalten der Kolonialherren gegenüber den Indern legitimiert. Dies wird exemplarisch durch den Kontrast zwischen dem Verhalten der Briten und dem der russischen Spione gegenüber dem Lama demonstriert. Während der Lama, der von den Indern als heiliger Mann verehrt wird, von den britischen Figuren herablassend, aber wohlwollend behandelt wird, begehen die russischen Spione in den Augen der Inder ein Sakrileg, indem sie den Lama schlagen. Dieser Vorfall kann metonymisch als Beweis für die Unfähigkeit der übrigen europäischen Völker, zum Wohl der indischen Bevölkerung über den Subkontinent zu herrschen, gelesen werden. Damit wird zugleich das *great game* als notwendig zur Sicherung des *Raj* gegen die Expansionsbestrebungen anderer europäischer Mächte legitimiert – und zwar zum Wohl der Inder.[9] Hier wird also das Ideal propagiert, daß die Kolonialherrschaft dem Vorteil der Beherrschten diene. Allerdings besitzen nur jene Briten, die schon länger in Indien leben oder sogar dort geboren sind, die für eine wohltätige Herrschaft notwendigen Kenntnisse über Indien.[10] Nur solche Briten werden von den Indern als Herrscher akzeptiert – eine pro-britische Auffassung, die einer indischen Figur unterschoben wird:

> 'These be the sort to oversee justice. They know the land and the customs of the land. The others, all new from Europe, suckled by white women and learning our tongues from books, are worse than the pestilence.' (S. 124)

Das Bild der britischen Herrschaft in Indien und des Verhältnisses zwischen Kolonialherren und einheimischer Bevölkerung ist durchgängig positiv gezeichnet und läßt kein Konfliktpotential erkennen. Dieses harmonische Verhältnis konkretisiert sich in der britisch-indischen Kooperation im *great game*, für das sich beispielsweise Mahbub Ali und Hurree Babu bereitwillig einsetzen, in dem sie sogar ihr Leben für die Sicherung des *Raj* riskieren.

Darüber hinaus wird die indische Rebellion gegen die britische Herrschaft von 1857, der einschneidende historische Konflikt zwischen Briten und Indern, in *Kim* auf der Basis imperialistischer Denkmuster umgedeutet und damit der politischen Brisanz beraubt.[11] Daß die pro-britische Interpretation dieses historischen Ereignisses einer indischen Figur in den Mund gelegt wird, trägt zur Integration dieser Deutung in die imperialistischen Legitimierungsbestrebungen bei.[12] Es ist ein indischer Veteran, der dem indischen Aufstand jegliche Berechtigung abspricht, was allein schon durch die Metaphorik zum Ausdruck gebracht wird; die von britischer Seite als "Mutiny" etikettierte Rebellion sei eine Krankheit gewesen, die ein Heilmittel ("remedy") erforderte:

> 'A madness ate into all the Army, and they turned against their officers. That was the first evil, but not past remedy if they had then held their hands. But they chose to kill the Sahibs' wives and children. Then came the Sahibs from over the sea and called them to most strict account.' (S. 100)

Da hier die mögliche Berechtigung der indischen Rebellion nicht einmal ansatzweise reflektiert wird, werden die historischen Ereignisse in einer verkürzten Weise dargestellt, in der gut und böse klar verteilt sind. Der Roman stellt somit historische Ereignisse in einer verzerrten Weise dar und leistet sowohl imperialistischen Rechtfertigungsstrategien als auch einseitigen Schuldzuweisungen Vorschub. Die Gegenposition – eine anti-britische Interpretation des indischen Aufstandes – wird nicht artikuliert. Damit wird ein

Bild der britischen Herrschaft in Indien entworfen, das mögliche Ansätze indischer Autonomiebestrebungen ausspart.[13] Said weist zudem auf die euphemistische Darstellung der britischen Vergeltungsmaßnahmen hin, die auf imperialistische Denkmuster Bezug nimmt:

> And when Kipling has the old soldier describe the British counter-revolt – with its horrendous reprisals by white men bent on 'moral' action – as 'calling' the Indian mutineers 'to strict account', we have left the world of history and entered the world of imperialist polemic, in which the native is naturally a delinquent, the white man a stern but moral parent and judge.[14]

Das Verhältnis der britischen Kolonialherren zu den Indern ist in Kiplings Roman als harmonische komplementäre Beziehung konzipiert, die auf der Dichotomie von Herrschenden und Beherrschten, Überlegenen und Unterlegenen beruht. Die überlegene Stellung der Kolonialherren birgt in Kiplings Indien kein Konfliktpotential in sich, da die Kolonialherren ihre Machtposition aus der Sicht der indischen Figuren nicht für egoistische Zwecke ausnutzen, sondern Indien zum Wohl aller regieren, und weil die Inder die Briten respektieren, ja sie sogar als Vorbilder imitieren. Die Versuche einer Anpassung an europäische Verhaltensweisen seitens indischer Figuren, wie z.B. Hurree Babu, sind Eingeständnis britischer Superiorität, zumal die Europäisierungsbestrebungen nur von mäßigem Erfolg gekrönt sind. Said betont, daß Hurree Babus Imitation von Creighton nicht aufgrund von mangelnder Kompetenz unvollkommen bleibt, ja sogar komisch wirkt, sondern lediglich aufgrund der Tatsache, daß er nicht weiß ist.[15] In dem Bild des Verhältnisses von britischen Kolonialherren und indischer Bevölkerung und der damit einhergehenden Aussparung anti-britischer Ansichten und möglichen Konfliktpotentials kommen also insgesamt Wunschprojektionen der Vertreter imperialistischer Ideen zum Ausdruck.

Da der Protagonist aufgrund seiner Herkunft und seiner Sozialisation zwischen zwei Kulturen, der Welt der britischen Kolonialherren und der der Inder steht, wird an dieser Figur das Aufeinandertreffen zweier gegensätzlicher Welten veranschaulicht. Während Kim zuvor in einer im wesentlichen indischen Umwelt gelebt hat, kommt er durch den Besuch der St. Xavier's School unter britischen bzw. anglo-indischen Einfluß. Dieser entfremdet ihn offenbar nicht von seiner früheren Lebensweise, denn es ist für Kim völlig ausreichend, seine inzwischen durch den Aufenthalt in geschlossenen Räumen heller gewordene Haut wieder dunkler zu färben, um von seinem Leben in der britischen Schule wieder zu seinem früheren Leben zurückzukehren. Damit wird Kim, dem "little Friend of all the World", die Flexibilität zugeschrieben, sich in beiden Welten sicher zu bewegen, problemlos von einer Welt in die andere hinüberzuwechseln. Allerdings beruhen diese Flexibilität sowie Kims ungebundene Wanderungen durch Indien letztlich auf der Macht der Kolonialmacht und sind Teil imperialistischer Phantasien.[16] Die Stellung des Protagonisten zwischen zwei Kulturen wird also kaum problematisiert – im Gegensatz zu vielen Werken postkolonialer Literatur, in denen gerade die Probleme einer solchen Situation im Mittelpunkt stehen.

In der Schule wird Kim ein Bewußtsein für die Hierarchie zwischen Kolonialherren und Kolonialisierten vermittelt, die der imperialistischen Mentalität zugrunde lag: "One must never forget that one is a Sahib, and that some day, when examinations are passed, one will command natives." (S. 173) Daß er gegenüber seinen Mitschülern seine bisherige Lebensweise verschweigt "for St. Xavier's looks down on boys who 'go native all-together'" (ebd.), zeigt, daß er die grundlegende Maxime britischen Verhaltens in Indien – "One must never forget that one is a Sahib" (ebd.) – zu einem gewissen Grad internalisiert hat. Doch dies bewirkt keineswegs eine Veränderung von Kims Zuneigung zu Mahbub Ali und insbesondere zu dem Lama, dem er trotz britischer Schulausbildung noch in der Rolle des *chela* (Schülers) folgt. Und es dürfte gerade diese konstante Zuneigung des Protagonisten zu diesen beiden Figuren sein (die ihn zeitweilig sogar seine Identität als Sahib vergessen läßt [z.B. S. 237, 319]), die bei den Rezipienten immer wieder den Eindruck erweckt, daß *Kim* imperialistischen Denkmustern weniger verhaftet sei als andere Kolonialromane. Da Kim dem Lama auch nach seiner Beeinflussung durch die britische Kolonialgesellschaft noch als Schüler dient, kommt es scheinbar zu einer Inversion des Hierarchieverhältnisses zwischen Kolonialherren und Kolonialisierten. Dennoch ändert die Titulierung Kims als *chela* nichts daran, daß Kim von Anfang an weniger die Rolle des Lernenden als die des Beschützers und Versorgers einnimmt – und damit letztlich metonymisch die Rolle des paternalistischen Beschützers Indiens, jene zur Rechtfertigung des Imperialismus häufig idealisierte und doch zugleich die einheimische Bevölkerung diskriminierende Rolle der Kolonialmacht. Sullivan sieht in der Beziehung Kims zu dem Lama eine Analogie zu imperialistischer Besitzergreifung: "Kim with the insight and intuition of the born colonialist, recognizes that the lama is a new territory worth annexing and possessing".[17] Durch die Überlegenheit des Protagonisten und die gleichzeitige aufrichtige Zuneigung zu dem Lama konkretisiert sich in Kim "a fantasy of integration between the oppositional roles of colonizer and colonized"[18], in der das diesen gegensätzlichen Rollen inhärente Konfliktpotential aufgelöst wird. Die harmonische Überbrückung der Kluft zwischen den Rassen, wie sie von Creighton explizit propagiert wird ("do not at any time be led to contemn the black men.", S. 167), stößt aber zumindest bei der Frage der Vermischung der Rassen an ihre Grenzen, wie die offen rassistischen Bemerkungen über Eurasier zeigen.[19]

In *Kim* zeigen sich trotz der grundsätzlich affirmativen Haltung zum imperialistischen Diskurs durchaus Ansätze zu einer Durchbrechung imperialistischer Denkweisen. So wird durch die Einschränkung, daß nur die lange in Indien lebenden Briten in der Lage sind, dem propagierten Idealbild des paternalistischen Herrschers zu entsprechen, eine gänzlich vorbehaltlose Akzeptanz der britischen Kolonialherren ausgeschlossen. Außerdem widerspricht die Tatsache, daß der stark durch die indische Umwelt geprägte Kim sehr positiv gezeichnet ist, dem Konzept der Minderwertigkeit des Fremden. Diese Ansätze zu einer Durchbrechung imperialistischer Denkmuster werden jedoch nicht zu einer Kritik an der Herrschaft genutzt, so daß insgesamt der Eindruck erweckt wird, daß die britische Herrschaft in Indien überaus gut und wohltätig sei.

In E. M. Forsters Indienroman *A Passage to India*, der über 20 Jahre nach *Kim* veröffentlicht wurde, werden Themen aufgegriffen, die schon bei Kipling von zentraler Bedeutung waren. Im Mittelpunkt beider Romane steht die Frage nach der Realisierbarkeit einer harmonischen Koexistenz zwischen britischen Kolonialherren und indischer Bevölkerung. Doch die Antworten, die beide Romane auf diese Frage geben, sind völlig verschieden. Während in *Kim* die Indienerfahrung der Anglo-Inder als Garant für eine harmonische Kooperation beider Gruppen erscheint, die auf einer beiderseitigen Akzeptanz der etablierten Hierarchie beruht, wird *A Passage to India* durch eine pessimistische Sichtweise des Verhältnisses von Briten und Indern geprägt.[20] Die Möglichkeit indischer Autonomie wird von indischen Figuren explizit thematisiert, und im Gegensatz zu Kiplings Roman artikulieren die indischen Figuren hier primär anti-britische Meinungen. Dem steht eine geschlossene anglo-indische Kolonialgesellschaft gegenüber, die durch die Perpetuierung rassistischer Vorstellungen und eines unumstößlichen Superioritätsgefühls eine Überbrückung der Kluft zwischen Kolonialherren und Kolonialisierten unmöglich macht. Das Bild der paternalistisch großzügigen britischen Herrscher in *Kim* weicht dem des despotischen und rassistischen Imperialisten. Das durchgängig arrogante Verhalten der Anglo-Inder gegenüber den Kolonialisierten sowie von einigen Mitgliedern der Kolonialgesellschaft offen geäußerte rassistische Ansichten bringen in drastischer Weise den imperialistischen Überlegenheitsdünkel zum Ausdruck, der Mrs Moore gegenüber folgendermaßen formuliert wird: "'You're superior to them, anyway. Don't forget that. You're superior to everyone in India except one or two of the ranis, and they're on an equality.'"[21] Das Superioritätsgefühl der britischen Kolonialgesellschaft zeigt sich in einem Spektrum von Verhaltensweisen, das von explizit geäußerter krasser Menschenverachtung, wie sie etwa in Mrs Callendars Kommentar "'Why, the kindest thing one can do to a native is to let him die...'" (S. 48) deutlich wird, bis zu subtileren Formen der Diskriminierung wie z.B. der Konvention, von Indern in einem anderen Tonfall zu sprechen als von Briten (S. 52), reicht. Es sind insbesondere die Frauen der britischen Kolonialbeamten, die durch rassistisches Verhalten auffallen und auf einer strengen Beibehaltung der Kluft zwischen Briten und Indern bestehen (siehe z.B. S. 66, 80, 217).

Die schon in *Kim* getroffene Differenzierung zwischen schon lange in Indien lebenden Anglo-Indern und Neuankömmlingen aus England findet sich auch in Forsters Roman – allerdings mit umgekehrten Vorzeichen, denn hier sind es nur die Neuankömmlinge, die Indern Interesse und Respekt entgegenbringen, während die Anglo-Inder die indische Kultur völlig mißachten. Die Schuldzuweisung für das antagonistische Verhältnis zwischen Kolonialherren und Kolonialisierten fällt in *A Passage to India* eindeutig aus; es ist offenbar das rigide hierarchische Denken der etablierten Kolonialgesellschaft, das die humanitären Einstellungen des Individuums korrumpiert:

> 'They come out intending to be gentlemen, and are told it will not do. [...] They all become exactly the same – not worse, not better. I give any Englishman two years, be he Turton or Burton. It is only the difference of a letter. And I give any Englishwoman six months.' (S. 34).

Durch die wiederholte Betonung des Anpassungsdrucks seitens der etablierten Kolonialgesellschaft wird implizit auch der Prozeß der Tradierung von Kollektivvorstellungen thematisiert. Selbst Fielding, den seine humanitären Überzeugungen und sein Gerechtigkeitsempfinden veranlassen, sich für Aziz einzusetzen und damit zugleich gegen die Normen der Kolonialgesellschaft zu verstoßen, kann sich schließlich dem von der Kolonialgesellschaft ausgeübten Druck nicht vollständig widersetzen, wie er bei der Wiederbegegnung mit Aziz erkennt:

> He had thrown in his lot with Anglo-India by marrying a countrywoman, and he was acquiring some of its limitations, and already felt surprise at his own past heroism. Would he today defy all his own people for the sake of a stray Indian? (S. 312f.)

Die rigiden Normen der Kolonialgesellschaft, sich solidarisch mit Anglo-Indern zu verhalten und die Kluft zwischen Kolonialherren und Kolonialisierten aufrechtzuerhalten, erlaubten dem Einzelnen kaum Kompromisse. Das zeigt sich exemplarisch an Fielding, dessen Einsatz für Aziz seine Isolierung von den Anglo-Indern zur Folge hat (S. 194ff.). Das Festhalten am Hierarchiedenken und das entsprechende Verhalten der Briten hat auch zur Folge, daß Inder ihrerseits stereotype Vorstellungen über Briten ausprägen, wie der folgende Erzählerkommentar zu erkennen gibt:

> He [Aziz] too generalized from his disappointments – it is difficult for members of a subject race to do otherwise. Granted the exceptions, he agreed that all Englishwomen are haughty and venal. (S. 36)

Im Unterschied zu *Kim* wird in *A Passage to India* das Überlegenheitsgefühl der Kolonialherren gegenüber den Indern sowie das daraus resultierende diskriminierende Verhalten kritisch dargestellt. Sowohl Inder als auch Briten, die als Sympathieträger konzipiert sind (vor allem Mrs Moore, in der Anfangsphase auch Adela Quested), sprechen sich explizit dagegen aus (z.B. S. 50, 68) und hinterfragen damit die Rechtmäßigkeit der britischen Herrschaft. Ronny Heaslop definiert in einem Gespräch mit seiner Mutter die Rolle der Kolonialherren folgendermaßen: "'We're not out here for the purpose of behaving pleasantly! [...] We're out here to do justice and keep the peace.'" (S. 69) – eine Rechtfertigung, die von Mrs. Moore als Anmaßung zurückgewiesen wird ("'...Englishmen like posing as gods.'", S. 69). Obige Definition der Funktion der Kolonialmacht legitimiert die britische Herrschaft in Indien als Grundlage für Gerechtigkeit und Frieden – und damit letztlich (ähnlich wie auch in *Kim*) als zum Wohle aller; durch Mrs Moores Zurückweisung wird diese Rechtfertigung jedoch ambivalent gezeichnet. Außerdem dienen interne Auseinandersetzungen zwischen Moslems und Hindus als Begründung für die britische Herrschaft, da diese die britische Präsenz in der Funktion einer Vermittlungsinstanz erforderlich zu machen scheinen (S. 110). Die Vorteile der Kolonie für das Mutterland bleiben nahezu unerwähnt. Mrs Moore kritisiert zwar die fehlende Humanität der Kolonialherrschaft ("One touch of regret – not the canny substitute but the true regret from the heart – would have made [...] the British Empire a different institution.", S. 70). Damit wird jedoch nicht die Legitimität des *Raj* an sich in Frage gestellt, sondern lediglich Kritik an der Art, wie die Kolonialherrschaft wahrgenommen wird, geübt – und dies, wie Parry betont, in sehr zurückhaltender Form.[22] Als Fielding von Aziz' Freunden auf die Legitimation der Kolonialherrschaft angesprochen wird, gibt dieser nicht die konventionelle Antwort "'England holds India for her good.'" (S. 124), sondern bleibt die Antwort schuldig, denn "[t]he zeal for honesty had eaten him up" (ebd.), und verweist damit auf eine Desillusionierung hinsichtlich der Legitimierbarkeit imperialistischer Expansion.

Während in *Kim* die soziale Kluft zwischen Kolonialherren und Kolonialisierten zwar einerseits von beiden Seiten akzeptiert wird, andererseits aber im *great game* und durch den Protagonisten immer wieder überbrückt wird, birgt diese Kluft in *A Passage to India* ein Konfliktpotential, das die Handlung vorantreibt. Sie wird von den Figuren immer wieder reflektiert und zeigt sich am deutlichsten in der Gerichtsverhandlung gegen Aziz. Die vermutete Vergewaltigung Adelas durch einen Inder in den *Marabar Caves* wird von der Kolonialgesellschaft nicht als Verbrechen gegen eine einzelne Frau gewertet, sondern wird im Kontext der imperialistischen Dichotomisierung von Britischem und Indischem rassistisch interpretiert. Was bei diesem Vorfall aus der Sicht der Kolonialgesellschaft im Vordergrund steht, sind folglich nicht individuelle Schicksale, sondern die unterschiedliche Hautfarbe von Aziz und Adela, die für die Kolonialisten die einzige Erklärungsgrundlage für die Vergewaltigung bildet. Sie glauben von dem (pseudo-)anthropologischen Faktum der „natürlichen" Attraktivität der Europäerin für den Inder aus:

> [...] the darker races are physically attracted by the fairer, but not vice versa – not a matter for bitterness this, not a matter for abuse, but just a fact which any scientific observer will confirm. (S. 222)[23]

Der Hinweis, daß derartige Gefühle bei der Niederschlagung des indischen Aufstandes im Jahr 1857 aufgebrochen seien, verweist darauf, daß die Vergewaltigung als Metonymie für den Widerstand gegen die britische Herrschaft gedeutet wird. In vielen Berichten über die indische Rebellion war von sexuellen Mißhandlungen und Vergewaltigungen britischer 'Ladies' durch indische Soldaten die Rede. Daß diese Berichte in offiziellen Untersuchungen schnell und eindeutig widerlegt wurden, beeinflußte den Glauben vieler Briten, daß solche Vergewaltigungen stattgefunden hätten, nicht. In der Reaktion auf die Anklage gegen Aziz sind in der Kolonialgesellschaft rassistische Züge mit misogynen Komponenten verknüpft, denn im Club ist es primär Ronny Heaslop, der bedauert wird, und nicht Adela. Sharpe kommentiert die Reaktionen der Anglo-Inder gegenüber Adela, die diese zum Objekt degradieren, folgendermaßen:

> Her fellow expatriates react to the news of the assault from within their code of honor and chivalry: they treat Adela as a mere cipher for a battle between men.[24]

Die Anklage der Vergewaltigung berührt also die "age-old equation of female chastity with male honor".[25] Daß Adela ihre Anklage zurücknimmt und der Prozeß gegen Aziz dadurch beendet wird, zeigt laut Sharpe, daß eigentlich Aziz das Opfer ist und das eigentliche Verbrechen in einem Mißbrauch der Macht seitens der Kolonialherren besteht.[26] Ängste, die auf keinerlei gültigen anthropologischen Theorien beruhen und die sich 1857 als völlig falsch erwiesen hatten, werden zur Grundlage von Haß und Rachegefühlen, die das britische Verhalten gegenüber Indern wie Aziz bestimmen.

Die Versuche einzelner Figuren, die Kluft zwischen Briten und Indern zu überbrücken, sind größtenteils zum Scheitern verurteilt. Dies verdeutlicht etwa die "Bridge Party" oder Fieldings Teilnahme an Aziz' Siegesfeier, bei der es ihm im Unterschied zu Kim nicht gelingt, durch indische Kleidung in die indische Welt einzutauchen (S. 250f.). Adelas Versuch, Indien kennenzulernen führt schließlich zur Katastrophe. Eine harmonische Beziehung zwischen Briten und Indern scheint in Forsters Indien nur außerhalb der Strukturen der Kolonialgesellschaft möglich zu sein und ist deshalb in der Kolonie allenfalls punktuell zwischen einzelnen Individuen realisierbar. Dies wird exemplarisch an der Freundschaft zwischen Aziz und Fielding gezeigt, die zwischen Annäherung und Entfremdung oszilliert und als dauerhafter Zustand erst in der Zukunft möglich scheint (S. 316). Lediglich Mrs Moores intuitiver Zugang zu Indien und Indern scheint ansatzweise erfolgreich zu sein. Doch auch Mrs Moore nimmt letzlich keine tatsächliche Vermittlungsposition zwischen beiden Welten ein, denn je näher sie Indien kommt, um so mehr entfremdet sie sich von der britischen Welt, bricht den Kontakt mit dieser ab.

Die andauernde Kluft zwischen der Welt der britischen Kolonialherren und der der Inder wird auch durch die Segmentierung des Raumes akzentuiert. Die Isolation des britischen Teils von Chandrapore, dessen sterile Anlage mit "roads that intersect at right angles" (S. 32) als metonymisch für das britische Ordnungsdenken gesehen werden kann, korreliert mit der Isolation der britischen Kolonialgesellschaft von der indischen Bevölkerung, mit dem Fehlen beiderseitiger Berührungspunkte: "it [the Civil Station] shares nothing with the city except the overarching sky" (S. 32). Außer der räumlichen Nähe gibt es zwischen beiden Welten nichts Verbindendes.

Obgleich die Darstellung der Inder im Vergleich in *A Passage to India* differenzierter ist, werden auch hier Kollektivvorstellungen über „den Orientalen" perpetuiert, der u.a. ineffizient, emotional und unpünktlich sei (S. 82, 88, 125, 154, 245, 276, 277f., 284, 296, 302).[27] Teils geschieht dies durch generalisierende Kommentare der Erzählinstanz. Im Unterschied zu Kiplings Roman werden jedoch auch einige der Kollektivvorstellungen über Inder gezielt dekonstruiert, und damit wird letztlich auch der Mythos britischer Überlegenheit unterminiert. Diese Dekonstruktion wird allein schon dadurch ermöglicht, daß das indische Personal sich im wesentlichen aus Mitgliedern der europäisch gebildeten indischen Mittelschicht zusammensetzt. Daher besteht das enorme Bildungsgefälle zwischen Kolonialherren und Kolonialisierten nicht mehr, das in *Kim* u.a. dazu diente, die britische Herrschaft über Indien zu legitimieren. So erweisen sich im Handlungsverlauf etwa Aziz oder die Juristen Das und Amritrao als zumindest ebenso qualifiziert wie ihre britischen Vorgesetzten. Aziz scheint sogar kompetenter zu sein als sein Vorgesetzter Major Callendar, wie in der Bewußtseinsdarstellung des letzteren deutlich wird:

> [...] in his heart he [Major Callendar] knew that if Aziz and not he had operated last year on Mrs Graysford's appendix the old lady would probably have lived. (S. 72)

Im letzten Teil (The Temple) wird allerdings das positive Bild von der Kompetenz der Inder und damit die Aufwertung der indischen intellektuellen Mittelschicht relativiert. So wird etwa die Fähigkeit der Inder, ohne britische Kontrolle ein Bildungssystem aufrechtzuerhalten, das europäischen Standards genügt, in Zweifel gezogen. Wenn Professor Godbole in dem selbständigen indischen Staat, in dem er Erziehungsminister ist, eine Schließung der Schule zugelassen hat (S. 310f.), so werden dadurch abermals Kollektivvorstellungen vom lethargischen Orientalen, dem Disziplin und Durchhaltevermögen fehlen, evoziert. Dennoch wird in *A Passage to India* abschätzigen Einstellungen gegenüber Indern wiederholt der Boden entzogen. Die pseudoanthropologische These des Polizeichefs McBryde, die besagt, daß ein Zusammenhang zwischen der Disposition zu Verbrechen und der geographischen Lage des Geburtsortes bestehe (S. 176), wird durch McBrydes eigenen Geburtsort ad absurdum geführt, denn "[b]orn at Karachi, he seemed to contradict his theory" (S. 176). Die Kollektivvorstellung von der indischen Nachlässigkeit wird ebenfalls dekonstruiert: Das Fehlen von Aziz' Kragenknopf wird von Ronny Heaslop als Zeichen von orientalischer Nachlässigkeit gewertet, als "'inattention to detail; the fundamental slackness that reveals the race'" (S. 97). Da die Rezipienten jedoch wissen, daß Aziz den Kragenknopf tatsächlich Fielding gegeben hat, wird das Stereotyp unterlaufen, und Heaslops Aussage entlarvt ihn daher als vorschnell urteilenden Rassisten. Der Umgang mit Kollektivvorstellungen zeigt also eine Ambivalenz des Romans in bezug auf den imperialistischen Diskurs, die Parry folgendermaßen zusammenfaßt: "*A Passage to India* can be seen as at once inheriting and interrogating the discourses of the Raj".[28]

Während in den beiden zuvor untersuchten Romanen die bereits etablierte britische Herrschaft in Indien im Mittelpunkt steht, geht es in Joseph Conrads *Heart of Darkness* um die Erschließung des „dunklen Kontinents", Afrika. Von den drei hier behandelten Romanen ist Conrads *Heart of Darkness* der Text, der am eindringlichsten die Ideologie des Imperialismus hinterfragt. Bereits in der Rahmenerzählung kommen die Legitimationen und Motivationen imperialistischer Herrschaft zur Sprache. Wenn auch in *Heart of Darkness* der belgische Kongo im Mittelpunkt steht, so wird die Handlung doch dadurch mit dem britischen Imperialismus in Verbindung gebracht, daß die Handlung der Rahmenerzählung auf einem Boot auf der Themse bei London situiert ist. Auch die Charakterisierung Londons ("the biggest, and the greatest, town on earth")[29] und der Themse ("a waterway leading to the uttermost ends of the earth", S. 28) verweist auf die Rolle der britischen Hauptstadt als Zentrum des Kolonialhandels und des *Empire*. Das *setting* evoziert beim Rahmenerzähler Erinnerungen an die Geschichte des *British Empire*, die er in verherrlichender Weise Revue passieren läßt (S. 28f.). In seinen Reflexionen werden bereits verschiedene Motivationen für imperialistische Expansion thematisiert, die sich im wesentlichen auf den Gegensatz zwischen Streben nach ökonomischem Gewinn und Macht und dem zivilisatorischen Sendungsbewußtsein, das durch die Formel "bearing [...] the torch" (S. 29) angesprochen wird, reduzieren lassen. In dieser Thematisierung unterschiedlicher Motivationen wird der zentrale Bildbereich des Werkes etabliert, der Gegensatz zwischen Licht und Dunkelheit, der mit dem Kontrast von Zivilisation und Barbarentum assoziiert wird. Zu Beginn der Binnenerzählung wird dem gegenüber das Bild der britischen Insel zur Zeit der Kolonialisierung durch die Römer evoziert, als England noch nicht Zivilisationsträger war, sondern "one of the dark places of the earth" (S. 29) und den römischen Kolonialherren als "very end of the world" (S. 30) bewohnt von "savages" (S. 30) erschien.

Den Unterschied zwischen römischem und britischem Imperialismus sieht der Ich-Erzähler Marlow in der Effizienz des letzteren ("'What saves us is efficiency – the devotion to efficiency.'", S. 31), die den Unterschied zwischen Eroberern und Kolonialherren im eigentlichen Sinne ausmache. Vor diesem Hintergrund erscheint die Kolonialisierung des belgischen Kongos, deren Zeuge Marlow in Afrika wird, als Rückfall in die römische Form der Expansion, denn Marlow konstatiert im Kongo immer wieder die überwältigende Ineffizienz des Vorgehens der Kolonialherren. Der Mythos europäischer Effizienz wird beispielsweise durch die Beschreibung der wirkungslos bleibenden Aktionen des französischen Kriegsschiffes dekonstruiert (S. 41). Ebenso stehen die verrostenden Maschinen und Geräte sowie die wirkungslos bleibenden Sprengungen für den Bau einer Eisenbahnstrecke (S. 42f.), die Marlow in einer der Handelsniederlassungen bemerkt, metonymisch für die völlige Ineffizienz der kolonialen Erschließung des Landes. Außerdem kommentieren sie ironisch die Rolle der Kolonialmacht als Überbringer europäischer Technik (S. 42ff.). Den Mythos europäischer Effizienz widerlegt schließlich auch die völlige Inaktivität der "pilgrims" (S. 52ff.).

Das ökonomische Gewinnstreben der europäischen Völker, das bei Kipling und Forster kaum erwähnt wird, erscheint in *Heart of Darkness* als zentrale Motivation imperialistischer Expansion. Im Handlungsverlauf wird immer wieder deutlich, daß die im Mutterland propagierte Multikausalität des Imperialismus, die Verbindung von missionarischer, altruistischer Tätigkeit und Profitstreben, wie sie exemplarisch von Marlows Tante formuliert wird (S. 39), sich in der realen Umsetzung zu einer Monokausalität verkürzt. Was in den Kolonien das Handeln der Kolonialherren bestimmt, ist ausschließlich ökonomisches Profitstreben, das in *Heart of Darkness* auf die einfache Formel „Elfenbein" gebracht wird. Damit wird aber der Kolonialisierung der ethische Anspruch entzogen – und gleichzeitig auch eine wesentliche Legitimierung, denn "[w]hat redeems it is the idea only" (S. 32).

Neben der Diskrepanz von ideologischer Legitimation und der tatsächlichen Motivation imperialistischer Expansion werden insbesondere die physischen und psychischen Gefährdungen, denen die Europäer in der Kolonie ausgesetzt sind, thematisiert. Bereits in *A Passage to India* wird die moralische Korrumpierung der Kolonialherren veranschaulicht, doch in *Heart of Darkness* rückt dieses Thema durch die Figur des Kurtz, aber auch durch verschiedene Nebenfiguren in den Mittelpunkt. Am Beispiel des Kurtz, des "first-class agent" (S. 46) seiner Handelsgesellschaft, wird der Verlust von ethisch-humanitären Idealen und die psychische Degenerierung besonders eindringlich dargestellt. Zunächst scheint Kurtz den Prototyp des vorbildlichen Kolonisten zu verkörpern, da er scheinbar in der Lage ist, die Rolle des erfolgreichen Händlers und die des Zivilisationsträgers, des "emissary of pity, and science, and progress" (S. 55) zu vereinbaren. Sein geschäftlicher Erfolg ist in der Kolonie schon legendär, und der ethische Anspruch, den er an sich selbst stellt, zeigt sich vor allem in dem von ihm gemalten Bild der "woman, draped and blindfolded, carrying a lighted torch" (S. 54) sowie in seiner Überzeugung, daß "'[e]ach station should be like a beacon on the road towards better things, a centre for trade of course, but also for humanizing, improving, instructing'" (S. 65). Kurtz propagiert also humanitäre Ideale, beruft sich aber dabei zugleich auf den imperialistischen Glauben an die Überlegenheit des Weißen. Durch Kurtz' Verfall in extreme Brutalität, in die „Dunkelheit", die er ursprünglich vertreiben wollte, wird die Legitimation der Kolonialisierung als Prozeß der Ausbreitung von Zivilisation dekonstruiert - zumal Marlow bereits vor der Begegnung mit Kurtz Europäer trifft, die psychisch degeneriert sind (z.B. S. 34, 52f., 59). Damit wird zugleich implizit eine generelle Feststellung über die negativen Folgen, die der Aufenthalt in der Kolonie auf die Psyche der Europäer hat, getroffen.

Während in den beiden zuvor behandelten Romanen die Stimme einer übergeordneten auktorialen Erzählinstanz (scheinbare) Objektivität suggeriert, wird in Conrads *Heart of Darkness* die Stimme eines am Geschehen als Beobachter beteiligten Individuums gewählt, die des Erzählers Marlow, der seine Erlebnisse im belgischen Kongo darstellt. Said sieht schon in dem Erzählen selbst einen Akt kolonialer Besitzergreifung, denn "in telling the story of his African journey Marlow repeats and confirms Kurtz's action: restoring Africa to European hegemony by historicizing and narrating its strangeness".[30] White weist hingegen darauf hin, daß sich gerade das Genre Abenteuerroman für Imperialismuskritik anbietet, die durch eine Verletzung der Genreerwartungen erzielt werden kann.[31] So wird laut White in *Heart of Darkness* etwa die Genrekonvention der Solidarität der Weißen in der Kolonie gebrochen;[32] dieses Fehlen von Solidarität korreliere darüber hinaus mit der "uneasy relationship between Marlow and his listeners".[33]

Da weder ein auktorialer Erzähler das Geschehen aus übergeordneter Perspektive beleuchtet noch Afrikaner als Fokalisierungsinstanzen dienen, wird die europäische Herrschaft nicht aus der Sicht der Kolonialisierten dargestellt. Die Beherrschten haben in *Heart of Darkness* keine eigene Stimme, und die Darstellung und Interpretation des Imperialismus bleibt auf die Sicht der Kolonialherren beschränkt. Diese Tatsache sowie die weitgehend fehlende Individualisierung der afrikanischen Figuren, die diese Figuren nahezu auf eine Funktion als Teil des *setting* reduziert, sind bereits Indikatoren für das völlige Fehlen von Kenntnissen über individuelle Züge, Sozialstrukturen u.ä. des Landes seitens der Kolonialherren. Dies hat zum einen zur Folge, daß das Fremde lediglich in den Kategorien der eigenen Kultur wahrgenommen und dargestellt werden kann. Zum anderen zeigt es die Distanz zwischen Europäern und Kolonialisierten. Die menschenunwürdige Behandlung der Afrikaner in der Kolonie, deren Ausbeutung und Versklavung, wird zwar in keiner

Weise beschönigt, doch die fehlende Spezifizierung des Fremden kann als Indikator imperialistischer Denkweisen gelten, da dies die Komplexität des Fremden reduziert. Collits weist zwar auf die Möglichkeit hin, das Fehlen von Individualisierung als "deep challenge to the old colonial novel's claim to cosmopolitan omniscience"[34] zu lesen, eine solche Lesart steht jedoch im Widerspruch zu der überaus stereotypen Darstellung der Afrikaner in *Heart of Darkness*. Der fremde Kontinent präsentiert sich Marlow vor allem als Gefahr, übt aber auch eine starke Faszination auf ihn aus, was bereits im Vergleich des Kongoflusses mit einer Schlange (S. 33, 36), dem archetypischen Sinnbild für die Verbindung von verführerischer Faszination und Gefahr, zum Ausdruck kommt. Diese ambivalente Einstellung des Erzählers zu Afrika schlägt sich auch in der Darstellung der afrikanischen Bevölkerung nieder, die er mit einer Mischung aus Angst und Faszination wahrnimmt. In Marlows Beschreibung der Bevölkerung, die von ihm als latente Bedrohung empfunden wird, dominieren aus Abenteuerromanen bekannte physische Attribute des Animalischen und des Exotischen, wie "faces like grotesque masks" (S. 40), "wild vitality" (S. 40), Antilopenhörner als Kopfschmuck (S. 106) oder bemalte Körper (S. 108). Die Sprache wird als "strings of amazing words that resembled no sounds of human language" (S. 109) beschrieben, und bezeichnenderweise finden sich unter den Afrikanern auch Kannibalen (S. 67, 74f.). Der Erzähler vergleicht die Afrikaner mit prähistorischen Menschen, weist ihnen also in Anlehnung an darwinistisches Denken eine niedere Entwicklungsstufe zu (S. 68, 75), und geht in seiner pejorativen Darstellung sogar so weit, darüber zu spekulieren, ob er tatsächlich noch Menschen vor sich habe (S. 69). Die Verabsolutierung europäischer Maßstäbe, die die Afrikaner defizitär erscheinen läßt, führt daher zu rassistischer Figurendarstellung. Die Abwertung der afrikanischen Bevölkerung macht eine umfassende Kritik an imperialistischer Expansion, die von der Anerkennung der Gleichwertigkeit der Rassen ausgeht, undenkbar. Damit wird in *Heart of Darkness* zwar die Rolle des Europäers als Zivilisationsträger, nicht aber die Überlegenheit des Weißen an sich in Frage gestellt. Die Europäer bleiben daher grundsätzlich zu imperialistischer Expansion, zum Erschließen der "blank spaces" (S. 33) der Welt, berechtigt.[35]

Insgesamt stellt sich Conrads *Heart of Darkness* als ambivalentester der drei behandelten Romane dar, denn hier steht eine systematische Dekonstruktion der Denkweisen, die imperialistische Expansion legitimieren, einer rassistischen Darstellung der Beherrschten gegenüber – eine Inkonsistenz und Begrenztheit der Imperialismuskritik, die Said folgendermaßen kommentiert und erklärt:

> Conrad's tragic limitation is that even though he could see clearly that on one level imperialism was essentially pure dominance and land-grabbing, he could not then conclude that imperialism had to end so that 'natives'

> could lead lives free from European domination. As a creature of his time, Conrad could not grant the natives their freedom, despite his severe critique of the imperialism that enslaved them.[36]

Die Ambivalenz und historisch bedingte Begrenztheit der Imperialismuskritik, die Said für *Heart of Darkness* konstatiert, kennzeichnet auch die anderen analysierten Werke. In der Auseinandersetzung mit dem Phänomen Imperialismus wird einerseits stets auf die dem Diskurs des Imperialismus inhärenten Denkstrukturen der Hierarchisierung und der Dichotomisierung des Eigenen und des Fremden zurückgegriffen; andererseits finden sich in jedem der Romane auch Strategien, mit denen eben diese Denkweisen dekonstruiert werden. So wird selbst in *Kim*, einem Roman, der sich ansonsten eher affirmativ zum imperialistischen Diskurs verhält, die Dichotomisierung von Eigenem und Fremdem mittels der Titelfigur, die eine Mittelposition zwischen beiden Polen einnimmt, zumindest ansatzweise unterlaufen. In den Romanen von Forster und Conrad findet sich darüber hinaus ein hohes Maß an expliziter Imperialismuskritik - Ausdruck einer zunehmenden Desillusionierung hinsichtlich der Legitimation imperialistischer Expansion, in der sich die im 20. Jahrhundert zunehmende Skepsis gegenüber der imperialistischen Vision eines *Greater Britain* und der allmähliche Wandel hin zu *Little England* abzeichnen.

Anmerkungen

1 E. Kreutzer: "Theoretische Grundlagen postkolonialer Literaturkritik".- In A. Nünning (Ed.): *Literaturwissenschaftliche Theorien, Modelle, Methoden: Eine Einführung.* Trier, 1995, S. 201.
2 Vgl. die kritische Bilanzierung der Forschungsmeinungen in P. Williams: "*Kim* and Orientalism". - In P. Williams, L. Chrisman (Eds.): *Colonial Discourse and Post-Colonial Theory: A Reader.* London, 1993, S. 480-497, hier S. 480f.
3 P. Williams: "*Kim* and Orientalism" sowie E. Said: *Culture and Imperialism.* Harmondsworth, 1978, S. 24-35, 79-82, 196-201. - Zur Rezeption von Kiplings Werken vgl. den Forschungsbericht von E. Mertner: *Rudyard Kipling und seine Kritiker.* Darmstadt, 1983.
4 Siehe z.B. Kipling, R.: *Kim.* Harmondsworth: Penguin, 1989 ([1]1901), S. 64, 70, 71, 77, 185, 190. Alle weiteren Angaben im Text beziehen sich auf diese Ausgabe.
5 Vgl. hierzu P. Williams "*Kim* and Orientalism", S. 493.
6 Z. T. Sullivan: *Narratives of Empire. The Fictions of Rudyard Kipling.* Cambridge, 1993, S. 151.
7 Siehe hierzu P. Williams: "*Kim* and Orientalism", S. 487.
8 Zu einer metonymischen Interpretation dieser Szene vgl. Z. T. Sullivan: *Narratives of Empire*, S. 153: "The gift further suggests the Englishman's power to

bestow upon the lama the gift of sight..." – Vgl. auch E. Said: *Culture and Imperialism*, S. 167f.

9 Vgl. hierzu auch P. Williams: "*Kim* and Orientalism", S. 494.

10 Zur Relation zwischen dem Wissen über fremde Kulturen und der Nutzbarmachung dieses Wissens im Imperialismus siehe Z. T. Sullivan: *Narratives of Empire*, S. 161. – Vgl. auch P. Williams, L. Chrisman: "Colonial Discourse and Post-Colonial Theory: An Introduction". – In P. Williams, L. Chrisman (eds.): *Colonial Discourse and Post-Colonial Theory: A Reader*. London, 1994, S. 8.

11 Zum indischen Aufstand und insbesondere der Belagerung und Befreiung von Lucknow und deren Bedeutung für die britisch-indischen Beziehungen in Indien siehe z.B. E. Said: *Culture and Imperialism*, S. 177f. – Vgl. auch den Artikel von V. Nünning in diesem Heft.

12 Siehe hierzu auch P. Williams: "*Kim* and Orientalism", S. 494.

13 Vgl. E. Said: *Culture and Imperialism*, S. 163 sowie 179.

14 E. Said: *Culture and Imperialism*, S. 178.

15 E. Said: *Culture and Imperialism*, S. 184f. – Vgl. auch P. Williams: "*Kim* and Orientalism", S. 483, der ebenfalls den bei den Europäisierungsversuchen implizierten pejorativen Aspekt herausstellt.

16 E. Said: *Culture and Imperialism*, S. 192-195.

17 Z. T. Sullivan: *Narratives of Empire*, S. 154.

18 Ebd., S. 148.

19 P. Williams: "*Kim* and Orientalism", S. 489-492 interpretiert in diesem Kontext auch die misogynen Äußerungen über indische Frauen als Abwehr einer Vermischung der Rassen.

20 G. K. Das: "*A Passage to India*: a Socio-historical Study". -In J. Beer (Ed.): *A Passage to India. Essays in Interpretation.* London and Basingstoke, 1985, S. 1-15 betont die Authentizität der Indiendarstellung in *A Passage to India*: "it registers the transitional moment of British India's transformation into a new India with a disenchantingly realistic and historical vision" (ebd., S. 1). – Vgl. auch G.K. Das: *E. M. Forster's India.* London, Basingstoke, 1977, hier insbesondere S. 75.

21 Forster, E.M.: *A Passage to India.* Harmondsworth: Penguin, 1988 ([1]1924), S. 61. Alle weiteren Angaben im Text beziehen sich auf diese Ausgabe.

22 B. Parry: "The Politics of Representation in *A Passage to India*". – In J. Beer (Ed.): *A Passage to India. Essays in Interpretation.* London, Basingstoke, 1985, S. 27-43, hier S. 28: "the overt criticism of colonialism is phrased in the feeblest of terms"; vgl. auch ebd., S. 29.

23 Vgl. J. Sharpe: "The Unspeakable Limits of Rape: Colonial Violence and Counter-Insurgency". – In P. Williams, L. Chrisman (eds.): *Colonial Discourse and Post-Colonial Theory: A Reader.* London, 1993, S. 221-243; Sharpe sieht hierin "the fears and fantasies of an imperial nation over the intermingling of two races, the colonizer and the colonized" (ebd., S. 221).

24J. Sharpe: "The Unspeakable Limits of Rape: Colonial Violence and Counter-Insurgency", S. 225.

25 Ebd., S. 225.

26 Ebd., S. 222.

27 Siehe hierzu auch B. Parry: "The Politics of Representation in *A Passage to India*", S. 28.

28 B. Parry: "The Politics of Representation in *A Passage to India*", S. 28.

29 Conrad, J.: *Heart of Darkness.* Harmondsworth: Penguin, 1987 ([1]1902), S. 27. Alle weiteren Angaben im Text beziehen sich auf diese Ausgabe.

30 E. Said: *Culture and Imperialism*, S. 198.

31 A. White: *Joseph Conrad and the Adventure Tradition. Constructing and Deconstructing the Imperial Subject.* Cambridge, 1993, S. 172ff.

32 Ebd., S. 178.

33 Ebd.

34 T. Collits: "Theorizing Racism". - In C. Tiffin, A. Lawson (Eds.): *De-scribing Empire. Post-colonialism and Textuality.* London, New York, 1994, S. 61-69, hier S. 68.

35 Vgl. hierzu C. Tiffin, A. Lawson: "Introduction. The Textuality of Empire". - In Dies. (Eds.): *De-scribing Empire. Post-colonialism and textuality.* London, New York, 1994, S. 1-11, hier insbesondere S. 5: "Colonialism conceptually depopulated countries either by acknowledging the native but relegating him or her to the category of the subhuman, or simply by looking through the native and denying his/her existence. [...] The blankness of the map is not an innocent ignorance because it enables, and therefore bears responsibility for, the subsequent practices of dispossession and annihilation."

36 E. Said: *Culture and Imperialism*, S. 34. - Zu einer ähnlichen Argumentation vgl. auch T. Collits: "Theorizing Racism", S. 66-69.

Jens-Ulrich Davids, Oldenburg

"Amazing Mix": 'East' und 'West' im indo-englischen Roman

> I want the cultures of all lands to be blown about my house as freely as possible. But I refuse to be blown off my feet by any.
>
> Mohandas K. Gandhi[1]

"Oh, East is East, and West is West, and never the twain shall meet" –:[2] Kiplings starke Worte waren schon im Jahre 1899 mehr dem imperialistischen Programm des *divide et impera* verpflichtet als der Wirklichkeit. Heute, in einer Welt vielfacher Migrationen und wachsender Kapital-, Waren- und Informationsströme gelten sie weniger denn je: wir leben in einer Zeit der Mischung. Dies bildet sich auch in der indo-englischen Literatur ab – also der Literatur, die von Indern und Inderinnen in englischer Sprache geschrieben wird -, die ich anhand einiger Beispiele hier besprechen möchte. Wie nutzen sie Konzepte von 'Ost' und 'West'? Wie bewerten sie sie? Wie benutzen sie in ihren fiktiven Welten Vorstellungen wie das Eigene und das Fremde, *the Self* und *the Other*? Europäer haben seit frühesten Zeiten die Welt in *Self* und *Other* eingeteilt. Die Griechen nannten alle Nichtgriechen Barbaren, das christliche Europa definierte sich gegen die Nichtgläubigen, und die Eroberung der Neuen Welt und die Sklavenhalterschaft wurden im Gegensatzpaar der zivilisierten Weißen und der nicht-zivilisierten Anderen (wenn sie denn als Menschen anerkannt wurden) legitimiert. Der Imperialismus der letzten zweihundert Jahre brachte mit einem als wissenschaftlich ausgegebenen Rassismus die ihm genehme Polarisierung hervor. Das gilt auch für die britischen Herren, die Indien mehr und mehr beherrschten. Ein frühes Beispiel aus dem Feld der Literatur mag genügen, um die ungeheure Arroganz, mit der die Kolonialisten die *Self/Other*-Dichotomie erfanden und bewerteten, zu zeigen. Thomas Babington Macaulay schrieb 1835 in seiner "Minute on Education", einem Planungspapier für die Einführung britischer Erziehung in Indien, "that a single shelf of a good European library was worth the whole native literature of India and Arabia".[3]

Die solcherweise aus den kolonialistischen Metropolen heraus Herabgesetzten haben sich von Anfang an gewehrt. Sie erhoben Gegenrede, in der sie dem imperialistischen Bild ihres *Self* ein eigenes entgegenstellten. Diese Anstrengung wird heute angesichts der kulturellen Hegemonie des 'Westens' fortgesetzt: "the Empire writes back with a vengeance".[4] Überall in der Welt, wo Europäer Kolonien besessen haben, sind eigene, regionale und nationale Literaturen entstanden, die auf verschiedenste Weisen ihre Welt repräsentieren und kommentieren, auch in Indien. In einer von Mary Louise Pratt entliehenen Metapher läßt sich die indo-englische Literatur möglicherweise, dies soll als These vorgetragen werden, mit Blick auf die *East-West*-Mischung auf folgende Weise charakterisieren: Indo-englische Literatur kann als Kontaktzone verstanden werden – "the space in which peoples geographically and historically separated come into contact with each other"[5] – zwischen östlichen (indischen) und westlichen (zunächst britischen) Kräften, Standpunkten, Werten, Normen, Weltanschauungen, Wörtern, die von Kolonisierung und anderen Berührungen zusammengebracht wurden, als Grenzland gewissermaßen. Dies ist ein Feld der Mischung, der gegenseitigen Beeinflussung und der Veränderung, ein Ort, der weder dem vor dem Kontakt wahrgenommenen England gleicht noch dem entsprechenden Indien, sondern etwas Drittes ist, an dem Neues entsteht, eine Arena der Erzählungen, in der Begriffe und Traditionen aufeinander einreden aus Europa und Asien, um ihre Streitigkeiten auszutragen in einer Sprache, die für den Austausch erdacht wurde. Die Stimmen, die hier zu hören sind, haben ihren Ursprung in verschiedenen Historien und Histörchen, sie haben je eigene Erinnerungen, sie reden oder schweigen, und so formen sie ein vielstimmiges Klangmuster, das keinem gleicht.

'Ost' und 'West' sind für diesen vielstimmigen Chor, mehr als für Kipling, Zeichen mit wandelbaren und komplexen Bedeutungen: alte Konnotationen ("der fatalistische Asiate") stehen neben neuen ("die jungen Tigerstaaten"). Der 'Westen' ist nicht länger nur identisch mit Europa. Er ist überhaupt kaum ein geographischer Begriff in diesem Zusammenhang, sondern, wie 'der Osten', ein Konzept.[6] Beide zusammen sind ein Deutungsmuster, mit dessen Hilfe die Welt geordnet wird. Wandelbar und komplex, ja, aber auch seltsam beständig in einer Konvention, in der 'Westen' Eigenschaften wie entwickelt, industrialisiert, urbanisiert, kapitalistisch, säkular, modern[7] und individualistisch bedeutet, 'Osten' ungefähr das Gegenteil. Die hier untersuchten Texte nehmen, wie zu zeigen sein wird, dieses binäre Muster auf und differenzieren und variieren es. Sie unterscheiden sich dabei erkennbar untereinander durch den Grad, zu dem sie sich jeweils stärker 'östlichen' oder stärker 'westlichen' Werten und Normen zuneigen. Sie führen geradezu in Versuchung, sie entlang einer gedachten Gleitskala anzuordnen, an derem einen Ende reine Essenzen stünden, am anderen ein "amazing mix".

1. India Aeterna?

Mit *The Vendor of Sweets* (1967) von R.K. Narayan und *A River Sutra* (1990) von Gita Mehta möchte ich zwei Romane betrachten, deren Veröffentlichungsdaten zwar über zwanzig Jahre auseinanderliegen, die sich aber darin überaus ähnlich sind, daß sie eine unverwechselbar indische – genauer: hinduistische – Werte- und Vorstellungswelt positiv besetzen und in den Vordergrund rücken. Die hier relevante Handlungsfolge des *Vendor of Sweets* ist schnell nachgezeichnet:

Jagan besitzt einen kleinen Laden für Süßwaren. Er liest täglich die *Bhagavad Gita* und versteht sich als Anhänger Gandhis. Seine Einkünfte teilt er in diejenigen bis sechs Uhr abends, die er versteuert, und die danach eingenommenen, die er in einem Versteck hortet. Nun kehrt sein Sohn Mali mit einer Freundin nach einigen Jahren in den USA nach Hause in die kleine südindische Stadt Malgudi zurück. Er bringt einen kühnen Plan mit: Er will eine Maschine fabrizieren und vertreiben, die Romane schreiben kann. Sein Vater, in dessen Haus er sich breitmacht, soll ihn mit 50 000 Dollar unterstützen. Vater Jagan kann sich nicht entschließen; die Ruhe verläßt ihn, weder *Gita* noch Geld können ihn befriedigen. Da entschließt er sich, im Alter von etwa fünfundfünfzig Jahren, all dem zu entfliehen und in eine neue Lebensphase einzutreten. Er übergibt sein Geschäft einem Cousin (der es später Mali überlassen soll) und zieht sich, zusammen mit einem religiös gesonnenen Bildhauer, in eine Art verwilderten Park auf der andern Seite des Flusses zurück, um in Bedürfnislosigkeit zu meditieren und bei der Herstellung einer Göttinnenstatue zur Hand zu gehen. Sein Scheckbuch indes nimmt er mit.

Zwei Wertesysteme werden einander gegenübergestellt: Mali steht für ein maliziös überzeichnetes Fortschrittsdenken, welches mit den USA verknüpft wird, während Jagan traditionelles hinduistisches Verhalten vorführt. Aber die Grenzziehung zwischen beiden wird durch Ironie und subtile Schattenspiele entschärft. Auf der einen Seite ist Mali ein flacher Charakter, auf den die Sympathie des Lesers überhaupt nicht gelenkt wird. Auf der andern Seite ist der komplizierte, runde Charakter Jagan, der zwar der traditionellen Rezeptur der heiligen Schriften folgt und sich im dritten Lebensabschnitt, *vanaprastya* (was wörtlich etwa 'Rückzug in den Wald' heißt)[8], aus dem Geschäftsleben zurückzieht, der aber beileibe kein moralischer Held und Vertreter hinduistischer Essenz ist: nicht nur, daß auch er ein Buch schreiben wollte (nicht mithilfe einer Maschine, aber ein diätetisches Kochbuch, was ihn auch lächerlich macht bei Mitbürgern und Lesern), daß seine gandhianischen Prinzipien mehrfach in Zweifel gezogen werden, daß er sich gegen Sohn und Freundin nicht zur Wehr setzen kann, um nur einiges zu nennen, nein, auch sein Eintritt in *vanaprastya* ist kein Akt in Reinheit: er nimmt sein Scheckbuch mit und bleibt so in Kontrolle von Geld und Geschäft. Zwar folgt er der traditionellen Rezeptur, aber gleichzeitig kapitalistischer Vernunft.

Der Protagonist in *River Sutra* verläßt ebenfalls Familie und Beruf und zieht sich in die Waldeinsamkeit zurück, folgt aber, wie Jagan auch, den Vorschriften nur in loser Manier: Nach einem Arbeitsleben als hochrangiger Verwaltungsbeamter läßt er sich die bescheidene Position als Verwalter eines staatlichen Rasthauses zuweisen. Es liegt inmitten tierreicher Wälder hoch über dem Fluß Narmada. Jetzt ist er "someone who has retired to the forest to reflect" (1), ein *vanaprastha* eben. Das Rasthaus liegt in einer stillen Region, fern aller Postämter, Telefone und Krankenhäuser, bevölkert hauptsächlich von Dorfbewohnern der Umgebung und Pilgern, die auf ihrer Reise von der Mündung zur Quelle des Flusses den Wallfahrtstempel Mahadeo aufsuchen, den er von seiner Terrasse aus weit unten liegen sieht. Auf der andern Flußseite lebt sein enger Freund Tariq Mia, Mullah einer Moschee, der ihn "little brother" nennt. Ihn besucht er oft, um Schach zu spielen und Geschichten und Betrachtungen auszutauschen.

Eines Tages trifft der Ich-Erzähler im Wald einen jungen Jain-Asketen, der ihm seine Lebensgeschichte erzählt: wie er der Nachfolger seines millionenschweren Vaters in der familieneigenen Firma werden sollte, sich aber von der Welt der Geschäfte sowie von seiner jungen Frau und seinen beiden kleinen Kindern abwandte und als Wandermönch lebt. Damit ist die Erzählstruktur des Romans eingeführt: In die stille Welt des Erzählers kommen Menschen oder Erzählungen von Menschen, und immer ist von großen Erschütterungen, Umbrüchen, Katastrophen oder Neuanfängen die Rede. Nach dem Jain hören wir von dem Musiklehrer, dessen begabter Schüler von einem Musikliebhaber umgebracht wird; von dem Manager, dem nur Narmada - die Fluß, aber auch Tochter Shivas ist - aus seiner Liebesnot helfen kann; von der Kurtisane, der das Kind geraubt wird; dem Musiker, der Musik als Liebe zu Gott begreift und zu einem traurigen Ende kommt; und schließlich vom Asketen Naga Baba und seiner Schülerin, der er die Hymnen zum Preis Shivas und Narmadas beibringt.

Diese letztgenannte Einzelerzählung ist besonders eng mit der Haupthandlung verwoben. In ihr wird berichtet, wie der Naga Baba - das ist ein sich dem Shiva weihender, kämpferischer und angesehener Asket - ein kleines Mädchen aus einem Bordell befreit und sie zu singen lehrt, damit sie den Narmada-Pilgern religiöse Lieder vortragen kann. Er nennt sie Uma, das ist einer der Namen für Shivas Ehefrau. Drei Jahre, so geht die Erzählung, leben beide in einer Höhle am Fluß, dann verschwinden sie. Im letzten Kapitel nun trifft eine ärchaologische Expedition im Rasthaus ein. Sie will frühe Zeugnisse menschlicher Siedlungen hier am Fluß ausgraben. Sie wird geleitet von Prof. Shankar (dies ist ein anderer Name für Shiva, genauso wie Mahadeo oder Rudra (so heißt ein Dorf in der Nähe)). Er macht das Rasthaus zu seinem Hauptquartier, einschließlich Feldtelephon, chemischem Labor, Mikroskopen und einer Handbibliothek. Als die Expedition für eine Woche zu Ausgrabungen unterwegs ist, taucht Uma auf und trägt dem Erzähler die ganze Hymne an Narmada vor, wie Shankaracharya sie im 9. Jahrhundert schrieb. Prof. Shankar kommt herzu, und es stellt sich heraus, daß er der verschwundene Naga Baba ist.

Von diesen Enthüllungen am Schluß her erschließt sich eine mythische und spirituelle Bedeutungsschicht des Romans: Shiva, einem der beiden wichtigsten Götter des Hinduismus, dem Gott der Schöpfung und des Todes, sind nicht nur die erwähnte Hymne (und andere kürzere Verse im Text) geweiht, sondern ihm, der in allem ist und der alles ist, gilt die Reflexion des Erzählers und der Autorin. Mahadeo, Rudra, Shankar, Narmada, Baba Naga, Uma: all das ist Shiva. Aber nicht zur Hauptsache die inkarnierte Gottheit, wie sie durch das Leben des *vanaprastha* spaziert, ist gemeint, sondern Shiva als Prinzip, als ewige Präsenz, als Ausdruck des All-Einen, höchste Sinnstiftung, als das Unwandelbare inmitten der irdischen Veränderungen, als Urgrund alles Seienden. Ist der Roman also ein langes Gebet? Ja, in gewisser Weise. Aber er illustriert nicht nur eine der traditionellen vedischen hinduistischen Weltanschauungen, er biegt den verehrenden Blick auf die Welt der Menschen zurück. Die ständig sich wandelnde Welt wird nämlich nicht als eine illusionäre dargestellt, als *maya*, die bedeutungslos ist neben dem als Eigentliches verstandenem Göttlichen, sondern als die wichtige Sphäre, in der sich menschliches und anderes Leben abspielt. Hier wird *moksha*, Erlösung, nicht in der völligen Abwendung von dieser Welt gesucht, sondern in der ebenfalls der Vedanta entstammenden Aufforderung „Erkenne dich selbst!“: Ihn, der sich zur Meditation zurückgezogen hatte, ihn weist ausgerechnet Shankar (= Shiva) zurecht: “If anything is sacred about this river, it is the individual experiences of the human beings who have lived here” (253). So kommt der Erzähler zu dieser Einsicht: “Perhaps destiny has brought me to the banks of the Narmada to understand the world” (255). Damit hat die Welt ihn wieder, in der sich Göttliches und Menschliches vielfach verschränken, durchdringen und bedingen, in der sowohl die Lebensfreude (in der Liebe, in der Musik) als auch das stille Ewige gewürdigt werden, und deren schließliches Einssein die Atmosphäre des Romans stark bestimmt. Dabei wird die Welt der Autos, der Geschäftemacher, der Verwaltung und der Teerstraßen angedeutet, bleibt aber im Hintergrund; auf unter ‘westlich’ zu subsumierende Werte (wie Profit, Besitz, individuelle Freiheit) wird aufmerksam gemacht, indem die wichtigsten Charaktere sich von ihnen abwenden. Die dominante Perspektive des Romans ist entschieden indisch (im Sinne von: hinduistisch, selbst wenn die Vertreter anderer Religionen wie Islam oder Jainismus ebenfalls voller Respekt behandelt werden).[9] Von den von mir ausgewählten Texten ist dieser derjenige, der am ehesten eine Art indischer Essentialität zu konstruieren versucht.[10]

2. *The British Raj Revisited*

Während *A River Sutra* Indien von religiös-philosophischem Blickwinkel aus entwirft, haben spätestens seit den dreißiger Jahren dieses Jahrhunderts indo-englische Romane Indien eher politisch bestimmt: als das Land, das von den

Engländern erobert, unterworfen, beherrscht und verändert wurde. Der antikolonialistische Gegendiskurs stemmte das aufmüpfige, widerständige und patriotische Selbst dem europäischen Anderen entgegen. Er setzt ein, als der nationale politische Widerstand gegen die Kolonialherren zwischen den Weltkriegen an Kraft, Reichweite, Wirksamkeit und internationalem Widerhall enorm zulegt. (Namen wie Gandhi, Nehru, Bose oder Jinnah mögen als Hinweis hier genügen). Mulk Raj Anand (*Untouchable*, 1935) und Raja Rao (*Kanthapura*, 1938) sind die beiden explizit anti-britischen der drei Gründerväter des indo-englischen Romans[11] (der dritte ist R.K.Narayan). In ihrer Nachfolge erschienen auch nach der 1947 erkämpften politischen Unabhängigkeit eine beträchtliche Anzahl indischer Romane, die die koloniale Vergangenheit aufnehmen[12] von einer nationalbewußten Perspektive aus. Ein jüngeres Glied in dieser Kette ist der historische Roman *Mistaken Identity* von Nayantara Sahgal, der 1988 veröffentlicht wurde.

Bombay 1929. Bhushan Singh kehrt nach eingen Jahren in Europa in seine Heimat zurück. In Bombay setzt er sich in den Zug nach Vijaygarh, weiter im Norden, wo sein Vater *talukdar* (erblicher Steuereinnehmer und Großgrundbesitzer) ist. Unterwegs wird er von Polizeibeamten des Raj verhaftet und unter Anklage wegen Hochverrats gestellt. Seine Mitgefangenen sind Gandhianer, Gewerkschaftler und Kommunisten. Ihnen erzählt er aus seinem Leben, das der Leserin und dem Leser in *flashbacks* präsentiert wird. Es beginnt mit seiner Kindheit und Jugend als Reicher, betreut und erzogen von Hauslehrer und Dienerschaft. Er selbst ist Hindu, verliebt sich jedoch in ein muslimisches Mädchen, die beiden werden zusammen erwischt, daraus entstehen blutige kommunale Auseinandersetzungen. Dann lernt er in Bombay Sylla kennen, die westlich orientierte, urbane und reiche Parsin; bis zu seinem Gefängnisaufenthalt unterhalten die beiden eine intime Freundschaft. Bhushan wird in die USA geschickt, um dort zu studieren, verbringt seine Zeit aber in einem Liebesverhältnis mit einer jungen Jüdin. Weder wählt noch erlernt er einen Beruf, sondern lebt als Mann von Welt, Bugattifahrer, Nichtstuer und Poet. Er versteht sich zwar als unpolitisch, immer wieder aber drängt sich die politische Dimension seines privaten Handelns auf. Beispiel: Seine Freundin Sylla engagiert sich in der Khilafat-Bewegung[13], die sich zwar hauptsächlich um die Wiederherstellung des Khalifats bemühte, gleichzeitig aber eine breite anti-britische Stoßrichtung hatte. Bei einem Treffen ihrer Bewegung tritt Bhushan, gereizt von Orthodoxen verschiedener Religionen, für die Auflösung religiöser Grenzziehungen und Ausgrenzungen auf und spricht visionär von einer Gesellschaft, in der alle Religionen gleich, mindestens aber gleichwertig, seien.

Der Prozeß findet in einer Zeit großer politischer Spannungen statt. Wir lesen von Gandhis Salzmarsch nach Dandi (1930), von Streiks, Protesten und Attentaten, von dem brutalen Vorgehen der britischen Kolonialbehörden und ihrer Ordnungskräfte und von der zunehmend bedeutenden Nationalbewegung, vor allem des *Indian National Congress.* Gleichzeitig nehmen wir Anteil am Leben der parsischen Schickeria im kosmopolitischen Bombay, dem noch feudalen Leben auf dem Gutshof des Raja, der Bhushans Vater ist, und hören die Gandhianer und Kommunisten, die mit Bhushan einsitzen, politische Diskussionen führen. Nach drei Jahren und vielen Eingaben des parsischen Anwalts wird Bhushan in zweiter Instanz freigesprochen.

Die Vergangenheit wird in diesem Roman durchleuchtet, um die Gegenwart zu erhellen, das Bild der Geschichte kommentiert die eigene Zeit: Vergangenheitsbewältigung. Die Briten, beschreibt der Roman, waren zwar barbarisch und repressiv, konnten indes nur herrschen, weil viele Inder das Herr-Knecht-Verhältnis mittrugen. Der erste Hauptankläger im Prozeß ist Inder; die Familie Bhushan hält ziemlich still, weil der Vater seinen Raja-Titel durch die Engländer erblich machen lassen will, die Reichen Bombays genießen Muße, Besitz und Privileg, ohne sich durch die Fremdherrschaft wesentlich eingeschränkt zu fühlen: ein simples Täter-Opfer-Modell der Kolonialzeit ist dies nicht. Auch keines, in dem den Kolonialherren die vollständige Definitionsmacht überlassen würde: Bhushans Hauslehrer zum Beispiel weist seinen Schüler, der zu den aristokratischen Rajputen gehört, an, Dokumente zur Geschichte der Familie zu lesen (wie sich etwa Mohammed Ghori 1192 zum Herren von Delhi machte) oder läßt ihn den Historiker al-Biruni über die Mongoleneinfälle lesen, da Hindus und Moslems in endlosen Schlachten aufeinander einschlugen, und so fort. Geschichte und Prägung Indiens, so impliziert der Roman, haben lange vor dem British Raj angefangen, die europäische Vorherrschaft erscheint als kurze Episode.

In verwandter Absicht werden die indischen Freiheitskämpfer den Reihen anderer Freiheitskämpfer zugezählt: Atatürk wird erwähnt, die Bolschewiken, Kropotkin, Garibaldi, die Karthager. Bequemes Denken in alten Schemata wird nicht zugelassen, kein harmonisches, monolithisches und geschlossenes Indien wird konstruiert: die Gesellschaft des Romans ist mehrfach hierarchisch strukturiert, nach Britisch und Indisch nicht nur, sondern gespalten und zerrissen auch nach Geschlecht, Klasse, Kaste, Religion, Alter, Stadt und Land, Arm und Reich. Die Überwindung der Frakturen wird nur privat möglich: Bhushan, in seiner Eigenschaft als Poet, versteigt sich, ausgehend von seiner verbotenen Liebe zu dem muslimischen Mädchen, zu utopischen Landschaften friedlichen Miteinanders:

> Fate meant the two of us for love, not war or separation. It meant us to roast our dogmas in the same bonfire. [...] I determinedly covered the landscape with Shiva temples sprouting minarets. In the mosque of my creation, *Om* flowed calm as a horizon along the muezzin's call to prayer. (129)

Wovon der Sohn nur träumt, verwirklicht seine Mutter spät in ihrem Leben: sie tut sich, selbst dem Hinduismus angehörend, mit einem Muslim zusammen, der Kommunist ist.

So vereint *Mistaken Identity* Kritik an den Briten des Raj, Absage an Raj-Nostalgie, Kampf gegen indische Selbstgerechtigkeit und verhaltenen Stolz auf den Freiheitskampf. Sahgal, die selbst aus einer Familie aktiver Freiheitskämpfer und -kämpferinnen stammt[14], nahm in einer vor kurzem gehaltenen Rede ausdrücklich Stellung zum "Puzzle of Identity":[15] Das Raj habe sie geprägt, die hochmütige "civilizing mission" der Briten, die "crude white arrogance" (4), die Marginalisierung der indischen Kultur – "the West was The World, and the rest of humanity a fringe on its edge" (5) – , die auch heute noch stattfände: "the West is still The World" (8). Dem sich fortzeugenden "vocabulary of colonial discourse" (5) wolle sie ebenso entgegentreten wie der heutigen "Raj nostalgia" (6). Sie müsse sich eine ganz neue Identität suchen zwischen dem "intractable Western grip on the world" (11) und den trennenden religiösen Fundamentalismen in Indien; diese eigene "cherished sense of Indianness" baue auf "religious diversity" and "cultural plurality". Sie selbst sei "a mix of cultures and influences, of Hinduism, Islam and Christianity, of East and West" , und diese "cultural confusion" sei "a blessing, not a curse" (14).

3. Sita in Delhi

Viney Kirpal weist in seinem Aufsatz "What is the Modern Third World Novel?"[16] auf eine Anzahl von Frauengestalten der neuesten indischen Literatur, die sich nach der Heirat in die neue Rolle als Ehefrau und Schwiegertochter nicht fügen wollen, dann aber, nach Nachdenken und neuen Erfahrungen, aus eigenem Antrieb diese Lebenssituation akzeptieren. Hier sieht er kulturelle Unabhängigkeit:

> These, then, are some of the ways in which the middle class Indian woman has found her freedom – not in the western sense but rather, freedom from inherited patterns of thought and action in favour of new modes, arrived at independently after much consideration of the various aspects of the problem, keeping also in view the kind of society she lives in. Thus, the third world novelist has to be aware of transformations and the manner in which they are occurring in his society. (148)

In der Kurzgeschichte *Bahu* – das bedeutet Schwiegertochter – von Anjana Appachana von 1991[17] verhält es sich nicht so. Diese Autorin stellt Ost und West, vertreten von einem patriarchalischen, traditionellen Indien und fortschrittlicher Modernität, in aller Klarheit gegenüber, wie sie sich in Konzepten von Femininität ausdrücken.

Am Anfang sind die Erzählerin Lakshmi und ihr Freund Siddarth irrsinnig verliebt ineinander und glücklich selbst im heißen Sommer von Delhi. Sie heiraten und ziehen in das Haus seiner Eltern. Lakshmi arbeitet weiter, aber ihr Leben wird zunehmend von ihrer Schwiegermutter kontrolliert. Es wird von ihr erwartet, daß sie alle Zeit mit der Familie verbringt; immer deutlicher weist man sie daraufhin, daß sie doch ihre Stellung im Büro aufgeben sollte. Sie wird schwanger, und die Familie ihres Mannes ist begeistert. Sie sind sicher, daß es ein Junge wird: " He would resemble Siddarth." Sie geben ihm, bevor er geboren wird, einen Namen, sie planen seine Zukunft, sie sagen "at least now you will give up your precious job. A child needs his mother" (18). Lakshmi erleidet eine Fehlgeburt und ist erleichtert. Siddarth hat weder Zeit für sie noch Verständnis. Ihre Liebe zu ihm schwindet, die Indienstnahme durch die Schwiegermutter verstärkt sich. Schließlich, mit Hilfe einer Freundin, flieht sie aus dem Haus und der Familie.

Die Trägerin der traditonellen Werte ist die Schwiegermutter. Ihr muß Lakshmi dienen. Das Wichtigste müsse ihr Ehemann sein, danach die Verwandtschaft. Sie kann weder verstehen noch dulden, daß die junge Frau gelegentlich allein sein möchte, entweder, um Sitar zu spielen, oder um mit dem Ehemann in Kino oder Bett zusammenzusein. Vor allem soll Lakshmi ein Kind bekommen, vorzugsweise einen Jungen. Dann haben sie reiche Geschenke von Lakshmis Eltern zu erwarten. Die meisten dieser Anmutungen erinnern an das konservative Frauenideal im viktorianischen England: die Frau als *angel in the house*, getrennt von der öffentlichen Sphäre, ohne erlernten Beruf, nicht-intellektuell, abhängig von Männern und für sie da – Mann, Sohn, Vater, Gott – a-sexuell und dekorativ. Aber die britische Kultur muß nicht der Ursprung dieser Vorstellungen sein, das hinduistische Indien hat seine eigenen patriarchalischen Vorstellungen entwickelt: sie werden vielfach in der Gestalt der Sita symbolisiert.

Sita ist die Protagonistin der *Ramayana*. Sie wird die Ehefrau des göttlichen Königs Rama. Als er ins Exil gehen muß, folgt sie ihm. Sie ist treu, rein und zärtlich. Als einmal Rama und sein Bruder Lakshmana zur Jagd sind, wird sie von Ravana entführt, dem mächtigen Herrscher von Lanka. Er wirbt um sie, aber sie hält Rama die Treue. Der Affenkönig Hanuman entdeckt sie in ihrer Gefangenschaft, und mit seiner Hilfe kann Rama sie befreien. Statt aber sie dankbar in die Arme zu schließen, sagt er: "How could ever one like me keep even for a moment a woman who has fallen into the hands of another." Er schickt sie fort: "I have no need for you". Sie beschwört ihre Unschuld und will sich verbrennen. Aber die Götter retten sie aus den Flammen, was für Rama allerdings nicht ihre Unschuld beweist. Sobald er wieder als König von Ayodhya eingesetzt ist, bittet er Lakshmana, Sita zu töten. Der aber überläßt sie lediglich ihrem Schicksal in den Wäldern. Bei dem Eremiten Valmiki lebt sie fünfzehn Jahre und bringt zwei Söhne zur Welt (der Vater ist Rama).

Dann besinnt sich Rama, verkündet öffentlich ihre Unschuld und bittet sie, zurückzukehren. Aber für Sita kommt das zu spät, sie bittet die Erdgöttin, ihre Mutter, sie zu sich zu nehmen.[18]

Gleich zu Beginn der Kurzgeschichte wird erzählt, wie die ganze Familie einen Film ansieht, der ein dem der Sita ähnliches Frauenschicksal erzählt. Die Frauen weinen gerührt, Lakshmi verläßt das Kino, hört aber noch, wie der Ehemann im Film zu seiner Frau sagt: "You are my Sita". Damit ist ein traditionelles indisches Deutungsmuster interpretierend eingeführt. Der Film, von dem erzählt wird, fungiert als Verbreiter eines bestimmten Frauenbildes. Hier sieht die Autorin offenbar die ideologisch-mythische Wurzel des Ideals der dienenden, rechtlosen, liebenden und selbstverleugnenden Ehefrau. (Vor nicht langer Zeit druckte *The Hindu*, die größte englischsprachige Zeitung Südindiens, regelmäßig im Kulturteil eine Spalte, mit der religiös fundierte moralische Vorstellungen konservativsten Zuschnitts an die Öffentlichkeit getragen wurden, darunter immer wieder Ermahnungen an indische Ehefrauen, sich Sita zum Vorbild zu nehmen.)

Die Männer kommen in dieser Kurzgeschichte schlecht weg, sie sind vor allem die Nutznießer patriarchalischer Privilegierung. Siddarth versteht zwar, als akademisch ausgebildeter junger Mann, zu einem gewissen Maß, was seine Frau bewegt, aber er macht keinen einzigen Schritt, ihr zu helfen. Denn das Arrangement paßt ihm – wie auch seinem Vater – gut, er bleibt verwöhnt, wie er es als Junge war. Der einzige Rat, den er Lakshmi geben kann, ist, sie solle sich stärker an die Gepflogenheiten seiner Familie, und das heißt: seiner Mutter, anpassen. Für ihn wie seinen Vater gilt, daß sie das Haus den Frauen überlassen und ihm in die Sphäre der Öffentlichkeit entfliehen: *separate spheres.*

Die Gegenposition zum Sita-Komplex wird von Lakshmi (und ihrer Freundin) vertreten. Ihre normativen Vorstellungen ruhen auf den Forderungen nach Gleichheit, freier individueller Entfaltung, dem Recht auf Privatheit, individueller Liebe, freier Bestimmung des eigenen Lebens, Werten also aus dem heutigen humanistisch-feministischen, aufgeklärten Wertekanon. Ihr einziger Weg zu seiner Verwirklichung besteht darin, Ehestand und Obhut aufzugeben und sich in eine gefährdete Existenz niedrigen Ansehens zu wagen.

4. Die Nase im Chutney

Mit *Midnight's Children* (1981) hat, darin sind sich wohl alle Kritiker einig, für den indo-englischen Roman eine neue Epoche begonnen. Wie sein späteres Buch *Satanic Verses*, welches die *fatwa*, die verbrecherische Todesdrohung des iranischen Ayatollah Khomeini, gegen ihn auslöste, zeichnet sich auch *Midnight's Children* durch eine weitgreifende Indienstnahme von Ideen und

Erzählformen, Bezügen und Bildern aus östlichen und westlichen Kulturregistern aus. Sein Stoff indes ist die Geschichte Indiens seit 1947.

Saleem Sinai, der Erzähler, wird zur selben Zeit geboren wie das unabhängige Indien unter seinem ersten Premierminister Jawaharlal Nehru: um Null Uhr in der Nacht vom 14. auf den 15. August 1947. Zu dieser Mitternacht erblikken 1001 Kinder das Licht der indischen Welt, die nicht nur besondere magische Kräfte besitzen, sondern auch das Schicksal des Landes bestimmen werden. Eine dieser Kräfte ist, daß sie, wo immer sie sich in Indien aufhalten, miteinander kommunizieren können. Die Relaisstation dieses eigenartigen Kommunikationsnetzes ist der Erzähler, in seinem Kopf versammeln sich die Stimmen der Mitternachtskinder. Saleems Leben verläuft in überraschender Parallelführung zu der seines Landes, von Geburt an. Die Situation, aus der heraus Saleem seine und des Landes abenteuerliche Entwicklung erzählt, ist dadurch gekennzeichnet, daß er der Manager einer Chutney-Fabrik geworden ist und das Abfüllen überwacht. Dabei schreibt er, was wir lesen, und diskutiert es mit Padma, seiner Zuhörerin, Mitarbeiterin und Geliebten.

Schon im Jahre 1938 formulierte Raja Rao im Vorwort zu seinem *Kanthapura* das Dilemma des in englischer Sprache schreibenden indischen Schriftstellers: "One has to convey in a language that is not one's own the spirit that is one's own."[19] Rushdies Lösung des Widerspruchs liegt in seiner atemberaubenden, alles miteinander verwirbelnden und verschlingenden und dabei verändernden Fusion der Kulturen, die ich hier lediglich in zwei Aspekten näher betrachten möchte.

(1) Geschichte, Autobiographie, Mythos. Nicht nur die englische Sprache – sie, in Rushdies Worten, "needs remaking for our own purposes"[20] -, auch die Geschichtsschreibung muß verändert werden: davon handelt dieser Roman. Aber es geht nicht allein um eine Neubewertung der Zeit britischer Kolonialherrschaft (wie etwa in Sahgals *Mistaken Identity*), sondern vor allem auch um die Befragung britischer (westlicher) Geschichts*auffassung* auf ihre Wirklichkeitshaltigkeit und Nützlichkeit hin. Der westlichen Vorstellung von Geschichte – die, darf man wohl zusammenfassen, rationalistisch ist, linear, teleologisch, die sich auf Logik verläßt, Chronologie, säkulare Kausalität und Kontinuität – wird eine andere an die Seite gestellt, eine diskontinuierliche, imaginative und mythische. Beide zusammen ergeben etwas Neues.

Es fängt damit an, daß Saleem Indien 'ist', verkörpert, zusammen mit 1001 Mitternachtskindern. Er sei "fathered by history" (118) und gleichzeitig mit Handschellen an sie gefesselt (9, 420). Das zeigt sich vor allem in den *cracks* : während er erzählt, entwickelt sein Körper Spalten, Bruchlinien, Anzeichen baldigen Auseinanderbrechens, und das ist auch als Aussage über das junge Indien gemeint. Auch die andern Kinder sind "a mirror of the nation" (255); die Zahl 1001 weist auf Erfundenes und Märchenhaftes. Indem Saleem die

Geschichte Indiens als Autobiographie erzählt, der er gleichzeitig manche Züge eines historischen Romans gibt, stellt er die "ballooning fantasy of history" zu Betrachtung und Bewertung aus. Dabei kehren in der Genealogie des Erzählers wichtige Charakteristika der indischen Geschichte, wie der Autor sie sieht, wieder: so ist zum Beispiel sein Vater William Methwold (dessen Urahn, wie der Roman vermeldet, bei der Gründung Bombays behilflich war), seine Mutter Inderin; sein "alter ego" (179) ist Shiva, ein Militär, der Macht ausübt, die nicht von Wissen temperiert wird (während Saleem Wissen besitzt, ohne Macht ausüben zu können).

Saleem stellt aber auch alles, was er erzählt, in Frage als der unzuverlässige Erzähler, der er ist, er verdreht und vergißt und erfindet waghalsige Begründungen für historische Prozesse.

> Let me state this quite unequivocally: it is my firm conviction that the hidden purpose of the Indo-Pakistani war of 1965 was nothing more or less than the elimination of my benighted family from the face of the earth. (338)

Rushdie selbst hat 1983 in einem Aufsatz auf die *unreliable narration* seines Erzählers hingewiesen: sie sei gewiß kein "authoritative guide to the history of post-Independence India", sei nicht "history", sondern spiele mit "historical shapes" und sei, glaube er, "a useful analogy for the way in which we all, every day, attempt to 'read' the world".[21] Geschichtsschreibung wird zur Fiktion, und aus Fiktion wird Geschichte. Wirklichkeit und Wahrheit erscheinen als Konstrukte der Vorstellungskraft, der Erfahrung und der Sprache.[22] Dieser Gedanke relativiert unter anderen auch die Geschichtsschreibung britischer Kolonialherren. Gut, aber wem soll man trauen? Etwa dem mythischen Geschichtsbild, das Rushdie als weitere Dimension in den Roman einflicht? Es beginnt mit Saleems gewaltiger Nase, die ihn mit dem elephantenköpfigen Gott Ganesh verbindet. Dieser Sohn Shivas und Parvatis ist der himmlische Patron der Schriftsteller, weil er, der Legende zufolge, vor langer Zeit zu Füßen des Weisen Vyasa saß und dessen Worte als das Epos *Mahabharata* zu Pergament brachte. (Dieser genealogischen Einbindung der Nase wird im übrigen noch eine zweite hinzugefügt, indem Saleem sie als "the legacy of a patrician French grandmother -. from Bergerac – whose blood ran aquamarinely in his veins" (95) bezeichnet. Damit tritt zum Verweis auf die göttergleiche Ausstattung spielerisch der auf Cyrano de Bergerac, aus europäischem Adel, der auch ein gewaltiger Geschichtenerzähler war.)

Mythische Zeit kommt auch durch Padma ins Spiel, die nicht nur eine Art Erstleserin ist, sondern auch alltagsverbundene Kritikerin und Dialogpartnerin, der erklärt wird, was uns, den Lesern, erklärt werden soll, sowie diejenige, mit der Saleem die Fiktionalität der Fiktion bespricht. Sie wird mythologisch verortet, wird "one of the Guardians of Life [...] Padma the Lotus calyx, which grew out of Vishnu's navel, and from which Brahma himself was born; Padma the Source, the mother of Time" (194-195). Und Zeit läßt sich auch anders rechnen als in westlicher Geschichtsschreibung:

> Think of this; history, in my version, entered a new phase on August 15th, 1947 – but in another version, that inescapable date is no more than one fleeting instant in the Age of Darkness, Kali-Yuga [...] will last a mere 432,000 years! Already feeling somewhat dwarfed, I should add nevertheless that the Age of Darkness is only the fourth phase of the present Maha-Yuga cycle which is, in total, ten times as long; and when you consider that it takes a thousand Maha-Yugas to make just one day of Brahma [...]. (194)

In diesen Ewigkeitsatem wird ein weiterer Erzählmodus eingeblendet, der des Films : "I permit myself to insert a Bombay-talkie-style close-up – a calendar ruffled by a breeze, its pages flying off in rapid succession to denote the passing of the years" (346): Mischung, wohin das lesende Auge fällt.

(2) Erzählen, Identität. Nicht nur Geschichte, auch das Erzählen von Geschichten wird in *Midnight's Children* reflektiert. Das wundert uns nicht, wenn wir uns an Rushdies Meinung erinnern, daß das Erzählen "a political act" sei: "redescribing a world is the necessary first step towards changing it".[23] Rushdie vollzieht erzählend nicht nur seine *abrogation*[24] eurozentrischer Historiographie, sondern auch europäischer Erzählweisen, vor allem wohl des bürgerlichen realistischen Romans. Die Form des Erzählens muß dem Gegenstand adäquat sein – "multitudinous, hinting at the infinite possibilities of the country"[25] – und immer wieder überprüft werden. Deshalb erläutert Saleem seiner Zuhörerschaft – erst Padma, dann uns –, was und vor allem wie er gerade erzählt. Beispielsweise plaziert er eine Liebesgeschichte in östliche wie westliche Traditionen: "Once upon a time there were Radha and Krishna, and Rama and Sita, and Laila and Majnu; also (because we are not unaffected by the West) Romeo and Juliet, and Spencer Tracy and Katherine Hepburn." (259)

Am auffälligsten spitzt Saleem die Reflexion eigenen Erzählens in der Großmetapher der *chutnification* zu. *Chutney* - das im Roman auch als *pickles* auftaucht – bedeutet eigentlich Gehacktes, und es bezeichnet Ein- und Zusammengekochtes oder auf andere Weise süß oder sauer Präserviertes, das gern als würzige Beilage zu allen möglichen Gerichten gegessen wird. Saleem managt eine Chutney-Fabrik, und er selbst versieht diesen Umstand mit Bedeutung:

> Symbolic value of the pickling process: all the six hundred million eggs which gave birth to the population of India could fit into a single, standard-sized pickle jar; six hundred million spermatozoa could be lifted on a

single spoon. Every pickle jar (you will forgive me if I become florid for a moment) contains, therefore, the most exalted of possibilities: the feasability of the chutnification of history; the grand hope of the pickling of time! I, however, have pickled chapters. Tonight, by screwing the lid firmly on to a jar bearing the legend *Special formula No. 30: Abracadabra* [dies steht im 30. Kapitel, das die Überschrift "Abracadabra" trägt, D.], I reach the end of my long-winded autobiography, in words and pickles, I have immortalized my memories, although distortions are inevitable in methods. (459)

Hoffentlich, sagt Saleem und neckt uns wieder als unzuverlässiger Erzähler und Historiker, wenn die Welt eines Tages die "pickles of history" zu schmecken bekommt, wird man sagen können, sie besäßen "the authentic taste of truth", seien sie doch "acts of love" (461) für eine ansonsten vergeßliche Nation ("nation of forgetters", 37). Während er das sagt, pulverisieren *fissures* und *cracks* seinen (und, wir erinnern uns, damit Indiens) ausgemergelten Körpers, und alles kommt zu einem Ende. Was bleibt, sind die dreißig Krüge präservierter Geschichte, das eingekochte indische nationale widersprüchliche Selbst dreier Dekaden, das, wie sein Erzähler, als Subjekt der Geschichte unverwechselbar ist.[26]

Rushdies Erzählmethoden, von magischem Realismus zur Metafiktion, haben, zusammen mit anderen Merkmalen wie Diskontinuität, Mehrstimmigkeit, Parodie und Absage an die *grand narratives*, dazu geführt, Rushdies Roman zur Postmoderne zu rechnen. Vielleicht zu recht. Bedeutsamer aber scheint mir zu sein, hier Formen des subversiven Gegen-Diskurses zu erkennen, des Widerstands gegen Formen von *Orientalism* und westlicher Kulturhegemonie. "Rushdie's art constantly and consistently jolts its readers into an awareness of their ethno- and linguo- centrism."[27] Das Etikett "postmodern" aber subsumiert tendenziell jeden Autor, auch diesen, unter eine 'westliche' Kategorie, die regionale Zugehörigkeit und postkoloniale Stoßrichtung nicht enthält.

5. Weltstadt Bombay

Auf der vorgestellten Gleitskala zwischen *„rein Indischem"* und *"amazing mix"* gelangen wir mit dem Roman *Trying to Grow* von Firdaus Kanga, publiziert 1990, zu einer Position, in der so etwas wie ein Ost-West-Kontrast unsichtbar zu werden beginnt. Während Rushdies *Midnight's Children* noch die koloniale Vergangenheit einbegriff und die vielschichtige Übernahme verschiedener kultureller Hinterlassenschaften imaginativ inszenierte, kann *Trying to Grow* dies als gleichsam bereits geleistete Arbeit voraussetzen und zur Präsentation des neuen Dritten fortschreiten. Dieses neue Dritte ist die Metropole Bombay: sie liefert das *setting* für diesen Bildungsroman:

Brit erzählt sein Leben zwischen seinem achten und seinem achtzehnten Lebensjahr. Mit seinen Eltern Sam und Sera und seiner Schwester Dolly wohnt er in Colaba Causeway wie viele andere parsische Familien auch. Brit ist behindert (Osteoporose), er hat bis weit in die Pubertät hinein zerbrechliche Knochen und muß im Rollstuhl sitzen. Die Art und Weise, wie er damit fertig wird, bildet den zentralen Entwicklungsstrang des Romans. Wie andere junge Menschen auch, muß er die Schwierigkeiten überwinden, die die Herausbildung eines ausgewogenen Selbstbewußtseins, das Erwachen der Sexualität und den Eintritt in das Erwachsensein insgesamt begleiten, nur erhalten sie für seine Entwicklung schärfere und schmerzhaftere Konturen. Mit Hilfe seiner weltläufigen und großzügigen Familie erreicht er das *happy end* dieses Lebensabschnitts: Sein erstes Manuskript wird von einem Londoner Verlag akzeptiert, und er kann die Liebe der geliebten Frau gewinnen.

Die Lebenswelt dieser Parsenfamilie hat deutliche Anteile aus verschiedenen Kulturen. Da ist die parsische Religion, deren Bestattungsriten vorgeführt werden; da sind hinduistische Asketen, die zur Heilung Brits (vergeblich) in Anspruch genommen werden; da ist der junge Muslim in New York, den Dolly heiratet. Auch beziehen sich die Charaktere, allen voran der belesene Protagonist, auf Themen, Bilder, Personen, Texte und Gedanken aus dem westlichen wie dem indischen Repertoire: "I wouldn't have given a damn if he looked like Shashi Kapoor or Sean Connery or whoever" (134); das Taj steht neben Hadrian's Wall (158), die *Times of India* neben *Rebecca*, Ravi Shankar neben Chopin und Mozart (118). Zusammen ergibt das einen ganzen Kosmos, und Brit lebt in seinem Mittelpunkt. Das alte *centre-periphery*-Modell, in dem London (oder heute New York) als Zentrum figurierte, ist abgelöst: hier ist das Zentrum das Bombay der Parsen. Von hier aus steht dem Erzähler die Welt zur Verfügung, aus ihr wählt seine Subjektivität aus, was sie zur Konstruktion des kulturellen Ichs amalgamieren will. Das Ergebnis ist keine fragmentierte, sondern eine zusammengesetzte, facettenreiche, zu einem urteils- und handlungsfähigen Menschen gehörige Identität.

Von diesem parsisch-bombayischen Selbst aus ist das Fremde, das Andere nicht etwa angesiedelt in Großbritannien – die britische Kultur wurde selektiv einverleibt – oder in den USA – die stehen offen –, sondern es liegt in Indien selbst. Vielleicht liegt hierin der stärkste Ausdruck des neuen Dritten, des selbstbewußten *third space*. "We are reluctant Indians" (28/29), sagt Brit und meint damit nicht nur die Nahrung; Sera kommentiert das Verschwinden eines jungen Mädchens: "They've taken her away, [...] somewhere deep in India. Don't you know how big India is? Endless forests and as many villages as – as the stars up there. God, we've lost her" (95); Sera: "The Muslims are the traditional, nay, the historical enemies of the Parsees" (141) (die Tochter heiratet trotzdem einen); Brits Freund: "What sensible man would leave Bombay? You know what New Delhi's like? It's monstrous."(112-113).

Sera, als ihr Gangeswasser als Heilmittel angeboten wird: "How dare you bring your Swami's *su-su* to my House? [...] The river floats with corpses and sewage. Don't you know?" (225). Zum Heranwachsen gehört für Brit auch, daß er kulturelle Angebote ausprobiert: Als zum Beispiel die alte Jeroo, die das Gangeswasser als Heilmittel propagiert, auch tägliche 108 Gebete empfiehlt, probiert Brit diesen Weg der Heilung einige Zeit aus. Brit selbst faßt beide, Unverwechselbarkeit und sich wandelnde kulturelle Zusammensetzung, in ein Bild, das sich die große Straße, an der er wohnt, zur Vorlage nimmt:

> Like great rivers everywhere the Causeway could take it all: the disappearance of its European restaurants and residents, the coming of the rich refugees from Sind with their gaudy sari shops, the march of the hippies and the Arab invasion, the whores who chase them like camp followers. With every tributary the Causeway sparkled and glittered, more cosmopolitan, more gay than any street in India. (19)

Die unauflösliche Mischung hat indes, das soll nicht unterschlagen werden, durchaus eine Vorliebe für 'Westliches' (die besonders von Mutter Sela verkörpert wird). Die Welt dieser Parsen mit dem Verhältnis zwischen Eltern und Kindern, mit Pubertät, Behinderung, Initiation, Sexualität, Freizeit und Arbeit, mit ihrer Wahrnehmungs- und Problemlösungsstruktur könnte fast auch in einer andern Riesenstadt angesiedelt sein. Das "theme of growth and search for identity as a human being"[28] ist eher universell als spezifisch indisch. Im Ethos dieser Parsen "English occupies a place of prestige".[29] Brits Haltung ist uns vertraut, in ihm wird das Parsische entweder westlich oder allgemein-menschlich: "I've got to be alone. I have got to be Osteo Brit and not mind." (224) Aber der Ort ist Bombay, eine Art globalisierte Region, erzählt wie als Beleg für die Idee von der *global village* und gleichzeitig mit unverwechselbaren Markierungen ausgestattet, die uns hören, riechen und sehen lassen, daß dies ein Teil Indiens ist.[30]

6. Marc Aurel in Madna

In *English, August* von Upamanyu Chatterjee, veröffentlicht 1988, signalisieren schon Titel und erste Seiten die hybride Identität des Protagonisten. Sein Vorname Agastya stammt von einem Asketen, der sowohl in der *Ramayana* als auch der *Mahabharata* auftritt (4). 'English' war sein Spottname in der Schule, von seinen Freunden wird er 'August' genannt und von seinem Vater 'Ogu', während manche Kollegen ihn mit seinem Familiennamen 'Sen' anreden. In seiner Genealogie (Mutter katholische Goanesin aus dem Westen Indiens, Vater hoher bengalischer Beamter, geliebter Onkel Hindu und Sanskrit-Gelehrter), seiner Erziehung (englischsprachige Eliteschule in Dehra Dun, Studium der englischen Literatur), seinen Musikvorlieben (Blues und

Tagore) und vielen Details seines Lebensstils wird es durchgehalten. Und in der Sprache:

> "Amazing mix, the English we speak, Hazaar fucked. Urdu and American", Agastya laughed, "a thousand fucked, really fucked. I'm sure nowhere else could languages be mixed *and* spoken with such ease [...]. And our accents are Indian [...]." (1)

Zum offensichtlichen Zeichen für ost-westliche Kulturverschränkung macht der Autor die beiden philosophischen Systeme, die Agastya immer wieder zu Rate zieht, die Stoa, vertreten durch die *Betrachtungen* des Marc Aurel, und die *Bhagavadgita.* Diese letztere wird ihm von seinem Freund Sathe – in einer englischsprachigen Fassung! – strengstens anempfohlen, von einem Mann, der als blasphemischer Freigeist, kritischer Karikaturist und witziger Marihuanaraucher in der Provinzstadt Madna, in die Agastya versetzt wird, ein Außenseiterleben führt. Die Bhagavadgita, als philosophischer Traktat eingebettet in die dramatische Handlungsfülle der *Mahabharata*, wird generell als einer der zentralen Texte hinduistischer Ethik gewertet. Ihre Form ist ein langer Dialog zwischen Krishna, einer Verkörperung des Vishnu, der hier als Lenker des Kriegswagens auftritt, und Arjuna, der in die Schlacht von Kurukshetra gefahren werden soll, sich aber sträubt, weil die Gegner seine Verwandten sind. Agastya solle sie lesen, mahnt Sathe, um dem verderblichen Einfluß britischer Kolonialherren entgegenzuwirken, nämlich "making us incapable of appreciating ourselves". Um dies zu sagen, Sathe "pitched his voice high, in mimicry" (83), offenbar nationalistische Mahner karikierend; er selbst zeigt Agastya den Entwurf einer Karikatur, "an easily recognizable Krishna on the battlefield of Kurukshetra, but a bald fat politician in Arjun's place, scratching his head, his face creased with incomprehension." (82) Trotz der ironisierenden Brechungen nimmt Agastya diesen indischen Bildungsauftrag an und stellt die *Gita* neben seinen Marc Aurel ins Bücherbord. Es ist klar, daß sie für ihn anders konnotiert ist als zum Beispiel für Jagan in Narayans *Vendor of Sweets.* Immer wieder liest er in beiden Büchern, und, ohne daß er die beiden Gedankengebäude ausdrücklich vergliche oder theoretisierte, wird doch deutlich, daß er in beiden vergleichbare Ansichten zu Konzepten wie „Pflicht“ und „der Geist beherrsche die Leidenschaften des Körpers“ findet, einmal rational begründet, einmal im Rahmen der Idee vom Karma.

Agastya Sen tritt seinen Dienst im *Indian Administrative Service* in der heißen Kleinstadt Madna an. Zwischen ungeliebten Dienstpflichten, in einer nicht nur sprachlich fremden Umgebung, fern von seinen Freunden und den Freuden der Großstadt, sucht er Sinn und Glück in sein Leben zu bringen. Oder eigentlich in seine drei Leben: sein offizielles als Beamter, sein privates als Freund, Liebhaber, Leser usw., und sein (geradezu autistisch versperrtes) geheimes Leben mit nächtlichem Jogging, Masturbation und Marihuana. Reisen und Briefe halten die Verbindung zu Freunden und Verwandten in Delhi und Calcutta. Seine innere Ruhelosigkeit können die als weitgehend ineffizient gezeigte Verwaltung, die meist unbefriedigenden Kontakte und die nur selten befriedigende Arbeit nicht aufheben. Schließlich, nach diesem Probejahr, entschließt er sich, den Dienst zu quittieren und ein Jahr der Selbstreflexion zu widmen, bevor er sich für diesen oder einen andern Beruf entscheidet.

Agastya leidet nicht post-modern an einer fragmentierten Identität, sondern sucht seinen Weg in einer post-kolonialen indischen Welt. Dieser Charakter – individualistisch, milde depressiv, frech, anti-autoritär, Kopfspielen zugeneigt und dauernd auf der Suche nach Liebe – könnte auch in einem westlichen Industriestaat leben, jedenfalls was seine Lebensproblematik angeht: jugendliche Einsamkeit, Sinnsuche und Selbstfindung scheinen Universalien der Moderne zu sein. In Form und Farbe sind sie jedoch genauso spezifisch indisch wie die vielgesichtige Kultur, in der sie stattfinden: Sich von der Elterngeneration absetzende Jugendliche gibt es wahrscheinlich überall, aber wo anders als in Indien könnte man sie "the generation that doesn't oil its hair" (47) nennen?

Spezifisch ist auch hier ein weiteres Mal das *Raj Revisited.* Das Raj, das seit 1858 über einen dem Vizekönig unterstellten Beamtenapparat verfügte (den *Indian Civil Service*), wurde vom unabhängigen Indien beerbt: aus dem ICS wurde nach 1947 der IAS (*Indian Administrative Service*), der wesentliche Strukturen beibehielt. Er ist das professionelle Milieu, in dem Agastya sich bewegt; seine Schwächen nimmt er aufs Korn (Ineffizienz, Korruption), seine Stärken lernt er schätzen (Idealismus, Mut, Opferbereitschaft). Die im Roman auftretenden IAS-Beamten werden durch den Widerschein des ICS der Raj-Vergangenheit gleichsam von hinten beleuchtet. Einmal durch Erinnerungen an britische Herablassung und Heuchelei, und dann durch intertextuelle Verweise: man wird erinnert an Ronny Heaslop aus E.M.Forsters *Passage to India* von 1924 (170), und einer der Beamten, Menon, benutzt sogar Ruth Prawer Jhabvalas Roman *Heat and Dust* (1975), der zur Hälfte in den dreißiger Jahren dieses Jahrhunderts spielt, um seine Rolle in Absetzung von der dort vorgeführten kolonialistischen Haltung des ICS-Beamten Douglas Rivers zu definieren (39).

7. Der Kreis der Vernunft

Gleich im ersten Kapitel seines Romans *Circle of Reason*, der 1986 publiziert wurde, beginnt Amitav Ghosh, das abendländische Konzept des wissenschaftlich-technischen Fortschritts dem sarkastischen Blick preiszugeben:

Balaram, der Lehrer ist in einem kleinen bengalischen Dorf, begeistert sich für zwei Wissenschaften, die ihm den Fortschritt zu versprechen scheinen: die eine ist die Phrenologie, das Vermessen von Schädeln, und die andere verkörpert sich in Louis Pasteur, dessen Biographie er andächtig liest und hegt. Wie in einer kleineren Version des indo-pakistanischen Kriegs, und zur selben Zeit, gerät er in einen Machtstreit mit dem Grundbesitzer Bhudeb Roy, den er verliert. Im zweiten Teil des dreiteiligen Romans tritt sein Pflegesohn Alu in den Mittelpunkt, Weber von Beruf und durch Beulen im Gesicht verunziert. Ihn jagt Jyoti Das, Polizist, und er verläßt Indien. Unter der Obhut Zindis reist er auf einem kleinen Schiff in die Ölstadt Al-Ghazira in der arabischen Welt. Um Zindi, die fürsorgliche Puffmutter, herum haben sich eine Anzahl versprengter Inderinnen und Inder versammelt. Die meisten von ihnen verdienen ihr Geld beim Bau eines neuen Einkaufszentrums. Sein Einsturz und andere Gründe veranlassen Zindi und Alu, sich mit Freunden auf den Weg nach Westen zu machen. Über Alexandria kommen sie nach Algerien, immer verfolgt von Jyoti Das (der aber inzwischen vor allem seltene Vögel sucht). Im Haus des indischen Ärzteehepaars Verma proben sie die dramatische Fassung einer Legende aus der *Mahabharata* ein, die den algerischen Kollegen vorgeführt werden soll. Am Schluß machen sich Alu und Zindi auf die Rückreise nach Indien, während Jyoti Das über Tanger nach Düsseldorf will.

Von allen bisher angebotenen Zusammenfassungen wird diese wahrscheinlich am wenigsten dem Roman gerecht. Sie kann die figurenreiche, zufällig erscheinende, sprunghafte und sich in zahlreichen, mit Hilfe von Parallelismen, Symbolen und Motiven verknüpften, Nebenhandlungen verschlingende Anlage dieses Romans ganz und gar nicht wiedergeben. Wenn Vinay Kirpal recht hat mit seiner Behauptung, daß der indo-englische Roman sich durch "two outstanding attributes" auszeichne, nämlich *digressiveness* und *episodicity*[31], dann ist *Circle of Reason* ein Musterexemplar dieser Gattung. Ich möchte an dieser Stelle vor allem ein Charakteristikum hervorheben, das ihm einen Platz nahe dem Ende meiner gedachten Gleitskala sichert: das ist seine vielgesichtige metafiktionale Reflexion des Erzählvorgangs (was ihn mit *Midnight's Children* verbindet).

Die Welt wird erzählt, und darum ist sie: so könnte der erkenntnistheoretische Leitsatz dieses Romans lauten. (1) Sie wird erzählt, konstruiert, vorgestellt und zu einem sinnfällig geordneten Gebilde gemacht in der europäischen aufklärerischen Vernunft, der sich Balaram verpflichtet fühlt. (2) Sie entsteht erst im Erzählen der fiktiven Gestalten des Romans. (3) Sie wird mit Sinn ausgestattet durch mythologische Erzählungen und philosophische Konstruktionen des Hinduismus.

(1) Louis Pasteur. Für Balaram wird Vallery-Radots Biographie *Life of Pasteur* zum Buch der Bücher spätestens dann, als es als einziges dem Buchverbrennungsdrang seiner Frau entkommt. Ihm entnimmt er die Anleitungen für seinen lebenslangen Kampf gegen den Schmutz ("a clean body is a new body,

a new body a new life" (143)). "Balaram, antiseptic and pungent with disinfectant, had never been so happy" (61); beim Einsatz von Karbolsäure gegen seinen schmutzigen Gegner Bhudeb Roy empfindet er "terrible joy" (141). Aber er unterliegt. In anderen Szenen und Ländern tauchen Pasteur und die Karbolsäure immer wieder auf. Zum Beispiel war *Life of Pasteur* für den Sozialisten Mishra, zusammen mit Büchern von Huxley und Darwin und Bänden von *Science Today*, ein "beacon" seines Bücherregals (378). Balarams Exemplar findet Alu Jahre später in Algerien; auf der ersten Seite liest er den Satz: "To remember Reason". Dieses Buch, sagt Alu, "is the only real brother I ever had" (395). Im letzten Kapitel, als während der Theateraufführung Kulfi gestorben ist, soll ein Stück Fußboden gesäubert werden, um sie dort hinzulegen. Mishra fordert dafür "Ganga-jal", Wasser des Ganges, Frau Verma aber benutzt Karbolsäure. Für sie sind beide austauschbar: "It's just a question of cleaning the place, isn't it?" (411).

Was hier der *abrogation* ausgesetzt wird, ist aber nicht die heutige, zeitgenössische Technologie und Naturwissenschaft, sondern die des vergangenen Jahrhunderts. Soll das die Unsinnigkeit des westlichen Fortschrittsglaubens hervorheben? Oder die Rückständigkeit provinzieller Eiferer von Balarams Zuschnitt anprangern? Gewiß ist, daß diese alten europäischen Anleitungen zu Verstehen und Handeln sich als untauglich erweisen.

(2) Erzählen. Das Erzählen von Geschichten erscheint im Roman als das hauptsächliche Instrument der Charaktere, ihrer Welt Sinn zuzumessen. Oder stärker noch: Erst durch das Erzählen werden die eigenen Erfahrungen wirklich, wie hier:

> They had lived through everything Zindi spoke of and had heard her talk of it time and again; yet it was only in her telling that it took shape; changed from mere incidents to a palpable thing, a block of time which was not hours or minutes or days, but something corporeal, with ist own malevolent wilfulness. That was Zindi's power: she could bring together empty air and give it a body just by talking of it. They could never tire of listening to her speak, in her welter of languages, though they knew every word, just as well as they knew lines of songs. And when sometimes she chose a different word or a new phrase it was like the pressure of the potter's thumb on clay – changing the thing itself and their knowledge of it. (212-213)

Dies eine Beispiel muß als Hinweis darauf genügen, wie Ghosh immer wieder auf der Schöpferkraft des Erzählens besteht. Dabei hat er wohl auch sein eigenes Erzählen im Sinn. Indem sie dauernd neue Bilder von der Welt erzählend entwerfen, schwimmen die Charaktere "in a sea of metaphors"[32] und bringen dadurch Ordnung in die Welt, mehr noch: Ihre Welt bestünde nicht, würde sie nicht erzählt (einschließlich der Motive für das eigene Handeln). Damit ist, andersherum betrachtet, die Arena der Bedeutungen frei. Es gibt keine feststehenden Oppositionen (wie Kiplings *East and West)*, Bewertungen müssen ausgehandelt werden, man muß sich verständigen. Die Welt ist in Fluß und ohne inhärenten Sinn, der wird jeweils erzählend hergestellt. Zugleich ist der Roman eine begeisterte Feier des Erzählens und seiner existentiellen Wichtigkeit, die auf eine andere Weise Salman Rushdie in seinem märchenhaften *Haroun or the Sea of Stories* (1990) betont.

(3) Mythos, Religion. Aber die indische *grand narrative* hinduistischer Prägung scheint erhalten zu bleiben. Wie schon *A River Sutra* hat auch *Circle of Reason* eine deutlich religiöse Dimension. (Louis James und Jan Shepard haben sie in einiger Ausführlichkeit entfaltet.[33]) Zeugnisse sind beispielsweise das Spiel um Saraswati im ersten und das Theaterstück um Chitrangada im letzten Teil, vor allem aber auch die Überschriften für die drei Teile des Romans: "Satwa: Reason", "Rajas: Passion" und "Tamas: Death". Während *A River Sutra* sich dem monistischen philosophischen System der Vedanta zuneigt, stammen diese drei Begriffe aus dem System der Samnkhya, welches dualistisch ist.[34] Dieses System ordnet die Natur nicht nur in 24 Kategorien, sondern auch in drei *gunas* (Stränge, Dimensionen), die alles Diesseitige vollständig durchdringen. Während in der Vedanta *moksha*, die Befreiung der Einzelseele, durch schließliche Vereinigung mit dem All-Einen geschieht, muß sie in der Samnkhya sich isolieren. Ob diese Vorstellung einen Schlüssel zum Verständnis des Romans liefert, sei dahingestellt. Sicher scheint, daß mit den drei *gunas* an so prominenter Stelle doch die Möglichkeit einer allumfassenden Welterklärung angedeutet wird. Damit stünde *Circle of Reason* gleichzeitig am Ende der vorgestellten Skala und wiese doch in einem Bogen auf ihren Anfang bei *A River Sutra* zurück.

8. *Schlußbetrachtung: Auf dem Weg zum* meeting place

Schon 1936 beschrieb Pundit Nehru sich als "a queer mixture of the East and the West" und war sich nicht sicher, "if I represent any one at all".[35] Diese Frage, die für einen Politiker sicher schmerzhaft ist, kann mit Nutzen auf eine Literaturgattung gerichtet werden.

Soziologisch gesehen, kommen die indo-englischen Schriftsteller und Schriftstellerinnen überwiegend aus dem städtischen Bürgertum. Ihre Stimmen geben nicht dem Indien der Dörfer Ausdruck, sondern hauptsächlich dem der kleinen und großen Städte. Keinesfalls repräsentieren sie irgend eine indische Gesamtheit, schon deshalb nicht, weil es neben der englischsprachigen eine ganze Reihe anderer hochentwickelter indischer Literaturen gibt, die in Bengali, Hindi, Urdu, Tamil und anderen Sprachen verfaßt sind. Vielmehr richten sie sich nach dem Satz Sathes aus *English, August*: "Great literature has to have its regional tang" (48). Sie gehören, indem sie über die englische

Sprache, "the national elite language"[36], verfügen, zu einer Elite. (Meenakshi Mukherjee erwähnt, daß die privaten Eliteschulen, wie zum Beispiel die in Dehra Dun, Englisch als Unterrichtssprache benutzen, und daß an der Universität, an der sie unterrichtet, Englisch sich mit hohem Status verbündet.)[37] Aber ihres ist nicht mehr einfach das britische Englisch, ist nicht, um die Formulierung von Ashcroft u.a. zu benutzen, *English*, sondern eines der vielen *englishes* der Welt, also ein kreolisiertes, regionalisiertes Englisch. Eben dieser Umstand, daß *English/english* seit den Zeiten des Empire die Sprache transkulturellen Austauschs ist, geeignet für Amalgamierung, Grenzüberschreitung, Erweiterung und Wandel, war wohl eine Voraussetzung dafür, daß wir heute im indischen Roman englischer Sprache diesen lustvollen und "amazing" "mix" vorfinden.

Diese Literatur ist vielleicht Teil einer *emerging culture* (Raymond Williams), die, aus dem Ost-West-Kontrast herauswachsend, in friedfertiger Verbindung das Lokale und das Globale verbindet, in der Lage, zwischen Kulturen, auch denen *in* Indien, zu vermitteln und zu verhandeln.[38] Ihr "controlling temper is synthesis", schreibt Vinay Kirpal, "polymorphism where all religions, all communal groups including the minorities have an important place".[39] Man kann sie lesen, alle meine Beispiele stützen das, als überregional verständliche Stimme des säkularen Indiens, eine Stimme, die zwar der Sprachelite angehört, sich aber weder als Sprachrohr des *Hindutva* – also des Hindu-Nationalismus – noch des kämpferischen Islams noch des Separatismus' der Sikhs eignet, sondern als literarische Intervention in den zerstörerischen Kommunalismus des Landes.[40] Die Waffen der Kritik, "part of the historical legacy of empire"[41], richten sich nicht nur gegen alten und neuen Imperialismus von außen, sondern auch gegen Aspekte der eigenen Gesellschaft, wie ihre patriarchalischen Strukturen (*Bahu*), ihre träge Administration (*English, August*), naiven Fortschrittsglauben (*Circle of Reason)*, und anderes. Das Ost-West-Thema ist durchdacht, abgehandelt und erledigt, jetzt geht es mehr und mehr um das kollektive und gleichwohl diverse Selbst auf dem zusammenwachsenden Globus, um neue indische Erfahrungen in der *time-space-compression* der weltweiten Moderne. Aus der *contact zone* der Einleitung ist ein anderes Bild geworden: der *meeting place* lokaler und globaler Energieströme, wie Doreen Massey das in "A global sense of place" beschreibt. Wir sollen uns vorstellen, fordert sie, von einem Satelliten hinunter auf die Erde zu sehen und den Fokus immer enger einzustellen,

> holding all those networks of social relations and movements and communications in one's head, then each 'place' can be seen as a particular, unique, point of their intersection. It is, indeed, a *meeting place*. Instead then, of thinking of places as areas with boundaries around, they can be imagined as articulated movements in networks of social relations and understandings, but where a large proportion of those relations, experiences and understandings are constructed on a far larger scale than what we happen

> to define for that moment as the place itself, whether that be a street, or a region or even a continent. And this in turn allows a sense of place which is extroverted, which includes a consciousness of its links with the wider world, which integrates in a positive way the global and the local.[42]

Diese Autoren und Autorinnen sind Grenzgänger zwischen dem Globalen und dem Lokalen, Wanderer und Vermittler zwischen verschiedenen Kulturen und Zeichensystemen, deren Umrisse sie aufweichen, ohne die Unterschiede zu mißachten. Für uns europäische Leser und Leserinnen stehen sie einerseits ebenso offen wie die englische Schreibtradition, aus der sie kommen; als authentische Ausdrucksformen hybrider Art aus einer anderen Weltregion aber erschließen sie sich, andererseits, nicht ganz von selbst. Sie speisen sich aus westlichen *und indischen* Quellen, und wir müssen Arun Mukherjee zustimmen, der überzeugt ist, daß "there is no short cut to the meaning of the text except through immersion into the narratives of a culture".[43] Die Spannung zwischen Globalisierung und regionaler Besonderheit, zwischen uns und ihnen, zwischen 'West' und 'Ost', bleibt in der Rezeption erhalten. Was sich geändert hat, ist, daß wir nicht mehr im Zentrum sitzen: "I figure the centre is everywhere. It goes with the discovery that the planet is round, not flat."[44]

Anmerkungen

1 Zit. in R. Bharucha: "Somebody's Other", S. 9.

2 R. Kipling: "The Ballad of East and West". – In R.Kipling: *Sixty Poems*, S. 97.

3 Zit. in S. Hay, I. H. Qureshi: *Sources*, S. 45.

4 Die Formulierung, inzwischen vielfach benutzt (vgl. z.B. Ashcroft u.a.), stammt ursprünglich von Salman Rushdie.

5 M. L. Pratt: *Imperial Eyes*, S. 6.

6 Vgl. E. Said: *Orientalism*, passim.

7 S. Hall: "West and Rest", 277.

8 Vgl. Stichwort "asrama" in: B. Walker: *Hindu World*, S.84-86. Nach dieser Anweisung für hochkastige Hindus hat das Leben vier Stadien: *brahmacharya*, in dem der Jüngling seinen Glauben erlernt; *grihastya*, in welchem der erwachsene Mann Haus und Familie führt; *vanaprastya*, während dessen der fromme Hindu sich von Besitz, Familie und dem Treiben der Welt zurückzieht, um betend und meditierend den vierten Lebensabschnitt anzusteuern: *samnyasa*, der ausgefüllt wird von weltabgewandter Meditation, sich so auf Tod und Wiedergeburt vorbereitend.

9 "All Indians are not Hindus but all Indians must reckon with Hinduism since it is the dominant setting, the social and psychological atmosphere." (N. Sahgal: "The Schizophrenic Imagination", S. 118.)

10 Der überaus interessanten Frage, ob die Autorin diesen Roman auch als Intervention in den Disput um die geplante Aufstauung der Narmada – die Hunderttausende aus ihren Dörfern vertreiben, vermutlich dem spirituellen Aspekt und sicher-

lich der Pilgertätigkeit abträglich sein würde – versteht, lohnte sich nachzugehen.
11 Vgl. W. Walsh: *Indian Literature in English*, S. 62-97.
12 Umfassend zusammengetragen in G.P.Sarma: *Nationalism in the Indo-Anglian Novel*. New Delhi 1978.
13 Die Siegermächte des ersten Weltkriegs schaffen, zusammen mit dem säkularistischen Kemal Pascha Atatürk, das Sultanat ab -: bis dahin war seit geraumer Zeit der Sultan in Istanbul das formelle Oberhaupt des Islam, der Stellvertreter des Propheten (Khalif).
14 Vgl. ihre Autobiographie *Prison and Chocolate Cake*. Bombay 1954.
15 Sahgal, "Some Thoughts on the Puzzle of Identity", 1993.
16 In *JCL* 1, 1988, 18-25.
17 A Appachana: *Incantations*.
18 nach Walker: *Hindu World*, S. 404-405.
19 Raja Rao: *Kanthapura*, Foreword.
20 S. Rushdie: "Homelands", S. 17.
21 S. Rushdie: "'Errata'", S. 23-25.
22 Vgl. A Srivastava: "The Empire Writes Back", S. 67.
23 Rushdie: "Homelands", S. 13-14.
24 Ashcroft, *The Empire*, S. 38.
25 Rushdie, "Homelands", S. 16.
26 Vgl. A Srivastava: "The Empire", S. 69.
27 A Srivastava: "The Empire", S. 75.
28 D. Kohli: "Different Mirrors", S. 182.
29 Ibid.
30 Vielleicht ist es kein Zufall, daß in jüngerer Zeit eine ganze Reihe von indo-englischen Romanen in Bombay spielen (beispielsweise: Anita Desai, *Baumgartner's Bombay*, 1988; Rohinton Mistry, *Such a Long Journey*, 1991; Shashi Deshpande, *That Long Silence*). Seit ihrer Gründung durch die Engländer im 17. Jahrhundert hat sich diese Stadt zu einer der bedeutendsten, international vernetzten urbanen Agglomerationen Indiens entwickelt. Es scheint sich anzubieten, sie als neue Metropole den alten westlichen entgegenzusetzen. Auch muß erwähnt werden, daß sich die Parsen, indem sie weder muslimisch noch hinduistisch noch christlich waren oder sind, als schon lange prosperierende und weltoffene städtische Minderheit wohl besonders gut als Einwohner eines *third place* eignen.
31 V. Kirpal: "Has the In dian Novel Been Understood", S. 313.
32 G. J. V. Prasad: "The Unfolding of a Raga", S. 101.
33 L. James, J. Shepard: "Shadow Lines: Cross-Cultural Perspectives in the Fiction of Amitav Ghosh".
34 Vgl. hierzu H. Zaehner: *Hinduism*, S. 91 ff.
35 J. Nehru: *An Autobiography*, S. 596.
36 R. W. Stein: *Changing India*, S. 200.
37 M. Mukherjee: "Growing up by the Ganga", S. 110.
38 Vgl. S. Hall: "Culture, Community, Nation".
39 V. Kirpal: *The New Indian Novel*, S. xxi.
40 Vgl. etwa R.W. Stein: *Changing India*, Kapitel 6.
41 E. Said: *Culture and Imperialism*, 295.
42 D. Massey: "A global sense of place", S. 238-239.
43 A. Mukherjee: "First World Readers", S. 34.
44 L. Murray, zitiert in L. Strongman: "The Transmodern Author", S. 150.

Texte

Appachana, Anjana: *Incantations and Other Stories.* London 1991.
Chatterjee, Upamanyu: *English, August.* London 1988.
Ghosh, Amitav: *The Circle of Reason.* London 1986.
Kanga, Firdaus: *Trying to Grow.* London 1991 (1990).
Mehta, Gita: *A River Sutra.* London 1994 (1993).
Narayan, R.K.: *The Vendor of Sweets.* Harmondsworth 1983 (1967).
Rushdie, Salman: *Midnight's Children.* London 1982 (1981).
Sahgal, Nayantara: *Mistaken Identity.* London 1989 (1988).

Benutzte Literatur

Ashton, B., Griffiths, G., Tiffin, H.: *The Empire Writes Back. Theory and practice in post-colonial literatures.* London, New York, 1989.
Bharucha, R.: "Somebody's Other: Disorientations in the Cultural Politics of our Times". *Third Text* 26, 1994, 3-10.
Chewe, S., Rutherford, A. (eds.): *Unbecoming Daughters of the Empire.* Hebden Bridge, Sidney, Mundelstrup, 1993.
Coomaraswamy, A.K., Sister Nivedita: *Myths of the Hindus and Buddhists.* New York 1967.
Cronin, R.: *Imagining India.* London, 1989.
Ghosh-Schellhorn, M.: "Post-Colonial Literature?". *Gulliver* 33, 1993, 37-43.
Hall, S.:"The West and the Rest: Discourse and Power". – In Hall, S., Gieben, B. (Eds.): *Formation of Society.* Oxford, 1992, S. 276-318.
Hall, S.: "Culture, Community, Nation". *Cultural Studies* 3, 1993, 349-363.
Hawes, C.: "Leading History by the Nose: The Eighteenth Century in *Midnight's Children*". *Modern Fiction Studies* 39/1, 1993, 147-168.
Hay, S., Qureshi, I.H. (Eds.): *Sources of Indian Tradition, vol. ii.* New York, London, 1958.
James, L., Shepard, J: "Shadow Lines: Cross-Cultural Perspectives in the Fiction of Amitav Ghosh". *Commonwealth* 14(1), 1991, 28-32.
Kapadia, N.: "Imagination and Politics in Amitav Ghosh's *The Shadow Lines*". – In Kirpal, V. (Ed.): T*he New Indian Novel.* S. 201-210.
Kapadia, N.: "Narrative Techniques in the New Indian Novel". – In Kirpal, V. (Ed.): *The New Indian Novel.* S. 239-250.
Kipling, R.: *Sixty Poems.* London, 1961.
Kirpal, V. (Ed.): *The New Indian Novel in English: A Study of the 1980s.* New Delhi, 1990.
Kirpal, V.: "Has the Indian Novel Been Understood?". – In Rutherford, A. (Ed.): *From Commonwelath to Post-Colonial.* S. 303-315.
Kohli, D.: "Different Mirrors, Different Faces: Search for Identity in Firdaus Kanga's *Trying to Grow* and Shashi Deshpande's *That Long Silence*". – In Reckwitz, E., Vennarini, L., Wegener, C. (Eds.): *Traditionalism vs. Modernism.* Essen, 1994, S. 181-187.
Kumar, T.V.: "I Can't Get No Satisfaction: Upamanyu Chatterjee's *English, August*". – In Kirpal, V. (Ed.): *The New Indian Novel.* New Delhi, 1990, S. 169-178.

Lakshmi, V.: "Rushdie's Fiction: The World Beyond the Looking Glass". – In Nelson, E.S. (Ed.): *Reworlding. The Literature of the Indian Diaspora.* New York, Westport (Connecticut), London, 1992, S. 149-168.

Massey, D.: "A global sense of place". – In Gray, A., McGuigan, J. (Eds.): *Studying Culture.* London, 1993. S. 232-240.

Michel, M., et al.: "Indian Women Between Tradition and Self-Determination: Problems in the Reception of Indo-English Short Stories Written by Women". – In Platz, N. (Ed.): *Mediating Cultures. Probleme des Kulturtransfers.* Essen, 1991. S. 118-137.

Michel, M.: Postcolonial Literatures: Use or Abuse of the Latest Post-Word?". *Gulliver* 33, 1993, 6-23.

Mukherjee, A.P.: "First World Readers, Third World Texts: Some Thoughts About Theory and Pedagogy". *Gulliver* 33, 1993, 24-36.

Mukherjee, M.: "Growing up by the Ganga". – In Chew, S., Rutherford, A. (Eds.): *Unbecoming Daughters of the Empire.* Hebden Bridge, 1993, S. 109-113.

Nehru, J.: *An Autobiography.* Bombay, New Delhi, Calcutta, 1962 (1936).

Nelson, E.S. (Ed.): *Reworlding. The Literature of the Indian Diaspora.* New York, Westport/CT, 1992.

Prasad, G.J.V.: "The Unfolding of a Raga: Narrative Structure in the *Circle of Reason*". – In V. Kirpal (Ed.): *The New Indian Novel.* S. 101-107.

Pratt, M. L.: *Imperial Eyes. Travel Writing and Transculturation.* London, 1992.

Riemenschneider, D.: "History and the Individual in Anita Desai's *Clear Light of Day* and Salman Rushdie's *Midnight's Children*". – In Kirpal, V. (Ed.): *The New Indian Novel.* S. 187-199.

Rübeling, H.: "Weaving Multicultural Strands: Upamanya Chatterjee and Amitav Ghosh". – In Collier, G. (Ed.): *Us/Them. Translation, Transcription and Identity in Post-Colonial Literary Cultures.* Amsterdam, Atlanta, 1992, S. 177-183.

Rushdie, S.: "'Errata': or, Unreliable Narration in *Midnight's Children*". – In Ders.: *Imaginary Homelands.* S. 22-25.

Rushdie, S.: "Imaginary Homelands". – In Ders.: *Imaginary Homelands.* S. 9-21.

Rushdie, S.: *Imaginary Homelands.* London, 1991.

Rutherford, A. (Ed.): *From Commonwealth to Post-Colonial.* Coventry, 1992.

Sampietro, L. (Ed.): *Declarations of Cultural Independence in the English-Speaking World.* Milano, 1989.

Srivastava, A.: "'The Empire Writes Back': Language and History in *Shame* and *Midnight's Children*". – In Adam, I., Tiffin, H. (Eds.): *Past The Last Post. Theorizing Post-Colonialism and Post-Modernism.* New York, London, 1991, S. 65-78.

Stein, Robert W.: *Changing India.* Cambridge, 1993.

Steinig, S.: "R.K.Narayan's *Mr Sampath – The Printer of Malgudi* and The Man-Eater of *Malgudi* – Indian Mythology/Metaphysics as a Response to Contemporary Crises?". – In Reckwitz, E., et al. (Eds.): *Traditionalism vs. Modernism. Proceedings of the Annual Conference of the Association for the Study of the New Literatures in English, Essen 1991.* Essen, 1994, S. 189-202.

Strongman, L.: "The Trans-Modern Author: Five Contemporary Writers". *Kunapipi* 3, 1993, 146-161.

Walker, B.: *Hindu World. An Encyclopedic Survey of Hinduism.* 2 vols. London, 1968.

Walsh, W.: *Indian Literature in English.* London, New York, 1990.

Wolpert, S.: *A New History of India.* Oxford, New York, 1989.

Zaehner, R.C.: *Hinduism.* London, 1962.

Ronald B. Hatch, Vancouver

Chinatown Ghosts in the White Empire

For some time now Canadians have liked to represent their country as a mosaic of peoples and to point, with pride, to the ways in which this mosaic differs from the melting pot of the United States. Yet when one looks at the historical development of Canada, the notion of a Canadian mosaic (in the sense that all peoples and races were welcomed and recognized as making a positive contribution) proves to be largely untrue. There has been and continues to be racism (the belief in the superiority of a particular race and the consequent prejudice against other races) or nativism (dislike of foreigners) in Canada. Indeed, one would have to be strangely naive not to expect to find in Canada's history the same sorts of racism that one finds in other Western countries. Moreover, when people today use the term "mosaic" to describe Canadian society, they often forget that John Porter (who originally applied the term to Canada as the title of his 1965 book *The Vertical Mosaic*) had spoken, not simply of a "mosaic", in which all the pieces are of equal importance, but of a "vertical mosaic", a hierarchy of classes and peoples.[1]

Although Canada's racism has taken different forms with different peoples, it has been most pronounced with people of colour. After the mid-nineteenth century, when Asians began arriving in the new world, those who regarded themselves as "white" denigrated and attempted to stop the entry of those to whom they referred as orientals: the Chinese, the Japanese, and the East Indians. As a result, Chinese Canadians, Japanese Canadians and Indo Canadians have been slow in creating a literature in English. In this paper, I shall discuss the history of one of these groups - the Chinese Canadians - and examine the effect of racism on the development of the literature in English produced by the Chinese Canadian community.

As one of the earliest non-Native peoples in British Columbia, the Chinese are of especial interest in understanding Canada's development and its literature. Unlike immigrant groups who came to Canada via the east coast and the St. Lawrence river, and then moved west across the country in a process of settlement, the Chinese came directly to the west coast and then gradually travelled eastwards. The Chinese and Japanese in Canada are sometimes lumped together, but in fact they are two distinct communities with different although overlapping histories. The Japanese began immigrating to Canada some thirty years after the first Chinese immigrants, and they then took up a unique place in the fishing and boat-building industries. Although the Chinese began arriving after news of the Fraser River gold rush in 1858, and have been a part of the country's history ever since, it has only been since about the 1970s that a strong Chinese Canadian literature has surfaced. Because racism in Canada in the 1990s is not nearly so strong or so open as it was in the period before World War II, and because there are now some well-known Chinese Canadian writers (such as Evelyn Lau, Sky Lee, Paul Yee and Denise Chong), it is easy enough for those with short memories to imagine that conditions in the early Chinese community were much the same as those of today. In fact, it requires an act of historical imagination to reconstruct the process by which Chinese Canadians were able to give voice to their own experiences in literature. For much of the time, the Chinese have been ghosts in a country that was determined to remain homogeneously white.

In presenting white attitudes to the Chinese, it is important to point out that Canada's racist attitudes have not been essentially different from those in Europe or the United States. Indeed, when one begins examining racist attitudes towards the Chinese during the early years of settlement on the west coast, one needs to remember that when the Chinese first began arriving there was no Canada as such. When whites and Chinese began to meet in the late 1850s and 1860s during the gold rush – in Victoria, New Westminster, in the smaller settlements of the interior or along the banks of the Fraser – they did so at first in what were the two British colonies – Vancouver Island and the British Columbia of the mainland – and only after 1871 (when British Columbia joined Confederation) in a province of Canada. The whites who arrived in the early days brought with them general patterns of nineteenth-century European Sinophobia. That such Sinophobia should exist may seem odd to those who recall that in eighteenth-century Europe, the Chinese were often held up as a model of civilization. However, after the British opium wars of 1839-1869, attitudes changed: the Chinese emperor and his court were seen as corruptly authoritarian, social conditions were depicted as backward, and the poor in the countryside were portrayed as poverty-stricken. As James Morton has pointed out, throughout the second half of the nineteenth century, Europeans regarded the Chinese as an inferior race. They were believed to be less intelligent, disease-ridden, and immoral. Perhaps most telling of all was the belief that they constituted a completely different culture that could never assimilate to Western traditions.[2]

The early miners and settlers on the west coast brought with them to British Columbia a Sinophobia that had also been deepened in the gold fields of California where widespread racism had resulted in numerous riots against the Chinese. Anti-Chinese feelings, which had been largely theoretical or second-hand in Europe, took on a lived character in the new land when the white population came into close competition with a large number of Chinese. Where it would have been rare in Britain or Germany in the nineteenth century for the ordinary person to meet many Chinese, on the west coast of

North America the Chinese were for a time one of the larger population groups. Population estimates in the early years suggest that the Chinese represented from 15 to 40 per cent of the total population on the west coast. For the Crown Colony of British Columbia, the *Catalogue* for 1862 lists the following figures: "White males – 20,000; White females – 500; Chinese – 4,000-10,000; Indians – 10,000-15,000".[3] Over the years, however, the percentage fell dramatically as the white population increased at a far faster rate than the Chinese.

To understand why large numbers of Chinese came to the west coast of North America in the nineteenth century, one has only to recognize how difficult conditions were in southern China at the time. Political unrest and economic problems drove many males abroad to try and supplement their families' incomes. In fact for several centuries before this period, they had been travelling to South East Asia to earn enough money to capitalize their farms.[4] With the news of the gold strikes on the west coast of North America, many decided to travel to "Gum San" (Gold Mountain) as it was called, to make their fortunes in the new land. Along with other gold seekers, they went first to California and then north to Victoria, when news spread of the Fraser River gold strikes. In fact, the first Chinese to arrive in Victoria as a result of the gold rush were merchants from California who came north as a result of Governor Douglas's reputation for fairness to minorities. They were soon joined by Chinese miners from California and other Chinese directly from China, lured to *Gum San* by the tales of easy money. Many of the Chinese did not actively mine for gold, finding it more lucrative to work as cooks, laundrymen, teamsters or in market gardens. Among the whites, the Chinese became known as "John Chinaman".[5]

As soon as it became clear that the gold rush was attracting significant numbers of Chinese, the whites felt threatened and began venting their prejudices. Moreover, once the gold rush was over and British Columbia entered Confederation, the whites continued to see the Chinese as a threat. This time however, it was as a threat to their idea of a "white Canada". For the next half century, a large proportion of British Columbia's immigration was directly from Britain, and the cry went up that the province should cultivate what was thought of as its British character. Unlike the prairies, which were populated by large numbers of farming people from the Ukraine, British Columbia – as its name indicates – attempted to preserve its British connection. The Europeans who came to Canada were determined to preserve it for "whites". At Fort Langley the United Farmers were convinced that the Chinese "do not assimilate with the white population – and it is not desirable that they should."[6]

The result was open opposition to the Chinese of a kind that is difficult to imagine today. Certainly immigration is a much discussed topic in the 1990s in Canada, and immigrants from minority communities often complain about racism. Nor would I wish to deny that racism still exists in Canada, especially with the swelling immigration to Canada from the 1960s on. The difference is that today one rarely encounters it openly in the legislature, in newspapers or on radio talkshows. Almost all public institutions have policies which forbid the promotion of racism in any form. Before World War II, however, racism was overt and ubiquitous. Few whites felt ashamed to hold racist opinions. Indeed, when one finds racist opinions among the wisest and most thoughtful thinkers of the time, one recognizes that the term (with all its present day connotations) needs to be applied with caution to the earlier period. Certainly white people of the nineteenth and early twentieth centuries believed that they had the backing of science (social-Darwinist to the core) to prove that the Chinese were an inferior race, and they felt little or no compunction about displaying their dislike of the Chinese. Most whites appeared to regard it as a fact of nature that "John Chinaman" was inferior to them, and this attitude was frequently promulgated into law by various levels of government.

From the 1870s onwards, a series of anti-Chinese organizations such as the Asiatic Exclusion League and the Oriental Exclusion Association were formed to curtail the immigration of the Chinese and to prevent them from owning land or engaging in public works. These movements were often led by local provincial politicians, and the British Columbia legislature was particularly active in attempting to pass laws that imposed penalties on the entry of Chinese immigrants.[7]

Yet at the same time the British Columbia legislature was devising legislation to stop Asians from entering the country, one finds increasing demands from industry leaders for Chinese labour. The need for Chinese labourers was particularly acute in the case of the Canadian Pacific Railway. British Columbia had entered Confederation in 1871 with the promise of a railway linking the country from coast to coast within ten years. The construction of the railway was a massive undertaking, but absolutely essential if Canada was to span the continent from sea to sea. In 1880 Andrew Onderdonk, who was in charge of the B.C. section of the railway, realized that there simply was not enough labour for the job, and he wrote to Sir John A. Macdonald and convinced him that he needed large numbers of Chinese labourers to complete the railway.[8] With his previous experience of railway building in the United States, Onderdonk knew that the Chinese were excellent workmen and that they would work for lower rates than whites. He also recognized that the Chinese could be persuaded to do some of the more dangerous work, especially the blasting of tunnels through the mountains along the Fraser River, work that white workers often refused.

As a result of the economic situation in British Columbia, there were two opposing forces at work. The general population of British Columbia wanted to restrict Chinese immigration, but an influential group within industry wanted cheap, industrious workers, and favoured allowing the Chinese into the country. The Chinese worked for about one-third to one-half of the wages of white workers. Moreover, they were known as being hard working, industrious, and loyal, so they were in high demand with many employers. Demand for Chinese labour came not only from the railway, but also coal mines around Nanaimo, logging camps on Vancouver Island, and fish canneries on the coast.

When one turns to consider the Chinese who came to Canada, it is a surprise to discover that they came almost entirely from the Sze-yap area in the province of Kwangtong, southwest of Canton, a tiny region, not more than fifty miles in radius. They came from communities having a strong kinship basis, and it was these kinship relations which allowed men to leave their wives and children in the care of close family members in order to travel abroad to better their family situation.[9] As a result, a very large proportion of the Chinese who came to Canada were men who came alone without their families. Nor did they initially think of themselves as immigrants in the normal sense of the term, since they had no intention of staying in Canada as settlers. The idea was to make their stake, send it back to their families, and then return themselves. The men were sojourners in a strange country. Although the numbers of Chinese who came were large, figures have to be treated with caution, since the Chinese population in Canada was highly mobile, with people continually entering and leaving the country. For example, Onderdonk imported some 15,000 Chinese labourers from 1880 to 1885, but at no time did he have more than about 7,500 people on the payroll.[10] The historian John Norris estimates that about half the Chinese who came to Canada before 1923 returned home.[11]

One of the major complaints by the white settlers about the Chinese sojourner was that he sent most of the money he made in Canada back to his family in China, and consequently the country did not benefit from his wages. Another charge was that the Chinese sojourners did not become part of the community, but stayed in their own settlements, Chinatowns. In truth, since most of the Chinese knew little English, they tended to form isolated communities, having been driven at first to accept the lowest paying jobs, on the railways, in the logging camps, the mines and the canneries. Of course, these were exactly the jobs the whites left to them, jobs they did not want themselves, especially at the level of wages for which the Chinese worked. And one must not forget that legislation made it impossible for the Chinese to gain important positions. Nevertheless, the Chinese soon developed a niche in the service industries. They became expert market gardeners, opened laundries or restaurants, and developed small family corner stores that stayed open long hours.

Calls for restrictions against the Chinese generally originated in British Columbia where, until after World War II, most Chinese lived. One of the first acts of the provincial legislature after Confederation was to deny the Chinese the provincial franchise, thus effectively barring the Chinese for the next 70 years from any real political power or social equality. Moreover, once it was clear that the railway was nearing completion, the Prime Minister of Canada instituted the 1884 Royal Commission on Chinese Immigration. The report of this Commission led to a bill in the Federal Parliament which disenfranchised all Chinese immigrants everywhere in Canada, and it was not until after World War II that the Chinese in Canada were given the vote.

Macdonald's Royal Commission also led to the first Chinese Immigration Act in July of 1885. The act stated that all Chinese on entry into Canada (except for diplomats, merchants, men of science and tourists) had to pay the sum of $50.00, a head tax. This was increased to $100.00 in 1901 and to $500.00 in 1903[12], and when even this did not prove enough to satisfy the whites, the second Chinese Immigration Act of 1923 was passed. Because the act prevented almost all Chinese immigration to Canada, it became known as the Chinese Exclusion Act, and is often referred to by that name even today.

Although the passing of the Chinese Immigration Acts is evidence enough of white hostility to the Chinese, they actually give little idea of the ongoing day-to-day harassment of the Chinese on the west coast. This is not to say that there were not people in British Columbia who defended the Chinese. For example, one finds comments by various individuals who recorded their esteem for their Chinese houseboys.[13] And as has already been mentioned, a number of industrialists praised them as workers. But these comments tend to be paternalistic, and it is apparent that public opinion was largely against the Chinese. Newspaper editors and politicians were of the opinion that Chinatowns were a blot on the map of white cities and the Chinese should be prevented from gaining a larger place in the country. It was always possible, especially in depressed economic times, to whip up animosity against the Chinese. In 1907, a riot in Vancouver's Chinatown caused great destruction of property. But the riot was only the culmination of a long list of daily insults.

The extent of hostility towards and fear of the Chinese (fear is the other side of hostility) can be seen in the ways in which, after having stopped Chinese immigration in 1923, the white population then tried to prevent those Chinese people already living in the country from owning land or gaining important positions. For example, the 1927 *Report on Oriental Activities Within the Province* that was prepared for the Legislative Assembly was clearly designed to prepare the way for a law denying all people of Asian descent the right to hold land. The report states: "Resolved, That the Legislature be requested to investigate as to whether legislation can be enacted to prevent Chinese and

Japanese from owning, selling, leasing, or renting land in British Columbia, or, in the alternative, imposing conditions upon their rights of ownership."[14] The Report went on to urge the Legislature that "the field of industrial and commercial activities of all Orientals now in Canada and particularly in British Columbia should be restricted by legislation."[15] Although the writers of the Report recognized that, over the three-year period from 1924 to 1927, "no Chinese have been admitted into Canada as immigrants," they were convinced that the Chinese already within Canada had "invaded" the commercial and industrial areas. Moreover, even though there were very few Chinese women in Canada in proportion to men, the writers of the report alleged that the "natural increase" of the Orientals was very high and that the chronic unemployment in B.C. could be traced to the Chinese. The reason: the Chinese would work for less than whites and were taking jobs that should be reserved for whites.

When one examines the conditions of Chinese life in Canada, one would expect to find a great deal of resentment at their treatment by the whites. And while there is no doubt that the Chinese disliked intensely the treatment meted out to them, most of their efforts went into building a viable community in the face of white hostility. It was a difficult task. Because the population consisted mostly of young, single men, the Chinese were unable to follow the usual immigrant pattern of using their family structure to recreate their cultural community. Moreover, because many regarded themselves as sojourners, and looked forward to the time when they would return to China, they thought of themselves as essentially Chinese and not Chinese Canadian. Leaders of the Chinese community created organizations that protected their members against white harassment, and the success of these benevolent organizations became a prime force in creating the Chinese Canadian community.[16]

Yet even within these benevolent organizations one finds an unusual development. In Canada, the developing elite among the Chinese tended to be the merchant class who had managed to bring their wives from China. Unlike in southern China where the merchant class had been disparaged, in Canada the merchants became wealthy and influential, the leaders of the community. Moreover, these merchant leaders were quick to see that it was in their own business interest to create a self-contained community which could function virtually independently of the white community. Thus they counselled their fellow Chinese to withdraw into their own community and to create themselves as a garrison within the white cities. There is a comparison here to what the Roman Catholic church in Quebec urged on the French Canadians so that they too could survive as a community with their own language and values – in the midst of a sea of English speakers. The merchant leaders counselled the Chinese people to keep to themselves, uphold their Confucian values and refuse to engage in activities which were seen as "white". The tactics, moreover, were clearly good ones, considering that the Chinese did not have political power in Canada until 1947 and that there was virtually no new Chinese immigration from 1923 to 1947.

Another aspect of Chinese thinking that needs to be mentioned in understanding the development of the Chinese community in Canada is the Chinese counterpart of white racism: many Chinese immigrants were themselves racist and regarded the whites of British Columbia as a race of barbarians. This "reverse racism" developed originally in China as a result of the British opium wars, but it also grew out of what the Chinese saw of the whites in Canada. Part of it sprang from the whites' xenophobic activities against the Chinese, but apart from this, the Chinese tended to view the whites as a race of uncultivated materialistic traders, interested only in making money. Earlier I used the term "ghosts" to characterize how the Chinese became ghostly, unwanted presences in British Columbia. Ironically, the Chinese use a similar term for white Canadians. They call them *Bok gwei*, or white ghosts. The Chinese saw white Canadians as ghosts because the whites appeared to have no sense of piety towards their ancestors. Fearing that they too might be contaminated by the white disease and lose their sense of culture and tradition, the Chinese avoided the whites whenever possible.

Consequently, the Chinese Canadian community withdrew into itself until the period after World War II. At this time white Canadians slowly realized the unacceptability of their racist attitudes towards Asians. This is not the place to discuss the reasons for this change, but the experience of World War II, with its atrocities, played a part. Another important factor lies in the disintegration of the great European empires after World War II. India won its independence in the same year that the Chinese gained the franchise in Canada. At the same time, the map of Africa also began to change drastically. In other words, after World War II, imperialism lost its sense of inevitability or naturalness. Westerners started on the long road toward seeing a world of independent nations, rather than colonial peoples. Of course with the rise of economic super powers we are now developing yet another type of colonialism, but that is a different story. Certainly once the Canadian government gave the Chinese the franchise in 1947, they began the slow process of integrating into mainstream Canadian life, entering the professions to become nurses, engineers, school teachers and lawyers. As was to be expected, it took almost two generations for the Chinese community to produce writers capable of telling its story. In this regard, it is interesting to note that the recent anthology of Chinese-Canadian writing, *Many-Mouthed Birds* (1991), takes as its title a phrase signifying people who talk too much and let out secrets. A many-mouthed bird is one who speaks out of turn when he should be quiet, one who endangers the entire community by telling the secrets of the tribe.

The writers in this anthology saw themselves in the eyes of their own communities as speaking out of turn, defiling their own nests. Yet it was just such outspoken people who were needed if the Chinese Canadian community was to break out of its isolation.

Turning now to the subject of Chinese Canadian literature, one should begin by mentioning briefly the earliest works. The first known writings are the short pieces scratched on the walls of the quarantine centre in Victoria in the 1860s and 1870s by Chinese immigrants on their first arrival. They are of course in Chinese, and they record the immigrants' feelings of desolation and homesickness. The next known piece is something of a curiosity, the *Chinese and English Phrase Book and Dictionary*, which may have been published as early as 1892. An edition of 1897 is noted and there is an extant edition with a preface by "T.J.G." from December 12, 1913.[17] This dictionary is of interest because it not only lists words and offers sample invoices and letters; it also presents short situations or conversations that resemble stories. A good example is the conversation in which a Chinese workman asks about the conditions of work on the railway. The author supplies information about the wages of the time and the living conditions and gives a lively impression of the Chinese situation – in both English and Chinese. The next stage in the creation of a Chinese Canadian literature is to be found in Chinese newspapers. The *New Citizen* appeared from 1949 to 1953 in Vancouver. It then moved to Toronto and was replaced in Vancouver by the *Chinatown News*, the longest running Chinese Canadian newspaper in English in Canada. From time to time, the *Chinatown News* included short literary pieces, especially serialized fiction.

Although this early evidence is important, Chinese Canadian writing in English could not really begin until the Chinese felt the possibility of acceptance into the mainstream of Canadian society and, as has been seen, this did not happen until after World War II. Even then, literature at first did not seem to hold out potential rewards for Chinese Canadians. During this period the families impressed upon their children that they must choose practical occupations that would bring in a steady salary. Behind this view lay the notion that the successful children would help to improve the family's position in society. The students who went to university at this period were thought of as pioneers venturing into strange territories of a potentially hostile white society.

Jim Wong-Chu, who has been active for many years in the Asian Canadian Writer's Workshop, attests that it was in the early 1960s that the first generation of Chinese Canadian writers emerged. He notes that these writers saw themselves as rebelling against their families and their traditions, which they perceived as restricting them to typically Chinese occupations and patterns of thought. These young writers were also helped by a series of events that coincided in the 1960s and that encouraged them to believe that they could rebel against their families and societies to become writers. Wong-Chu notes:

> In Vancouver, the Cultural Revolution in China influenced local politics and unleashed the first of a series of Asian immigrant waves beginning with those who fled the 1967 riots of Hong Kong. During those heady times, a group of UBC students, inspired by a radicalized visiting Asian American professor began the process of re-examining their history and identity. They formed the Asian Canadian Coalition, hosted a conference and created historical exhibitions on campus. The ACC's Chinese component was called *Gah Hing*, the Japanese component was the *Wakayama group.*[18]

Wong-Chu indicates that there were also other, perhaps less obvious, social influences on the development of emerging writers in the Chinese Canadian community. Curiously enough, one of the more important may have been the "hippie" movement. With their criticisms of conventions, the hippies showed young Chinese Canadians that there were other people struggling to break out of traditional societies. Another influence in the 1960s was the protest movement against the American war in Vietnam, which revealed that people from different backgrounds could join together against racism of different kinds. A fourth important influence was the Afro-American movement and other Third World minority movements which showed that people of colour could work together to advance their own goals. All of these influences together formed a critical mass of Chinese Canadian youth who believed that they could become writers and do something different for themselves and their community.[19]

One of the immediate developments of this radicalization was the development of the Chinese Canadian Writer's Workshop which published the magazine *Gum San Po* in 1974. Although the magazine lasted for only two issues, it included Sean Gunn's well-known satirical piece "Lofaantown", a tour guide to white Vancouver, based on, but reversing, the many tourist articles about Chinatown that were proving so tiresome to the new generation of Chinese. Gunn's satire shows the Chinese gaining confidence in their ability to see themselves as the centre instead of merely a margin. In the following years, "Pender Guy", an English-language Chinese Canadian radio programme, was developed on Vancouver's Co-op radio, under the leadership of Garrick Chu.[20] This ran for five years, from 1976-1981, and included many literary pieces that remain uncollected.

In 1976 the Chinese and Japanese writers groups joined forces to begin creating the first anthology of Asian Canadian writing, which appeared in 1979 under the title of *Inalienable Rice*. In the same year the Asian Canadian Writer's Workshop was founded, a collective organized to help writers. Its membership included names that were to become well known in only a few years: Paul Yee, Sean Gunn, Rick Shiomi and Jim Wong-Chu. This organization was crucial in enabling Chinese Canadian writers to exchange ideas and eventually to blossom with their own books.

There is not time to offer a full-scale discussion of the explosion of Chinese Canadian literature that has taken place since the 1970s and which is producing new publications every year, but the best place for someone new to the subject is undoubtedly the anthology edited by Bennett Lee and Jim Wong-Chu, *Many-Mouthed Birds* (1991), which collects some of the finer writing from the previous two decades. As with much immigrant writing, many of the pieces in the volume are designed to record the memories of the older members of the community before they die. In turn, this process of retrieval tends to position the writer between the older traditions and the newer values. For example, Lucy Ng's poems work to recapture a sense of the past, of the memories of her parents and grandparents. But as with many children of immigrants, Ng finds that the very process of retrieval leaves her feeling that she stands outside the earlier tradition in a space that is empty.

The novel which to this point best captures both the historical development of the Chinese Canadian community and the feeling of being Chinese-Canadian – a hyphenated being – is Sky Lee's *Disappearing Moon Cafe* (1990). As both a feminist and a postmodernist, Sky Lee (pseudonym) offers an historicist account of a Chinese extended family in Canada from 1882 to the present, and yet is able to do so without being linear or suggesting that the narrator is the sum total of the historic narrative line. In fact, the novel's emphasis upon the role of the reader situates both the narrator and reader, not within an historical continuum that naturally contains meaning, but within fragments of time from which meaning is always to be constructed. The postmodern element of the novel also means that Sky Lee rejects any easy assimilation to what more conventional critics would term the mainstream of Canadian culture. Recently Sky Lee has followed up her success in *Disappearing Moon Cafe* with a collection of short stories, *Belly Dancer* (1994). An eclectic series, the stories concern both white and coloured women. While a number of the stories are fine, it would appear that some of them are early work, in a much more mimetic style than her experimental novel.

The most famous Chinese Canadian writer today is probably Evelyn Lau, although this is partly a result of the notoriety she gained for *Runaway* (1989), a kind of diary-memoir of her life as a teenage prostitute and drug addict. Lau ran away from home at age fourteen, but was already at this period writing poems and having them accepted in magazines. When she found an editor and published her journal of life on the streets as *Runaway*

(1989), it was an instant best-seller, making Lau one of the better known authors in Canada – before she was twenty-one. She has also published two books of poetry and a collection of short stories *Fresh Girls* (1993). Centering on sado-masochistic relationships, the stories are sometimes dazzling in their imagery.

Curiously enough, Lau seldom mentions in her writing that she is Chinese Canadian; when asked, she says that she thinks of herself as a writer rather than an ethnic writer. While understandable, this stance sometimes creates problems in her writing. In *Runaway*, for example, she never explains her reasons for running away from home. When a film was recently made of the book, the film-makers explained the mystery by indicating that Lau is the daughter of immigrant parents. The mother in particular is depicted as someone who tries to force her daughter to succeed in order to assure her own sacrifice, thus placing enormous pressures on the teenager. Whether in fact this is the real explanation for Lau's running away into the hell of Vancouver's streets remains unclear.

In fact, some writers from minority backgrounds now see the emphasis on their ethnic background as a trap. Joy Kogawa, the most celebrated Japanese Canadian writer, has made it clear that she dislikes the fact that she is expected to continue writing about her experiences as a Japanese Canadian, as if that is her only theme. Certainly many of the Chinese Canadian writers choose to write about subjects that have nothing to do with being a Chinese Canadian. Ben Soo, for example, does not mention his Chinese heritage. Nor does Jam Ismail. On the other hand, a writer like Fred Wah, one of the original TISHites in the 1960s, who began writing in the Black Mountain vein, without giving a thought to ethnic issues, became interested in the subject many years later when multiculturalism became valued. In *Waiting for Saskatchewan* (1985), he documents the search for his Chinese grandfather, a subject that caught the critics' attention and won the volume the Governor General's award.

Another important genre for Chinese Canadian literature is children's literature. Works for children are especially important in giving the new generation role models. Here the first in the field was Sing Lim with *West Coast Chinese Boy* (1979), which was so successful that it recently went into a second printing. For slightly older children, Paul Yee's *Breakaway* (1994) is a fine story of a young Chinese Canadian determined to succeed in the world beyond the Chinese community through the sport of soccer.

Among the poets, Jim Wong-Chu, in his poems, *Chinatown Ghosts* (1986), offers one of the subtler evocations of life in Canada. A "paper son", Wong-Chu was brought to Canada by his aunt in place of her own son who had died. With the quota system still in place until the 1960s, the Canadian government had given her the right to bring only one person with her, and the family decided that the important paper should be used by her nephew, which accounts for Wong-Chu's hyphenated name. Most interesting about Wong-Chu's poetry is the way he shows how the search for Chinese Canadian history is the means of opening his own identity. In the poem "Tradition", the opening of a bundle to find the "sweet rice within", signals the moment when he finds himself beginning "to open".[21] The transformation of the self comes once the protective leaves are stripped away.

In observing Chinese Canadian writing, one naturally expects to find the writer placing the emphasis on the Chinese experience within Canada, as does Wong-Chu's poem. While this is the usual emphasis, it hides the fact that the Chinese immigration experience changed not only the immigrants in Canada but also the family left behind in China. In her award-winning novel/social history, *The Concubine's Children: Portrait of a Family Divided* (1994), Denise Chong draws on her own experience to offer a view of the two-family system. Chong, a former senior economic adviser to Pierre Trudeau, tells of her grandfather Chan Sam and his arrival in Canada in 1913 and of his difficult life in Vancouver's Chinatown. Although he was married in China, Chan wanted sons and thus had a "concubine", seventeen-year-old May-ying, a servant girl, sent over from China to Vancouver. With May-ying, Chan had three daughters. When the first two daughters were of school age Chan and May-ying took them back to his village in China to be looked after by his at-home wife, Huangbo. When May-ying became pregnant again, she convinced Chan to return to Canada and this is where Hing, the mother of the author is born. Thus it is that the two families are separated. Chong does a superb job of conveying the village world in China, with Chan returning to build the great house of his dreams. But she also tells the story of May-ying in Vancouver and Nanaimo, working as a waitress and sending a large part of her earnings to help Chan build his house. Part of May-ying's reasoning for doing this involves the Confucian deference to the male; the other part is that Maiying enjoys her freedom in Canada. Sending a part of her wages to China seems a small price to pay. As she says, "Naturally, I'll send him what he's asking for. I'll borrow. Anything to keep him in the village and out of my way".[22] Although Chan returned to Canada when conditions in China became desperate, his two families – in China and Canada – never met again. At least not until 1987 when Denise Chong and her mother finally visited the other side of the family, and for the first time in 50 years the family was rejoined. As Chong tells the story of this divided family, we see the Chinese in Canada as a people truly caught between two countries, with family in each, and each going its separate way.

The increasing interest in conveying the Chinese part of the Chinese-Canadian experience has meant that a number of works by Chinese Canadian artists have begun to use both Cantonese and English. Betty Quan's play *Mother Tongue* (produced, but as yet unpublished) centres on a Chinese Canadian family and the difficulties the family have in communicating in an English-speaking environment. The mother in the play can speak only Cantonese; her sixteen-year-old son Steve lost his hearing at age eleven and speaks in sign language. The daughter, who has been able to bridge the different languages, is about to leave to go to graduate school, and as a result it looks as though the family will lose its only connecting thread. In order to symbolize the need to build bridges between the languages and the generations to keep the family together, Quan includes from Chinese folklore the symbol of the Jingwei bird. The Jingwei drops twigs and stones into the ocean to build a bridge to her land-bound family. Strengthening the sense of the divided family, Quan includes flashbacks to the mother's family in China from whom she was separated in the time of Mao. As the play reveals, the family died in Mao's work camps.

Since Chinese Canadian drama in English is wholly new, it requires the construction of an infrastructure. The Vancouver Firehall production of the play featured actress Alannah Ong, who recently played in the film "Double Happiness". In order to improve the possibilities for Chinese Canadian actors, Ong plans to teach at the newly formed Greater Vancouver Academy of Performing Arts in Richmond where, she said, she "hopes to train a lot of wonderful Asian actors".[23]

As should be evident from this brief survey, one of the main features of Chinese Canadian literature is the manner in which it explores its own community in its relations to the white community. Given all the earlier overt racism directed against the Chinese by the whites, it is surprising to find so little animosity by Chinese Canadians in their writing. In part this is the result of the community deciding to get on with their lives within Canada. Given the chance finally to join the mainstream, they have generally taken it, while maintaining some of their own traditions. Most have decided not to use the past as a weapon against the white population, but as a means of healing.

The Canadian government's initiatives to move the country in a multicultural direction have also helped Chinese Canadians to develop their own literature. As was mentioned earlier, although some Canadians assume that the country has always been multicultural in focus, in fact the focus on multiculturalism developed only in the 1960s – at the very time when Chinese Canadians were beginning to find their voices. The two are in fact closely connected, and tied to an interesting development in Canada's history. Howard Palmer has noted that in the 1960s the Pearson government wanted to have French recognized as an "official" language. To this end, the Royal Commission on Bilingualism and Biculturalism was formed in 1963. But as the commissioners travelled around the country, they discovered that the minority groups, the Chinese included, resented the fact that only English Canadian and French Canadians were being valorized. To meet these complaints, the commissioners decided that they would have to extend biculturalism to multiculturalism. The complaints of the minorities were given partial redress by Trudeau's government in October 1971 with the introduction of "a multicultural policy within a bilingual framework".[24]

The Multiculturalism Act itself, which came into law only in July of 1988, has been enormously helpful to minority communities. Not only does the act give the stamp of approval to the preservation of minority traditions, the Programs Branch of Multiculturalism and Citizenship Canada makes funds available to help the various communities. One cannot help noticing how many of the more prominent books of the Chinese Canadian community were published soon after the Multicultural Act was passed – with help from this fund. Sky Lee's *Disappearing Moon Cafe* and *Many-Mouthed Birds* are only two of the more prominent. Publishers cannot, however, apply to the Department of Heritage for funds for just any kind of ethnic minority book. For example, one could not obtain funds under this program for a book about the Holocaust. The guidelines state that the purpose is to "promote the development and expression of heritage cultures as an integral part of Canadian artistic and cultural life."[25] In other words the book must show how a minority adapts/contributes to Canada itself. Thus the guidelines of the Heritage Cultures and Languages Program have been wisely aimed at helping minorities relate their experiences of joining the larger Canadian nation.

While there is no doubt that the Chinese Canadian community is presently making a major contribution to Canadian literature, there are also some unexpected complications that should be briefly mentioned. In the 1960s, at the very moment when Canada's Chinese writers were beginning to find their voices, Canada changed its immigration quotas significantly. Many new immigrant groups came in that decade, including a new wave of Chinese immigration. Since then, there have been at least five major waves of Chinese immigration from different countries, and at the moment there are a great many Chinese immigrants arriving from Hong Kong, people who are leaving Hong Kong because they fear what will happen to the British colony when it is handed over to China in 1997. The new Chinese immigrants are vastly different from those in the established Chinese community, and there is frequently friction between the two groups. As immigration continues, there is also a danger of older forms of racism reasserting themselves among whites. Presently in Vancouver about one resident in six is of Asian ancestry.[26] Moreover, many of the new immigrants are relatively wealthy and have taken a leading role in Canadian industry and commerce. It is a far cry from the days of the sojourner Chinese immigrant alone in Chinatown. At the moment British Columbia's highest government position, the Lieutenant Governor, is filled by David Lam. As well, the Chancellor of British Columbia's largest university is currently Robert Lee.

While it will probably take at least a generation or two for the children of the new Chinese immigrants from Hong Kong to begin writing fiction and poetry, some of the Chinese from other areas have already begun writing about their experiences. Lydia Kwa, who emigrated from Singapore in 1980 has recently published her first book of poems, *The Colours of Heroines* (1994). Similarly, Thuong Vuong-Riddick, from the Chinese minority community in Vietnam, recounts in her poems in *Two Shores / Deux rives* (1995) her flight from Vietnam to Paris, to Montreal, and finally to Vancouver, in search of a new home. For a country like Canada, composed as it is of immigrants, the Chinese Canadian story looks as though it will be told with numerous fresh beginnings.

Notes

1 J. Porter: *The Vertical Mosaic*, pp. 60-98.
2 J. Morton: *In the Sea of Sterile Mountains*, pp. xi-xii.
3 R. W. Wynne: *Reaction to the Chinese*, p. 130.
4 J. Norris: *Strangers Entertained*, p. 211.
5 W. P. Ward: *White Canada Forever*, p. 3.
6 P. Roy: "The Oriental 'Menace' in British Columbia", p. 246
7 R. W. Wynne: *Reaction to the Chinese*, pp. 148-170.
8 A. Chan: *Gold Mountain*, p. 60.
9 W.P. Ward: *White Canada Forever*, p. 15.
10 Ibid., p. 36.
11 J. Norris: *Strangers Entertained*, p. 210.
12 J. Barman: *The West Beyond the West*, p. 146.
13 W. P. Ward: *White Canada Forever*, p. 12.
14 *Report*: p. 1
15 *Report*: p. 2.
16 J. Norris: *Strangers Entertained*, p. 211.
17 *Chinese and English Phrasebook and Dictionary.*
18 *Rice Paper*, p. 1.
19 J. Wong-Chu: "Interview".
20 *Rice Paper*, p. 1.
21 J. Wong-Chu: *Chinatown Ghosts*, p. 11.
22 D. Chong: *The Concubine's Children*, p. 82.
23 *Firehall Arts Centre Newsletter*, 4.
24 H. Palmer: "Mosaic Versus Melting Pot?", p. 171.
25 "Guide for Applicants", p. 1.
26 W. P. Ward: *White Canada Forever*, p. xvii.

Bibliography

Barman, Jean: *The West Beyond the West: A History of British Columbia.* Toronto: University of Toronto Press, 1991.
Chan, Anthony B.: *Gold Mountain: The Chinese in the New World.* Vancouver: New Star Books, 1983.
Chinese and English Phrasebook and Dictionary. Vancouver, 1913.
Chong, Denise: *The Concubine's Children: Portrait of a Family Divided.* Toronto & New York: Viking/Penguin, 1994.
Chuenyan Lai, David: *Chinatowns: Towns within Cities in Canada.* Vancouver: University of British Columbia Press, 1988.
–: *The Forbidden City within Victoria.* Victoria: Orca, 1991.
Firehall Arts Centre Newsletter. Vancouver, 1995.
"Guide for Applicants." Programs Branch, Multiculturalism and Citizenship, September 1991.
Huang, Evelyn & Jeffery, Lawrence (Eds.): *Chinese Canadians: Voices from a Community.* Vancouver/Toronto: Douglas & McIntyre, 1992.
Inalienable Rice: A Chinese & Japanese Canadian Anthology. Vancouver, 1979.
Kim, Elaine H.: *Asian American Literature.* Philadelphia: Temple University Press, 1982.
Kwa, Lydia: *The Colours of Heroines.* Toronto: Women's Press, 1994.
Lau, Evelyn: *Fresh Girls.* Toronto: Harper Collins, 1993.
–: *Oedipal Dreams.* Victoria: Beach Holme Press, 1992.
–: *Runaway: Diary of a Street Kid.* Toronto: Harper Collins, 1989.
–: *You Are Not Who You Claim.* Victoria: Porcepic Books, 1990.
Lee, Bennett & Wong-Chu, Jim (Eds.): *Many-Mouthed Birds.* Vancouver/Toronto: Douglas & McIntyre, 1991.
Lee, Sky: *Disappearing Moon Cafe.* Vancouver/Toronto: Douglas & McIntyre, 1990.
–: *Bellydancer.* Vancouver: Press Gang, 1994.
Lim, Sing: *West Coast Chinese Boy.* 1st ed. 1979. Montreal: Tundra, 1991.
Morton, James: *In the Sea of Sterile Mountains: The Chinese in British Columbia.* Vancouver: J.J. Douglas, 1974.
Norris, John: *Strangers Entertained: A History of the Ethnic Groups of British Columbia.* Vancouver, 1971.
Palmer, Howard: "Mosaic versus Melting Pot?: Immigration and Ethnicity in Canada and the United States," repr. in *A Passion for Identity*, ed. David Taras, B. Rasporich, & Eli Mandel, 2nd ed. Scarborough, Ont: Nelson, 1993, pg. 162-174.
Porter, John: *The Vertical Mosaic: An Analysis of Social Class and Power in Canada.* Toronto: University of Toronto Press, 1965.
Report on Oriental Activities within the Province. Victoria: Legislative Assembly, 1927.
Rice Paper: the Newsletter of the Asian Canadian Writer's Workshop Vol 1, no 1, Fall 1994, 1-12.
Roy, Patricia. "The Oriental 'Menace' in British Columbia" in *Historical Essays on British Columbia* ed. J. Friesen & H.K. Ralston. Toronto: McClelland & Stewart, 1974, pg. 243-255.
Vancouver Sun. Weekend Edition, September 18, 1993.
Vuong-Riddick, Thuong. *Two Shores / Deux rives.* Vancouver: Ronsdale Press, 1995.
Wah, Fred. *Waiting for Saskatchewan.* Winnipeg: Turnstone, 1985.

Ward, W. Peter: *White Canada Forever.* 1st ed. 1978. Montreal: McGill Queen's University Press, 1990.
Wong-Chu, Jim: *Chinatown Ghosts.* Vancouver: Pulp Press, 1986.
–. Interview, unpublished. Vancouver, 26 February, 1995.
Wynne, Robert Edward: *Reaction to the Chinese in the Pacific Northwest and British Columbia 1850 to 1910.* University of Washington Dissertation, 1964.
Yee, Paul: *Breakaway.* Toronto: Groundwood Books, 1994.
–. *Roses Sing on New Snow: a Delicious Tale.* Vancouver/Toronto: Douglas & McIntyre, 1991.
–. *Saltwater City: An Illustrated History of the Chinese in Vancouver.* Vancouver: Douglas & McIntyre, 1988.

Angelika Köhler, Dresden

Die Kompromisse und die Vermittlungen der *Popular Culture:* Das Gibson Girl und die *New Woman*

Das ausgehende 19. Jahrhundert wird Zeuge eines bemerkenswerten kulturhistorischen Phänomens - der Eroberung Amerikas durch das Gibson Girl. Renommierte Zeitschriften und Magazine wie *Life, Time, The Ladies' Home Journal, Scribner's,* und *Collier's Weekly* präsentieren (nicht selten sogar auf ihren Titelseiten) Zeichnungen, in deren Mittelpunkt eine selbstsichere, modisch gekleidete und frisierte junge amerikanische Frau steht. Sie ist von hochgewachsener, schlanker Statur und strahlt entschlossenes Selbstbewußtsein aus. Mit ihrem Stolz und ihrem sicheren Auftreten (in Gesellschaft, im Theater, auf dem Sportplatz, nie aber am heimischen Herd) verkörpert sie offenbar eine Emanzipation von den Konventionen weiblicher Häuslichkeit und Unterordnung. Sie scheint die traditionellen Kriterien für die Beurteilung einer Frau geradezu herauszufordern, denn was sie auszeichnet, ist Durchsetzungsvermögen (sogar gegenüber ihren Eltern), Schlagfertigkeit und Überlegenheit (nicht selten gegenüber den Männern).

Damit gewinnt die Figur des Gibson Girl ein exemplarisches Interesse. Ganz offensichtlich verdankt sie ihren Erfolg einer *Popular Culture,* die sich am Ende des vergangenen Jahrhunderts in eine höchst „progressive" und gemeinhin mit anspruchsvoller Literatur assoziierte Debatte einmischte: die amerikanische Debatte um die *New Woman.* Wie die folgenden Beispiele im einzelnen illustrieren - und wie nicht überraschen wird -, kann es die Stimme der populären Kultur natürlich nicht mit den radikaleren Bildern neuer Weiblichkeit aufnehmen, wie sie z. B. in den Romanen mancher zeitgenössischen Autorinnen zu finden waren. Vielmehr bleibt diese Stimme, eben weil sie auf Akzeptanz bei einem großen Publikum (und bei Zeitschriften-Herausgebern) angewiesen war, dem strategischen Kompromiß zwischen Altem und Neuem, der Harmonisierung von schwer vereinbaren Rollenmodellen, verpflichtet. Und doch beansprucht eine Kunstfigur wie das famose Gibson Girl damit innerhalb der angedeuteten Debatte eine Bedeutung, die man nicht einfach auf die Funktion einer verlogenen Beschwichtigung reduzieren kann. Die folgende Skizze stellt so auch einen Versuch dar, an einem besonders instruktiven Fall zu demonstrieren, wie wichtig die Einbeziehung populärer Kultur überall dort ist, wo es um die Formierung neuen Bewußtseins, neuer Mythologien (im Sinne von Barthes[1]) und neuer sozialer Modelle geht. Gerade auch die feministisch orientierte Literaturwissenschaft tut sich keinen

Dienst, wenn sie die Spuren des allmählichen Emanzipationsprozesses nur in den zwar besonders fortschrittlichen, aber häufig eben auch exklusiven und zum Zeitpunkt ihrer Veröffentlichung nur wenig rezipierten Texten von Autorinnen sucht, die ihrer Zeit voraus waren. Solche Spuren finden sich auch in der *Popular Culture* jener Jahre, teilweise entstellt und verschüttet von ideologischen Kompromissen, aber zuweilen besonders aussagekräftig, wenn es um die jeweilige Stimmungslage einer Gesellschaft zu einem bestimmten historischen Zeitpunkt geht.

Die Abbildung 1[2] gibt zunächst einen ersten Eindruck von der Kultfigur, die die Amerikaner so begeisterte. Die dargestellte weibliche Person richtet ihren forschenden Blick in die Welt. Zu diesem Zweck hält sie in ihrer rechten Hand ein Fernglas, über ihrer Schulter hängt eine kleine Tasche, auf der die linke Hand liegt – eine vieldeutig interpretierbare Geste. Zum einen entsteht dadurch eine relative innere Geschlossenheit der Darstellung: Indem diese Hand am eigenen Körper ruht, existiert die Gestalt eigenständig, ohne Stütze von außen. Zum anderen ist diese Hand frei zur Bewegung, zum Erfassen ihrer Umwelt. Der einzige unmittelbare Bezug zu einem außerhalb ihrer Person liegenden Gegenstand wird durch ihren Blick hergestellt, eine Beziehung, die ihrer eigenen Initiative entspringt und von ihr gesteuert wird. Dieser Blick verrät Entschlossenheit, gleichzeitig hat er auch eine verführerische Qualität,

Abb. 1

die durch die kecke Stupsnase sowie die schwungvoll gezeichnete Form der Lippen noch weiter erhöht wird.

Der Gegenstand dieser Lithographie, nach seinem Schöpfer Charles Dana Gibson (1867-1944) Gibson Girl genannt, wird zum Leitbild einer ganzen Generation junger Amerikanerinnen ungeachtet ihrer sozialen Stellung, die in der Anmut, Eleganz, Sportlichkeit sowie Weltoffenheit dieser Figur ihre heimlichen Sehnsüchte künstlerisch realisiert finden. Dank der vom Maler genutzten Technik der Schwarzweißzeichnung sind seine Werke einfach zu reproduzieren; das Identifikationsobjekt kann daher ohne große finanzielle Aufwendungen an der Wand angebracht werden, die Kissenhülle, den Frühstücksteller oder das Taschentuch zieren. Es entstehen Theaterstücke und Revuen mit dem Gibson Girl als Protagonistin, die Figur wird in Liedern besungen und von der sich rasch entwickelnden Werbebranche gewinnbringend vermarktet. Ob Reklame für neue Haushaltsgegenstände, Dessous, Trendfrisuren oder die Mode der Saison – die Verkaufsstrategien nutzen dieses Symbol scheinbarer weiblicher Freiheit[3].

Das Gibson Girl avanciert schnell zur "Miss America": "[S]he was a national sensation by 1894, when the first folio edition of Gibson's book was published."[4] Die Darstellung einer jungen, selbstbewußten amerikanischen Frau hatte Charles Dana Gibson über Nacht nationale Anerkennung gebracht. 1867 im neuenglischen Roxbury, Massachusetts, geboren, war er in bescheidenen Verhältnissen aufgewachsen. Für seine frühen künstlerisch-kreativen Neigungen fand er jedoch in seinem Elternhaus Offenheit und Unterstützung. Er besuchte die High School und vervollständigte anschließend von 1884-85 seine Ausbildung als Bleistift- und Tuschezeichner an der Art Students' League in New York. Nach anfänglichen Mißerfolgen gelang es ihm schließlich, mit politischen und sozialkritischen Karikaturen für *Life* und *Tid-Bits* (später *Time*) seine Existenz aufzubauen und eine langersehnte Reise nach Paris und London, in die Zentren europäischer Kunst, zu unternehmen. In der britischen Hauptstadt besuchte er George Du Maurier, dessen feinlinige Technik ihn seit frühester Jugend stark beeinflußt und inspiriert hatte. Der englische Künstler, Zeichner und Schriftsteller zugleich, wurde anfangs der 90er Jahre auch in den Vereinigten Staaten sehr bekannt mit *Trilby*, jener legendären Heldin seines gleichnamigen Romans, die im Pariser Quartier Latin beheimatet war und mit ihrem *vie Bohême* das puritanisch-provinzielle Amerika schockte[5].

Du Maurier gehörte zu den bedeutendsten Karikaturisten seiner Zeit und war vor allem in dem Magazin *Punch* als spöttischer Vertreter des Aesthetic Movement hervorgetreten. Diese Bewegung, eine heterogene Gruppe von Künstlern, begann in den 80er Jahren des 19. Jahrhunderts etablierte, konventionelle Werte zu hinterfragen und kritisierte damit die bestehende viktorianische Ordnung. Ihre Lebensphilosophie erfaßte weite Kreise Englands. Ein wesentliches Charakteristikum des Ästhetizismus der weiblichen Anhänger dieser Bewegung war ihre unkonventionelle Art sich zu kleiden. Zwar bevorzugten sie nach wie vor eine schlanke Taille, doch verzichteten sie auf Korsett und Turnüre, und betonten auf diese Weise die ursprüngliche Schönheit und Grazie des weiblichen Körpers.[6] Du Maurier, der sich in erster Linie von der natürlichen Anmut der Frau inspiriert fühlte, fand hier zunächst eine Bestätigung seines Konzeptes. Erst später wurde er sich der sozialkritischen Komponente dieser Konzeption bewußt: Eine Kritik an einengender und unpraktischer Kleidung implizierte gleichzeitig eine Kritik an der der Frau dadurch aufgezwungenen Lebensweise. Die eingeschränkte körperliche Bewegungsfreiheit schien ihre gesellschaftliche Ausgrenzung aus zahlreichen Bereichen des Lebens widerzuspiegeln.

Zwischen Du Maurier und Charles Dana Gibson entwickelte sich eine produktive Freundschaft, die den jüngeren Künstler schließlich befähigte, sein Modell weiblicher Schönheit zu kreieren. Obwohl eine Ähnlichkeit zwischen beiden Frauentypen nicht zu übersehen ist, wirken die jungen Frauen in Gibsons Zeichnungen lebendiger und natürlicher als in Du Mauriers, aus denen neben Zuneigung auch bewundernde Ehrfurcht zu sprechen scheint[7]. Gibson war diese Distanz fremd. Er kannte die lebenden Vorbilder seiner Zeichnungen persönlich, denn für ihn – den gutaussehenden jungen Amerikaner, der durch Fleiß und Beharrlichkeit seine künstlerische Karriere begründet hatte, – gehörten sie zum unmittelbaren Erlebnisbereich. In die USA zurückgekehrt, begann 1890 der beispiellose Triumphzug des Künstlers durch die nationalen Medien. Nahezu jede renommierte Zeitschrift zeigte sich bestrebt, Zeichnungen des Gibson Girl zu veröffentlichen. Darüber hinaus widmete sich der Maler der Illustration von Büchern, wobei seine Werke vor allem in den Romanen des zur damaligen Zeit außerordentlich populären Schriftstellers Richard Harding Davis überwältigende Erfolge feierten.[8]

Das zu Beginn der 90er Jahre entstandene Gibson Girl scheint die Veränderungen, die sich im traditionellen Bild der amerikanischen Frau im Laufe der zweiten Hälfte des 19. Jahrhunderts vollzogen haben, zu reflektieren. In ihrer 1898 publizierten Studie *Women and Economics* bezeichnete Charlotte Perkins Gilman das Gibson Girl als repräsentatives Zeugnis eines Prozesses, als dessen Ergebnis sich eine von konventionellen Wertvorstellungen befreiende *New Woman*[9] konstituierte. Die Vertreterinnen der neuen Frauengeneration unterschieden sich bereits äußerlich vom bisherigen Ideal amerikanischer Weiblichkeit: "[they were] growing honester, braver, stronger, more healthful and skilful and able and free, more human in all ways."[10]

Entspricht also das Gibson Girl, dieses neue Modell amerikanischer Weiblichkeit, wirklich der *New Woman*, die ihr Selbstwertgefühl aus den eigenen

Fähigkeiten und Stärken bezieht und sich von den Rollenzwängen einer männlich definierten Welt befreit hat? Die Untersuchung ausgewählter Zeichnungen von Charles Dana Gibson soll versuchen, diese Frage provisorisch zu beantworten und somit zu den spezifischen Funktionen des Gibson Girls im kulturhistorischen Kontext des ausgehenden 19. Jahrhunderts beizutragen. Aus der Beschreibung der äußeren Erscheinung der Figur ist bereits deutlich geworden, daß neue amerikanische Weiblichkeit in der Kunst von Attributen wie Selbständigkeit und Entschlossenheit bestimmt wird. Von diesen Prinzipien ist das öffentliche Auftreten des Gibson Girl geprägt. Es präsentiert sich gern in Gesellschaft und genießt es, bei öffentlichen Veranstaltungen wie Pferderennen, Theateraufführungen und sportlichen Wettkämpfen im Mittelpunkt zu stehen.

"Advice to Caddies" (Abb. 2) zeigt im Vordergrund eine junge Amerikanerin als Golfspielerin, während im Hintergrund acht männliche Gestalten zu

Abb. 2: Advice to Caddies.
You will save time by keeping your eye on the ball, not on the Player.

erkennen sind, die mehr oder weniger intensiv mit der Suche nach dem Ball beschäftigt scheinen und sich gleichsam alle zu Caddies degradiert haben. Die optische Überlegenheit der Frauenfigur ist von Gibson geradezu extrem herausgearbeitet: Sie erscheint überproportional groß, sehr gerade und aufrecht (während die meisten der männlichen Figuren sich beugen oder sogar zu ihren Füßen kriechen), überaus kontrolliert und kühl, gerade auch im Gegensatz zu dem einzigen „aufrechten" Mann des Bildes, der sich – verwirrt oder resigniert? – den Schweiß von der Stirne wischt. Außerdem sind die Blicke aller Männer auf die Frau gerichtet, was sie zu einer Kopfhaltung zwingt, die zum Teil zu der durch die vergebliche Ballsuche definierten Körperhaltung in unnatürlichem Gegensatz steht. Dagegen wirkt die Protagonistin unberührt durch ihre Umgebung und durch die bewundernden Männer, die sie ihrerseits keines Blickes würdigt. Ihre Kopfhaltung und die Handbewegung, mit der sie ihr Haar ordnet, suggerieren (und sollen offenbar auch suggerieren), daß sie in sich selbst ruht und mit sich selbst beschäftigt ist. Ihre witzige Bemerkung schließlich, die durch die zum Teil verrenkten Männerfiguren mit ihren verstohlenen Blicken völlig gerechtfertigt erscheint – "You will save time by keeping your eye on the ball, not on the player" – läßt sie endgültig als überlegene Herrin der Lage erscheinen, während die Männer eher den Eindruck von unreifen Halbwüchsigen machen. Freilich zögert man bei genauer Betrachtung, hier von einer "emanzipierten" jungen Frau zu sprechen. Bereits die Bezeichnung Golfspielerin ist nicht ganz ernst zu nehmen; denn die Heldin, die offenbar den Ball unwiederbringlich ins *rough* geschlagen hat, hält den Golfschläger wie einen Sonnenschirm nur mit den Fingerspitzen. Sportlich-modern gekleidet in Rock und Hemdbluse, dem typisch amerikanischen Freizeit-Outfit des Gibson Girl, setzt sie auf den ersten Blick ein Ziel der sogenannten *dress reformer* jener Zeit praktisch um. Auf den zweiten Blick wird aber auch hier ihre Kompromißbereitschaft sichtbar, denn ihre Wespentaille verrät von vornherein nur eingeschränkte sportliche Ambitionen und läßt ihre ganze Aufmachung geziert, auf konventionell „weibliche" Wirkung bedacht, erscheinen. Vor allem ist ihre Pose so eindeutig von Koketterie geprägt, daß sie von der Ironie des Zeichners nicht ausgenommen bleibt. Ihre klassische, d. h. auch: ihre künstliche Armhaltung, mit der Fotomodelle noch heute ihre Büste vorteilhaft zur Geltung bringen, ist offenbar auf Wirkung angelegt und straft die scheinbare Unnahbarkeit Lügen.

Mit anderen Worten: Die Dominanz und Überlegenheit des Gibson Girl, die nicht nur auf Attraktivität, sondern auch auf Witz und kalkulierter Strategie beruht, ist einerseits provokativ neu (im Vergleich zur traditionellen Zurückhaltung der *True Woman*[11]); jedoch bleibt dieses Selbstbewußtsein nach wie vor „kokett" auf den Mann bezogen und damit von fortschrittlichen Vorstellungen der weiblichen Autonomie bzw. Selbstfindung weit entfernt. Typisch ist auch das Ambiente, in dem sich hier das Gibson Girl bewegt: eine Welt nämlich, aus der alle Hinweise auf die Sphäre der Macht und des Berufs ausgespart bleiben. Das Gibson Girl begegnet dem anderen Geschlecht im Bereich luxoriöser Muße. Innerhalb dieses Bereichs aber zeigt sie sich den Männern (und zwar sowohl den gleichaltrigen wie den älteren) turmhoch überlegen. Die Zweideutigkeit dieser Modellfigur wird damit deutlicher beschreibbar. Sie wird vom Zeichner bewußt in einer nur teilweise realistischen Sphäre angesiedelt, einer Sphäre des Spiels, des Entertainment und des Rituals, in der Macht, Verantwortung oder Beruf keine Rolle spielen. Die Bilder erhalten damit etwas Augenzwinkerndes; sie nehmen die eigentlich unbestreitbare Überlegenheit des Gibson Girl nur zum Teil ernst. Andererseits verdankt eine Zeichnung wie "Advice to Caddies" ihren Erfolg aber eben doch der provokanten Botschaft, daß hier eine neue Generation von amerikanischen Frauen den Männern an Geist, Witz, Entschlossenheit, Strategie und Diplomatie deutlich überlegen war.

Eine ähnliche Zweideutigkeit bestimmt auch Gibsons Folge von Zeichnungen unter dem Titel "The Weaker Sex". Die spöttisch-ironische Sicht auf das Thema wird bereits aus dem Kontrast zu den Zeichnungen sichtbar, in denen sich das "schwache Geschlecht" meist in Gestalt von souveränen, kraftvoll-verführerischen Frauen vorstellt. Ein besonders extremes Beispiel ist die Abb. 3. Gibson zeichnet hier vier attraktive junge Damen im heiratsfähigen

Abb. 3: The Weaker Sex. – II.

Alter, die mit süffisantem Blick einen schmächtigen Vertreter des männlichen Geschlechts „unter die Lupe nehmen". Mit scheinbar wissenschaftlicher Akribie untersuchen sie ihren winzigen, auf Knien ums Überleben bettelnden Gegenstand mittels einer Lupe und einer Präpariernadel – doch diese erweist sich bei genauem Hinsehen als Stricknadel! Die für die *Popular Culture* typische Vermittlung zwischen Konvention und Provokation ist hier besonders instruktiv verwirklicht. Es ist ja keine Frage, daß Gibson die neuen Ansprüche der Frauen „zitiert": Seine überlegenen *Girls* spiegeln diese Ambitionen wider, aber sie scheinen sie auch wiederum zu parodieren, wie die ins Groteske verzerrten Größenverhältnisse à la *Gullivers Travels* suggerieren. Umgekehrt werden natürlich auch die Ansprüche des „starken" Geschlechts nicht mehr ernst genommen, vor allem von den weiblichen Figuren nicht; aber die Stricknadel signalisiert dem Publikum zugleich, daß die neuen Frauen ihre Überlegenheit nur im häuslichen und im gesellschaftlichen Bereich, nicht aber in der Welt politischer und beruflicher Macht (die in den Zeichnungen überhaupt nicht vorzukommen scheint) ausüben wollen.

Intelligenz erweist sich als „notwendige Zutat" in einer Zeichnung gleichen Titels (Abb. 4). Ein junger Mann, offenbar ein Hobby-Maler aus besseren

Abb. 4: A Necessary Ingredient.
He: I wonder why I can never obtain the same color effects as Reynolds and Rembrandt.
She: Perhaps it's in preparing the colors: I've heard that they used to mix them with brains.

Kreisen (vgl. seine Kleidung), bemüht sich verzweifelt, das Gibson Girl so zu porträtieren, daß seine Farben den Vergleich mit denen Rembrandts aushalten. Da ihm dies natürlich nicht gelingt, läßt er entmutigt Palette und Pinsel sinken. Sein Blick ist ins Leere gerichtet; sein zusammengesunkener Körper bildet wiederum einen extremen Kontrast zu der aufrechten und selbstbewußten Haltung seines jungen Modells. Das Gibson Girl reagiert, übrigens in einer ganz ähnlichen Pose wie die Golfspielerin, auf die Verzweiflung des törichten Dilettanten mit beißendem Spott. Nicht das geeignete Modell, Farbe und Pinsel schaffen einen erfolgreichen Künstler, sein Verstand und seine Kreativität sind entscheidend. So präsentiert sich diese Figur nicht nur als hinreißend attraktiv, sondern auch als witzig, kultiviert und intelligent. Wiederum besteht an der Überlegenheit des Gibson Girl kein Zweifel. Doch erneut wird diese „Machtkonstellation" auf den Bereich beschränkt, der durch Muße und Kultur, aber eben nicht durch Herrschaft und Verantwortung gekennzeichnet ist. Die Ansprüche der *New Woman* auf Emanzipation werden zitiert, zugleich allerdings durch ihre Zurückdrängung auf die Nebenschauplätze der Macht verharmlost. Dennoch bleiben sie präsent, sozusagen „im Gespräch", und künden von dem Vertrauen des Künstlers in die junge Amerikanerin, mit gesundem Urteilsvermögen und Engagement ihr Leben selbst zu gestalten. Keine von Gibsons Zeichnungen thematisiert den Mann – als Vater oder Bewerber – in der Rolle des Entscheidungsträgers. Damit setzt er durchaus bemerkenswerte Akzente.

Im Gefolge des Gilded Age war in der zweiten Hälfte des 19. Jahrhunderts eine neue Schicht entstanden: die *nouveaux riches* der Vereinigten Staaten, die über beträchtlichen materiellen Reichtum verfügten, jedoch aufgrund fehlender Familientradition ihre soziale Stellung als unbefriedigend empfanden. Sie entwickelten eine Vorliebe für ausgedehnte Reisen nach Europa, auf denen sie ihre Töchter im heiratsfähigen Alter in die sogenannte „Gesellschaft" einführten mit dem Ziel, einen meist schon in die Jahre gekommenen Adligen als Schwiegersohn zu „ködern" und auf diese Weise in die Nobilität einzuheiraten.

Die humorvoll-kritische Auseinandersetzung mit diesen Praktiken nimmt verhältnismäßig breiten Raum in Gibsons Schaffen ein. Der Künstler stellt ein geradezu exemplarisches Beispiel für das Funktionieren des *American Way of Life* dar. Mit seinem *Girl* hatte er eine nationale Alternative zu dem bis dahin in Amerika dominierenden europäischen Modell von Weiblichkeit geschaffen. Die bewußt forcierte Suche amerikanischer Väter und Mütter nach einem Schwiegersohn, der dem europäischen Adel entstammte, verletzte somit gleichermaßen seine nationalen Gefühle und seine Vorstellungen von Natürlichkeit und romantischer Partnerschaft. Sollen Jugend und Liebe als Preis für den sozialen Aufstieg geopfert werden, erhebt er seinen Zeichenstift und läßt sein Gibson Girl unzweideutig rebellieren (Abb. 5). Im Gespräch mit dem Vater vermeidet es die offene Auseinandersetzung, aber die Situation, in der Gibson Vater und Tochter agieren läßt, impliziert zukünftige Konflikte. Er spricht mit ihr, doch sie wendet sich ab, dreht ihm den Rücken zu. Eine Hand auf die Hüfte gestützt, die andere zum aufrecht getragenen Kopf erhoben (auch hier

Abb. 5: "If we go to Europe, Cynthia, I don't want you to marry any of them Counts or Dukes. You just wait until we run across some King in reduced circumstances."

wieder eine Variante der bereits erwähnten klassischen Pose), drückt ihre Haltung alles andere als die Bereitschaft zu Akzeptanz und Unterordnung aus. Es entsteht der Eindruck, als beabsichtige die junge Frau mit der linken Hand ihre Gehirntätigkeit in Gang zu setzen mit dem Ziel, durch clevere List den Plan ihres alten Herrn zu vereiteln. Deshalb verrät ihr Blick keine Niedergeschlagenheit ob dieser Information, sondern sagt deutlicher als Worte, daß sie in puncto Heirat eigene Wege verfolgt.

Der Künstler unterstreicht die Botschaft seines Bildes zusätzlich durch die ihm technisch-kompositorisch zur Verfügung stehenden Mittel. Der Vater macht sich mit seinem Plan in den Augen der Tochter lächerlich – ikonographisch agiert er im doppelten Sinne im Hintergrund. Er befindet sich zum einen im hinteren Teil des gezeichneten Raumes; zum anderen hüllt die dunkle Tönung der Wand ihn insgesamt in eine düstere Atmosphäre ein. Anders die junge Frau, die im vorderen Teil des Bildes gezeigt wird. Bereits rein proportional beherrscht sie die Szene, ein Eindruck, der noch durch die auffällige Helligkeit ihrer unmittelbaren Umgebung unterstrichen wird. Sie bevorzugt das Licht des Tages, in dem sie ihre anmutige Gestalt, ihre natürliche Schönheit präsentieren kann. Licht bedeutet Leben, und genau daran will sie teilhaben. Der scharfe Kontrast von Hell und Dunkel materialisiert den Gegensatz von Natürlichkeit und Zwang zeichnerisch und zeigt die Sympathien des Malers auf Seiten seines Gibson Girl.

Alle untersuchten Zeichnungen weisen ein gemeinsames Merkmal auf: In ihrem Mittelpunkt steht eine selbstsichere junge Frau, die ihre Überlegenheit aus einer Mischung von natürlicher Schönheit, Koketterie und geistvollem Witz schöpft. Charles Dana Gibson reagiert damit auf Veränderungen im Verhalten der jungen Amerikanerinnen und kommentiert sie mit Zeichnungen, in denen das Gibson Girl immer wieder seinen Anspruch auf einen selbst gewählten, eigenständigen Platz in der von traditionellen Werten bestimmten Welt des Mannes durch seine aktive Teilnahme an einem zumindest weiten Bereich des öffentlichen Lebens behauptet und seine Fähigkeiten und Fertigkeiten sichtbar präsentiert. Es fordert keine gleichberechtigte Repräsentanz, doch es hat sich unübersehbar – und wie die weitere historische Entwicklung bestätigen wird -unumkehrbar aus der *domestic sphere* der *true woman* befreit.

Natürlich kann auch schon allein die Tatsache, daß dieser Frauentyp nationale Aufmerksamkeit findet, als deutliches Zeichen eines sich wandelnden weiblichen Lebensanspruchs und eines sich verändernden Selbstwertempfindens der Frau verstanden werden. Die Wurzeln der besonderen kulturhistorischen Bedeutung des Gibson Girl liegen allerdings weiter zurück. Bereits seit dem Bürgerkrieg hatte eine grundlegende Neuaufteilung der Rollen von Mann und Frau begonnen, ein Prozeß, der immer mehr junge Amerikanerinnen veranlaßte, Zweifel an der „Natürlichkeit“ ihrer Unterordnung – als Tochter, als Ehefrau, als Mutter – zu äußern. Sie sahen ihre Ideale vielmehr in den Zeichnungen Charles Dana Gibsons verwirklicht, in denen eine junge Frau scheinbar unabhängig ihre Geschicke selbstbewußt und erfolgreich in die Hand nahm.

Mit dieser spezifischen Form der künstlerischen Umsetzung weiblicher Befindlichkeit traf der Maler den Nerv seiner Zeit. Die Vereinigten Staaten hatten im letzten Drittel des 19. Jahrhunderts einen rasanten wirtschaftlichen Aufschwung genommen. Industrialisierung und Urbanisierung veränderten das Antlitz des Landes grundlegend, brachten aber auch neue soziale Probleme hervor. In den industriellen Ballungszentren wurden immer mehr Arbeitskräfte benötigt, vor allem auch solche, die über eine grundlegende Schulbildung verfügten. Die Infrastruktur in den Städten war nur mangelhaft entwickelt, und die Gefahr der Bildung erster Slums wurde akut.

All dies erschütterte auch die bürgerliche Idealkonzeption häuslicher Geborgenheit. Bereits Mitte des 19. Jahrhunderts hatte die Frauenbewegung mit abolitionistischen und prohibitionistischen Aktivitäten den häuslichen Bereich gleichsam auf Probe verlassen, im letzten Drittel des Jahrhunderts begann sie sich nun verstärkt bei der Lösung sozialer Fragen zu engagieren und kämpfte gezielt gegen die Diskriminierung der Frauen in Erziehung, Beruf und vor dem Gesetz. Damit rüttelte sie zu einer Zeit an den Grundfesten des patriarchalischen Systems, zu der das fortschreitende industrielle Wachstum auf seiner Suche nach Arbeitskräften das Potential der Frauen benötigte. Die immer größere Zahl von Schulen machte die jungen Amerikanerinnen als Lehrkräfte bald unentbehrlich. Diese Entwicklung löste einen wahren Ansturm der heranwachsenden weiblichen Generation auf höhere Schulen, Colleges und schließlich Universitäten aus, und im Ergebnis dieses enormen Aufschwungs wurde die uneingeschränkte, gleichberechtigte aktive Teilnahme der Frauen am öffentlichen Leben zu einer unüberhörbaren Forderung. Das jahrzehntelang erfolgreich praktizierte Konzept, daß der Platz der amerikanischen Frau am häuslichen Herd und in der Familie sei, schien nicht mehr zu funktionieren.

In dieser „kritischen" Phase tauchten die ersten Gibson Girls auf, die sich rasch den amerikanischen Markt eroberten. Die Ursache für diese Popularität lag gerade in der ihnen eigenen Ambiguität. Als eine Mischung von Konventionellem und frecher „Dekonstruktion" schienen die Zeichnungen von Charles Dana Gibson die „Not" mit den sich emanzipierenden Frauen in eine „Tugend" umzuwandeln. Im Kontext der amerikanischen Kulturgeschichte des ausgehenden 19. Jahrhunderts funktionierten sie auf zweierlei Weise: Mit einer Frauenfigur, die nicht einmal auf den Gedanken kam, sich durch einen Beruf zu emanzipieren, die statt dessen ausschließlich bei *leisured activities* „kokett" agierte und die nach wie vor von ihren Relationen zum Mann her definiert wurde, kam Gibson mit seinem Modell moderner amerikanischer Weiblichkeit gewissen traditionellen Vorstellungen durchaus entgegen. Andererseits ging er in seinen Zeichnungen erstaunlich provokant mit diesen konventionellen Konzepten um, indem er eine weibliche Figur schuf, die den sie umgebenden Männern intellektuell eindeutig überlegen war, die witziger, intelligenter, schlagfertiger auftrat, die wußte, was sie wollte, und diesen Willen auch gegenüber Vätern und potentiellen Partnern durchsetzte. Das Gibson Girl stellt somit eine Art Kompromiß dar, der "at once pleased the crowd and satisfied the critical"[12], was nichts anderes heißt, als daß es als Produkt der *Popular Culture* wohl in vielerlei Weise den konventionellen Vorstellungen von der Rolle der Frau verpflichtet bleibt, aber eben gleichzeitig innerhalb dieser Grenzen erstaunlich neue Konstellationen entwirft, die gerade in der sozusagen verharmlosten Form deutliche Aspekte der *New Woman* verschlüsselt erkennen lassen.

Anmerkungen

1 Vgl. Roland Barthes, *Die Mythen des Alltags,* Frankfurt/M. (Suhrkamp Verlag), 1964, S. 85 ff.

2 Alle Zeichnungen Gibsons entstammen *The Gibson Book. A Collection of the Published Works of Charles Dana Gibson.* In Two Volumes, New York (Charles Scribner's Sons), 1907.

3 Vgl. z. B. Werbeanzeigen in *Life* März/April 1901 sowie Fairfax Downey, *Portrait of an Era as Drawn by C. D. Gibson,* New York (Charles Scribner's Sons), 1936, S. 200-206.

4 Louis Banner, *The American Beauty,* Chicago (The University of Chicago Press), 1983, S. 154. Bei dem hier erwähnten Buch Charles Dana Gibsons handelt es sich um die im Herbst 1894 in New York erfolgte erstmalige Herausgabe einer Sammlung von 84 der besten Zeichnungen Gibsons (vgl. Robert Howard Russel, "How Charles Dana Gibson Started." *The Ladies' Home Journal* 10, 1902, S. 8.

5 Vgl. Fairfax Downey, *Portrait of an Era as Drawn by C. D. Gibson.* S. 206/08.

6 Vgl. Leonceè Ormond, *George Du Maurier,* Pittsburgh (University of Pittsburgh Press), 1969, S. 247/48 bzw. 267/68.

7 Zum Vergleich beider Frauentypen siehe Fairfax Downey, *Portrait of an Era as Drawn by C. D. Gibson.* S. 86.

8 Aus dieser Zusammenarbeit ging der als Gibson-Davis Man bekannt gewordene ideale Partner des Gibson Girl, der *new man*, hervor.

9 Dieser erstmals in journalistischen Kreisen verwendete Begriff beschreibt das Ideal der modernen Frau, die sich ihr Leben selbständig, frei von jeglicher männlicher Abhängigkeit aufbaut und sich in ihrer Beziehung zum Mann als gleichberechtigte Partnerin versteht. (Vgl. Carolyn Forrey, "The new woman revisited". *Women's Studies* 2/1, 1974, S.38/39.

10 Charlotte Perkins Gilman, *Women and Economics,* ed. Carl N. Degler, New York (Harper & Row), 1966, S. 148.

11 Dieser Begriff bezeichnet das Ideal der viktorianischen Frau des 19. Jahrhunderts, die in der Erfüllung ihrer Pflichten als Ehefrau und Mutter den Sinn ihres Lebens erkannte. (Vgl. Barbara Welter, "The Cult of True Womanhood: 1820-1860", *American Quarterly* 18/2, 1966, S. 151-174.

12 Zitiert nach Fairfax Downey, *Portrait of an Era as Drawn by C. D. Gibson.* S. 3.

Anschriften der Autoren

Dr. Jens-Ulrich Davids. Universität Oldenburg. Fachbereich 11. Postfach 2503, 26129 Oldenburg.

Marion Gymnich, MA. Universität zu Köln. Englisches Seminar. Albertus-Magnus-Platz, 50923 Köln.

Prof. Dr. Ronald B. Hatch. The University of British Columbia. Department of English. No. 397–1873 East Mall, Vancouver, B.C., V6T 1Z1, Kanada.

Prof. Dr. John M. MacKenzie. Lancaster University. Department of History. Lancaster LA1 4YW

Prof. Dr. Ansgar Nünning. Justus-Liebig-Universität Giessen. Institut für Anglistik und Amerikanistik. Otto-Behaghel-Str. 10, 35394 Giessen.

PD Dr. Vera Nünning. Universität zu Köln. Anglo-Amerikanische Abteilung des Historischen Seminars. Albertus-Magnus-Platz, 50923 Köln.

Prof. Dr. Erhard Reckwitz. Universität Gesamthochschule Essen. Fachbereich 3: Literatur- und Sprachwissenschaften, Anglistik. Gebäude R 12, Universitätsstraße 12, 45117 Essen.

Prof. Dr. Bernhard Reitz, Seminar für Englische Philologie. Johannes-Gutenberg-Universität Mainz. Jakob-Welder-Weg 18, 55099 Mainz.

Dr. Phil. Angelika Köhler. Technische Universität Dresden. Fakultät für Sprach- und Literaturwissenschaften. Institut für Anglistik/Amerikanistik, 01062 Dresden.

Neuerscheinungen:

Dagmar Flinspach

Das Bild des Künstlers im zeitgenössischen englischen Roman

Untersuchungen zum Problem von Künstlertum und Mediokrität in Iris Murdochs »The Black Prince«, Anthony Burgess' Enderby-Zyklus und John Fowles' »Daniel Martin«

1996. X, 244 Seiten. Kart. DM 124.– / ÖS 918.– / SFr 110.–. ISBN 3-484-45033-9 (Band 33)

Seit dem Aufkommen des Kœnstlerromans gegen Ende des 18. Jahrhunderts in Deutschland gehören Künstler aller Art zum festen Figurenrepertoire der internationalen Literatur. Anhand ausgewählter englischer Romane der Gegenwart wird in dieser Arbeit detailliert untersucht, welches Künstlerbild in zeitgenössischen Romanen vorherrscht und inwiefern sich dieses Künstlerbild von denen früherer Epochen unterscheidet. Ein radikal veränderter Kunstbegriff und die Desavouierung des Subjektbegriffs durch den Poststrukturalismus sind in diesem Zusammenhang von zentraler Bedeutung. Symptomatisch für das Selbstverständnis des zeitgenössischen Künstlers ist außerdem dessen zwiespältiges Verhältnis zur künstlerischen Tradition, das zwischen Bewunderung und Minderwertigkeitsgefühl anzusiedeln ist. Das Wechselspiel von künstlerischer Traditionsverbundenheit und Innovationswunsch schreibt sich in die Figurenkonzeption und Plot-Struktur der Romane selbst ein. Bei allen untersuchten Texten können daher sowohl Elemente des traditionellen Künstlerromans als auch der zeitgenössischen Metafiktion nachgewiesen werden. Dabei, das belegen die Textanalysen, reden sie aber der Postmoderne keineswegs das Wort, sondern erteilen ihr im Gegenteil eine ironische Absage. Schließlich kulminiert die Auseinandersetzung des zeitgenössischen Künstlers mit der künstlerischen Tradition in einem Rückgriff auf mythische Identifikationsmodelle. Doch die Wahl der zeitgenössischen Künstler fällt nicht auf die romantische Identifikationsfigur Prometheus, sondern auf den von Apoll im künstlerischen Wettstreit besiegten Satyr Marsyas, der in der Interpretation des zeitgenössischen Künstlers zur Symbolgestalt künstlerischer Mediokrität ›verformt‹ wird.

Lothar Jordan

Bibliographie zur europäischen und amerikanischen Gegenwartslyrik im deutschen Sprachraum

Sekundärliteratur 1945–1988

1996. XIX, 215 Seiten. Kart. DM 86.– / ÖS 636.– / SFr 78.–. ISBN 3-484-63012-4 (Communicatio. Band 12)

Die Bibliographie will die Forschungen zu den internationalen Zusammenhängen der Gegenwartslyrik unterstützen. Das ursprünglich literarhistorische, vor allem rezeptionsgeschichtliche Sammelinteresse wurde im Laufe der Arbeit erweitert um andere komparatistische Fragestellungen, die eine weite Auslegung des Ausdrucks ›literarische Beziehungen‹ erfordern, von verschiedenen Aspekten der Intertextualität, des typologischen Vergleichs, der Vermittlung, der Übersetzung bis zu methodologischen und literaturpolitischen Fragen. Das Buch versteht sich als Ergänzung zu »Europäische und nordamerikanische Gegenwartslyrik im deutschen Sprachraum 1920–1970. Studien zu ihrer Vermittlung und Wirkung« vom gleichen Verfasser, doch ist es so angelegt, daß es eigenständig benutzbar ist. Die Arbeit ordnet sich in die Perspektiven einer international orientierten, insbesondere einer europäischen Literaturwissenschaft ein. Erstmals werden gleichermaßen west- und osteuropäische Poesien, tatsächlich zahlreiche ›große‹ und ›kleine‹ Sprachen berücksichtigt. Hinzu kommen Titel zur englischsprachigen nordamerikanischen und zur lateinamerikanischen Lyrik.

Lothar Jordan

Europäische und nordamerikanische Gegenwartslyrik im deutschen Sprachraum 1920–1970

Studien zu ihrer Vermittlung und Wirkung

1994. VIII, 223 Seiten. Kart. DM 116.– / ÖS 905.– / SFr 116.–. ISBN 3-484-63008-6 (Communicatio. Band 8)

Niemeyer 

THE FATAL GIFT OF BEAUTY
THE ITALIES OF BRITISH TRAVELLERS
An Annotated Anthology

Ed. by Manfred Pfister

Amsterdam/Atlanta, GA 1996. 554 pp.
(Internationale Forschungen zur Allgemeinen und Vergleichenden Literaturwissenschaft 15)
ISBN: 90-5183-981-2 Bound Hfl. 250,-/US-$ 165.-
ISBN: 90-5183-943-X Paper Hfl. 60,-/US-$ 40.-

This is the first anthology of British travel writing on Italy which traces the development of the genre and the history of the British perception of Italy from the Renaissance to the present. As an *anthologie raissonnée* it presents the texts in thematic clusters and chronological order, providing commentary and annotations for each of them and their nearly hundred authors (some of them, like Smollett, Byron, Dickens or Huxley, well-known, others virtually unknown, amongst them many unduly neglected women writers). Further features are a substantial introduction to the travelogue and the writing of Italy, more than thirty illustrations visualizing the British experience of Italy, and an extensive bibliography of primary and secondary sources.

USA/Canada: Editions Rodopi B.V., 2015 South Park Place, Atlanta, GA 30339, Tel. (770) 933-0027, *Call toll-free* (U.S. only) 1-800-225- 3998, Fax (770) 933-9644, *E-mail:* F.van.der.Zee@rodopi.nl
All Other Countries: Editions Rodopi B.V., Keizersgracht 302-304, 1016 EX Amsterdam, The Netherlands. Tel. + + 31 (0)20-622-75-07, Fax + + 31 (0)20-638-09-48, *E-mail:* F.van.der.Zee@rodopi.nl